139
GIBBON'S
AUTOBIOGRAPHY

Oxford University Press, Walton Street, Oxford OX2 6DP

OXFORD LONDON GLASGOW
NEW YORK TORONTO MELBOURNE WELLINGTON
KUALA LUMPUR SINGAPORE JAKARTA HONG KONG TOKYO
DELHI BOMBAY CALCUTTA MADRAS KARACHI
IBADAN NAIROBI DAR ES SALAAM CAPE TOWN

AUTOBIOGRAPHY OF
EDWARD GIBBON
AS ORIGINALLY EDITED BY
LORD SHEFFIELD

WITH AN INTRODUCTION BY
J. B. BURY

OXFORD UNIVERSITY PRESS

EDWARD GIBBON

Born, Putney . . . . 27 April 1737
Died, St. James's Street, London 16 January 1794

The Miscellaneous Works of Edward Gibbon, Esq.,
with Memoirs of his Life and Writings composed by
himself, *illustrated from his letters, with occasional
notes and narrative, by the Right Honourable John,
Lord Sheffield, were first published in two volumes in*
1796, *and a second edition, in five volumes, appeared
in* 1814. *In* The World's Classics *the Autobiography,
forming the greater part of Vol. I of the second edition
of* 1814, *was first published in* 1907 *and reprinted in*
1923, 1931, 1935, 1950, 1959, 1962, 1972, 1978

ISBN 0 19 250139 9

*Printed in Great Britain
at the University Press, Oxford
by Vivian Ridler
Printer to the University*

INTRODUCTION

THE title under which Gibbon intended that his autobiography should appear was *Memoirs of my Life and Writings*, but it will always be known as the *Autobiography*, the name under which, posthumously published by his friend and executor Lord Sheffield, it became a classic. Lord Sheffield gave the work its final shape and, though he performed the task, which was not an easy one, with laudable skill, we must deeply regret that the author had not himself arranged the material for publication. He left six sketches of his life, which partly supplement each other and partly cover the same ground. They were printed some years ago [1], and enable us to appreciate the dexterity with which Lord Sheffield pieced together the consecutive narrative, adhering, he states, ' with scrupulous fidelity to the very words of the author.' The sketches show that this statement, though generally true, is not accurate. The editor made a number of changes for various reasons. One or two cases are interesting and characteristic.

Speaking of his absences from Magdalen College, Oxford, Gibbon wrote : ' I was too young and bashful to enjoy, like a manly Oxonian, the taverns and bagnios of Convent Garden.' The last words were euphemistically changed by Lord Sheffield into ' the pleasures of London'. Describing · the *pension* of M. de Mesery at Lausanne, the author had simply observed that ' the boarders were numerous ' ; the editor makes him pretentiously tell us that ' the boarders were select '.

[1] *The Autobiographies of Edward Gibbon.* Edited by John Murray, 1896.

In his solicitude not to offend contemporary English prejudices, Lord Sheffield also cut out some characteristic remarks. Referring to his essay on *The Age of Sesostris*, the historian had written : ' In my supposition the high priest is guilty of a voluntary error : flattery is the prolific parent of falsehood ; and falsehood, I will now add, is not incompatible with the sacerdotal character.' Coming from the author of the *Decline and Fall* the remark was assuredly mild ; but the editor protected the sacerdotal order, and consulted the feelings of its admirers, by eliminating the last clause. That the name of the Oxford tutor who ' well remembered that he had a salary to receive and only forgot that he had a duty to perform ' (Dr. Winchester) should have been suppressed is intelligible, but in most cases the editorial pruning-knife was directed by English prejudices which were alien to Gibbon and with which we have no sympathy now.[1]

When Gibbon finished his *Decline and Fall of the Roman Empire*, he was far from being an old man, but he had made up his mind that his life-work was completed. He composed his memoirs because he was the author of the history, and he never forgets that the historian of the *Decline and Fall* is telling an interested public the story of his life. He is on a stage, addressing an audience ; he never lets himself go, like other great autobiographers, Cellini, or Rousseau, or Goethe. But, saturated though it is with self-consciousness, the Memoir is actual ; the pose was nature. ' Style is the image of character,' he observes at the beginning of the *Autobiography* ; and of him this generality is perfectly true. The same full dress which he had worn in describing the fortunes of the Roman Empire, he assumed to trace the vicissitudes of his own career. He took himself and his life as

---

[1] Attention was called to these and other instances of editorial tampering with the text by Dr. Birkbeck Hill in the preface to his learned edition of the *Autobiography* (1900). I am indebted to this work for a number of references.

seriously as his *magnum opus*; he never lost himself in his labour; he was not one of those who think of nothing but the advancement of knowledge and work till they fall. He had his own ideal of the life of a literary man, and he had models. At the age of fifty-four he calculated on grounds of statistical probability that he might hope to enjoy for about fifteen years the ' autumnal felicity' which had been the lot of ' Voltaire, Hume, and many other men of letters'. He hoped to bequeath to the admiration of posterity not only a great book, but a vision of the fortunate life of an eminent writer. This self-consciousness moves high above the range of vulgar vanity. Of his intellectual powers and his achievements as a writer, he had a just and not excessive opinion. His work had placed him at once in the same rank with Hume and Robertson, whose fame was established when he had begun to write. ' I will frankly own,' he wrote, ' that my pride is elated as often as I find myself ranked in the triumvirate of British Historians of the present age, and though I feel myself the Lepidus, I contemplate with pleasure the superiority of my colleagues.' He never shows a trace of jealousy in his appreciation of the intellectual merits of others.

In his intercourse with his fellow creatures, indeed, Gibbon was exceedingly vain, sensitive, and ready to take offence. Austere moralists will perhaps discover an index of deplorable vanity in his scrupulous attention to the adornment of his person. In a letter to his friend Holroyd (Lord Sheffield) he describes himself as ' writing at Boodle's [Club] in a fine velvet coat with ruffles of My Lady's choosing '. His attire on one occasion was criticized by an observer as ' a little overcharged perhaps, if his *person* be considered '. He was always anxious to make a good impression; he was worldly and suave, inclined to be all things to all men. In almost every point he was the antithesis of his great contemporary, Dr. Samuel Johnson, and the idolizers of that rugged, uncompromising, ruthlessly sincere, thoroughly un-

conventional hero, will not extend much sympathy
to Gibbon as a man. One who in his boyhood met
them together in society has thus recorded the contrasted impressions they produced upon him:

'On the day I first sat down with Johnson, in his
rusty brown, and his black worsteds, Gibbon was
placed opposite to me in a suit of flower'd velvet, with
bag and sword. Each had his measured phraseology,
and Johnson's famous parallel between Dryden and
Pope might be loosely parodied in reference to himself
and Gibbon. Johnson's style was grand and Gibbon's
elegant; the stateliness of the former was sometimes
pedantic, and the polish of the latter was occasionally
finical. Johnson march'd to kettle-drums and trum-
pets; Gibbon moved to flutes and hautboys; Johnson
hew'd passages through the Alps, while Gibbon
levell'd walks through parks and gardens. Maul'd as
I had been by Johnson, Gibbon pour'd balm upon
my bruises, by condescending once or twice, in the
course of the evening, to talk with me; the great
historian was light and playful; suiting his matter
to the capacity of the boy; but it was done *more suo*;
still his mannerism prevail'd; still he tapp'd his
snuff-box, still he smirk'd and smiled; and rounded
his periods with the same air of good breeding, as if
he were conversing with men.—His mouth, mellifluous
as Plato's, was a round hole, nearly in the centre of his
visage [1].'

This anecdote shows the historian as a fop. He
records himself in his *Diary* how the lady to whom
he had been engaged, Mademoiselle Curchod, rallied
him on his ' ton de petit maître '. But the anecdote
also reveals him in an amiable light, and it would be
very unfair to construe his desire to please as the trait
of an insincere character. He is always reproached with
a cold nature, and he certainly was not capable of
a romantic affection. His relations with Mademoiselle

---

[1] This passage from the *Random Records* of George
Colman (i. 121, 1830) is quoted by Mr. R. Prothero in
his edition of Gibbon's *Correspondence* (i. 213, 1896).

Curchod attest this. He broke off his engagement
with her (in August, 1762) on account of the opposition
of his father, and Rousseau thought that she would
not have been happy with a man of such cold temperament. In the *Autobiography* Gibbon says that
his cure ' was accelerated by a faithful report of the
tranquillity and cheerfulness of the lady herself ',
but his *Diary* reveals that he was deeply mortified at
the time by the calmness with which the lady had
accepted the rupture. He heard with resentment that
she shared in the social amusements of Lausanne, was
surrounded by admirers, and listened to them with
complaisance. When he returned to Lausanne in
1763, she wrote to him assurances that she had been
constant, and that his image had never for a moment
been effaced from her heart. Her protestations failed
to convince her former lover. Commenting on her
letter in his *Diary*, he says : Her ' amusements convict
her of the most odious dissimulation, and if infidelity
is sometimes a weakness, duplicity is always a vice.
This episode, curious throughout, has been of great
use to me ; it has opened my eyes to the character of
women, and will serve me long as a preservative against
the seductions of love.' It is probable that he never
thought very seriously of matrimony again. Once
indeed he wrote to Lady Sheffield (in 1784) : Should
you be very much surprised to hear of my being
married ? Amazing as it may seem, I do assure you
that the event is less improbable than it would have
appeared to myself a twelvemonth ago. Deyverdun
and I have often agreed, in jest and in earnest, that
a house like ours would be regulated, and graced, and
enlivened, by an agreeable female Companion ; but
each of us seems desirous that his friend should sacrifice
himself for the public good. Since my residence here
I have lived much in women's company ; and, to
your credit be it spoken, I like you better the more
I see of you. Not that I am in love with any particular
person. I have discovered about half a dozen *Wives*
who would please me in different ways, and by various

merits : one as a mistress ; a second, a lively entertaining acquaintance ; a third, a sincere good-natured
friend ; a fourth, who would represent with grace and
dignity at the head of my table and family ; a fifth,
an excellent economist and housekeeper ; and a sixth,
a very useful nurse. Could I find all these qualities
united in a single person, I should dare to make my
addresses, and should deserve to be refused.' Some
two years later he writes that ' I was in some danger '
from the charms of Madame de Montolieu. Her mother,
Madame de Genlis, said that he proposed, and described
the scene—Gibbon on his knees, her daughter declining
his proposal, Gibbon unable to rise until a servant,
summoned by the lady, came to his assistance. But
the story is undoubtedly a fiction ; it was contra-
dicted by Madame de Montolieu.

The little drama of his early affection had an epi-
logue. Mademoiselle Curchod married the French
statesman, M. Necker, and when Gibbon was in Paris
in the autumn of 1763, they both paid him most friendly
attentions. A letter to Holroyd thus describes their
civilities. ' The Curchod (Madame Necker) I saw at
Paris. She was very fond of me, and the husband
particularly civil. Could they insult me more cruelly ?
Ask me every evening to supper ; go to bed and leave
me alone with his wife—what an impertinent security !
It is making an old lover of mighty little consequence.
She is as handsome as ever, and much genteeler ;
seems pleased with her fortune rather than proud of
it. I was (perhaps indiscreetly enough) exalting
Nanette de Illens's good luck and the fortune. "What
fortune ?" said she, with an air of contempt, "not
above 20,000 livres a year." I smiled, and she caught
herself immediately. "What airs I give myself in
despising 20,000 livres a year, who a year ago looked
upon 800 as the summit of my wishes."' Madame
Necker also wrote to a friend about these visits of her
old lover. ' They gave me pleasure beyond all expression ; not that I retain any sentiment for a man who,
I see, does not deserve it ; but my feminine vanity

has never had a triumph juster or more complete.' Gibbon thoroughly appreciated the opulence which surrounded her; 'till then,' she writes, 'it had only made upon me a disagreeable impression.'

But if Gibbon did not shine as a lover, he was capable of warm and faithful friendships, as with the Holroyds and Deyverdun.

During the parliamentary period of his life (1774–83), he went much into society in London. 'The militia, my travels, the House of Commons, the fame of an author, contributed to multiply my connexions; I was chosen a member of the fashionable clubs, and, before I left England in 1783, there were few persons in the literary or political world to whom I was a stranger.' Among these clubs was a weekly society known as the Literary Club, instituted in 1764, of which Burke, Johnson, Goldsmith, Garrick, Sir Joshua Reynolds, Fox, Sheridan, Adam Smith, and many other distinguished people were members. It is to be regretted that we have no record of a conversation between Gibbon and Johnson. The nearest approach we have is an anecdote told by Boswell. At a dinner of the Literary Club, the subject of bears was introduced. ' "We are told," said Johnson, "that the black bear is innocent; but I should not like to trust myself with him." Mr. Gibbon muttered, in a low tone of voice, "I should not like to trust myself with *you*." ' The dislike of Gibbon was returned by Johnson and his satellite.

Boswell wrote: 'Gibbon is an ugly, affected, disgusting fellow, and poisons our literary club to me.' Again, in his *Life of Johnson*, we read: 'Johnson certainly was vain of the society of ladies, and could make himself very agreeable to them when he chose it; Sir Joshua Reynolds agreed with me that he could. Mr. Gibbon, with his usual sneer, controverted it, perhaps in resentment of Johnson's having talked with some disgust of his ugliness, which one would think a *philosopher* would not mind.' The name of Johnson is not mentioned in the *Autobiography*, but in the

Decline and Fall the author sometimes refers to his
writings, and almost always for the purpose of a hit.

We cannot look with much complacency on Gibbon's
career as a politician. He was a silent member of the
House of Commons during the years in which England
was engaged in the war with her American colonies,
and he cast the weight of his votes for the disastrous
policy of Lord North. 'I took my seat,' he says, 'at
the beginning of the memorable contest between Great
Britain and America, and supported with many a sincere
and silent vote, the rights, though not, perhaps, the
interest, of the mother country.' He was, no doubt,
sincerely convinced of the abstract justice of the
English cause, but he certainly came to disbelieve in
the policy of the measures which he supported. He
reveals this frankly in his *Correspondence*. 'Upon the
whole I find it much easier to defend the justice than
the policy of our measures, but there are certain cases
where whatever is repugnant to sound policy ceases to
be just.' And later on he condemns North strongly
and unequivocally: 'I still repeat that in my opinion
Lord N. does not deserve pardon for the past, applause
for the present, or confidence for the future.' He knew
that the war would result in failure and was exhausting
the country. But he sacrificed his real opinions to
loyalty to his leader and party, and was rewarded by
a sinecure worth £750 a year (1780). Gibbon had
never to struggle with poverty; he had always a competence; but his ideas of ease and luxury prevented
him from being satisfied with his means. On an
income, however, which had to be husbanded in
London, he found himself able to live handsomely
when he retired to Lausanne on the termination of
his parliamentary career; and he looked forward to
'the deaths of aged ladies', whose inheritances would
secure him affluence and enable him to return to
London and live at his ease. One of these ladies,
Mrs. Gibbon, his stepmother, proved to have a better
life than his own.

Gibbon's wisdom in choosing what he calls his

'voluntary banishment' to Lausanne was fully approved by the results. 'If every day has not been equally soft and serene, not a day, not a moment, has occurred in which I have repented of my choice.' He had felt his political life as 'a chain of duty and dependence'; his conduct had been swayed by what he conceived to be his obligations to Lord North, and by his hopes of a share 'in the division of the spoil'. On the shores of Lake Leman he enjoyed complete independence, uninterrupted leisure to complete his history, and a climate which agreed with his health. We have few glimpses of his life there from other sources than his own epistles. The visit of Fox, to which he refers in the *Autobiography*, is thus more graphically described in a letter: 'I have eat, drank, and conversed, and sat up all night with Fox in England; but it has never happened, perhaps it never can happen again, that I should enjoy him, as I did that day, alone, from ten in the morning till ten at night. We had little politics; though he gave me in a few words such a character of Pitt as one great man should give to another his rival; much of books, from my own, on which he flattered me very pleasantly, to Homer and the *Arabian Nights*; much about the country, and my garden (which he understands far better than I do); and, upon the whole, I think he envies me, and would do so were he minister.' Here is Fox's impression of the visit, recorded by Rogers: 'Gibbon talked a great deal, walking up and down the room, and generally ending his sentences with a genitive case; every now and then, too, casting a look of complacency on his own portrait by Sir Joshua Reynolds, which hung over the chimney-piece—that wonderful portrait, in which, while the oddness and vulgarity of the features are refined away, the likeness is perfectly preserved.'

Byron visited the historian's house in 1816, and saw the summer-house, in which the conclusion of the *Decline and Fall* was written, in a state of dilapidation. I enclose you,' he wrote to Mr. Murray, 'a sprig of

Gibbon's acacia and some rose leaves from his garden, which, with part of his house, I have just seen. The garden and summer-house, where he composed, are neglected, and the last utterly decayed ; but they still show it as his " cabinet ", and seem perfectly aware of his memory.'

The biography of an historian is valuable for the study of his work. It is slowly being recognized that history is in the last resort somebody's image of the past, and the image is conditioned by the mind and experience of the person who forms it. Only such things as dates, names, documents, can be considered purely objective facts. The reconstruction, which involves the discovery of causes and motives, which it is the historian's business to attempt, depends on subjective elements, which cannot be eliminated. Further, he can only realize, fully and vitally, the time in which he lives ; this is really, however uncon- sciously, the starting-point for his travels in the ages of the past ; he inevitably takes present values and modern measures with him ; and the conscious allow- ances which he makes for difference of conditions cannot remove, though it may disguise or mitigate, this limitation of his mind. We cannot separate a history from its writer, or the writer from his time ; and to appreciate the particular interpretation of the past which his work presents, it is of the highest importance to know the influences which moulded him and the external circumstances of his life.

It is pertinent, for instance, to know that Gibbon, before he became a Rationalist, had become first a Roman Catholic, and then a Protestant, through intellectual conviction, and that in embracing the former faith he had preferred, as he says, ' conscience to interest ', and made himself liable to the severe penalties with which English statutes menaced such conversion. ' The gates of Magdalen College were for ever shut ' against him ; his father threatened to disown him, and sent him to Lausanne. More than this he did not suffer ; but even this, along with the

fact that he might have come within the range of the
tyrannical laws of a state unemancipated from ecclesi-
asticism, was enough to bring home to him acutely the
meaning of freedom of conscience. Afterwards, as an
infidel, he might legally have been oppressed under
statutes which had been enacted at no remote date,
if he had openly declared the opinions which he more
effectively insinuated. For in our country, which
boasted of its freedom, three years' imprisonment
without bail was, for the second offence, the penalty
imposed on any one who, brought up as a Christian,
should deny the truth of Christianity. The irony
which he had learned from Pascal was the historian's
defensive armour against these barbarous laws.

The *Autobiography* confirms the influence exercised
on Gibbon by Bayle and Montesquieu, which we might
surmise from the *Decline and Fall*, and it teaches us
the interesting fact that he had received a special
stimulus from the work of Giannone. This Neapolitan
lawyer exposed in his *Civil History of Naples* the evils
of sacerdotal power. His enlightened work procured
him the hatred and persecution of the Jesuits; he
sought refuge at Geneva from the pursuit of his implacable foes, was basely lured into Savoy territory,
and ended his days in a Piedmontese prison. But his
book had a far-reaching influence on the higher classes,
and even on the governments, in Italy, in discrediting
sacerdotalism and the Canon Law and affirming the
complete independence of the State in relation to the
Church. Along with the later writings of Genovesi,
Beccaria, and Filangieri, it prepared the way for the
victories of liberty in the nineteenth century. Giannone helped to form Gibbon's standard in surveying
universal history.

His standard is also illustrated by his deep interest
in the fortunes of the Swiss republic and the early
struggles of the cantons. One of the youthful designs
which he never realized, recorded in the *Autobiography*,
was to write *The History of the Liberty of the Swiss*,
' of that independence which a brave people rescued

from the House of Austria, defended against a Dauphin of France, and finally sealed with the blood of Charles of Burgundy.' Liberty was in fact his ultimate standard; perhaps there was no deeper feeling in his breast than jealousy of personal freedom and independence which he describes as the first of earthly blessings.

But in regard to the realization of the liberty of the individual within the State, he was not in advance of his times; he was not a democrat or a believer in equality. His ideal did not involve more than such free institutions, or such a measure of freedom, as were to be found in the happier countries in the eighteenth century. But paternal governments, however well-meaning and efficient they might be, did not satisfy him, if they excluded political liberty. He perceived that without such liberty there was no security for the future. This view is clearly shown in his famous judgement on the age of Nerva and his successors, to the death of Marcus Aurelius, which he holds up (in the third chapter of the *Decline and Fall*) as the period of history in which the human race was most happy and prosperous. But two remarks which follow signalize the defect of the happiness thus procured. 'Such princes deserved the honour of restoring the republic, had the Romans of their days been capable of enjoying a rational freedom.' 'They must often have recollected the instability of a happiness which depended on the character of a single man.'

The happiness of mankind, including liberty as an essential ingredient and an indispensable condition, is the standard by which Gibbon judged the past, and condemned the Middle Ages, the era of 'the triumph of religion'. He does not attempt to do what historians of the following century were to attempt to do, by acquiring what is called 'historical sense',—to judge an age by its own ideas and ideals.

He was thus deeply imbued with the humanity which characterized the enlightenment of the eighteenth century. Porson said maliciously: 'Nor does his humanity ever slumber unless when women are ravished or the Christians persecuted.' The criticism is hardly fair. All cruelty and persecution were odious to Gibbon, and even in the sixteenth chapter, to which it specially refers, he makes this perfectly plain. At the same time, he does assume a pointed indifference to the sufferings of the Christians; and lets us see that he could not help feeling a wicked satisfaction that the Christians who have been merciless in plaguing infidels should themselves have been plagued. He cannot be acquitted of sometimes affecting cynicism; but it must be remembered that it was not incumbent on him to express horror or indignation on every occasion that he had to commemorate acts of violence or inhumanity. He displays his detestation of the murder of Hypatia; he might merely have recorded the fact, if it had not inflicted ' an indelible stain on the character and religion ' of a Christian bishop; but if he had made no comment, it would not be fair to say that his humanity slumbered.

His humanity is shown by his horror of ' the abominable slave-trade '. His friend, Lord Sheffield, was opposed to its abolition, and published a tract on the subject. Gibbon wrote to him: ' You have such a knack of turning a nation that I am afraid you will triumph (perhaps by the force of argument) over justice and humanity. But do you not expect to work at Beelzebub's sugar plantations in the infernal regions, under the tender government of a negro-driver ? ' Two years later, when the gradual abolition of the trade was voted in the House (1792), he wrote more coolly, showing his dread of the Revolution : ' In the slave question you triumphed last session ; in this you have been defeated. What is the cause of the alteration ? If it proceeded only from an impulse of humanity, I cannot be displeased, even with an error ; since it is very likely that my own vote (had I possessed one) would have been added to the Majority. But in this rage against slavery, in the numerous petitions against the Slave-trade, was there no leaven of new democratical principles? no wild ideas of the rights and natural equality of man?'

In the last years of his life, Gibbon conceived the idea of an interesting biographical work. He communicated the literary secret to the private ear of Lord Sheffield. 'I have long resolved in my mind another scheme of biographical writing: the lives, or rather, the characters, of the most eminent persons in arts and arms, in Church and State, who have flourished in Britain from the reign of Henry VIII to the present age. This work, extensive as it may be, would be an amusement rather than a toil: the materials are accessible in our own language, and for the most part ready to my hands; but the subject, which could afford a rich display of human nature and domestic history, would powerfully address itself to the feelings of every Englishman. The taste or fashion of the times seems to delight in picturesque decorations; and this series of British portraits might aptly be accompanied by the respective heads, taken from originals, and engraved by the best masters.' He asks his friend to sound a bookseller in Pall Mall on the subject as if the idea came from himself—'as it is most essential that I be solicited and do not solicit'. He tells Lord Sheffield how to conduct the negotiation. 'If he (the publisher) kindles at the thought, and eagerly claims my alliance; you will begin to hesitate. "I am afraid, Mr. Nichols, that we shall hardly persuade my friend to engage in so great a work. Gibbon is old, and rich, and lazy. However you may make the trial."' Lord Sheffield promised to speak to Nichols, but we hear no more of the matter, and a twelvemonth later Gibbon died. We cannot think without chagrin that if he had survived to enjoy the full period of 'autumnal felicity' to which he looked forward, we might have had from his brilliant pen portraits of Elizabeth and Cromwell, Wolsey and Laud, Marlborough and Bolingbroke, to name but half a dozen of the host that crowd to one's mind.

J. B. BURY.

CONTENTS

LETTERS

FROM LORD SHEFFIELD'S ADVERTISEMENT

TO THE

FIRST EDITION OF GIBBON'S MISCELLANEOUS WORKS

THE melancholy duty of examining the papers of my deceased friend devolved upon me at a time when I was depressed by severe afflictions.

In that state of mind, I hesitated to undertake the task of selecting and preparing his manuscripts for the press. The warmth of my early and long attachment to Mr. Gibbon made me conscious of a partiality, which it was not proper to indulge, especially in revising many of his juvenile and unfinished compositions. I had to guard, not only against a sentiment like my own, which I found extensively diffused, but also against the eagerness occasioned by a very general curiosity to see in print every literary relic, however imperfect, of so distinguished a writer.

Being aware how disgracefully authors of eminence have been often treated, by an indiscreet posthumous publication of fragments and careless effusions; when I had selected those papers which to myself appeared the fittest for the public eye, I consulted some of our common friends, whom I knew to be equally anxious with myself for Mr. Gibbon's fame, and fully competent, from their judgement, to protect it.

Under such a sanction it is, that, no longer suspecting myself to view through too favourable a medium the

compositions of my friend, I now venture to publish
them : and it may here be proper to give some information to the reader respecting the contents of these
volumes.

The most important part consists of Memoirs of
Mr. Gibbon's Life and Writings, a work which he seems
to have projected with peculiar solicitude and attention, and of which he left six different sketches, all in
his own handwriting. One of these sketches, the
most diffuse and circumstantial, so far as it proceeds,
ends at the time when he quitted Oxford. Another
at the year 1764, when he travelled to Italy. A third,
at his father's death, in 1770. A fourth, which he
continued to March, 1791, appears in the form of
annals, much less detailed than the others. The two
remaining sketches are still more imperfect. But it
is difficult to discover the order in which these several
pieces were written. From all of them the following
Memoirs have been carefully selected, and put together.

My hesitation in giving these Memoirs to the world
arose, principally, from the circumstance of Mr.
Gibbon's seeming, in some respect, not to have been
quite satisfied with them, as he had so frequently
varied their form : yet, notwithstanding this diffidence,
the compositions, though unfinished, are so excellent,
that I think myself justified in permitting my friend
to appear as his own biographer, rather than to have
that office undertaken by any other person less qualified
for it.

This opinion has rendered me anxious to publish
the present Memoirs, without any unnecessary delay ;
for I am persuaded that the author of them cannot
be made to appear in a truer light than he does in the
following pages. In them, and in his different letters,
which I have added, will be found a complete picture
of his talents, his disposition, his studies, and his
attainments.

Those slight variations of character, which naturally
arose in the progress of his life, will be unfolded in
a series of letters, selected from a correspondence

between him and myself, which continued full thirty years, and ended with his death.

It is to be lamented, that all the sketches of the Memoirs, except that composed in the form of annals, cease about twenty years before Mr. Gibbon's death; and consequently, that we have the least detailed account of the most interesting part of his life. His correspondence during that period will, in great measure, supply the deficiency. It will be separated from the Memoirs and placed in an appendix, that those who are not disposed to be pleased with the repetitions, familiarities, and trivial circumstances of epistolary writing, may not be embarrassed by it. By many, the letters will be found a very interesting part of the present publication. They will prove how pleasant, friendly, and amiable Mr. Gibbon was in private life; and if, in publishing letters so flattering to myself, I incur the imputation of vanity, I shall meet the charge with a frank confession, that I am indeed highly vain of having enjoyed, for so many years, the esteem, the confidence, and the affection of a man, whose social qualities endeared him to the most accomplished society, and whose talents, great as they were, must be acknowledged to have been fully equalled by the sincerity of his friendship.

Whatever censure may be pointed against the editor, the public will set a due value on the letters for their intrinsic merit. I must, indeed, be blinded, either by vanity or affection, if they do not display the heart and mind of their author, in such a manner as justly to increase the number of his admirers.

I have not been solicitous to garble or expunge passages which, to some, may appear trifling. Such passages will often, in the opinion of the observing reader, mark the character of the writer, and the omission of them would materially take from the ease and familiarity of authentic letters.

Few men, I believe, have ever so fully unveiled their own character, by a minute narrative of their sentiments and pursuits, as Mr. Gibbon will here be found to have done; not with study and labour—not with an affected frankness—but with a genuine confession of his little foibles and peculiarities, and a good-humoured and natural display of his own conduct and opinions.

Mr. Gibbon began a journal, a work distinct from the sketches already mentioned, in the early part of his life, with the following declaration:

'I propose from this day, August 24, 1761, to keep an exact journal of my actions and studies, both to assist my memory, and to accustom me to set a due value on my time. I shall begin by setting down some few events of my past life, the dates of which I can remember.'

This industrious project he pursued occasionally in French, with the minuteness, fidelity, and liberality of a mind resolved to watch over and improve itself.

The journal is continued under different titles, and is sometimes very concise, and sometimes singularly detailed. One part of it is entitled 'My Journal', another 'Ephemerides, or Journal of my Actions, Studies, and Opinions'. The other parts are entitled, 'Ephémérides, ou Journal de ma Vie, de mes Études, et de mes Sentimens'. In this journal, among the most trivial circumstances, are mixed very interesting observations and dissertations on a satire of Juvenal, a passage of Homer, or of Longinus, or of any other author whose works he happened to read in the course of the day; and he often passes from a remark on the most common event, to a critical disquisition of considerable learning, or an inquiry into some abstruse point of Philosophy.

It certainly was not his intention that this private and motley diary should be presented to the public; nor have I thought myself at liberty to present it, in the shape in which he left it. But when reduced to an account of *his literary occupations*, it forms so singular and so interesting a portrait of an indefatigable student, that I persuade myself it will be regarded as a valuable acquisition by the Literary World, and as an accession of fame to the memory of my friend. With the extracts from Mr. Gibbon's journal will be printed his dissertations entitled 'Extraits Raisonnés de mes Lectures': and 'Recueil de mes Observations, et Pièces détachées sur différens Sujets' A few other passages from other parts of the journals, introduced in notes, will make a curious addition to the Memoirs.

It remains only to express a wish, that in discharging this latest office of affection, my regard to the memory of my Friend may appear, as I trust it will do, proportioned to the high satisfaction which I enjoyed for many years in possessing his entire confidence, and very partial attachment.

SHEFFIELD

Sheffield Place,
   Aug. 6, 1795.

MEMOIRS

OF

MY LIFE AND WRITINGS

In the fifty-second year of my age, after the completion of an arduous and successful work, I now propose to employ some moments of my leisure in reviewing the simple transactions of a private and literary life. Truth, naked, unblushing truth, the first virtue of more serious history, must be the sole recommendation of this personal narrative. The style shall be simple and familiar: but style is the image of character; and the habits of correct writing may produce, without labour or design, the appearance of art and study. My own amusement is my motive, and will be my reward: and if these sheets are communicated to some discreet and indulgent friends, they will be secreted from the public eye till the author shall be removed beyond the reach of criticism or ridicule.[1]

[1] This passage is found in one only of the six sketches, and in that which seems to have been the first written, and which was laid aside among loose papers. Mr. Gibbon, in his communications with me on the subject of his Memoirs, a subject which he had not mentioned to any other person, expressed a determination of publishing them in his lifetime; and never appears to have departed from that resolution, excepting in one of his letters annexed, in which he intimates a doubt, though rather carelessly, whether in his time, or at any time, they would meet the eye of the public. In a conversation, however, not long

A lively desire of knowing and of recording our
ancestors so generally prevails, that it must depend
on the influence of some common principle in the
minds of men. We seem to have lived in the persons
of our forefathers; it is the labour and reward of
vanity to extend the term of this ideal longevity.
Our imagination is always active to enlarge the narrow
circle in which nature has confined us. Fifty or
an hundred years may be allotted to an individual;
but we step forward beyond death with such hopes
as religion and philosophy will suggest; and we fill
up the silent vacancy that precedes our birth, by
associating ourselves to the authors of our existence.
Our calmer judgement will rather tend to moderate,
than to suppress, the pride of an ancient and worthy
race. The satirist may laugh, the philosopher may
preach; but reason herself will respect the prejudices
and habits, which have been consecrated by the
experience of mankind. Few there are who can
sincerely despise in others, an advantage of which
they are secretly ambitious to partake. The knowledge of our own family from a remote period, will
be always esteemed as an abstract pre-eminence,
since it can never be promiscuously enjoyed; but the
longest series of peasants and mechanics would not
afford much gratification to the pride of their descendant. We wish to discover our ancestors, but we
wish to discover them possessed of ample fortunes,
adorned with honourable titles, and holding an eminent
rank in the class of hereditary nobles, which has been
maintained for the wisest and most beneficial purposes, in almost every climate of the globe, and in
almost every modification of political society.

Wherever the distinction of birth is allowed to
form a superior order in the state, education and

before his death, I suggested to him, that, if he should
make them a full image of his mind, he would not have
nerves to publish them, and therefore that they should
be posthumous. He answered, rather eagerly, that he
was determined to publish them *in his lifetime*. S.

example should always, and will often, produce among them a dignity of sentiment and propriety of conduct, which is guarded from dishonour by their own and the public esteem. If we read of some illustrious line so ancient that it has no beginning, so worthy that it ought to have no end, we sympathize in its various fortunes; nor can we blame the generous enthusiasm, or even the harmless vanity, of those who are allied to the honours of its name. For my own part, could I draw my pedigree from a general, a statesman, or a celebrated author, I should study their lives with the diligence of filial love. In the investigation of past events, our curiosity is stimulated by the immediate or indirect reference to ourselves; but in the estimate of honour we should learn to value the gifts of nature above those of fortune; to esteem in our ancestors the qualities that best promote the interests of society; and to pronounce the descendant of a king less truly noble than the offspring of a man of genius, whose writings will instruct or delight the latest posterity. The family of Confucius is, in my opinion, the most illustrious in the world. After a painful ascent of eight or ten centuries, our barons and princes of Europe are lost in the darkness of the middle ages; but, in the vast equality of the empire of China, the posterity of Confucius have maintained, above two thousand two hundred years, their peaceful honours and perpetual succession. The chief of the family is still revered, by the sovereign and the people, as the lively image of the wisest of mankind. The nobility of the Spencers has been illustrated and enriched by the trophies of Marlborough; but I exhort them to consider the *Fairy Queen* [1] as the most precious jewel of their coronet. Our immortal Fielding was of the younger branch of the Earls of Denbigh, who draw their origin from

---

[1] Nor less praiseworthy are the ladies three,
    The honour of that noble familie,
    Of which I meanest boast myself to be.
                    Spenser, *Colin Clout*, &c., v. 538.

the Counts of Habsburg, the lineal descendants of Eltrico, in the seventh century, Duke of Alsace. Far different have been the fortunes of the English and German divisions of the family of Habsburg: the former, the knights and sheriffs of Leicestershire, have slowly risen to the dignity of a peerage; the latter, the Emperors of Germany, and Kings of Spain, have threatened the liberty of the old, and invaded the treasures of the new world. The successors of Charles the Fifth may disdain their brethren of England; but the romance of *Tom Jones*, that exquisite picture of human manners, will outlive the palace of the Escurial, and the imperial eagle of the house of Austria.

That these sentiments are just, or at least natural, I am the more inclined to believe, as I am not myself interested in the cause; for I can derive from my ancestors neither glory nor shame. Yet a sincere and simple narrative of my own life may amuse some of my leisure hours; but it will subject me, and perhaps with justice, to the imputation of vanity. I may judge, however, from the experience both of past and of the present times, that the public are always curious to know the men who have left behind them any image of their minds: the most scanty accounts of such men are compiled with diligence, and perused with eagerness; and the student of every class may derive a lesson, or an example, from the lives most similar to his own. My name may hereafter be placed among the thousand articles of a *Biographia Britannica*; and I must be conscious that no one is so well qualified as myself to describe the series of my thoughts and actions. The authority of my masters, of the grave Thuanus, and the philosophic Hume, might be sufficient to justify my design; but it would not be difficult to produce a long list of ancients and moderns who, in various forms, have exhibited their own portraits. Such portraits are often the most interesting, and sometimes the only interesting parts of their writings; and, if they be sincere, we seldom complain of the minuteness or prolixity of these personal memorials. The lives of the younger Pliny, of Petrarch, and of Erasmus, are expressed in the epistles which they themselves have given to the world. The essays of Montaigne and Sir William Temple bring us home to the houses and bosoms of the authors: we smile without contempt at the headstrong passions of Benvenuto Cellini, and the gay follies of Colley Cibber. The confessions of St. Austin and Rousseau disclose the secrets of the human heart: the commentaries of the learned Huet have survived his evangelical demonstration; and the memoirs of Goldoni are more truly dramatic than his Italian comedies. The heretic and the churchman are strongly marked in the characters and fortunes of Whiston and Bishop Newton; and even the dullness of Michael de Marolles and Anthony Wood acquires some value from the faithful representation of men and manners. That I am equal or superior to some of these, the effects of modesty or affectation cannot force me to dissemble.

My family is originally derived from the county of Kent. The southern district, which borders on Sussex and the sea, was formerly overspread with the great forest Anderida, and even now retains the denomination of the *Weald*, or Woodland. In this district, and in the hundred and parish of Rolvenden, the Gibbons were possessed of lands in the year one thousand three hundred and twenty-six; and the elder branch of the family, without much increase or diminution of property, still adheres to its native soil. Fourteen years after the first appearance of his name, John Gibbon is recorded as the Marmorarius or architect of King Edward the Third: the strong and stately castle of Queensborough, which guarded the entrance of the Medway, was a monument of his skill; and the grant of an hereditary toll on the passage from Sandwich to Stonar, in the Isle of Thanet, is the reward of no vulgar artist. In the visitations of the heralds, the Gibbons are frequently mentioned: they held the rank of Esquire in an age when that title was less promiscuously assumed: one of them, in the reign of Queen Elizabeth, was captain of the militia of Kent; and a free school, in the neighbouring town of Benenden, proclaims the charity and opulence of its founder. But time, or their own obscurity, has cast a veil of oblivion over the virtues and vices of my Kentish ancestors; their character or station confined them to the labours and pleasures of a rural life; nor is it in my power to follow the advice of the poet, in an inquiry after a name—

> Go! search it there, where to be born, and die,
> Of rich and poor makes all the history,

so recent is the institution of our parish registers. In the beginning of the seventeenth century a younger branch of the Gibbons of Rolvenden migrated from the country to the city; and from this branch I do not blush to descend. The law requires some abilities; the church imposes some restraints; and before our army and navy, our civil establishments, and India empire, had opened so many paths of fortune, the mercantile profession was more frequently chosen by youths of a liberal race and education, who aspired to create their own independence. Our most respectable families have not disdained the counting-house, or even the shop; their names are enrolled in the Livery and Companies of London; and in England, as well as in the Italian commonwealths, heralds have been compelled to declare that gentility is not degraded by the exercise of trade.

The armorial ensigns which, in the times of chivalry, adorned the crest and shield of the soldier, are now become an empty decoration, which every man, who has money to build a carriage, may paint according to his fancy on the panels. My family arms are the same which were borne by the Gibbons of Kent in an age when the College of Heralds religiously guarded the distinctions of blood and name: a lion rampant gardant, between three escallop-shells Argent, on a field Azure.[1] I should not, however, have been tempted to blazon my coat of arms, were it not connected with a whimsical anecdote. About the reign of James the First, the three harmless escallop-shells were changed by Edmund Gibbon, Esq., into three *Ogresses*, or female cannibals, with a design of stigmatizing three ladies, his kinswomen, who had provoked him by an unjust lawsuit. But this singular mode of revenge, for which he obtained the sanction of Sir William Seagar, king-at-arms, soon expired with its author; and, on his own monument in the Temple Church, the monsters vanish, and the three escallop-shells resume their proper and hereditary place.

Our alliances by marriage it is not disgraceful to mention. The chief honour of my ancestry is James Fiens, Baron Say and Seale, and Lord High Treasurer of England, in the reign of Henry the Sixth; from whom by the Phelips, the Whetnalls, and the Cromers, I am lineally descended in the eleventh degree. His dismission and imprisonment in the Tower were insufficient to appease the popular clamour; and the Treasurer, with his son-in-law Cromer, was beheaded (1450), after a mock trial by the Kentish insurgents. The black list of his offences, as it is exhibited in Shakespeare, displays the ignorance and envy of a plebeian tyrant. Besides the vague reproaches of selling Maine and Normandy to the Dauphin, the Treasurer is specially accused of luxury, for riding on a foot-cloth, and of treason, for speaking French, the language of our enemies: 'Thou hast most traiterously corrupted the youth of the realm', says Jack Cade to the unfortunate lord, 'in erecting a grammar school; and whereas before, our forefathers had no other books than the score and the tally, thou

---

[1] The father of Lord Chancellor Hardwicke married an heiress of this family of Gibbon. The Chancellor's escutcheon in the Temple Hall quarters the arms of Gibbon, as does also that, in Lincoln's Inn Hall, of Charles York, Chancellor in 1770. S.

hast caused printing to be used; and, contrary to
the king, his crown, and dignity, thou hast built
a paper-mill. It will be proved to thy face, that
thou hast men about thee who usually talk of a noun
and a verb, and such abominable words, as no Christian
ear can endure to hear.' Our dramatic poet is generally
more attentive to character than to history; and
I much fear that the art of printing was not introduced
into England till several years after Lord Say's death:
but of some of these meritorious crimes I should
hope to find my ancestor guilty; and a man of letters
may be proud of his descent from a patron and martyr
of learning.

In the beginning of the last century, Robert Gibbon,
Esq., of Rolvenden in Kent[1] (who died in 1618),
had a son of the same name of Robert, who settled
in London, and became a member of the Clothworkers'
Company. His wife was a daughter of the Edgars,
who flourished about four hundred years in the county
of Suffolk, and produced an eminent and wealthy
serjeant-at-law, Sir Gregory Edgar, in the reign of
Henry the Seventh. Of the sons of Robert Gibbon
(who died in 1643), Matthew did not aspire above the
station of a linen-draper in Leadenhall Street; but
John has given to the public some curious memorials
of his existence, his character, and his family. He
was born on the 3rd of November, in the year 1629;
his education was liberal, at a grammar school, and
afterwards in Jesus College at Cambridge; and he

---

[1] Robert Gibbon, my lineal ancestor, in the fifth degree,
was captain of the Kentish militia, and as he died in the
year 1618, it may be presumed that he had appeared in
arms at the time of the Spanish invasion. His wife was
Margaret Phillips, daughter of Edward Phillips de la Weld
in Tenterden, and of Rose his wife, daughter of George
Whitnell, of East Peckham, Esquire. Peckham, the seat
of the Whitnells of Kent, is mentioned, not indeed much
to its honour, in the *Mémoires du Comte de Grammont,*
a classic work, the delight of every man and woman of
taste to whom the French language is familiar.

celebrates the retired content which he enjoyed at Allesborough in Worcestershire, in the house of Thomas Lord Coventry, where he was employed as a domestic tutor. But the spirit of my kinsman soon immerged into more active life; he visited foreign countries as a soldier and a traveller, acquired the knowledge of the French and Spanish languages; passed some time in the Isle of Jersey, crossed the Atlantic, and resided upwards of a twelvemonth (1659) in the rising colony of Virginia. In this remote province, his taste, or rather passion, for heraldry found a singular gratification at a war-dance of the native Indians. As they moved in measured steps, brandishing their tomahawks, his curious eye contemplated their little shields of bark, and their naked bodies, which were painted with the colours and symbols of his favourite science. 'At which (says he) I exceedingly wondered; and concluded that heraldry was ingrafted *naturally* into the sense of human race. If so, it deserves a greater esteem than nowadays is put upon it.' His return to England after the restoration was soon followed by his marriage —his settlement in a house in St. Catherine's Cloister, near the Tower, which devolved to my grandfather —and his introduction into the Heralds' College (in 1671) by the style and title of Blue-mantle Pursuivant-at-Arms. In this office he enjoyed near fifty years the rare felicity of uniting, in the same pursuit, his duty and inclination: his name is remembered in the College, and many of his letters are still preserved. Several of the most respectable characters of the age, Sir William Dugdale, Mr. Ashmole, Dr. John Betts, and Dr. Nehemiah Grew, were his friends; and in the society of such men, John Gibbon may be recorded without disgrace as the member of an astrological club. The study of hereditary honours is favourable to the Royal prerogative; and my kinsman, like most of his family, was a high Tory both in church and state. In the latter end of the reign of Charles the Second, his pen was exercised in the cause of

the Duke of York: the Republican faction he most
cordially detested; and as each animal is conscious
of its proper arms, the herald's revenge was emblazoned
on a most diabolical escutcheon. But the triumph of
the Whig government checked the preferment of
Blue-mantle; and he was even suspended from his
office till his tongue could learn to pronounce the oath
of abjuration. His life was prolonged to the age of
ninety; and, in the expectation of the inevitable
though uncertain hour, he wishes to preserve the
blessings of health, competence, and virtue. In the
year 1682 he published at London his *Introductio ad
Latinam Blasoniam,* an original attempt, which
Camden had desiderated, to define, in a Roman idiom,
the terms and attributes of a Gothic institution.
It is not two years since I acquired, in a foreign land,
some domestic intelligence of my own family; and
this intelligence was conveyed to Switzerland from
the heart of Germany. I had formed an acquaintance
with Mr. Langer, a lively and ingenious scholar,
while he resided at Lausanne as preceptor to the
Hereditary Prince of Brunswick. On his return to
his proper station of Librarian to the Ducal Library
of Wolfenbuttel, he accidentally found among some
literary rubbish a small old English volume of heraldry,
inscribed with the name of John Gibbon. From the
title only Mr. Langer judged that it might be an
acceptable present to his friend; and he judged
rightly. His manner is quaint and affected; his
order is confused: but he displays some wit, more
reading, and still more enthusiasm; and if an enthu-
siast be often absurd, he is never languid. An English
text is perpetually interspersed with Latin sentences
in prose and verse; but in his own poetry he claims
an exemption from the laws of prosody. Amidst
a profusion of genealogical knowledge, my kinsman
could not be forgetful of his own name; and to him
I am indebted for almost the whole information concerning the Gibbon family.[1] From this small work

---

[1] Mr. Gibbon seems, after this was written, to have

(a duodecimo of one hundred and sixty-five pages)
the author expected immortal fame: and at the conclusion of his labour he sings, in a strain of self-
exultation;

> Usque huc corrigitur Romana Blasonia per me;
> Verborumque dehinc barbara forma cadat.
> Hic liber, in meritum si forsitan incidet usum,
> Testis rite meae sedulitatis erit.
> Quicquid agat Zoilus, ventura fatebitur aetas
> Artis quod fueram non Clypearis inops.

Such are the hopes of authors! In the failure of
those hopes John Gibbon has not been the first of
his profession, and very possibly may not be the last
of his name. His brother, Matthew Gibbon, the draper,
had one daughter and two sons—my grandfather,
Edward, who was born in the year 1666, and Thomas,
afterwards Dean of Carlisle. According to the mercantile creed, that the best book is a profitable ledger,
the writings of John the herald would be much less
precious than those of his nephew Edward: but
an author professes at least to write for the public
benefit; and the slow balance of trade can be pleasing
to those persons only to whom it is advantageous.
The successful industry of my grandfather raised him
above the level of his immediate ancestors; he appears
to have launched into various and extensive dealings:
even his opinions were subordinate to his interest;
and I find him in Flanders clothing King William's
troops, while he would have contracted with more
pleasure, though not perhaps at a cheaper rate, for
the service of King James. During his residence
abroad, his concerns at home were managed by his
mother Hester, an active and notable woman. Her
second husband was a widower, of the name of Acton:
they united the children of their first nuptials. After
his marriage with the daughter of Richard Acton,

collected much additional information respecting his
family; as appears from a number of manuscripts in
my possession. S.

goldsmith in Leadenhall Street, he gave his own sister
to Sir Whitmore Acton, of Aldenham; and I am
thus connected, by a triple alliance, with that ancient
and loyal family of Shropshire baronets. It consisted
about that time of seven brothers, all of gigantic
stature; one of whom, a pigmy of six feet two inches,
confessed himself the last and the least of the seven;
adding, in the true spirit of party, that such men
were not born since the Revolution. Under the Tory
administration of the last four years of Queen Anne
(1710–4), Mr. Edward Gibbon was appointed one of
the Commissioners of the Customs; he sat at that
Board with Prior: but the merchant was better
qualified for his station than the poet; since Lord
Bolingbroke has been heard to declare that he never
conversed with a man who more clearly understood
the commerce and finances of England. In the year
1716 he was elected one of the directors of the South
Sea Company; and his books exhibited the proof
that, before his acceptance of this fatal office, he had
acquired an independent fortune of sixty thousand
pounds.

But his fortune was overwhelmed in the shipwreck
of the year twenty, and the labours of thirty years
were blasted in a single day. Of the use or abuse
of the South Sea scheme, of the guilt or innocence
of my grandfather and his brother directors, I am
neither a competent nor a disinterested judge. Yet
the equity of modern times must condemn the violent
and arbitrary proceedings, which would have disgraced
the cause of justice, and would render injustice still
more odious. No sooner had the nation awakened
from its golden dream than a popular and even a
parliamentary clamour demanded their victims: but
it was acknowledged on all sides that the South Sea
directors, however guilty, could not be touched by
any known laws of the land. The speech of Lord
Molesworth, the author of *The State of Denmark*,
may show the temper, or rather the intemperance,
of the House of Commons. 'Extraordinary crimes

(exclaimed that ardent Whig) call aloud for extraordinary remedies. The Roman lawgivers had not
foreseen the possible existence of a parricide: but as
soon as the first monster appeared he was sewn in
a sack, and cast headlong into the river; and I shall
be content to inflict the same treatment on the authors
of our present ruin.' His motion was not literally
adopted; but a bill of pains and penalties was introduced, a retroactive statute, to punish the offences,
which did not exist at the time they were committed.
Such a pernicious violation of liberty and law can be
excused only by the most imperious necessity; nor
could it be defended on this occasion by the plea of
impending danger or useful example. The legislature
restrained the persons of the directors, imposed an
exorbitant security for their appearance, and marked
their characters with a previous note of ignominy:
they were compelled to deliver, upon oath, the strict
value of their estates; and were disabled from making
any transfer or alienation of any part of their property.
Against a bill of pains and penalties it is the common
right of every subject to be heard by his counsel at
the bar: they prayed to be heard; their prayer was
refused; and their oppressors, who required no
evidence, would listen to no defence. It had been at
first proposed that one-eighth of their respective
estates should be allowed for the future support of
the directors; but it was speciously urged, that in
the various shades of opulence and guilt such an
unequal proportion would be too light for many,
and for some might possibly be too heavy. The
character and conduct of each man were separately
weighed; but, instead of the calm solemnity of
a judicial inquiry, the fortune and honour of three
and thirty Englishmen were made the topic of hasty
conversation, the sport of a lawless majority; and
the basest member of the committee, by a malicious
word or a silent vote, might indulge his general spleen
or personal animosity. Injury was aggravated by
insult, and insult was embittered by pleasantry.

Allowances of twenty pounds, or one shilling, were facetiously moved. A vague report that a director had formerly been concerned in *another* project, by which some unknown persons had lost their money, was admitted as a proof of his actual guilt. One man was ruined because he had dropped a foolish speech, that his horses should feed upon gold; another because he was grown so proud, that, one day at the Treasury, he had refused a civil answer to persons much above him. All were condemned, absent and unheard, in arbitrary fines and forfeitures, which swept away the greatest part of their substance. Such bold oppression can scarcely be shielded by the omnipotence of parliament: and yet it may be seriously questioned, whether the judges of the South Sea directors were the true and legal representatives of their country. The first parliament of George the First had been chosen (1715) for three years: the term had elapsed, their trust was expired; and the four additional years (1718–22), during which they continued to sit, were derived not from the people, but from themselves; from the strong measure of the septennial bill, which can only be paralleled by *il serar di consiglio* of the Venetian history. Yet candour will own that to the same parliament every Englishman is deeply indebted: the septennial act, so vicious in its origin, has been sanctioned by time, experience, and the national consent. Its first operation secured the House of Hanover on the throne, and its permanent influence maintains the peace and stability of government. As often as a repeal has been moved in the House of Commons, I have given in its defence a clear and conscientious vote.

My grandfather could not expect to be treated with more lenity than his companions. His Tory principles and connexions rendered him obnoxious to the ruling powers: his name is reported in a suspicious secret; and his well-known abilities could not plead the excuse of ignorance or error. In the first proceedings against the South Sea directors,

Mr. Gibbon is one of the few who were taken into custody; and, in the final sentence, the measure of his fine proclaims him eminently guilty. The total estimate which he delivered on oath to the House of Commons amounted to one hundred and six thousand five hundred and forty-three pounds, five shillings, and sixpence, exclusive of antecedent settlements. Two different allowances of fifteen and of ten thousand pounds were moved for Mr. Gibbon; but, on the question being put, it was carried without a division for the smaller sum. On these ruins, with the skill and credit, of which parliament had not been able to despoil him, my grandfather at a mature age erected the edifice of a new fortune: the labours of sixteen years were amply rewarded; and I have reason to believe that the second structure was not much inferior to the first. He had realized a very considerable property in Sussex, Hampshire, Buckinghamshire, and the New River Company; and had acquired a spacious house,[1] with gardens and lands, at Putney, in Surrey, where he resided in decent hospitality. He died in December, 1736, at the age of seventy; and by his last will, at the expense of Edward, his only son (with whose marriage he was not perfectly reconciled), enriched his two daughters, Catherine and Hester. The former became the wife of Mr. Edward Elliston: their daughter and heiress Catherine was married in the year 1756 to Edward Eliot, Esq. (now Lord Eliot), of Port Eliot, in the county of Cornwall; and their three sons are my nearest male relations on the father's side. A life of devotion and celibacy was the choice of my aunt, Mrs. Hester Gibbon, who, at the age of eighty-five, still resides in a hermitage at Cliffe, in Northamptonshire; having long survived her spiritual guide and faithful companion Mr. William Law, who, at an advanced age, about the year 1761, died in her house. In our family he had left the reputation of a worthy and pious man,

[1] Since inhabited by Mr. Wood, Sir John Shelley, the Duke of Norfolk, &c. S.

who believed all that he professed, and practised all that he enjoined. The character of a non-juror, which he maintained to the last, is a sufficient evidence of his principles in church and state ; and the sacrifice of interest to conscience will be always respectable. His theological writings, which our domestic connexion has tempted me to peruse, preserve an imperfect sort of life, and I can pronounce with more confidence and knowledge on the merits of the author. His last compositions are darkly tinctured by the incomprehensible visions of Jacob Behmen ; and his discourse on the absolute unlawfulness of stage entertainments is sometimes quoted for a ridiculous intemperance of sentiment and language. ' The actors and spectators must all be damned : the playhouse is the porch of hell, the place of the devil's abode, where he holds his filthy court of evil spirits : a play is the devil's triumph, a sacrifice performed to his glory, as much as in the heathen temples of Bacchus or Venus ', &c., &c. But these sallies of religious frenzy must not extinguish the praise which is due to Mr. William Law as a wit and a scholar. His argument on topics of less absurdity is specious and acute, his manner is lively, his style forcible and clear ; and, had not his vigorous mind been clouded by enthusiasm, he might be ranked with the most agreeable and ingenious writers of the times. While the Bangorian controversy was a fashionable theme, he entered the lists on the subject of Christ's kingdom, and the authority of the priesthood : against the plain account of the sacrament of the Lord's Supper he resumed the combat with Bishop Hoadley, the object of Whig idolatry, and Tory abhorrence ; and at every weapon of attack and defence the nonjuror, on the ground which is common to both, approves himself at least equal to the prelate. On the appearance of the Fable of the Bees, he drew his pen against the licentious doctrine that private vices are public benefits, and morality as well as religion must join in his applause. Mr. Law's master-work, the *Serious Call*, is still read as a popular and powerful book of devotion. His precepts are rigid, but they are founded on the gospel: his satire is sharp, but it is drawn from the knowledge of human life; and many of his portraits are not unworthy of the pen of La Bruyere. If he finds a spark of piety in his reader's mind, he will soon kindle it to a flame; and a philosopher must allow that he exposes, with equal severity and truth, the strange contradiction between the faith and practice of the Christian world. Under the names of Flavia and Miranda he has admirably described my two aunts—the heathen and the Christian sister.

My father, Edward Gibbon, was born in October, 1707: at the age of thirteen he could scarcely feel that he was disinherited by Act of Parliament; and, as he advanced towards manhood, new prospects of fortune opened to his view. A parent is most attentive to supply in his children the deficiencies of which he is conscious in himself: my grandfather's knowledge was derived from a strong understanding, and the experience of the ways of men; but my father enjoyed the benefits of a liberal education as a scholar and a gentleman. At Westminster School, and afterwards at Emmanuel College in Cambridge, he passed through a regular course of academical discipline; and the care of his learning and morals was entrusted to his private tutor, the same Mr. William Law. But the mind of a saint is above or below the present world; and while the pupil proceeded on his travels, the tutor remained at Putney, the much-honoured friend and spiritual director of the whole family. My father resided some time at Paris to acquire the fashionable exercises; and as his temper was warm and social, he indulged in those pleasures, for which the strictness of his former education had given him a keener relish. He afterwards visited several provinces of France; but his excursions were neither long nor remote; and the slender knowledge, which he had gained of the French language, was gradually obliterated. His passage through Besançon is marked by a singular consequence in the chain of human events. In a dangerous illness Mr. Gibbon was attended, at his own request, by one of his kinsmen of the name of Acton, the younger brother of a younger brother, who had applied himself to the study of physic. During the slow recovery of his patient, the physician himself was attacked by the malady of love: he married his mistress, renounced his country and religion, settled at Besançon, and became the father of three sons; the eldest of whom, General Acton, is conspicuous in Europe as the principal Minister of the King of the Two Sicilies. By an uncle whom another stroke of fortune had transplanted to Leghorn, he was educated in the naval service of the Emperor; and his valour and conduct in the command of the Tuscan frigates protected the retreat of the Spaniards from Algiers. On my father's return to England he was chosen, in the general election of 1734, to serve in Parliament for the borough of Petersfield: a burgage tenure, of which my grandfather possessed a weighty share, till he alienated (I know not why) such important property. In the opposition to Sir Robert Walpole and the Pelhams, prejudice and society connected his son with the Tories,—shall I say Jacobites? or, as they were pleased to style themselves, the country gentlemen? with them he gave many a vote; with them he drank many a bottle. Without acquiring the fame of an orator or a statesman, he eagerly joined in the great opposition, which, after a seven years' chase, hunted down Sir Robert Walpole: and in the pursuit of an unpopular minister, he gratified a private revenge against the oppressor of his family in the South Sea persecution.

I was born at Putney, in the county of Surrey, the 27th of April, O. S. in the year one thousand seven hundred and thirty-seven; the first child of the marriage of Edward Gibbon, Esq., and of Judith Porten.[1] My lot might have been that of a slave,

---

[1] The union to which I owe my birth was a marriage of inclination and esteem. Mr. James Porten, a merchant

a savage, or a peasant; nor can I reflect without pleasure on the bounty of Nature, which cast my birth in a free and civilized country, in an age of science and philosophy, in a family of honourable rank, and decently endowed with the gifts of fortune. From my birth I have enjoyed the right of primogeniture; but I was succeeded by five brothers and one sister, all of whom were snatched away in their infancy. My five brothers, whose names may be found in the parish register of Putney, I shall not pretend to lament: but from my childhood to the present hour I have deeply and sincerely regretted my sister, whose life was somewhat prolonged, and whom I remember to have seen an amiable infant. The relation of a brother and a sister, especially if they do not marry, appears to me of a very singular nature. It is a familiar and tender friendship with a female, much about our own age; an affection perhaps softened by the secret influence of sex, but pure from any mixture of sensual desire, the sole species of Platonic love that can be indulged with truth, and without danger.

At the general election of 1741, Mr. Gibbon and Mr. Delmé stood an expensive and successful contest at Southampton, against Mr. Dummer and Mr. Henly, afterwards Lord Chancellor and Earl of Northington. The Whig candidates had a majority of the resident voters; but the corporation was firm in the Tory interest: a sudden creation of one hundred and seventy new freemen turned the scale; and a supply was readily obtained of respectable volunteers, who flocked from all parts of England to support the

of London, resided with his family at Putney, in a house adjoining to the bridge and churchyard, where I have passed many happy hours of my childhood. He left one son (the late Sir Stanier Porten) and three daughters: Catherine, who preserved her maiden name, and of whom I shall hereafter speak; another daughter married Mr. Darrel of Richmond, and left two sons, Edward and Robert: the youngest of the three sisters was Judith, my mother.

cause of their political friends. The new Parliament opened with the victory of an opposition, which was fortified by strong clamour and strange coalitions. From the event of the first divisions, Sir Robert Walpole perceived that he could no longer lead a majority in the House of Commons, and prudently resigned (after a dominion of one and twenty years) the guidance of the state (1742). But the fall of an unpopular minister was not succeeded, according to general expectation, by a millennium of happiness and virtue: some courtiers lost their places, some patriots lost their characters, Lord Orford's offences vanished with his power; and after a short vibration, the Pelham government was fixed on the old basis of the Whig aristocracy. In the year 1745, the throne and the constitution were attacked by a rebellion, which does not reflect much honour on the national spirit: since the English friends of the Pretender wanted courage to join his standard, and his enemies (the bulk of the people) allowed him to advance into the heart of the kingdom. Without daring, perhaps without desiring, to aid the rebels, my father invariably adhered to the Tory opposition. In the most critical season he accepted, for the service of the party, the office of alderman in the city of London: but the duties were so repugnant to his inclination and habits, that he resigned his gown at the end of a few months. The second Parliament in which he sat was prematurely dissolved (1747): and as he was unable or unwilling to maintain a second contest for Southampton, the life of the senator expired in that dissolution.

The death of a new-born child before that of its parents may seem an unnatural, but it is strictly a probable event: since of any given number the greater part are extinguished before their ninth year, before they possess the faculties of the mind or body. Without accusing the profuse waste or imperfect workmanship of Nature, I shall only observe, that this unfavourable chance was multiplied against my infant existence. So feeble was my constitution, so

precarious my life, that, in the baptism of my brothers'
my father's prudence successively repeated my Christian name of Edward, that, in case of the departure
of the eldest son, this patronymic appellation might
be still perpetuated in the family.

—— Uno avulso non deficit alter.

To preserve and to rear so frail a being, the most
tender assiduity was scarcely sufficient; and my
mother's attention was somewhat diverted by her
frequent pregnancies, by an exclusive passion for her
husband, and by the dissipation of the world, in which
his taste and authority obliged her to mingle. But
the maternal office was supplied by my aunt, Mrs.
Catherine Porten; at whose name I feel a tear of
gratitude trickling down my cheek. A life of celibacy
transferred her vacant affection to her sister's first
child: my weakness excited her pity; her attachment
was fortified by labour and success: and if there be
any, as I trust there are some, who rejoice that I live,
to that dear and excellent woman they must hold
themselves indebted. Many anxious and solitary
days did she consume in the patient trial of every
mode of relief and amusement. Many wakeful nights
did she sit by my bedside in trembling expectation
that each hour would be my last. Of the various and
frequent disorders of my childhood my own recollection is dark; nor do I wish to expatiate on so disgusting a topic. Suffice it to say, that while every
practitioner, from Sloane and Ward to the Chevalier
Taylor, was successively summoned to torture or
relieve me, the care of my mind was too frequently
neglected for that of my health: compassion always
suggested an excuse for the indulgence of the master,
or the idleness of the pupil; and the chain of my
education was broken as often as I was recalled from
the school of learning to the bed of sickness.

As soon as the use of speech had prepared my infant
reason for the admission of knowledge, I was taught
the arts of reading, writing, and arithmetic. So

remote is the date, so vague is the memory of their origin in myself, that, were not the error corrected by analogy, I should be tempted to conceive them as innate. In my childhood I was praised for the readiness with which I could multiply and divide, by memory alone, two sums of several figures: such praise encouraged my growing talent; and had I persevered in this line of application, I might have acquired some fame in mathematical studies.

After this previous institution at home, or at a day-school at Putney, I was delivered at the age of seven into the hands of Mr. John Kirkby, who exercised about eighteen months the office of my domestic tutor. His own words, which I shall here transcribe, inspire in his favour a sentiment of pity and esteem. ' During my abode in my native county of Cumberland, in quality of an indigent curate, I used now and then in a summer, when the pleasantness of the season invited, to take a solitary walk to the seashore, which lies about two miles from the town where I lived. Here I would amuse myself, one while in viewing at large the agreeable prospect which surrounded me, and another while (confining my sight to nearer objects) in admiring the vast variety of beautiful shells thrown upon the beach, some of the choicest of which I always picked up, to divert my little ones upon my return. One time among the rest, taking such a journey in my head, I sat down upon the declivity of the beach with my face to the sea, which was now come up within a few yards of my feet, when immediately the sad thought of the wretched condition of my family, and the unsuccessfulness of all endeavours to amend it, came crowding into my mind, which drove me into a deep melancholy, and ever and anon forced tears from my eyes.' Distress at last forced him to leave the country. His learning and virtue introduced him to my father; and at Putney he might have found at least a temporary shelter, had not an act of indiscretion again driven him into the world. One day, reading prayers in the parish church, he most unluckily

forgot the name of King George : his patron, a loyal
subject, dismissed him with some reluctance and
a decent reward ; and *how* the poor man ended his
days I have never been able to learn. Mr. John Kirkby
is the author of two small volumes—the *Life of Automathes* (London, 1745) and an *English and Latin
Grammar* (London, 1746), which, as a testimony of
gratitude, he dedicated (November 5, 1745) to my
father. The books are before me : from them the
pupil may judge the preceptor ; and, upon the whole,
his judgement will not be unfavourable. The grammar
is executed with accuracy and skill, and I know not
whether any better existed at the time in our language :
but the *Life of Automathes* aspires to the honours of
a philosophical fiction. It is the story of a youth, the
son of a shipwrecked exile, who lives alone on a desert
island from infancy to the age of manhood. A hind
is his nurse ; he inherits a cottage, with many useful
and curious instruments ; some ideas remain of the
education of his two first years ; some arts are borrowed from the beavers of a neighbouring lake ; some
truths are revealed in supernatural visions. With
these helps, and his own industry, Automathes becomes
a self-taught though speechless philosopher, who had
investigated with success his own mind, the natural
world, the abstract sciences, and the great principles
of morality and religion. The author is not entitled
to the merit of invention, since he has blended the
English story of *Robinson Crusoe* with the Arabian
romance of *Hai Ebn Yokhdan*, which he might have
read in the Latin version of Pocock. In the *Automathes* I cannot praise either the depth of thought
or elegance of style ; but the book is not devoid of
entertainment or instruction ; and among several
interesting passages I would select the discovery of
fire, which produces by accidental mischief the discovery of conscience. A man who had thought so
much on the subjects of language and education was
surely no ordinary preceptor : my childish years, and
his hasty departure, prevented me from enjoying the

full benefit of his lessons; but they enlarged my knowledge of arithmetic, and left me a clear impression of the English and Latin rudiments.

In my ninth year (January, 1746), in a lucid interval of comparative health, my father adopted the convenient and customary mode of English education; and I was sent to Kingston-upon-Thames, to a school of about seventy boys, which was kept by Dr. Wooddeson and his assistants. Every time I have since passed over Putney Common, I have always noticed the spot where my mother, as we drove along in the coach, admonished me that I was now going into the world, and must learn to think and act for myself. The expression may appear ludicrous; yet there is not, in the course of life, a more remarkable change than the removal of a child from the luxury and freedom of a wealthy house, to the frugal diet and strict subordination of a school; from the tenderness of parents and the obsequiousness of servants, to the rude familiarity of his equals, the insolent tyranny of his seniors, and the rod, perhaps, of a cruel and capricious pedagogue. Such hardships may steel the mind and body against the injuries of fortune; but my timid reserve was astonished by the crowd and tumult of the school; the want of strength and activity disqualified me for the sports of the playfield; nor have I forgotten how often in the year forty-six I was reviled and buffeted for the sins of my Tory ancestors. By the common methods of discipline, at the expense of many tears and some blood, I purchased the knowledge of the Latin syntax: and not long since I was possessed of the dirty volumes of Phaedrus and Cornelius Nepos, which I painfully construed and darkly understood. The choice of these authors is not injudicious. The *Lives* of Cornelius Nepos, the friend of Atticus and Cicero, are composed in the style of the purest age: his simplicity is elegant, his brevity copious: he exhibits a series of men and manners; and with such illustrations, as every pedant is not indeed qualified to give, this classic biographer may

initiate a young student in the history of Greece and
Rome. The use of fables or apologues has been approved
in every age, from ancient India to modern Europe.
They convey in familiar images the truths of morality
and prudence ; and the most childish understanding
(I advert to the scruples of Rousseau) will not suppose
either that beasts *do* speak, or that men *may* lie.
A fable represents the genuine characters of animals ;
and a skilful master might extract from Pliny and
Buffon some pleasing lessons of natural history, a
science well adapted to the taste and capacity of
children. The Latinity of Phaedrus is not exempt
from an alloy of the silver age ; but his manner is
concise, terse, and sententious : the Thracian slave
discreetly breathes the spirit of a freeman ; and when
the text is sound, the style is perspicuous. But his
fables, after a long oblivion, were first published by
Peter Pithou, from a corrupt manuscript. The labours
of fifty editors confess the defects of the copy, as well
as the value of the original ; and the schoolboy may
have been whipped for misapprehending a passage
which Bentley could not restore, and which Burman
could not explain.

My studies were too frequently interrupted by
sickness ; and after a real or nominal residence at
Kingston school of near two years, I was finally
recalled (December, 1747) by my mother's death,
which was occasioned, in her thirty-eighth year, by
the consequences of her last labour. I was too young
to feel the importance of my loss ; and the image of
her person and conversation is faintly imprinted in
my memory. The affectionate heart of my aunt,
Catherine Porten, bewailed a sister and a friend ; but
my poor father was inconsolable, and the transport
of grief seemed to threaten his life or his reason.
I can never forget the scene of our first interview,
some weeks after the fatal event ; the awful silence,
the room hung with black, the midday tapers, his
sighs and tears ; his praises of my mother, a saint in
heaven ; his solemn adjuration that I would cherish

her memory and imitate her virtues; and the fervour with which he kissed and blessed me as the sole surviving pledge of their loves. The storm of passion insensibly subsided into calmer melancholy. At a convivial meeting of his friends, Mr. Gibbon might affect or enjoy a gleam of cheerfulness; but his plan of happiness was for ever destroyed: and after the loss of his companion he was left alone in a world, of which the business and pleasures were to him irksome or insipid. After some unsuccessful trials he renounced the tumult of London and the hospitality of Putney, and buried himself in the rural or rather rustic solitude of Buriton; from which, during several years, he seldom emerged.

As far back as I can remember, the house near Putney Bridge and churchyard, of my maternal grandfather, appears in the light of my proper and native home. It was there that I was allowed to spend the greatest part of my time, in sickness or in health, during my school vacations and my parents' residence in London, and finally after my mother's death. Three months after that event, in the spring of 1748, the commercial ruin of her father, Mr. James Porten, was accomplished and declared. As his effects were not sold, nor the house evacuated, till the Christmas following, I enjoyed during the whole year the society of my aunt, without much consciousness of her impending fate. I feel a melancholy pleasure in repeating my obligations to that excellent woman, Mrs. Catherine Porten, the true mother of my mind as well as of my health. Her natural good sense was improved by the perusal of the best books in the English language; and if her reason was sometimes clouded by prejudice, her sentiments were never disguised by hypocrisy or affectation. Her indulgent tenderness, the frankness of her temper, and my innate rising curiosity, soon removed all distance between us; like friends of an equal age, we freely conversed on every topic, familiar or abstruse; and it was her delight and reward to observe the first shoots of my young ideas. Pain and languor were often soothed by the voice of instruction and amusement; and to her kind lessons I ascribe my early and invincible love of reading, which I would not exchange for the treasures of India. I should perhaps be astonished, were it possible to ascertain the date, at which a favourite tale was engraved, by frequent repetition, in my memory: the Cavern of the Winds; the Palace of Felicity; and the fatal moment, at the end of three months or centuries, when Prince Adolphus is overtaken by Time, who had worn out so many pair of wings in the pursuit. Before I left Kingston school I was well acquainted with Pope's *Homer* and the *Arabian Nights' Entertainments*, two books which will always please by the moving picture of human manners and specious miracles: nor was I then capable of discerning that Pope's translation is a portrait endowed with every merit, excepting that of likeness to the original. The verses of Pope accustomed my ear to the sound of poetic harmony: in the death of Hector, and the shipwreck of Ulysses, I tasted the new emotions of terror and pity; and seriously disputed with my aunt on the vices and virtues of the heroes of the Trojan war. From Pope's *Homer* to Dryden's *Virgil* was an easy transition; but I know not how, from some fault in the author, the translator, or the reader, the pious Aeneas did not so forcibly seize on my imagination; and I derived more pleasure from Ovid's *Metamorphoses*, especially in the fall of Phaeton, and the speeches of Ajax and Ulysses. My grandfather's flight unlocked the door of a tolerable library; and I turned over many English pages of poetry and romance, of history and travels. Where a title attracted my eye, without fear or awe I snatched the volume from the shelf; and Mrs. Porten, who indulged herself in moral and religious speculations, was more prone to encourage than to check a curiosity above the strength of a boy. This year (1748), the twelfth of my age, I shall note as the most propitious to the growth of my intellectual stature.

The relics of my grandfather's fortune afforded a bare annuity for his own maintenance; and his daughter, my worthy aunt, who had already passed her fortieth year, was left destitute. Her noble spirit scorned a life of obligation and dependance; and after revolving several schemes, she preferred the humble industry of keeping a boarding-house for Westminster School,[1] where she laboriously earned a competence for her old age. This singular opportunity of blending the advantages of private and public education decided my father. After the Christmas holidays, in January, 1749, I accompanied Mrs. Porten to her new house in College Street; and was immediately entered in the school, of which Dr. John Nicoll was at that time head master. At first I was alone: but my aunt's resolution was praised; her character was esteemed; her friends were numerous and active: in the course of some years she became the mother of forty or fifty boys, for the most part of family and fortune; and as her primitive habitation was too narrow, she built and occupied a spacious mansion in Dean's Yard. I shall always be ready to join in the common opinion, that our public schools, which have produced so many eminent characters, are the best adapted to the genius and constitution of the English people. A boy of spirit may acquire a previous and practical experience of the world; and his playfellows may be the future friends of his heart or his interest. In a free intercourse with his equals, the habits of truth, fortitude, and prudence will insensibly be matured. Birth and riches are measured by the standard of personal merit; and the mimic scene of a rebellion has displayed, in their true colours, the ministers and patriots of the rising generation. Our seminaries of learning do not exactly correspond with the precept of a Spartan king, 'that

[1] It is said in the family that she was principally induced to this undertaking by her affection for her nephew, whose weak constitution required her constant and unremitted attention. S.

the child should be instructed in the arts which will be useful to the man '; since a finished scholar may emerge from the head of Westminster or Eton, in total ignorance of the business and conversation of English gentlemen in the latter end of the eighteenth century. But these schools may assume the merit of teaching all that they pretend to teach, the Latin and Greek languages: they deposit in the hands of a disciple the keys of two valuable chests; nor can he complain, if they are afterwards lost or neglected by his own fault. The necessity of leading in equal ranks so many unequal powers of capacity and application will prolong to eight or ten years the juvenile studies, which might be dispatched in half that time by the skilful master of a single pupil. Yet even the repetition of exercise and discipline contributes to fix in a vacant mind the verbal science of grammar and prosody: and the private or voluntary student, who possesses the sense and spirit of the classics, may offend, by a false quantity, the scrupulous ear of a well-flogged critic. For myself, I must be content with a very small share of the civil and literary fruits of a public school. In the space of two years (1749, 1750), interrupted by danger and debility, I painfully climbed into the third form; and my riper age was left to acquire the beauties of the Latin, and the rudiments of the Greek tongue. Instead of audaciously mingling in the sports, the quarrels, and the connexions of our little world, I was still cherished at home under the maternal wing of my aunt; and my removal from Westminster long preceded the approach of manhood.

The violence and variety of my complaints, which had excused my frequent absence from Westminster School, at length engaged Mrs. Porten, with the advice of physicians, to conduct me to Bath: at the end of the Michaelmas vacation (1750) she quitted me with reluctance, and I remained several months under the care of a trusty maid-servant. A strange nervous affection, which alternately contracted my legs, and

produced, without any visible symptoms, the most
excruciating pain, was ineffectually opposed by the
various methods of bathing and pumping. From
Bath I was transported to Winchester, to the house
of a physician; and after the failure of his medical
skill, we had again recourse to the virtues of the Bath
waters. During the intervals of these fits, I moved
with my father to Buriton and Putney; and a short
unsuccessful trial was attempted to renew my attendance at Westminster School. But my infirmities
could not be reconciled with the hours and discipline
of a public seminary; and instead of a domestic tutor,
who might have watched the favourable moments,
and gently advanced the progress of my learning, my
father was too easily content with such occasional
teachers as the different places of my residence could
supply. I was never forced, and seldom was I persuaded, to admit these lessons: yet I read with
a clergyman at Bath some odes of Horace, and several
episodes of Virgil, which gave me an imperfect and
transient enjoyment of the Latin poets. It might
now be apprehended that I should continue for life
an illiterate cripple: but, as I approached my sixteenth year, nature displayed in my favour her
mysterious energies: my constitution was fortified
and fixed; and my disorders, instead of growing with
my growth and strengthening with my strength, most
wonderfully vanished. I have never possessed or
abused the insolence of health: but since that time
few persons have been more exempt from real or
imaginary ills; and, till I am admonished by the
gout, the reader will no more be troubled with the
history of my bodily complaints. My unexpected
recovery again encouraged the hope of my education;
and I was placed at Esher, in Surrey, in the house of
the Reverend Mr. Philip Francis, in a pleasant spot,
which promised to unite the various benefits of air,
exercise, and study (January, 1752). The translator
of Horace might have taught me to relish the Latin
poets had not my friends discovered in a few weeks

that he preferred the pleasures of London to the instruction of his pupils. My father's perplexity at this time, rather than his prudence, was urged to embrace a singular and desperate measure. Without preparation or delay he carried me to Oxford; and I was matriculated in the University as a gentleman-commoner of Magdalen College, before I had accomplished the fifteenth year of my age (April 3, 1752).

The curiosity which had been implanted in my infant mind was still alive and active; but my reason was not sufficiently informed to understand the value, or to lament the loss, of three precious years from my entrance at Westminster to my admission at Oxford. Instead of repining at my long and frequent confinement to the chamber or the couch, I secretly rejoiced in those infirmities, which delivered me from the exercises of the school and the society of my equals. As often as I was tolerably exempt from danger and pain, reading, free desultory reading, was the employment and comfort of my solitary hours. At Westminster my aunt sought only to amuse and indulge me; in my stations at Bath and Winchester, at Buriton and Putney, a false compassion respected my sufferings, and I was allowed, without control or advice, to gratify the wanderings of an unripe taste. My indiscriminate appetite subsided by degrees in the *historic* line: and since philosophy has exploded all innate ideas and natural propensities, I must ascribe this choice to the assiduous perusal of the *Universal History*, as the octavo volumes successively appeared. This unequal work, and a treatise of Hearne, the *Ductor historicus*, referred and introduced me to the Greek and Roman historians, to as many at least as were accessible to an English reader. All that I could find were greedily devoured, from Littlebury's lame Herodotus, and Spelman's valuable Xenophon, to the pompous folios of Gordon's Tacitus, and a ragged Procopius of the beginning of the last century. The cheap acquisition of so much knowledge confirmed my dislike to the study of languages; and I argued

with Mrs. Porten, that, were I master of Greek and
Latin, I must interpret to myself in English the thoughts
of the original, and that such extemporary versions
must be inferior to the elaborate translations of professed scholars; a silly sophism, which could not easily
be confuted by a person ignorant of any other language
than her own.   From the ancient I leaped to the
modern world: many crude lumps of Speed, Rapin,
Mezeray, Davila, Machiavel, Father Paul, Bower, &c.,
I devoured like so many novels; and I swallowed
with the same voracious appetite the descriptions of
India and China, of Mexico and Peru.

My first introduction to the historic scenes, which
have since engaged so many years of my life, must be
ascribed to an accident. In the summer of 1751 I
accompanied my father on a visit to Mr. Hoare's, in
Wiltshire; but I was less delighted with the beauties
of Stourhead than with discovering in the library
a common book, the *Continuation of Echard's Roman
History*, which is indeed executed with more skill and
taste than the previous work. To me the reigns of
the successors of Constantine were absolutely new;
and I was immersed in the passage of the Goths over
the Danube when the summons of the dinner-bell
reluctantly dragged me from my intellectual feast.
This transient glance served rather to irritate than to
appease my curiosity; and as soon as I returned to
Bath I procured the second and third volumes of
Howel's *History of the World*, which exhibit the
Byzantine period on a larger scale. Mahomet and his
Saracens soon fixed my attention; and some instinct
of criticism directed me to the genuine sources. Simon
Ockley, an original in every sense, first opened my
eyes; and I was led from one book to another, till
I had ranged round the circle of Oriental history.
Before I was sixteen, I had exhausted all that could
be learned in English of the Arabs and Persians, the
Tartars and Turks; and the same ardour urged me
to guess at the French of D'Herbelot, and to construe
the barbarous Latin of Pocock's *Abulfaragius*.

Such vague and multifarious reading could not teach me to think, to write, or to act; and the only principle, that darted a ray of light into the indigested chaos, was an early and rational application to the order of time and place. The maps of Cellarius and Wells imprinted in my mind the picture of ancient geography: from Stranchius I imbibed the elements of chronology: the Tables of Helvicus and Anderson, the Annals of Usher and Prideaux, distinguished the connexion of events, and engraved the multitude of names and dates in a clear and indelible series. But in the discussion of the first ages I overleaped the bounds of modesty and use. In my childish balance I presumed to weigh the systems of Scaliger and Petavius, of Marsham and Newton, which I could seldom study in the originals; and my sleep has been disturbed by the difficulty of reconciling the Septuagint with the Hebrew computation. I arrived at Oxford with a stock of erudition that might have puzzled a doctor, and a degree of ignorance of which a schoolboy would have been ashamed.

At the conclusion of this first period of my life, I am tempted to enter a protest against the trite and lavish praise of the happiness of our boyish years, which is echoed with so much affectation in the world. That happiness I have never known, that time I have never regretted; and were my poor aunt still alive, she would bear testimony to the early and constant uniformity of my sentiments. It will indeed be replied that *I* am not a competent judge; that pleasure is incompatible with pain; that joy is excluded from sickness; and that the felicity of a schoolboy consists in the perpetual motion of thoughtless and playful agility, in which I was never qualified to excel. My name, it is most true, could never be enrolled among the sprightly race, the idle progeny of Eton or Westminster,

> Who foremost might delight to cleave,
> With pliant arm, the glassy wave,
> Or urge the flying ball.

The poet may gaily describe the short hours of recreation; but he forgets the daily tedious labours of the school, which is approached each morning with anxious and reluctant steps.

A traveller who visits Oxford or Cambridge is surprised and edified by the apparent order and tranquillity that prevail in the seats of the English muses. In the most celebrated Universities of Holland, Germany, and Italy, the students, who swarm from different countries, are loosely dispersed in private lodgings at the houses of the burghers: they dress according to their fancy and fortune; and in the intemperate quarrels of youth and wine, their *swords*, though less frequently than of old, are sometimes stained with each other's blood. The use of arms is banished from our English Universities; the uniform habit of the academics, the square cap and black gown, is adapted to the civil and even clerical professions; and from the doctor in divinity to the undergraduate, the degrees of learning and age are externally distinguished. Instead of being scattered in a town, the students of Oxford and Cambridge are united in colleges; their maintenance is provided at their own expense, or that of the founders; and the stated hours of the hall and chapel represent the discipline of a regular, and, as it were, a religious community. The eyes of the traveller are attracted by the size or beauty of the public edifices; and the principal colleges appear to be so many palaces, which a liberal nation has erected and endowed for the habitation of science. My own introduction to the University of Oxford forms a new era in my life; and at the distance of forty years I still remember my first emotions of surprise and satisfaction. In my fifteenth year I felt myself suddenly raised from a boy to a man: the persons, whom I respected as my superiors in age and academical rank, entertained me with every mark of attention and civility; and my vanity was flattered by the velvet cap and silk gown, which distinguish a gentleman-commoner from a plebeian student. A decent allowance, more money than a schoolboy had ever seen, was at my own disposal; and I might command, among the tradesmen of Oxford, an indefinite and dangerous latitude of credit. A key was delivered into my hands, which gave me the free use of a numerous and learned library: my apartment consisted of three elegant and well-furnished rooms in the new building, a stately pile, of Magdalen College; and the adjacent walks, had they been frequented by Plato's disciples, might have been compared to the Attic shade on the banks of the Ilissus. Such was the fair prospect of my entrance (April 3, 1752,) into the University of Oxford.

A venerable prelate, whose taste and erudition must reflect honour on the society in which they were formed, has drawn a very interesting picture of his academical life:—'I was educated (says Bishop Lowth) in the University of Oxford. I enjoyed all the advantages, both public and private, which that famous seat of learning so largely affords. I spent many years in that illustrious society, in a well-regulated course of useful discipline and studies, and in the agreeable and improving commerce of gentlemen and of scholars; in a society where emulation without envy, ambition without jealousy, contention without animosity, incited industry, and awakened genius; where a liberal pursuit of knowledge and a genuine freedom of thought was raised, encouraged and pushed forward by example, by commendation, and by authority. I breathed the same atmosphere that the Hookers, the Chillingworths, and the Lockes had breathed before; whose benevolence and humanity were as extensive as their vast genius and comprehensive knowledge; who always treated their adversaries with civility and respect; who made candour, moderation, and liberal judgement as much the rule and law as the subject of their discourse. And do you reproach me with my education in this place, and with my relation to this most respectable body, which I shall always esteem my greatest advantage and my highest honour?' I transcribe with pleasure this

eloquent passage, without examining what benefits or
what rewards were derived by Hooker, or Chillingworth, or Locke, from their academical institution;
without inquiring, whether in this angry controversy
the spirit of Lowth himself is purified from the intolerant
zeal which Warburton had ascribed to the genius of
the place. It may indeed be observed that the atmosphere of Oxford did not agree with Mr. Locke's constitution, and that the philosopher justly despised
the academical bigots, who expelled his person and
condemned his principles. The expression of gratitude
is a virtue and a pleasure: a liberal mind will delight
to cherish and celebrate the memory of its parents;
and the teachers of science are the parents of the
mind. I applaud the filial piety, which it is impossible
for me to imitate; since I must not confess an imaginary debt, to assume the merit of a just or generous
retribution. To the University of Oxford I acknowledge no obligation; and she will as cheerfully renounce
me for a son, as I am willing to disclaim her for a
mother. I spent fourteen months at Magdalen College;
they proved the fourteen months the most idle and
unprofitable of my whole life: the reader will pronounce between the school and the scholar: but
I cannot affect to believe that nature had disqualified
me for all literary pursuits. The specious and ready
excuse of my tender age, imperfect preparation, and
hasty departure, may doubtless be alleged; nor do
I wish to defraud such excuses of their proper weight.
Yet in my sixteenth year I was not devoid of capacity
or application; even my childish reading had displayed an early though blind propensity for books;
and the shallow flood might have been taught to flow
in a deep channel and a clear stream. In the discipline
of a well-constituted academy, under the guidance of
skilful and vigilant professors, I should gradually
have risen from translations to originals, from the
Latin to the Greek classics, from dead languages to
living science: my hours would have been occupied
by useful and agreeable studies, the wanderings of

fancy would have been restrained, and I should have escaped the temptations of idleness, which finally precipitated my departure from Oxford.

Perhaps in a separate annotation I may coolly examine the fabulous and real antiquities of our sister universities, a question which has kindled such fierce and foolish disputes among their fanatic sons. In the meanwhile it will be acknowledged that these venerable bodies are sufficiently old to partake of all the prejudices and infirmities of age. The schools of Oxford and Cambridge were founded in a dark age of false and barbarous science; and they are still tainted with the vices of their origin. Their primitive discipline was adapted to the education of priests and monks; and the government still remains in the hands of the clergy, an order of men whose manners are remote from the present world, and whose eyes are dazzled by the light of philosophy. The legal incorporation of these societies by the charters of popes and kings had given them a monopoly of the public instruction; and the spirit of monopolists is narrow, lazy, and oppressive: their work is more costly and less productive than that of independent artists; and the new improvements so eagerly grasped by the competition of freedom, are admitted with slow and sullen reluctance in those proud corporations, above the fear of a rival, and below the confession of an error. We may scarcely hope that any reformation will be a voluntary act; and so deeply are they rooted in law and prejudice, that even the omnipotence of Parliament would shrink from an inquiry into the state and abuses of the two Universities.

The use of academical degrees, as old as the thirteenth century, is visibly borrowed from the mechanic corporations; in which an apprentice, after serving his time, obtains a testimonial of his skill, and a licence to practise his trade and mystery. It is not my design to depreciate those honours, which could never gratify or disappoint my ambition; and I should applaud the institution, if the degrees of bachelor or licentiate were bestowed as the reward of manly and successful study: if the name and rank of doctor or master were strictly reserved for the professors of science, who have approved their title to the public esteem.

In all the Universities of Europe, excepting our own, the languages and sciences are distributed among a numerous list of effective professors: the students, according to their taste, their calling, and their diligence, apply themselves to the proper masters; and in the annual repetition of public and private lectures, these masters are assiduously employed. Our curiosity may inquire what number of professors has been instituted at Oxford (for I shall now confine myself to my own University)? by whom are they appointed, and what may be the probable chances of merit or incapacity? how many are stationed to the three faculties, and how many are left for the liberal arts? what is the form, and what the substance, of their lessons? But all these questions are silenced by one short and singular answer, 'That in the University of Oxford, the greater part of the public professors have for these many years given up altogether even the pretence of teaching'. Incredible as the fact may appear, I must rest my belief on the positive and impartial evidence of a master of moral and political wisdom, who had himself resided at Oxford. Dr. Adam Smith assigns as the cause of their indolence, that, instead of being paid by voluntary contributions, which would urge them to increase the number, and to deserve the gratitude of their pupils, the Oxford professors are secure in the enjoyment of a fixed stipend, without the necessity of labour, or the apprehension of control. It has indeed been observed, nor is the observation absurd, that excepting in experimental sciences, which demand a costly apparatus and a dexterous hand, the many valuable treatises that have been published on every subject of learning may now supersede the ancient mode of oral instruction. Were this principle true in its utmost latitude, I should only infer that the offices and salaries, which

are become useless, ought without delay to be abolished.
But there still remains a material difference between
a book and a professor; the hour of the lecture enforces
attendance; attention is fixed by the presence, the
voice, and the occasional questions of the teacher;
the most idle will carry something away; and the
more diligent will compare the instructions which
they have heard in the school, with the volumes
which they peruse in their chamber. The advice of
a skilful professor will adapt a course of reading to
every mind and every situation; his authority will
discover, admonish, and at last chastise the negligence
of his disciples; and his vigilant inquiries will ascertain the steps of their literary progress. Whatever
science he professes he may illustrate in a series of
discourses, composed in the leisure of his closet, pronounced on public occasions, and finally delivered
to the press. I observe with pleasure that in the
University of Oxford Dr. Lowth, with equal eloquence
and erudition, has executed this task in his incomparable *Praelectiones* on the Poetry of the Hebrews.
The College of St. Mary Magdalen was founded in
the fifteenth century by Wainfleet, Bishop of Winchester; and now consists of a president, forty fellows,
and a number of inferior students. It is esteemed one
of the largest and most wealthy of our academical corporations, which may be compared to the Benedictine
abbeys of Catholic countries; and I have loosely
heard that the estates belonging to Magdalen College,
which are leased by those indulgent landlords at small
quit-rents and occasional fines, might be raised, in
the hands of private avarice, to an annual revenue
of nearly *thirty thousand pounds.* Our colleges are
supposed to be schools of science, as well as of education; nor is it unreasonable to expect that a body
of literary men, devoted to a life of celibacy, exempt
from the care of their own subsistence, and amply
provided with books, should devote their leisure to
the prosecution of study, and that some effects of
their studies should be manifested to the world. The

shelves of their library groan under the weight of the Benedictine folios, of the editions of the fathers, and the collections of the middle ages, which have issued from the single abbey of St. Germain de Préz at Paris. A composition of genius must be the offspring of one mind; but such works of industry, as may be divided among many hands, and must be continued during many years, are the peculiar province of a laborious community. If I inquire into the manufactures of the monks of Magdalen, if I extend the inquiry to the other colleges of Oxford and Cambridge, a silent blush, or a scornful frown, will be the only reply. The fellows or monks of my time were decent easy men, who supinely enjoyed the gifts of the founder; their days were filled by a series of uniform employments; the chapel and the hall, the coffee-house and the common room, till they retired, weary and well satisfied, to a long slumber. From the toil of reading, or thinking, or writing, they had absolved their conscience; and the first shoots of learning and ingenuity withered on the ground, without yielding any fruits to the owners or the public. As a gentleman-commoner, I was admitted to the society of the fellows, and fondly expected that some questions of literature would be the amusing and instructive topics of their discourse. Their conversation stagnated in a round of college business, Tory politics, personal anecdotes, and private scandal: their dull and deep potations excused the brisk intemperance of youth: and their constitutional toasts were not expressive of the most lively loyalty for the house of Hanover. A general election was now approaching: the great Oxfordshire contest already blazed with all the malevolence of party zeal. Magdalen College was devoutly attached to the old interest! and the names of Wenman and Dashwood were more frequently pronounced, than those of Cicero and Chrysostom. The example of the senior fellows could not inspire the undergraduates with a liberal spirit or studious emulation; and I cannot describe, as I never knew, the discipline of college.

Some duties may possibly have been imposed on the poor scholars, whose ambition aspired to the peaceful honours of a fellowship (*ascribi quietis ordinibus . . . Deorum*) ; but no independent members were admitted below the rank of a gentleman-commoner, and our velvet cap was the cap of liberty. A tradition prevailed that some of our predecessors had spoken Latin declamations in the hall ; but of this ancient custom no vestige remained : the obvious methods of public exercises and examinations were totally unknown ; and I have never heard that either the president or the society interfered in the private economy of the tutors and their pupils.

The silence of the Oxford professors, which deprives the youth of public instruction, is imperfectly supplied by the tutors, as they are styled, of the several colleges. Instead of confining themselves to a single science, which had satisfied the ambition of Burman or Bernoulli, they teach, or promise to teach, either history or mathematics, or ancient literature, or moral philosophy ; and as it is possible that they may be defective in all, it is highly probable that of some they will be ignorant. They are paid, indeed, by private contributions ; but their appointment depends on the head of the house : their diligence is voluntary, and will consequently be languid, while the pupils themselves, or their parents, are not indulged in the liberty of choice or change. The first tutor into whose hands I was resigned appears to have been one of the best of the tribe : Dr. Waldegrave was a learned and pious man, of a mild disposition, strict morals, and abstemious life, who seldom mingled in the politics or the jollity of the college. But his knowledge of the world was confined to the University ; his learning was of the last, rather than of the present age ; his temper was indolent ; his faculties, which were not of the first rate, had been relaxed by the climate, and he was satisfied, like his fellows, with the slight and superficial discharge of an important trust. As soon as my tutor had sounded the insufficiency of his disciple in school-learning, he proposed that we should read every morning from ten to eleven the comedies of Terence. The sum of my improvement in the University of Oxford is confined to three or four Latin plays; and even the study of an elegant classic, which might have been illustrated by a comparison of ancient and modern theatres, was reduced to a dry and literal interpretation of the author's text. During the first weeks I constantly attended these lessons in my tutor's room; but as they appeared equally devoid of profit and pleasure, I was once tempted to try the experiment of a formal apology. The apology was accepted with a smile. I repeated the offence with less ceremony; the excuse was admitted with the same indulgence: the slightest motive of laziness or indisposition, the most trifling avocation at home or abroad, was allowed as a worthy impediment; nor did my tutor appear conscious of my absence or neglect. Had the hour of lecture been constantly filled, a single hour was a small portion of my academic leisure. No plan of study was recommended for my use; no exercises were prescribed for his inspection; and, at the most precious season of youth, whole days and weeks were suffered to elapse without labour or amusement, without advice or account. I should have listened to the voice of reason and of my tutor; his mild behaviour had gained my confidence. I preferred his society to that of the younger students; and in our evening walks to the top of Headington Hill, we freely conversed on a variety of subjects. Since the days of Pocock and Hyde, oriental learning has always been the pride of Oxford, and I once expressed an inclination to study Arabic. His prudence discouraged this childish fancy; but he neglected the fair occasion of directing the ardour of a curious mind. During my absence in the summer vacation, Dr. Waldegrave accepted a college living at Washington in Sussex, and on my return I no longer found him at Oxford. From that time I have lost sight of my first tutor; but at the end of thirty years (1781) he was still alive;

and the practice of exercise and temperance had entitled him to a healthy old age.

The long recess between the Trinity and Michaelmas terms empties the colleges of Oxford, as well as the courts of Westminster. I spent, at my father's house at Buriton in Hampshire, the two months of August and September. It is whimsical enough that as soon as I left Magdalen College, my taste for books began to revive; but it was the same blind and boyish taste for the pursuit of exotic history. Unprovided with original learning, unformed in the habits of thinking, unskilled in the arts of composition, I resolved—to write a book. The title of this first essay, *The Age of Sesostris*, was perhaps suggested by Voltaire's *Age of Lewis XIV*, which was new and popular; but my sole object was to investigate the probable date of the life and reign of the conqueror of Asia. I was then enamoured of Sir John Marsham's *Canon Chronicus*; an elaborate work, of whose merits and defects I was not yet qualified to judge. According to his specious, though narrow plan, I settled my hero about the time of Solomon, in the tenth century before the Christian era. It was therefore incumbent on me, unless I would adopt Sir Isaac Newton's shorter chronology, to remove a formidable objection; and my solution, for a youth of fifteen, is not devoid of ingenuity. In his version of the Sacred Books, Manetho the high priest has identified Sethosis, or Sesostris, with the elder brother of Danaus, who landed in Greece, according to the Parian Marble, fifteen hundred and ten years before Christ. But in my supposition the high priest is guilty of a voluntary error; flattery is the prolific parent of falsehood. Manetho's *History of Egypt* is dedicated to Ptolemy Philadelphus, who derived a fabulous or illegitimate pedigree from the Macedonian kings of the race of Hercules. Danaus is the ancestor of Hercules; and after the failure of the elder branch, his descendants, the Ptolemies, are the sole representatives of the royal family, and may claim by inheritance the kingdom which they hold by

conquest. Such were my juvenile discoveries; at
a riper age, I no longer presume to connect the Greek,
the Jewish, and the Egyptian antiquities, which are
lost in a distant cloud. Nor is this the only instance,
in which the belief and knowledge of the child are
superseded by the more rational ignorance of the
man. During my stay at Buriton, my infant labour
was diligently prosecuted, without much interruption
from company or country diversions; and I already
heard the music of public applause. The discovery
of my own weakness was the first symptom of taste.
On my return to Oxford, *The Age of Sesostris* was
wisely relinquished; but the imperfect sheets remained
twenty years at the bottom of a drawer, till, in a general
clearance of papers (November, 1772), they were
committed to the flames.

After the departure of Dr. Waldegrave, I was
transferred, with his other pupils, to his academical
heir, whose literary character did not command the
respect of the college. Dr. **** well remembered
that he had a salary to receive, and only forgot that
he had a duty to perform. Instead of guiding the
studies, and watching over the behaviour of his
disciple, I was never summoned to attend even the
ceremony of a lecture; and, excepting one voluntary
visit to his rooms, during the eight months of his
titular office, the tutor and pupil lived in the same
college as strangers to each other. The want of
experience, of advice, and of occupation, soon betrayed
me into some improprieties of conduct, ill-chosen company, late hours, and inconsiderate expense. My
growing debts might be secret; but my frequent
absence was visible and scandalous: and a tour to
Bath, a visit into Buckinghamshire, and four excursions to London in the same winter, were costly and
dangerous frolics. They were, indeed, without a
meaning, as without an excuse. The irksomeness of
a cloistered life repeatedly tempted me to wander;
but my chief pleasure was that of travelling; and I
was too young and bashful to enjoy, like a manly

Oxonian in town, the pleasures of London. In all these excursions I eloped from Oxford; I returned to college; in a few days I eloped again, as if I had been an independent stranger in a hired lodging, without once hearing the voice of admonition, without once feeling the hand of control. Yet my time was lost, my expenses were multiplied, my behaviour abroad was unknown; folly as well as vice should have awakened the attention of my superiors, and my tender years would have justified a more than ordinary degree of restraint and discipline.

It might at least be expected that an ecclesiastical school should inculcate the orthodox principles of religion. But our venerable mother had contrived to unite the opposite extremes of bigotry and indifference: an heretic, or unbeliever, was a monster in her eyes; but she was always, or often, or sometimes, remiss in the spiritual education of her own children. According to the statutes of the University, every student, before he is matriculated, must subscribe his assent to the thirty-nine articles of the Church of England, which are signed by more than read, and read by more than believe them. My insufficient age excused me, however, from the immediate performance of this legal ceremony; and the Vice-Chancellor directed me to return, as soon as I should have accomplished my fifteenth year; recommending me, in the meanwhile, to the instruction of my college. My college forgot to instruct: I forgot to return, and was myself forgotten by the first magistrate of the University. Without a single lecture, either public or private, either Christian or Protestant, without any academical subscription, without any episcopal confirmation, I was left by the dim light of my catechism to grope my way to the chapel and communion-table, where I was admitted, without a question, how far, or by what means, I might be qualified to receive the Sacrament. Such almost incredible neglect was productive of the worst mischiefs. From my childhood I had been fond of religious disputation: my poor aunt has been often puzzled by the mysteries which she strove to believe ; nor had the elastic spring been totally broken by the weight of the atmosphere of Oxford. The blind activity of idleness urged me to advance without armour into the dangerous mazes of controversy ; and at the age of sixteen, I bewildered myself in the errors of the Church of Rome.

The progress of my conversion may tend to illustrate, at least, the history of my own mind. It was not long since Dr. Middleton's *Free Inquiry* had sounded an alarm in the theological world ; much ink and much gall had been spilt in the defence of the primitive miracles ; and the two dullest of their champions were crowned with academic honours by the University of Oxford. The name of Middleton was unpopular ; and his proscription very naturally led me to peruse his writings, and those of his antagonists. His bold criticism, which approaches the precipice of infidelity, produced on my mind a singular effect ; and had I persevered in the communion of Rome, I should now apply to my own fortune the prediction of the Sibyl,

—— Via prima salutis,
Quod minimè reris, Graiâ, pandetur ab urbe.

The elegance of style and freedom of argument were repelled by the shield of prejudice. I still revered the character, or rather the names, of the saints and fathers whom Dr. Middleton exposes ; nor could he destroy my implicit belief, that the gift of miraculous powers was continued in the Church during the first four or five centuries of Christianity. But I was unable to resist the weight of historical evidence, that within the same period most of the leading doctrines of Popery were already introduced in theory and practice : nor was my conclusion absurd, that miracles are the test of truth, and that the Church must be orthodox and pure, which was so often approved by the visible interposition of the Deity. The marvellous tales which are so boldly attested by the Basils and Chrysostoms, the Austins and Jeroms, compelled me to embrace the superior merits of celibacy, the institution of the monastic life, the use of the sign of the cross, of holy oil, and even of images, the invocation of saints, the worship of relics, the rudiments of purgatory in prayers for the dead, and the tremendous mystery of the sacrifice of the body and blood of Christ, which insensibly swelled into the prodigy of transubstantiation. In these dispositions, and already more than half a convert, I formed an unlucky intimacy with a young gentleman of our college. With a character less resolute, Mr. Molesworth had imbibed the same religious opinions; and some Popish books, I know not through what channel, were conveyed into his possession. I read, I applauded, I believed: the English translations of two famous works of Bossuet, Bishop of Meaux, the *Exposition of the Catholic Doctrine*, and the *History of the Protestant Variations*, achieved my conversion, and I surely fell by a noble hand.[1] I have since examined the originals with a more discerning eye, and shall not hesitate to pronounce, that Bossuet is indeed a master of all the weapons of controversy. In the *Exposition*, a specious apology, the orator assumes, with consummate art, the tone of candour and simplicity; and the ten-horned monster is transformed, at his magic touch, into the milk-white hind, who must be loved as soon as she is seen. In the *History*, a bold and well-aimed attack, he displays, with a happy mixture of narrative and argument, the faults and follies, the changes and contradictions of our first reformers; whose variations (as he dexterously contends) are the mark of historical error, while the perpetual unity of the Catholic Church is the sign and test of infallible truth. To my present feelings it seems incredible that I should ever believe

---

[1] Mr. Gibbon never talked with me on the subject of his conversion to Popery but once: and then, he imputed his change to the works of Parsons the Jesuit, who lived in the reign of Elizabeth, and who, he said, had urged all the best arguments in favour of the Roman Catholic religion. S.

that I believed in transubstantiation. But my conqueror oppressed me with the sacramental words,
'Hoc est corpus meum', and dashed against each
other the figurative half-meanings of the Protestant
sects: every objection was resolved into omnipotence;
and after repeating, at St. Mary's, the Athanasian
creed, I humbly acquiesced in the mystery of the real
presence.

> To take up half on trust, and half to try,
> Name it not faith, but bungling bigotry.
> Both knave and fool, the merchant we may call,
> To pay great sums, and to compound the small,
> For who would break with Heaven, and would not
>   break for all?

No sooner had I settled my new religion than I resolved
to profess myself a Catholic. Youth is sincere and
impetuous; and a momentary glow of enthusiasm
had raised me above all temporal considerations.[1]

By the keen Protestants, who would gladly retaliate
the example of persecution, a clamour is raised of the
increase of Popery: and they are always loud to
declaim against the toleration of priests and jesuits,
who pervert so many of his majesty's subjects from
their religion and allegiance. On the present occasion,
the fall of one or more of her sons directed this clamour
against the University; and it was confidently affirmed
that Popish missionaries were suffered, under various
disguises, to introduce themselves into the colleges of
Oxford. But justice obliges me to declare that, as
far as relates to myself, this assertion is false; and
that I never conversed with a priest, or even with
a Papist, till my resolution from books was absolutely
fixed. In my last excursion to London, I addressed
myself to Mr. Lewis, a Roman Catholic bookseller in
Russell Street, Covent Garden, who recommended
me to a priest, of whose name and order I am at

---

[1] He described the letter to his father, announcing his
conversion, as written with all the pomp, the dignity, and
self-satisfaction of a martyr. S.

present ignorant.[1] In our first interview he soon discovered that persuasion was needless. After sounding the motives and merits of my conversion, he consented to admit me into the pale of the Church; and at his feet, on the 8th of June, 1753, I solemnly, though privately, abjured the errors of heresy. The seduction of an English youth of family and fortune was an act of as much danger as glory; but he bravely overlooked the danger, of which I was not then sufficiently informed. 'Where a person is reconciled to the See of Rome, or procures others to be reconciled, the offence (says Blackstone) amounts to high treason.' And if the humanity of the age would prevent the execution of this sanguinary statute, there were other laws of a less odious cast, which condemned the priest to perpetual imprisonment, and transferred the proselyte's estate to his nearest relation. An elaborate controversial epistle, approved by my director, and addressed to my father, announced and justified the step which I had taken. My father was neither a bigot nor a philosopher; but his affection deplored the loss of an only son; and his good sense was astonished at my strange departure from the religion of my country. In the first sally of passion he divulged a secret which prudence might have suppressed, and the gates of Magdalen College were for ever shut against my return. Many years afterwards, when the name of Gibbon was become as notorious as that of Middleton, it was industriously whispered at Oxford, that the historian had formerly 'turned Papist': my character stood exposed to the reproach of inconstancy; and this invidious topic would have been handled without mercy by my opponents, could they have separated my cause from that of the University. For

---

[1] His name was Baker, a Jesuit, and one of the chaplains of the Sardinian Ambassador. Mr. Gibbon's conversion made some noise; and Mr. Lewis, the Roman Catholic bookseller of Russell Street, Covent Garden, was summoned before the Privy Council, and interrogated on the subject. This was communicated by Mr. Lewis's son. 1814. S.

my own part, I am proud of an honest sacrifice of interest to conscience. I can never blush, if my tender mind was entangled in the sophistry that seduced the acute and manly understandings of Chillingworth and Bayle, who afterwards emerged from superstition to scepticism.

While Charles the First governed England, and was himself governed by a Catholic queen, it cannot be denied that the missionaries of Rome laboured with impunity and success in the court, the country, and even the Universities. One of the sheep,

> —— Whom the grim wolf with privy paw
> Daily devours apace, and nothing said,

is Mr. William Chillingworth, Master of Arts, and Fellow of Trinity College, Oxford; who, at the ripe age of twenty-eight years, was persuaded to elope from Oxford to the English seminary at Douay in Flanders. Some disputes with Fisher, a subtle Jesuit, might first awaken him from the prejudices of education; but he yielded to his own victorious argument, 'that there must be somewhere an infallible judge; and that the Church of Rome is the only Christian society which either does or can pretend to that character'. After a short trial of a few months, Mr. Chillingworth was again tormented by religious scruples: he returned home, resumed his studies, unravelled his mistakes, and delivered his mind from the yoke of authority and superstition. His new creed was built on the principle that the Bible is our sole judge, and private reason our sole interpreter: and he ably maintains this principle in *The Religion of a Protestant,* a book which, after startling the doctors of Oxford, is still esteemed the most solid defence of the Reformation. The learning, the virtue, the recent merits of the author, entitled him to a fair preferment: but the slave had now broken his fetters; and the more he weighed, the less was he disposed to subscribe to the thirty-nine articles of the Church of England. In a private letter he declares, with all the energy of language, that he could not subscribe to them without subscribing to his own damnation; and that if ever he should depart from his immovable resolution, he would allow his friends to think him a madman or an atheist. As the letter is without a date, we cannot ascertain the number of weeks or months that elapsed between this passionate abhorrence and the Salisbury Register, which is still extant. 'Ego Gulielmus Chillingworth, . . . omnibus hisce articulis, . . . et singulis in iisdem contentis, volens et ex animo subscribo, et consensum meum iisdem praebeo. 20 die Julii 1638.' But, alas! the chancellor and prebendary of Sarum soon deviated from his own subscription: as he more deeply scrutinized the article of the Trinity, neither scripture nor the primitive fathers could long uphold his orthodox belief; and he could not but confess, 'that the doctrine of Arius is either a truth, or at least no damnable heresy'. From this middle region of the air, the descent of his reason would naturally rest on the firmer ground of the Socinians: and if we may credit a doubtful story, and the popular opinion, his anxious inquiries at last subsided in philosophic indifference. So conspicuous, however, were the candour of his nature and the innocence of his heart, that this apparent levity did not affect the reputation of Chillingworth. His frequent changes proceeded from too nice an inquisition into truth. His doubts grew out of himself; he assisted them with all the strength of his reason: he was then too hard for himself; but finding as little quiet and repose in those victories, he quickly recovered, by a new appeal to his own judgement: so that in all his sallies and retreats, he was in fact his own convert.

Bayle was the son of a Calvinist minister in a remote province in France, at the foot of the Pyrenees. For the benefit of education, the Protestants were tempted to risk their children in the Catholic Universities; and in the twenty-second year of his age young Bayle was seduced by the arts and arguments of the Jesuits of Toulouse. He remained about seventeen months

(March 19, 1699—August 19, 1670) in their hands, a
voluntary captive ; and a letter to his parents, which
the new convert composed or subscribed (April 15,
1670), is darkly tinged with the spirit of Popery. But
nature had designed him to think as he pleased, and
to speak as he thought : his piety was offended by
the excessive worship of creatures ; and the study
of physics convinced him of the impossibility of transubstantiation, which is abundantly refuted by the
testimony of our senses. His return to the communion
of a falling sect was a bold and disinterested step, that
exposed him to the rigour of the laws ; and a speedy
flight to Geneva protected him from the resentment
of his spiritual tyrants, unconscious as they were of
the full value of the prize which they had lost. Had
Bayle adhered to the Catholic Church, had he embraced
the ecclesiastical profession, the genius and favour of
such a proselyte might have aspired to wealth and
honours in his native country : but the hypocrite
would have found less happiness in the comforts of
a benefice, or the dignity of a mitre, than he enjoyed
at Rotterdam in a private state of exile, indigence,
and freedom. Without a country, or a patron, or
a prejudice, he claimed the liberty and subsisted by
the labours of his pen : the inequality of his voluminous
works is explained and excused by his alternately
writing for himself, for the booksellers, and for posterity ; and if a severe critic would reduce him to
a single folio, that relic, like the books of the Sibyl,
would become still more valuable. A calm and lofty
spectator of the religious tempest, the philosopher of
Rotterdam condemned with equal firmness the persecution of Lewis the Fourteenth, and the republican
maxims of the Calvinists ; their vain prophecies, and
the intolerant bigotry which sometimes vexed his
solitary retreat. In reviewing the controversies of
the times, he turned against each other the arguments
of the disputants ; successively wielding the arms of
the Catholics and Protestants, he proves that neither
the way of authority nor the way of examination can

afford the multitude any test of religious truth ; and
dexterously concludes that custom and education must
be the sole grounds of popular belief.   The ancient
paradox of Plutarch, that atheism is less pernicious
than superstition, acquires a tenfold vigour when it is
adorned with the colours of his wit, and pointed with
the acuteness of his logic.   His critical dictionary is
a vast repository of facts and opinions ; and he balances
the *false* religions in his sceptical scales, till the opposite
quantities (if I may use the language of algebra)
annihilate each other.   The wonderful power which
he so boldly exercised, of assembling doubts and
objections, had tempted him jocosely to assume the
title of the νεφεληγερετα Ζευς, the cloud-compelling
Jove ; and in a conversation with the ingenious Abbé
(afterwards Cardinal) de Polignac, he freely disclosed
his universal Pyrrhonism.   'I am most truly (said
Bayle) a Protestant ; for I protest indifferently against
all systems and all sects.'

The academical resentment, which I may possibly
have provoked, will prudently spare this plain narrative
of my studies, or rather of my idleness ; and of the
unfortunate event which shortened the term of my
residence at Oxford.   But it may be suggested, that
my father was unlucky in the choice of a society and
the chance of a tutor.   It will perhaps be asserted that
in the lapse of forty years many improvements have
taken place in the college and in the University.
I am not unwilling to believe that some tutors might
have been found more active than Dr. Waldegrave
and less contemptible than Dr. ****.   At a more
recent period, many students have been attracted by
the merit and reputation of Sir William Scott, then
a tutor in University College, and now conspicuous in
the profession of the civil law : my personal acquaintance with that gentleman has inspired me with a just
esteem for his abilities and knowledge ; and I am
assured that his lectures on history would compose,
were they given to the public, a most valuable treatise.
Under the auspices of the late Deans, a more regular

discipline has been introduced, as I am told, at Christ Church ; [1] ' a course of classical and philosophical studies is proposed, and even pursued, in that numerous

---

[1] This was written on the information Mr. Gibbon had received, and the observation he had made, previous to his late residence at Lausanne.   During his last visit to England, he had an opportunity of seeing at Sheffield Place some young men of the college above alluded to ; he had great satisfaction in conversing with them, made many inquiries respecting their course of study, applauded the discipline of Christ Church, and the liberal attention shown by the Dean, to those whose only recommendation was their merit.   Had Mr. Gibbon lived to revise this work, I am sure he would have mentioned the name of Dr. Jackson with the highest commendation : and also that of Dr. Bagot, Bishop of St. Asaph, whose attention to the duties of his office while he was Dean of Christ Church was unremitted ;   and to whom, perhaps, that college is more indebted for the good discipline introduced there, than to any other person whatever.   There are other colleges at Oxford, with whose discipline my friend was unacquainted, to which, without doubt, he would willingly have allowed their due praise, particularly Brasenose and Oriel Colleges ;   the former under the care of Dr. Cleaver, Bishop of Chester, the latter under that of Dr. Eveleigh. It is still greatly to be wished that the general expense, or rather extravagance, of young men at our English Universities may be more effectually restrained.   The expense, in which they are permitted to indulge, is inconsistent not only with a necessary degree of study, but with those habits of morality which should be promoted, by all means possible, at an early period of life.   An academical education in England is at present an object of alarm and terror to every thinking parent of moderate fortune. It is the apprehension of the expense, of the dissipation, and other evil consequences, which arise from the want of proper restraint at our own Universities, that forces a number of our English youths to those of Scotland, and utterly excludes many from any sort of academical instruction.   If a charge be true, which I have heard insisted on, that the heads of our colleges in Oxford and Cambridge are vain of having under their care chiefly men of opulence,

seminary : learning has been made a duty, a pleasure, and even a fashion ; and several young gentlemen do honour to the college in which they have been educated. According to the will of the donor, the profit of the second part of Lord Clarendon's *History* has been applied to the establishment of a riding-school, that the polite exercises might be taught, I know not with what success, in the University. The Vinerian professorship is of far more serious importance ; the laws of his country are the first science of an Englishman of rank and fortune, who is called to be a magistrate, and may hope to be a legislator. This judicious institution was coldly entertained by the graver doctors, who complained (I have heard the complaint) that it would take the young people from their books : but Mr. Viner's

who may be supposed exempt from the necessity of economical control, they are indeed highly censurable ; since the mischief of allowing early habits of expense and dissipation is great, in various respects, even to those possessed of large property ; and the most serious evil from this indulgence must happen to youths of humbler fortune, who certainly form the majority of students both at Oxford and Cambridge. S.

Since these observations appeared, a Sermon, with very copious notes, has been published by the Reverend Dr. Parr, wherein he complains of the scantiness of praise bestowed on those who were educated at the Universities of England. I digressed merely to speak of the few heads of colleges of whom I had at that time heard, or with whom I was acquainted, and I did not allude to any others educated there. I have further to observe, that I have not met with any person who lived at the time to which Mr. Gibbon alludes, who was not of opinion that his representation, at least of his own college, was just : and such was the opinion of that accomplished, ingenious, and zealous friend of the University, the late Mr. Windham : but every man, acquainted with the former and present state of the University, will acknowledge the vast improvements which have of late been introduced into the plan and conduct of education in the University. S.

benefaction is not unprofitable, since it has at least produced the excellent commentaries of Sir William Blackstone.

After carrying me to Putney, to the house of his friend Mr. Mallet [1], by whose philosophy I was rather scandalized than reclaimed, it was necessary for my father to form a new plan of education, and to devise some method which, if possible, might effect the cure of my spiritual malady. After much debate it was determined, from the advice and personal experience of Mr. Eliot (now Lord Eliot), to fix me, during some years, at Lausanne in Switzerland. Mr. Frey, a Swiss gentleman of Basil, undertook the conduct of the journey: we left London the 19th of June, crossed the sea from Dover to Calais, travelled post through several provinces of France, by the direct road of St. Quentin, Rheims, Langres, and Besançon, and arrived the 30th of June at Lausanne, where I was immediately settled under the roof and tuition of Mr. Pavilliard, a Calvinist minister.

The first marks of my father's displeasure rather astonished than afflicted me: when he threatened to banish, and disown, and disinherit, a rebellious son, I cherished a secret hope that he would not be able or willing to effect his menaces; and the pride of conscience encouraged me to sustain the honourable and important part which I was now acting. My spirits were raised and kept alive by the rapid motion of my journey, the new and various scenes of the Continent, and the civility of Mr. Frey, a man of sense, who was not ignorant of books or the world. But after he had resigned me into Pavilliard's hands, and I was fixed in my new habitation, I had leisure to contemplate the strange and melancholy prospect before me. My first complaint arose from my ignorance

[1] The author of a *Life of Bacon*, which has been rated above its value; of some forgotten poems and plays; and of the pathetic ballad of William and Margaret. His tenets were deistical; perhaps a stronger term might have been used. S.

of the language. In my childhood I had once studied the French grammar, and I could imperfectly understand the easy prose of a familiar subject. But when I was thus suddenly cast on a foreign land, I found myself deprived of the use of speech and of hearing; and, during some weeks, incapable not only of enjoying the pleasures of conversation, but even of asking or answering a question in the common intercourse of life. To a home-bred Englishman every object, every custom was offensive; but the native of any country might have been disgusted with the general aspect of his lodging and entertainment. I had now exchanged my elegant apartment in Magdalen College for a narrow, gloomy street, the most unfrequented of an unhandsome town, for an old inconvenient house, and for a small chamber ill-contrived and ill-furnished, which, on the approach of winter, instead of a companionable fire, must be warmed by the dull, invisible heat of a stove. From a man I was again degraded to the dependence of a schoolboy. Mr. Pavilliard managed my expenses, which had been reduced to a diminutive state: I received a small monthly allowance for my pocket-money; and helpless and awkward as I have ever been, I no longer enjoyed the indispensable comfort of a servant. My condition seemed as destitute of hope as it was devoid of pleasure: I was separated for an indefinite, which appeared an infinite term from my native country; and I had lost all connexion with my Catholic friends. I have since reflected with surprise, that as the Romish clergy of every part of Europe maintain a close correspondence with each other, they never attempted, by letters or messages, to rescue me from the hands of the heretics, or at least to confirm my zeal and constancy in the profession of the faith. Such was my first introduction to Lausanne; a place where I spent nearly five years with pleasure and profit, which I afterwards revisited without compulsion, and which I have finally selected as the most grateful retreat for the decline of my life.

But it is the peculiar felicity of youth that the most unpleasing objects and events seldom make a deep or lasting impression; it forgets the past, enjoys the present, and anticipates the future. At the flexible age of sixteen I soon learned to endure, and gradually to adopt, the new forms of arbitrary manners: the real hardships of my situation were alienated by time. Had I been sent abroad in a more splendid style, such as the fortune and bounty of my father might have supplied, I might have returned home with the same stock of language and science which our countrymen usually import from the Continent. An exile and a prisoner as I was, their example betrayed me into some irregularities of wine, of play, and of idle excursions: but I soon felt the impossibility of associating with them on equal terms; and after the departure of my first acquaintance, I held a cold and civil correspondence with their successors. This seclusion from English society was attended with the most solid benefits. In the *Pays de Vaud*, the French language is used with less imperfection than in most of the distant provinces of France: in Pavilliard's family, necessity compelled me to listen and to speak; and if I was at first disheartened by the apparent slowness, in a few months I was astonished by the rapidity of my progress. My pronunciation was formed by the constant repetition of the same sounds; the variety of words and idioms, the rules of grammar, and distinctions of genders, were impressed in my memory: ease and freedom were obtained by practice; correctness and elegance by labour; and before I was recalled home, French, in which I spontaneously thought, was more familiar than English to my ear, my tongue, and my pen. The first effect of this opening knowledge was the revival of my love of reading, which had been chilled at Oxford; and I soon turned over, without much choice, almost all the French books in my tutor's library. Even these amusements were productive of real advantage: my taste and judgement were now somewhat riper. I was introduced to a new mode of style and literature : by the comparison of manners and opinions, my views were enlarged, my prejudices were corrected, and a copious voluntary abstract of the *Histoire de l'Eglise et de l'Empire*, by le Sueur, may be placed in a middle line between my childish and my manly studies. As soon as I was able to converse with the natives, I began to feel some satisfaction in their company : my awkward timidity was polished and emboldened ; and I frequented, for the first time, assemblies of men and women. The acquaintance of the Pavilliards prepared me by degrees for more elegant society. I was received with kindness and indulgence in the best families of Lausanne ; and it was in one of these that I formed an intimate and lasting connexion with Mr. Deyverdun, a young man of an amiable temper and excellent understanding. In the arts of fencing and dancing, small indeed was my proficiency ; and some months were idly wasted in the riding-school. My unfitness to bodily exercise reconciled me to a sedentary life, and the horse, the favourite of my countrymen, never contributed to the pleasures of my youth.

My obligations to the lessons of Mr. Pavilliard, gratitude will not suffer me to forget : he was endowed with a clear head and a warm heart ; his innate benevolence had assuaged the spirit of the Church ; he was rational, because he was moderate : in the course of his studies he had acquired a just though superficial knowledge of most branches of literature ; by long practice, he was skilled in the arts of teaching ; and he laboured with assiduous patience to know the character, gain the affection, and open the mind of his English pupil.[1] As soon as we began to understand

---

[1] EXTRACT OF A LETTER FROM M. PAVILLIARD TO
EDWARD GIBBON, ESQ.

À Lausanne, ce 25 Juillet 1753.

Monsieur de Gibbon se porte très bien par la grace de Dieu, et il me paroit qu'il ne se trouve pas mal de notre Maison ; j'ai même lieu de penser qu'il prend de

each other, he gently led me, from a blind and undistinguishing love of reading, into the path of

l'attachement pour moi, ce dont je suis charmé et que je travaillerai à augmenter, parcequ'il aura plus de confiance en moi, dans ce que je me propose de lui dire.

Je n'ai point encore entrepris de lui parler sur les matières de religion, parceque je n'entends pas assez la langue Angloise pour soutenir une longue conversation en cette langue, quoique je lise les auteurs Anglois avec assez de facilité; et Monsieur de Gibbon n'entend pas assez de François, mais il y fait beaucoup de progrès.

Je suis fort content de la politesse et de la douceur de caractère de Monsieur votre fils, et je me flatte que je pourrai toujours vous parler de lui avec éloge; il s'applique beaucoup à la lecture.

FROM THE SAME TO THE SAME.

À Lausanne, ce 13 Août 1753.

Monsieur de Gibbon se porte bien par la grace de Dieu; je l'aime, et je me suis extrèmement attaché à lui parcequ'il est doux et tranquille. Pour ce qui regarde ses sentimens, quoique je ne lui aye encore rien dit là-dessus, j'ai lieu d'espérer qu'il ouvrira les yeux à la vérité. Je le pense ainsi, parcequ'étant dans mon cabinet, il a choisi deux livres de controversie qu'il a pris dans sa chambre, et qu'il les lit. Il m'a chargé de vous offrir ses très humbles respects, et de vous demander la permission de le laisser monter au manège: cet exercice pourroit contribuer à donner de la force à son corps, c'est l'idée qu'il en a.

FROM THE SAME TO THE SAME.

À Lausanne, ce 31 Octobre 1753.

MONSIEUR,

Depuis ma lettre du 15me Août, je reçus le 18me du même mois la lettre que vous m'avez fait l'honneur de m'écrire en datte du 24e Juillet. Je l'ai lue avec attention: permettez moi de vous marquer les réflexions que j'y ai fait.

Vous souhaitez que je tienne Monsieur votre fils à la maison attaché à ses études, et qu'il sorte peu. Vous êtes père, par là même, Monsieur, vous avez droit de prescrire la manière dont vous voulez qu'on le conduise. Sans doute vous ne prenez ce parti, que parceque vous

instruction. I consented with pleasure that a portion of the morning hours should be consecrated to a plan

croyez qu'on réussira mieux par cette voie, à le ramener des prejugés auxquels il s'est livré. Mais je vous prie de considérer que Monsieur votre fils est d'un caractère sérieux, qu'il se plait à refléchir, qu'étant dans sa chambre occupé à lire, il suivra ses idées, et il s'y attachera toujours plus, parceque personne ne le contredira : d'ailleurs regardant comme une peine l'obligation qu'on lui impose, il sera toujours moins porté à écouter favorablement ce que je lui dirai : il envisagera tous mes discours, comme venant d'un homme qui est dans des idées qu'il désapprouve, et qui veut, cependant, les lui faire recevoir, parcequ'il est paié pour cela.

Je crois, Monsieur, qu'il seroit plus à propos de le distraire un peu, de l'égaier un peu, pour lui faire passer ce qu'il a de trop sombre dans le caractère : en voyant bonne compagnie, il appercevroit qu'on pense juste sur bien de sujets : il s'accoutumeroit à être contredit quelquefois, et à céder aussi dans l'occasion, il examineroit avec plus de soin et avec moins de préoccupation les principes qu'il adopte, et les voyant souvent condamnés par des personnes qu'il voit qui ont du goût pour la verité, il ne les regarderoit pas comme infaillibles, et convaincu qu'on ne le hait pas à cause de ses sentiments, il écouteroit ce qu'on lui diroit avec plus de confiance. Tout ce que je viens de dire est une suite des remarques que j'ai fait sur son caractère, et sur ce que vous m'avez fait l'honneur de m'en dire dans votre lettre. Je me suis apperçu qu'il étoit attaché au parti du Prétendant : il s'en est déclaré assez ouvertement dans la suite. J'ai combattu ses idées sans faire semblant que c'étoit les siennes, et sans marquer aucune intention de lui faire de la peine : il a répliqué plusieurs fois, mais à la fin j'ai tellement renversé tous ses raisonnemens qu'il n'en parle plus, et qu'il s'exprime sur le sujet du roi d'une manière bien différente de ce qu'il faisoit autrefois. Je n'assurerai pas cependant qu'il ait entièrement changé d'idées, parcequ'il parle peu, et que je n'ai pas voulu faire connoître que j'avois dessein de l'emporter sur lui.

Monsieur,

Votre très humble et obéissant Serviteur,

PAVILLIARD, PASTEUR.

of modern history and geography, and to the critical
perusal of the French and Latin classics ; and at each
step I felt myself invigorated by the habits of application and method. His prudence repressed and dis-
sembled some youthful sallies ; and as soon as I was
confirmed in the habits of industry and temperance,
he gave the reins into my own hands. His favourable
report of my behaviour and progress gradually obtained
some latitude of action and expense ; and he wished
to alleviate the hardships of my lodging and entertainment. The principles of philosophy were associated
with the examples of taste ; and by a singular chance,
the book, as well as the man, which contributed the
most effectually to my education, has a stronger claim
on my gratitude than on my admiration. Mr. De
Crousaz, the adversary of Bayle and Pope, is not distinguished by lively fancy or profound reflection ;
and even in his own country, at the end of a few years,
his name and writings are almost obliterated. But
his philosophy had been formed in the school of Locke,
his divinity in that of Limborch and Le Clerc ; in
a long and laborious life, several generations of pupils
were taught to think, and even to write ; his lessons
rescued the academy of Lausanne from Calvinistic
prejudice ; and he had the rare merit of diffusing a
more liberal spirit among the clergy and people of
the Pays de Vaud. His system of logic, which in the
last editions has swelled to six tedious and prolix
volumes, may be praised as a clear and methodical
abridgement of the art of reasoning, from our simple
ideas to the most complex operations of the human
understanding. This system I studied, and meditated,
and abstracted, till I obtained the free command of an
universal instrument, which I soon presumed to
exercise on my Catholic opinions. Pavilliard was not
unmindful that his first task, his most important duty,
was to reclaim me from the errors of Popery. The
intermixture of sects has rendered the Swiss clergy
acute and learned on the topics of controversy ; and
I have some of his letters in which he celebrates the

dexterity of his attack, and my gradual concessions, after a firm and well-managed defence.[1] I was willing, and I am now willing, to allow him a handsome share of the honour of my conversion : yet I must observe that it was principally effected by my private reflections ; and I still remember my solitary transport at the discovery of a philosophical argument against the doctrine of transubstantiation : *that* the text of Scripture, which seem to inculcate the real presence, is attested only by a single sense—our sight ; while the real presence itself is disproved by three of our senses—the sight, the touch, and the taste. The various articles of the Romish creed disappeared like a dream ; and after a full conviction, on Christmas Day, 1754, I received the sacrament in the church of Lausanne. It was here that I suspended my religious inquiries, acquiescing with implicit belief in the tenets and mysteries which are adopted by the general consent of Catholics and Protestants.[2]

---

[1] M. Pavilliard has described to me the astonishment with which he gazed on Mr. Gibbon standing before him : a thin little figure, with a large head, disputing and urging, with the greatest ability, all the best arguments that had ever been used in favour of Popery. Mr. Gibbon many years ago became very fat and corpulent, but he had uncommonly small bones, and was very slightly made. S.

[2] LETTER FROM M. PAVILLIARD TO EDWARD GIBBON, ESQ.

MONSIEUR, Juin 26, 1754.

J'espère que vous pardonnerez mon long silence en faveur des nouvelles que j'ai à vous apprendre. Si j'ai tant tardé, ce n'a été ni par oubli, ni par négligence, mais je croyois de semaine en semaine pouvoir vous annoncer que Monsieur votre fils avoit entièrement renoncé aux fausses idées qu'il avoit embrassées ; mais il a fallu disputer le terrein pied à pied, et je n'ai pas trouvé en lui un homme léger, et qui passe rapidement d'un sentiment à un autre. Souvent après avoir détruit toutes ses idées sur un article, de manière qu'il n'avoit rien à répliquer,

Such, from my arrival at Lausanne, during the first eighteen or twenty months (July 1753—March 1755),

ce qu'il avouoit sans détour, il me disoit qu'il ne croioit pas qu'il n'y eût rien à me répondre. Là-dessus je n'ai pas jugé qu'il fallût le pousser à bout, et extorquer de lui un aveu que son cœur désavoueroit ; je lui donnois alors du tems pour réfléchir ; tous mes livres étoient à sa disposition ; je revenois à la charge quand il m'avouoit qu'il avoit étudié la matière aussi bien qu'il l'avoit pu, et enfin j'établissois une verité.

Je me persuadois que, quand j'aurois détruit les principales erreurs de l'église Romaine, je n'aurois qu'à faire voir que les autres sont des conséquences des premières, et qu'elles ne peuvent subsister quand les fondamentales sont renversées ; mais, comme je l'ai dit, je me suis trompé, il a fallu traiter chaque article dans son entier. Par la grace de Dieu, je n'ai pas perdu mon tems, et aujourdhui, si même il conserve quelques restes de ses pernicieuses erreurs, j'ose dire qu'il n'est plus membre de l'église Romaine ; voici donc où nous en sommes.

J'ai renversé l'infaillibilité de l'église ; j'ai prouvé que jamais St. Pierre n'a été chef des apôtres ; que quand il l'auroit été, le pape n'est point son successeur ; qu'il est douteux que St. Pierre ait jamais été à Rome, mais supposé qu'il y ait été, il n'a pas été évêque de cette ville : que la transubstantiation est une invention humaine, et peu ancienne dans l'église ; que l'adoration de l'Eucharistie et le retranchement de la coupe sont contraires à la parole de Dieu : qu'il y a des saints, mais que nous ne savons pas qui ils sont, et par conséquent qu'on ne peut pas les prier ; que le respect et le culte qu'on rend aux reliques est condamnable ; qu'il n'y a point de purgatoire, et que la doctrine des indulgences est fausse : que le Carême et les jeunes du Vendredi et du Samedi sont ridicules aujourdhui, et de la manière que l'église Romaine les prescrit : que les imputations que l'église de Rome nous fait de varier dans notre doctrine, et d'avoir pour réformateurs des personnes dont la conduite et les mœurs ont été un scandale, sont entièrement fausses.

Vous comprenez bien, Monsieur, que ces articles sont d'une longue discussion, qu'il a fallu du tems à Monsieur votre fils pour méditer mes raisons, et pour y chercher

were my useful studies, the foundation of all my future improvements. But every man who rises above the

des réponses. Je lui ai demandé plusieurs fois si mes preuves et mes raisons lui paroissoient convainquantes ; il m'a toujours assuré qu'oui, de façon que j'ose assurer aussi, comme je le lui ai dit à lui-même il y a peu de tems, qu'il n'étoit plus catholique Romain. Je me flatte qu'après avoir obtenu la victoire sur ces articles, je l'aurai sur le reste avec le secours de Dieu. Tellement que je compte vous marquer dans peu que cette ouvrage est fini ; je dois vous dire encore que, quoique j'ai trouvé M^r votre fils très ferme dans ses idées, je l'ai trouvé raisonnable, qu'il s'est rendu à la lumière, et qu'il n'est pas, ce qu'on appelle, chicaneur. Par rapport à l'article du jeune le Vendredi et Samedi, long tems après que je vous eus écrit qu'il n'avoit jamais marqué qu'il voulût l'observer, environs le commencement du mois de Mars je m'apperçus un Vendredi qu'il ne mangeoit point de viande ; je lui parlai en particulier pour en savoir la raison, craignant que ce ne fut par indisposition ; il me répondit qu'il l'avoit fait à dessein, et qu'il avoit cru être obligé de se conformer à la pratique d'une église dont il étoit membre : nous parlâmes quelque tems sur ce sujet ; il m'assura qu'il n'envisageoit cela que comme une pratique bonne à la vérité, et qu'il devoit suivre, quoiqu'il ne la crût pas sainte en elle même, ni d'institution divine. Je ne crus pas devoir insister pour lors, ni le forcer à agir contre ses lumières : j'ai traité cet article qui est certainement un des moins importans, des moins fondés ; et cependant il m'a fallu un tems considérable pour le détromper, et pour lui faire comprendre qu'il avoit tort de s'assujettir à la pratique d'une église qu'il ne reconnoissoit plus pour infaillible ; que si même cette pratique avoit eu quelque utilité dans son institution, cependant elle n'en avoit aucune en elle même, puisqu'elle ne contribuoit en rien à la pureté des mœurs, qu'ainsi il n'y avoit aucune raison, ni dans l'institution de cette pratique, ni dans la pratique elle même, qui l'autorisât à s'y soumettre : qu'aujourdhui ce n'étoit qu'une affaire d'intérêt, puisqu'avec de l'argent on obtenoit des dispenses pour manger gras, &c. de manière que je l'ai ramené à la liberté Chretienne avec beaucoup de peine et seulement depuis quelques semaines. Je l'ai engagé

common level has received two educations : the first from his teachers ; the second, more personal and

à vous écrire, pour vous manifester les sentiments où il est, et l'état de sa santé ; et je crois qu'il l'a fait.

From Mr. Gibbon to Mrs. Porten.[1]

DEAR MADAM,

I have at length good news to tell you. I am now good Protestant, and am extremely glad of it. I have in all my letters taken notice of the different movements of my mind, entirely Catholic when I came to Lausanne, wavering long time between the two systems, and at last fixed for the Protestant—when that conflict was over, I had still another difficulty—brought up with all the ideas of the Church of England, I could scarce resolve to communion with Presbyterians, as all the people of this country are. I at last got over it, for considering that whatever difference there may be between their churches and ours, in the government and discipline, they still regard us as brethren and profess the same faith as us—determined then in this design, I declared it to the ministers of the town, assembled at Mr. Pavilliard's, who having examined me, approved of it, and permitted me to receive the communion with them, which I did Christmas day from the hands of Mr. Pavilliard, who appeared extremely glad of it. I am so extremely myself—and do assure you feel a joy extremely pure, and the more so, as I know it to be not only innocent but laudable.

M. Pavilliard to Mrs. Porten.

Lausanne, January 28, 1755.

MADAM,

As I have a piece of news extremely interesting to acquaint you with, I cannot any longer defer answering to the letter you honoured me with. God has at length blessed my cares, and heard your prayers ; I have had the satisfaction of bringing back Mr. Gibbon to the bosom

---

[1] This letter is curious : as it shows in how short a time (not more than a year and a half) he had adopted the idiom of the French language and lost that of his own. S.

important, from himself. He will not, like the fanatics
of the last age, define the moment of grace ; but he
cannot forget the era of his life in which his mind
has expanded to its proper form and dimensions. My
worthy tutor had the good sense and modesty to
discern how far he could be useful : as soon as he felt
that I advanced beyond his speed and measure, he
wisely left me to my genius ; and the hours of lesson
were soon lost in the voluntary labour of the whole
morning, and sometimes of the whole day. The
desire of prolonging my time gradually confirmed
the salutary habit of early rising, to which I have
always adhered, with some regard to seasons and

of our Reformed Church ; he has communicated with us
Christmas Day last, with devotion : he appears satisfied
with what he has done, and I am persuaded is at present
as little inclined to the sentiments of the Church of Rome,
as I am myself. I have made use with him, neither of
rigour nor artifice. I have never hurried him in his
decisions, but have always left him the time to reflect on
every article ; he has been persuaded of the integrity of
my intentions, he has heard me as a friend, and I have
served him as guide to enter into the road of the truth.
God Almighty be blessed for it ; I pray that God to
strengthen him more and more in the right way, and to
make him a faithful member of his Church. I ought to
render him the justice to say, I never found him obstinate ;
he has been fixed in his ideas, but when he has seen the
light, he has rendered himself. His behaviour has been
very regular and has made no slips, except that of gaming
twice and losing much more than I desired. I hope,
Madam, you will acquaint Mr. Gibbon with your satisfaction and restore him your affection, which, though his
errors may have shaken, they have not, I am sure,
destroyed. As his father has allowed him but the bare
necessaries, but nothing more, I dare beg you to grant
him some tokens of your satisfaction. I am convinced
he will employ them well, and I ever flatter myself he
will give me the direction of them, for he has promised
me never to play any more games of chance. I wish you,
Madam, all kinds of prosperity.

situations ; but it is happy for my eyes and my health, that my temperate ardour has never been seduced to trespass on the hours of the night. During the last three years of my residence at Lausanne, I may assume the merit of serious and solid application ; but I am tempted to distinguish the last eight months of the year 1755 as the period of the most extraordinary diligence and rapid progress.[1] In my French and Latin translations I adopted an excellent method, which, from my own success, I would recommend to the imitation of students. I chose some classic writer, such as Cicero and Vertot, the most approved for purity and elegance of style. I translated, for instance, an epistle of Cicero into French ; and after throwing it aside, till the words and phrases were obliterated from my memory, I re-translated my French into such Latin as I could find ; and then compared each sentence of my imperfect version with the ease, the grace, the propriety of the Roman orator. A similar experiment was made on several pages of the Revolutions of Vertot ; I turned them into Latin, returned them after a sufficient interval into my own French,

[1] JOURNAL, December 1755.—In finishing this year, I must remark how favourable it was to my studies. In the space of eight months, from the beginning of April, I learnt the principles of drawing ; made myself complete master of the French and Latin languages, with which I was very superficially acquainted before, and wrote and translated a great deal in both ; read Cicero's *Epistles ad Familiares*, his *Brutus*, all his *Orations*, his *Dialogues de Amicitiâ*, and *De Senectute* ; Terence, twice ; and Pliny's *Epistles*. In French, Giannone's *History of Naples*, and l'Abbé Bannier's *Mythology*, and M. De Boehat's *Mémoires sur la Suisse*, and wrote a very ample relation of my tour. I likewise began to study Greek, and went through the Grammar. I began to make very large collections of what I read. But what I esteem most of all, from the perusal and meditation of De Crousaz's *Logic*, I not only understood the principles of that science, but formed my mind to a habit of thinking and reasoning I had no idea of before.

and again scrutinized the resemblance or dissimilitude of the copy and the original. By degrees I was less ashamed, by degrees I was more satisfied with myself; and I persevered in the practice of these double translations, which filled several books, till I had acquired the knowledge of both idioms, and the command at least of a correct style. This useful exercise of writing was accompanied and succeeded by the more pleasing occupation of reading the best authors. The perusal of the Roman classics was at once my exercise and reward. Dr. Middleton's *History*, which I then appreciated above its true value, naturally directed me to the writings of Cicero. The most perfect editions, that of Olivet, which may adorn the shelves of the rich, that of Ernesti, which should lie on the table of the learned, were not within my reach. For the familiar epistles I used the text and English commentary of Bishop Ross; but my general edition was that of Verburgius, published at Amsterdam in two large volumes in folio, with an indifferent choice of various notes. I read, with application and pleasure, *all* the epistles, *all* the orations, and the most important treatises of rhetoric and philosophy; and as I read, I applauded the observation of Quintilian, that every student may judge of his own proficiency, by the satisfaction which he receives from the Roman orator. I tasted the beauties of language, I breathed the spirit of freedom, and I imbibed from his precepts and examples the public and private sense of a man. Cicero in Latin, and Xenophon in Greek, are indeed the two ancients whom I would first propose to a liberal scholar; not only for the merit of their style and sentiments, but for the admirable lessons, which may be applied almost to every situation of public and private life. Cicero's *Epistles* may in particular afford the models of every form of correspondence, from the careless effusions of tenderness and friendship, to the well-guarded declaration of discreet and dignified resentment. After finishing this great author, a library of eloquence and reason, I formed a more extensive plan of reviewing the Latin classics [1], under the four divisions of—(1) historians, (2) poets, (3) orators, and (4) philosophers, in a chronological series, from the days of Plautus and Sallust, to the decline of the language and empire of Rome: and this plan, in the last twenty-seven months of my residence at Lausanne (January, 1756—April, 1758), I *nearly* accomplished. Nor was this review, however rapid, either hasty or superficial. I indulged myself in a second and even a third perusal of Terence, Virgil, Horace, Tacitus, &c., and studied to imbibe the sense and spirit most congenial to my own. I never suffered a difficult or corrupt passage to escape, till I had viewed it in every light of which it was susceptible: though often disappointed, I always consulted the most learned or ingenious commentators, Torrentius and Dacier on Horace, Catrou and Servius on Virgil, Lipsius on Tacitus, Meziriac on Ovid, &c.; and in the ardour of my inquiries, I embraced a large circle of historical and critical erudition. My abstracts of each book were made in the French language: my observations often branched into particular essays; and I can still read, without contempt, a dissertation of eight folio pages on eight lines (287–294) of the fourth *Georgic* of Virgil. Mr. Deyverdun, my friend, whose name will be frequently repeated, had joined with equal zeal, though not with equal perseverance, in the same undertaking. To him every thought, every composition, was instantly communicated; with him I enjoyed the benefits of a free conversation on the topics of our common studies.

But it is scarcely possible for a mind endowed with any active curiosity to be long conversant with the Latin classics without aspiring to know the Greek

[1] JOURNAL, January 1756.—I determined to read over the Latin authors in order; and read this year, Virgil, Sallust, Livy, Velleius Paterculus, Valerius Maximus, Tacitus, Suetonius, Quintus Curtius, Justin, Florus, Plautus, Terence, and Lucretius. I also read and meditated Locke upon the Understanding.

originals, whom they celebrate as their masters, and of whom they so warmly recommend the study and imitation ;

—— Vos exemplaria Graeca
Nocturnâ versate manu, versate diurnâ.

It was now that I regretted the early years which had been wasted in sickness or idleness, or mere idle reading ; that I condemned the perverse method of our schoolmasters, who, by first teaching the mother language, might descend with so much ease and perspicuity to the origin and etymology of a derivative idiom. In the nineteenth year of my age I determined to supply this defect ; and the lessons of Pavilliard again contributed to smooth the entrance of the way, the Greek alphabet, the grammar, and the pronunciation according to the French accent. At my earnest request we presumed to open the *Iliad* ; and I had the pleasure of beholding, though darkly and through a glass, the true image of Homer, whom I had long since admired in an English dress. After my tutor had left me to myself, I worked my way through about half the *Iliad*, and afterwards interpreted above a large portion of Xenophon and Herodotus. But my ardour, destitute of aid and emulation, was gradually cooled, and, from the barren task of searching words in a lexicon, I withdrew to the free and familiar conversation of Virgil and Tacitus. Yet in my residence at Lausanne I had laid a solid foundation, which enabled me, in a more propitious season, to prosecute the study of Grecian literature.

From a blind idea of the usefulness of such abstract science, my father had been desirous, and even pressing, that I should devote some time to the mathematics [1] ;

[1] EXTRACT OF A LETTER FROM M. PAVILLIARD TO EDWARD GIBBON, ESQ.

Je n'ai point changé de sentimens pour Monsieur votre fils. Il vous rend compte de ses études, et je puis vous

nor could I refuse to comply with so reasonable a wish.
During two winters I attended the private lectures

assurer qu'il ne vous dit rien qui ne soit très vrai.   Il
emploie très bien son temps, et il s'applique extrêmement,
aussi a-t-il fait beaucoup de progrès.   Il entend très bien
le Latin, et il a lu les meilleurs auteurs que nous ayons,
et cela plus d'une fois : il a lu la Logique de Mr. de Crousaz
et l'Essai sur l'Entendement humain de Mr. Locke, dont
il a fait des extraits : il a commencé le Grec, et il s'y
attache : il va commencer l'algèbre, comme vous le lui
ordonnez.   Vous jugerez par ses lettres s'il entend le
François, car je vous assure que je n'y ai fait aucune
correction.

Par rapport à la religion, il n'a pas laissé échapper un
seul mot, qui ait pu me faire soupçonner qu'il eut encore
quelque attachement pour la religion Romaine, et quoique
nous parlions souvent sur ces matières je le trouve toujours
penser très juste sur toutes les questions qu'on traite.
Le petit voyage que nous avons fait lui a beaucoup valu
à cet égard : il a été témoin des superstitions épouvant-
ables, qui y régnent : il en a été d'autant plus frappé
qu'il ne le connoissoit pas, et qu'il ne pouvoit s'imaginer
qu'elles fussent aussi grandes.   Quand il n'auroit pas déjà
renoncé à cette communion, il l'auroit fait indubitablement,
tant elles lui ont paru excessives et déraisonnables.   Je
suis persuadé qu'il a embrassé le parti Protestant par
raison, et qu'il y a peu de personnes qui aient plus examiné
et mieux senti la force de nos preuves que lui.   Je lui dois
ce témoignage, et je le lui rends avec plaisir, de même que
sur sa bonne conduite.

P.S.—La lettre que vous avez écrit à Monsieur votre
fils l'a extrèmement touché parce qu'elle lui a fait voir
que vous étiez mécontent de lui.   Rien ne peut le mortifier
davantage que cette idée.   Rendez lui, je vous supplie,
votre affection, il la mérite, par l'attachement qu'il a
pour vous.

FROM THE SAME TO THE SAME.

Janvier 12, 1757.

MONSIEUR,
        Vous avez souhaité que Monsieur votre fils s'appliquât
à l'algèbre ; le goût qu'il a pour les belles lettres lui

of Monsieur de Traytorrens, who explained the elements of algebra and geometry, as far as the conic

faisoit appréhender que l'algèbre ne nuisât à ses études favorites ; je lui ai persuadé qu'il ne se faisoit pas une juste idée de cette partie des mathématiques ; l'obéissance qu'il vous doit, jointe à mes raisons, l'ont déterminé à en faire un cours. Je ne croiois pas qu'avec cette répugnance il y fît de grands progrès ; je me suis trompé : il fait bien tout ce qu'il fait ; il est exact à ses leçons ; il s'applique à lire avant sa leçon, et il repasse avec soin, de manière qu'il avance beaucoup, et plus que je ne serois attendu : il est charmé d'avoir commencé, et je pense qu'il fera un petit cours de géométrie, ce qui en tout ne lui prendra que sept à huit mois. Pendant qu'il fait ses leçons, il ne s'est point relaché sur ses autres études ; il avance beaucoup dans le Grec, et il a presque lu la moitié de l'Iliade d'Homère ; je lui fais régulièrement des leçons sur cet auteur : il a aussi fini les historiens Latins ; il en est à présent aux poëtes ; et il a lu entièrement Plaute et Terence, et bientôt il aura fini Lucrèce. Au reste, il ne lit pas ces auteurs à la légère, il veut s'éclaircir sur tout ; de façon qu'avec le génie qu'il a, l'excellente mémoire et l'application, il ira loin dans les sciences.

J'ai eu l'honneur de vous dire ci-devant, que malgré ses études il voyoit compagnie ; je puis vous le dire encore aujourdhui.

From the Same to the Same.

Jan. 14, 1758.

Monsieur,

J'ai eu l'honneur de vous écrire le 27 Juillet et le 26 8bre passés, et je vous ai rendu compte de la santé, des études, et de la conduite de Monsieur votre fils. Je n'ai rien à ajouter à tout ce que je vous en ai dit : il se porte parfaitement bien par la grace de Dieu : il continue à étudier avec application, et je puis vous assurer qu'il fait des progrès considérables dans les études, et il se fait extrêmement estimer par tous ceux qui le connoissent, et j'espère que quand il vous montrera en détail ce qu'il sait, vous en serez très content. Les Belles Lettres qui sont son étude favorite ne l'occupent pas entièrement ;

sections of the Marquis de l'Hôpital, and appeared
satisfied with my diligence and improvement.[1]   But
as my childish propensity for numbers and calculations was totally extinct, I was content to receive the
passive impression of my professor's lectures, without
any active exercise of my own powers.   As soon as
I understood the principles, I relinquished for ever the
pursuit of the mathematics ; nor can I lament that
I desisted, before my mind was hardened by the habit
of rigid demonstration, so destructive of the finer
feelings of moral evidence, which must, however,
determine the actions and opinions of our lives.   I listened with more pleasure to the proposal of studying
the law of nature and nations, which was taught in

il continue les mathématiques, et son professeur m'assure
qu'il n'a jamais vu personne avancer autant que lui, ni
avoir plus d'ardeur et d'application qu'il n'en a.   Son
génie heureux et pénétrant est secondé par une mémoire
des plus heureuses, tellement qu'il n'oublie presque rien
de ce qu'il apprend.   Je n'ai pas moins lieu d'être content
de sa conduite ; quoiqu'il étudie beaucoup, il voit cependant compagnie, mais il ne voit que des personnes dont le
commerce peut lui être utile.

[1] JOURNAL, January, 1757.—I began to study algebra
under M. de Traytorrens, went through the elements of
algebra and geometry, and the three first books of the
Marquis de l'Hôpital's *Conic Sections.*   I also read Tibullus,
Catullus, Propertius, Horace (with Dacier's and Torrentius's notes), Virgil, Ovid's *Epistles,* with Meziriac's
Commentary, the *Ars Amandi,* and the *Elegies ;* likewise
the Augustus and Tiberius of Suetonius, and a Latin
translation of Dion Cassius, from the death of Julius
Caesar to the death of Augustus.   I also continued my
correspondence begun last year with M. Allamand of Bex,
and the Professor Breitinger of Zurich ; and opened a new
one with the Professor Gesner of Gottingen.
    N.B.—Last year and this, I read St. John's Gospel,
with part of Xenophon's *Cyropaedia ;* the *Iliad,* and
Herodotus : but, upon the whole, I rather neglected my
Greek.

the academy of Lausanne by Mr. Vicat, a professor of some learning and reputation. But, instead of attending his public or private course, I preferred in my closet the lessons of his masters, and my own reason. Without being disgusted by Grotius or Puffendorf, I studied in their writings the duties of a man, the rights of a citizen, the theory of justice (it is, alas! a theory), and the laws of peace and war, which have had some influence on the practice of modern Europe. My fatigues were alleviated by the good sense of their commentator, Barbeyrac. Locke's *Treatise of Government* instructed me in the knowledge of Whig principles, which are rather founded in reason than experience; but my delight was in the frequent perusal of Montesquieu, whose energy of style, and boldness of hypothesis, were powerful to awaken and stimulate the genius of the age. The logic of De Crousaz had prepared me to engage with his master Locke, and his antagonist Bayle; of whom the former may be used as a bridle, and the latter as a spur, to the curiosity of a young philosopher. According to the nature of their respective works, the schools of argument and objection, I carefully went through the *Essay on Human Understanding*, and occasionally consulted the most interesting articles of the *Philosophic Dictionary*. In the infancy of my reason I turned over, as an idle amusement, the most serious and important treatise: in its maturity, the most trifling performance could exercise my taste or judgement; and more than once I have been led by a novel into a deep and instructive train of thinking. But I cannot forbear to mention three particular books, since they may have remotely contributed to form the historian of the Roman empire. (1) From the *Provincial Letters* of Pascal, which almost every year I have perused with new pleasure, I learned to manage the weapon of grave and temperate irony, even on subjects of ecclesiastical solemnity. (2) *The Life of Julian*, by the Abbé de la Bleterie, first introduced me to the man and the times; and I should be glad

to recover my first essay on the truth of the miracle
which stopped the rebuilding of the Temple of Jerusalem. (3) In Giannone's *Civil History of Naples* I
observed with a critical eye the progress and abuse
of sacerdotal power, and the revolutions of Italy in the
darker ages. This various reading, which I now
conducted with discretion, was digested, according to
the precept and model of Mr. Locke, into a large
commonplace book; a practice, however, which I do
not strenuously recommend. The action of the pen
will doubtless imprint an idea on the mind as well as
on the paper: but I much question whether the
benefits of this laborious method are adequate to the
waste of time; and I must agree with Dr. Johnson
(*Idler*, No. 74), ' that what is twice read is commonly
better remembered than what is transcribed '.

During two years, if I forget some boyish excursions
of a day or a week, I was fixed at Lausanne; but at
the end of the third summer, my father consented
that I should make the tour of Switzerland with
Pavilliard: and our short absence of one month
(September 21—October 20, 1755) was a reward and
relaxation of my assiduous studies.[1] The fashion of

---

[1] FROM EDWARD GIBBON TO MRS. PORTEN.

. . . Now for myself. As my father has given me
leave to make a journey round Switzerland, we set out
to-morrow. Buy a map of Switzerland, it will cost you
but a shilling, and follow me. I go by Iverdun, Neufchâtel, Bienne or Biel, Soleurre or Solothurn, Bale or
Basil, Bade, Zurich, Lucerne, and Bern. The voyage
will be of about four weeks; so that *I hope to find a letter
from you waiting for me.* As my father had given me
leave to learn what I had a mind, I have learned to ride,
and learn actually to dance and draw. Besides that,
I often give ten or twelve hours a day to my studies.
I find a great many agreeable people here; see them
sometimes, and can say upon the whole, without vanity,
that though I am the Englishman here who spends the
least money, I am he who is the most generally liked.
I told you that my father had promised to send me into

climbing the mountains and reviewing the *Glaciers* had not yet been introduced by foreign travellers, who seek the sublime beauties of nature. But the political face of the country is not less diversified by the forms and spirit of so many various republics, from the jealous government of the *few* to the licentious freedom of the *many*. I contemplated with pleasure the new prospects of men and manners; though my conversation with the natives would have been more free and instructive had I possessed the German, as well as the French language. We passed through most of the principal towns in Switzerland; Neufchâtel, Bienne, Soleurre, Arau, Baden, Zurich, Basil, and Bern. In every place we visited the churches

France and Italy. I have thanked him for it; but if he would follow my plan, he won't do it yet awhile. I never liked young travellers; they go too raw to make any great remarks, and they lose a time which is (in my opinion) the most precious part of a man's life. My scheme would be, to spend this winter at Lausanne: for though it is a very good place to acquire the air of good company and the French tongue, we have no good professors. To spend (I say) the winter at Lausanne; go into England to see my friends for a couple of months, and after that, finish my studies, either at Cambridge (for after what has passed one cannot think of Oxford), or at an University in Holland. If you liked the scheme, *could you not propose it to my father by Metcalf, or somebody* who has *a certain credit over him?* I forgot to ask you whether, in case my father writes to tell me of his marriage, would you advise me to compliment my mother-in-law? I think so. My health is so very regular, that I have nothing to say about it.

I have been the whole day writing you this letter; the preparations for our voyage gave me a thousand interruptions. Besides that, I was obliged to write in English. This last reason will seem a paradox, but I assure you the French is much more familiar to me.

I am, &c.,

E. GIBBON.

Lausanne, Sept. 20, 1755.

arsenals, libraries, and all the most eminent persons; and after my return, I digested my notes in fourteen or fifteen sheets of a French journal, which I dispatched to my father, as a proof that my time and his money had not been misspent. Had I found this journal among his papers, I might be tempted to select some passages; but I will not transcribe the printed accounts, and it may be sufficient to notice a remarkable spot, which left a deep and lasting impression on my memory. From Zurich we proceeded to the Benedictine Abbey of Einsidlen, more commonly styled Our Lady of the Hermits. I was astonished by the profuse ostentation of riches in the poorest corner of Europe; amidst a savage scene of woods and mountains a palace appears to have been erected by magic; and it was erected by the potent magic of religion. A crowd of palmers and votaries was prostrate before the altar. The title and worship of the Mother of God provoked my indignation; and the lively naked image of superstition suggested to me, as in the same place it had done to Zuinglius, the most pressing argument for the reformation of the Church. About two years after this tour, I passed at Geneva a useful and agreeable month; but this excursion, and some short visits in the Pays de Vaud, did not materially interrupt my studious and sedentary life at Lausanne.

My thirst of improvement, and the languid state of science at Lausanne, soon prompted me to solicit a literary correspondence with several men of learning, whom I had not an opportunity of personally consulting. (1) In the perusal of Livy (xxx, 44) I had been stopped by a sentence in a speech of Hannibal, which cannot be reconciled by any torture with his character or argument. The commentators dissemble, or confess their perplexity. It occurred to me, that the change of a single letter, by substituting *otio* instead of *odio*, might restore a clear and consistent sense; but I wished to weigh my emendation in scales less partial than my own. I addressed myself to

M. Crevier, the successor of Rollin, and a professor in the University of Paris, who had published a large and valuable edition of Livy. His answer was speedy and polite ; he praised my ingenuity, and adopted my conjecture. (2) I maintained a Latin correspondence, at first anonymous, and afterwards in my own name, with Professor Breitinger of Zurich, the learned editor of a Septuagint Bible. In our frequent letters we discussed many questions of antiquity, many passages of the Latin classics. I proposed my interpretations and amendments. His censures, for he did not spare my boldness of conjecture, were sharp and strong ; and I was encouraged by the consciousness of my strength, when I could stand in free debate against a critic of such eminence and erudition. (3) I corresponded on similar topics with the celebrated Professor Matthew Gesner, of the University of Göttingen ; and he accepted, as courteously as the two former, the invitation of an unknown youth. But his abilities might possibly be decayed ; his elaborate letters were feeble and prolix ; and when I asked his proper direction, the vain old man covered half a sheet of paper with the foolish enumeration of his titles and offices. (4) These professors of Paris, Zurich, and Göttingen were strangers, whom I presumed to address on the credit of their name ; but Mr. Allamand, Minister at Bex, was my personal friend, with whom I maintained a more free and interesting correspondence. He was a master of language, of science, and, above all, of dispute ; and his acute and flexible logic could support, with equal address, and perhaps with equal indifference, the adverse sides of every possible question. His spirit was active, but his pen had been indolent. Mr. Allamand had exposed himself to much scandal and reproach, by an anonymous letter (1745) to the Protestants of France, in which he labours to persuade them that *public* worship is the exclusive right and duty of the state, and that their numerous assemblies of dissenters and rebels were not authorized by the law or the gospel. His style is animated, his arguments

specious; and if the Papist may seem to lurk under
the mask of a Protestant, the philosopher is concealed
under the disguise of a Papist. After some trials in
France and Holland, which were defeated by his
fortune or his character, a genius that might have
enlightened or deluded the world, was buried in a
country living, unknown to fame, and discontented
with mankind. 'Est sacrificulus in pago, et rusticos
decipit.' As often as private or ecclesiastical business
called him to Lausanne, I enjoyed the pleasure and
benefit of his conversation, and we were mutually
flattered by our attention to each other. Our correspondence, in his absence, chiefly turned on Locke's
metaphysics, which he attacked, and I defended; the
origin of ideas, the principles of evidence, and the
doctrine of liberty;

> And found no end, in wandering mazes lost.

By fencing with so skilful a master, I acquired some
dexterity in the use of my philosophic weapons; but
I was still the slave of education and prejudice. He
had some measures to keep; and I much suspect that
he never showed me the true colours of his secret
scepticism.

Before I was recalled from Switzerland, I had the
satisfaction of seeing the most extraordinary man of
the age; a poet, an historian, a philosopher, who has
filled thirty quartos, of prose and verse, with his various
productions, often excellent, and always entertaining.
Need I add the name of Voltaire? After forfeiting,
by his own misconduct, the friendship of the first of
kings, he retired, at the age of sixty, with a plentiful
fortune, to a free and beautiful country, and resided
two winters (1757 and 1758) in the town or neighbourhood of Lausanne. My desire of beholding Voltaire,
whom I then rated above his real magnitude, was
easily gratified. He received me with civility as an
English youth; but I cannot boast of any peculiar
notice or distinction, *Virgilium vidi tantum*.

The ode which he composed on his first arrival on

the banks of the Leman Lake, *O Maison d'Aristippe !* *O Jardin d'Epicure*, &c., had been imparted as a secret to the gentleman by whom I was introduced. He allowed me to read it twice ; I knew it by heart ; and as my discretion was not equal to my memory, the author was soon displeased by the circulation of a copy. In writing this trivial anecdote, I wished to observe whether my memory was impaired, and I have the comfort of finding that every line of the poem is still engraved in fresh and indelible characters. The highest gratification which I derived from Voltaire's residence at Lausanne was the uncommon circumstance of hearing a great poet declaim his own productions on the stage. He had formed a company of gentlemen and ladies, some of whom were not destitute of talents. A decent theatre was framed at Monrepos, a country-house at the end of a suburb ; dresses and scenes were provided at the expense of the actors ; and the author directed the rehearsals with the zeal and attention of paternal love. In two successive winters his tragedies of *Zayre, Alzire, Zulime*, and his sentimental comedy of the *Enfant Prodigue*, were played at the theatre of Monrepos. Voltaire represented the characters best adapted to his years, Lusignan, Alvaréz, Benassar, Euphemon. His declamation was fashioned to the pomp and cadence of the old stage ; and he expressed the enthusiasm of poetry, rather than the feelings of nature. My ardour, which soon became conspicuous, seldom failed of procuring me a ticket. The habits of pleasure fortified my taste for the French theatre, and that taste has perhaps abated my idolatry for the gigantic genius of Shakespeare, which is inculcated from our infancy as the first duty of an Englishman. The wit and philosophy of Voltaire, his table and theatre, refined, in a visible degree, the manners of Lausanne ; and, however addicted to study, I enjoyed my share of the amusements of society. After the representation of Monrepos I sometimes supped with the actors. I was now familiar in some, and acquainted in many houses ;

and my evenings were generally devoted to cards and conversation, either in private parties or numerous assemblies.

I hesitate, from the apprehension of ridicule, when I approach the delicate subject of my early love. By this word I do not mean the polite attention, the gallantry, without hope or design, which has originated in the spirit of chivalry, and is interwoven with the texture of French manners. I understand by this passion the union of desire, friendship, and tenderness, which is inflamed by a single female, which prefers her to the rest of her sex, and which seeks her possession as the supreme or the sole happiness of our being. I need not blush at recollecting the object of my choice ; and though my love was disappointed of success, I am rather proud that I was once capable of feeling such a pure and exalted sentiment. The personal attractions of Mademoiselle Susan Curchod were embellished by the virtues and talents of the mind. Her fortune was humble, but her family was respectable. Her mother, a native of France, had preferred her religion to her country. The profession of her father did not extinguish the moderation and philosophy of his temper, and he lived content with a small salary and laborious duty in the obscure lot of minister of Crassy, in the mountains that separate the Pays de Vaud from the county of Burgundy.[1] In the solitude of a sequestered village he bestowed a liberal, and even learned,

---

[1] EXTRACTS FROM THE JOURNAL.

March 1757.   I wrote some critical observations upon Plautus.

March 8th.   I wrote a long dissertation on some lines of Virgil.

June.   I saw Mademoiselle Curchod—*Omnia vincit amor, et nos cedamus amori.*

August.   I went to Crassy, and staid two days.

Sept. 15th.   I went to Geneva.

Oct. 15th.   I came back to Lausanne, having passed through Crassy.

education on his only daughter. She surpassed his
hopes by her proficiency in the sciences and languages;
and in her short visits to some relations at Lausanne,
the wit, the beauty, and erudition of Mademoiselle
Curchod were the theme of universal applause. The
report of such a prodigy awakened my curiosity;
I saw and loved. I found her learned without pedantry,
lively in conversation, pure in sentiment, and elegant
in manners; and the first sudden emotion was fortified
by the habits and knowledge of a more familiar acquaintance. She permitted me to make her two or
three visits at her father's house. I passed some
happy days there, in the mountains of Burgundy, and
her parents honourably encouraged the connexion.
In a calm retirement the gay vanity of youth no
longer fluttered in her bosom; she listened to the
voice of truth and passion, and I might presume to
hope that I had made some impression on a virtuous
heart. At Crassy and Lausanne I indulged my dream
of felicity: but on my return to England, I soon discovered that my father would not hear of this strange
alliance, and that without his consent I was myself
destitute and helpless. After a painful struggle
I yielded to my fate: I sighed as a lover, I obeyed

Nov. 1st.	I went to visit M. de Watteville at Loin, and saw Mademoiselle Curchod in my way through Rolle.
Nov. 17th.	I went to Crassy, and staid there six days.
Jan. 1758.	In the three first months of this year I read Ovid's *Metamorphoses*, finished the conic sections with M. de Traytorrens, and went as far as the infinite series; I likewise read Sir Isaac Newton's *Chronology*, and wrote my critical observations upon it.
Jan. 23rd.	I saw *Alzire* acted by the society at Monrepos. Voltaire acted Alvarez; D'Hermanches, Zamore; de St. Cierge, Gusman; M. de Gentil, Monteze; and Madame Denys. Alzire.

as a son ;[1] my wound was insensibly healed by time,
absence, and the habits of a new life. My cure was
accelerated by a faithful report of the tranquillity and
cheerfulness of the lady herself, and my love subsided
in friendship and esteem. The minister of Crassy soon
afterwards died ; his stipend died with him : his
daughter retired to Geneva, where, by teaching young
ladies, she earned a hard subsistence for herself and her
mother ; but in her lowest distress she maintained
a spotless reputation, and a dignified behaviour.
A rich banker of Paris, a citizen of Geneva, had the
good fortune and good sense to discover and possess
this inestimable treasure ; and in the capital of taste
and luxury she resisted the temptations of wealth, as
she had sustained the hardships of indigence. The
genius of her husband has exalted him to the most
conspicuous station in Europe. In every change of
prosperity and disgrace he has reclined on the bosom
of a faithful friend ; and Mademoiselle Curchod is now
the wife of M. Necker, the minister, and perhaps the
legislator, of the French monarchy.

Whatsoever have been the fruits of my education,
they must be ascribed to the fortunate banishment
which placed me at Lausanne. I have sometimes
applied to my own fate the verses of Pindar, which
remind an Olympic champion that his victory was the
consequence of his exile ; and that at home, like
a domestic fowl, his days might have rolled away
inactive or inglorious.

> . . . ἤτοι καὶ τεά κεν,
> Ἐνδομάχας ἅτ᾽ ἀλέκτωρ,
> Συγγόνῳ παρ᾽ ἑστίᾳ

[1] See *Oeuvres de Rousseau*, tom. xxxiii, pp. 88, 89, octavo
edition. As an author I shall not appeal from the judgement, or taste, or caprice of *Jean Jacques* : but that
extraordinary man, whom I admire and pity, should have
been less precipitate in condemning the moral character
and conduct of a stranger.

'Ακλεὴς τιμὰ κατεφυλλορόησε ποδῶν·
Εἰ μὴ στάσις ἀντιάνειρα
Κνωσίας ἄμερσε πάτρας.[1]   *Olymp.* xii.

If my childish revolt against the religion of my country
had not stripped me in time of my academic gown,
the five important years, so liberally improved in the
studies and conversation of Lausanne, would have
been steeped in port and prejudice among the monks
of Oxford. Had the fatigue of idleness compelled me
to read, the path of learning would not have been
enlightened by a ray of philosophic freedom. I should
have grown to manhood ignorant of the life and
language of Europe, and my knowledge of the world
would have been confined to an English cloister. But
my religious error fixed me at Lausanne, in a state
of banishment and disgrace. The rigid course of
discipline and abstinence, to which I was condemned,
invigorated the constitution of my mind and body ;
poverty and pride estranged me from my countrymen.
One mischief, however, and in their eyes a serious
and irreparable mischief, was derived from the success
of my Swiss education : I had ceased to be an Englishman. At the flexible period of youth, from the age
of sixteen to twenty-one, my opinions, habits, and
sentiments were cast in a foreign mould ; the faint
and distant remembrance of England was almost
obliterated ; my native language was grown less
familiar ; and I should have more cheerfully accepted the
offer of a moderate independence on the terms of
perpetual exile. By the good sense and temper of

---

[1] Thus, like the crested bird of Mars, at home
    Engag'd in foul domestic jars,
    And wasted with intestine wars,
  Inglorious hadst thou spent thy vig'rous bloom ;
    Had not sedition's civil broils
    Expell'd thee from thy native *Crete*,
    And driv'n thee with more glorious toils
  Th' *Olympic* crown in *Pisa's* plain to meet.
                                        West's *Pind.* S.

Pavilliard my yoke was insensibly lightened: he left me master of my time and actions; but he could neither change my situation, nor increase my allowance, and with the progress of my years and reason I impatiently sighed for the moment of my deliverance. At length, in the spring of the year 1758, my father signified his permission and his pleasure that I should immediately return home. We were then in the midst of a war: the resentment of the French at our taking their ships without a declaration had rendered that polite nation somewhat peevish and difficult. They denied a passage to English travellers, and the road through Germany was circuitous, toilsome, and, perhaps in the neighbourhood of the armies, exposed to some danger. In this perplexity, two Swiss officers of my acquaintance in the Dutch service, who were returning to their garrisons, offered to conduct me through France as one of their companions; nor did we sufficiently reflect that my borrowed name and regimentals might have been considered, in case of a discovery, in a very serious light. I took my leave of Lausanne on the 11th of April, 1758, with a mixture of joy and regret, in the firm resolution of revisiting, as a man, the persons and places which had been so dear to my youth. We travelled slowly, but pleasantly, in a hired coach, over the hills of Franche-compté and the fertile province of Lorraine, and passed, without accident or inquiry, through several fortified towns of the French frontier: from thence we entered the wild Ardennes of the Austrian duchy of Luxemburg; and after crossing the Meuse at Liège, we traversed the heaths of Brabant, and reached, on the fifteenth day, our Dutch garrison of Bois le Duc. In our passage through Nancy, my eye was gratified by the aspect of a regular and beautiful city, the work of Stanislaus, who, after the storms of Polish royalty, reposed in the love and gratitude of his new subjects of Lorraine. In our halt at Maestricht I visited Mr. de Beaufort, a learned critic, who was known to me by his specious arguments against the five first centuries of the *Roman*

History. After dropping my regimental companions, I stepped aside to visit Rotterdam and the Hague. I wished to have observed a country, the monument of freedom and industry; but my days were numbered, and a longer delay would have been ungraceful. I hastened to embark at the Brill, landed the next day at Harwich, and proceeded to London, where my father awaited my arrival. The whole term of my first absence from England was four years ten months and fifteen days.

In the prayers of the Church our personal concerns are judiciously reduced to the threefold distinction of *mind, body,* and *estate.* The sentiments of the mind excite and exercise our social sympathy. The review of my moral and literary character is the most interesting to myself and to the public; and I may expatiate, without reproach, on my private studies; since they have produced the public writings, which can alone entitle me to the esteem and friendship of my readers. The experience of the world inculcates a discreet reserve on the subject of our person and estate, and we soon learn that a free disclosure of our riches or poverty would provoke the malice of envy, or encourage the insolence of contempt.

The only person in England whom I was impatient to see was my aunt Porten, the affectionate guardian of my tender years. I hastened to her house in College Street, Westminster; and the evening was spent in the effusions of joy and confidence. It was not without some awe and apprehension that I approached the presence of my father. My infancy, to speak the truth, had been neglected at home; the severity of his look and language at our last parting still dwelt on my memory; nor could I form any notion of his character, or my probable reception. They were both more agreeable than I could expect. The domestic discipline of our ancestors has been relaxed by the philosophy and softness of the age; and if my father remembered that he had trembled before a stern parent, it was only to adopt with his own son an

opposite mode of behaviour. He received me as
a man and a friend; all constraint was banished at
our first interview, and we ever afterwards continued
on the same terms of easy and equal politeness. He
applauded the success of my education; every word
and action was expressive of the most cordial affection;
and our lives would have passed without a cloud, if
his economy had been equal to his fortune, or if his
fortune had been equal to his desires. During my
absence he had married his second wife, Miss Dorothea
Patton, who was introduced to me with the most
unfavourable prejudice. I considered his second
marriage as an act of displeasure, and I was disposed
to hate the rival of my mother. But the injustice was
in my own fancy, and the imaginary monster was an
amiable and deserving woman. I could not be mistaken in the first view of her understanding, her
knowledge, and the elegant spirit of her conversation:
her polite welcome, and her assiduous care to study
and gratify my wishes, announced at least that the
surface would be smooth; and my suspicions of art
and falsehood were gradually dispelled by the full
discovery of her warm and exquisite sensibility. After
some reserve on my side, our minds associated in
confidence and friendship; and as Mrs. Gibbon had
neither children nor the hopes of children, we more
easily adopted the tender names and genuine characters of mother and of son. By the indulgence of
these parents, I was left at liberty to consult my taste
or reason in the choice of place, of company, and of
amusements; and my excursions were bounded only
by the limits of the island, and the measure of my
income. Some faint efforts were made to procure me
the employment of secretary to a foreign embassy;
and I listened to a scheme which would again have
transported me to the continent. Mrs. Gibbon, with
seeming wisdom, exhorted me to take chambers in
the Temple, and devote my leisure to the study of
the law. I cannot repent of having neglected her
advice. Few men, without the spur of necessity, have

resolution to force their way through the thorns and thickets of that gloomy labyrinth. Nature had not endowed me with the bold and ready eloquence which makes itself heard amidst the tumult of the bar; and I should probably have been diverted from the labours of literature, without acquiring the fame or fortune of a successful pleader. I had no need to call to my aid the regular duties of a profession; every day, every hour, was agreeably filled; nor have I known, like so many of my countrymen, the tediousness of an idle life.

Of the two years (May, 1758—May, 1760), between my return to England and the embodying of the Hampshire militia, I passed about nine months in London, and the remainder in the country. The metropolis affords many amusements, which are open to all. It is itself an astonishing and perpetual spectacle to the curious eye; and each taste, each sense may be gratified by the variety of objects which will occur in the long circuit of a morning walk. I assiduously frequented the theatres at a very propitious era of the stage, when a constellation of excellent actors, both in tragedy and comedy, was eclipsed by the meridian brightness of Garrick in the maturity of his judgement and vigour of his performance. The pleasures of a town-life are within the reach of every man who is regardless of his health, his money, and his company. By the contagion of example I was sometimes seduced; but the better habits, which I had formed at Lausanne, induced me to seek a more elegant and rational society; and if my search was less easy and successful than I might have hoped, I shall at present impute the failure to the disadvantages of my situation and character. Had the rank and fortune of my parents given them an annual establishment in London, their own house would have introduced me to a numerous and polite circle of acquaintance. But my father's taste had always preferred the highest and the lowest company, for which he was equally qualified; and after a twelve years' retirement, he was no longer in

the memory of the great with whom he had associated.
I found myself a stranger in the midst of a vast and
unknown city; and at my entrance into life I was
reduced to some dull family parties, and some scattered
connexions, which were not such as I should have
chosen for myself. The most useful friends of my
father were the Mallets: they received me with
civility and kindness at first on his account, and
afterwards on my own; and (if I may use Lord
Chesterfield's words) I was soon *domesticated* in their
house. Mr. Mallet, a name among the English poets,
is praised by an unforgiving enemy, for the ease and
elegance of his conversation, and his wife was not
destitute of wit or learning. By his assistance I was
introduced to Lady Hervey, the mother of the present
Earl of Bristol. Her age and infirmities confined her
at home; her dinners were select; in the evening
her house was open to the best company of both sexes
and all nations; nor was I displeased at her preference
and affectation of the manners, the language, and the
literature of France. But my progress in the English
world was in general left to my own efforts, and those
efforts were languid and slow. I had not been endowed
by art or nature with those happy gifts of confidence
and address, which unlock every door and every
bosom; nor would it be reasonable to complain of
the just consequences of my sickly childhood, foreign
education, and reserved temper. While coaches were
rattling through Bond Street, I have passed many
a solitary evening in my lodging with my books. My
studies were sometimes interrupted by a sigh, which
I breathed towards Lausanne; and on the approach
of spring, I withdrew without reluctance from the
noisy and extensive scene of crowds without company,
and dissipation without pleasure. In each of the
twenty-five years of my acquaintance with London
(1758-83), the prospect gradually brightened; and
this unfavourable picture most properly belongs to
the first period after my return from Switzerland.

My father's residence in Hampshire, where I have

passed many light, and some heavy hours, was at
Buriton, near Petersfield, one mile from the Portsmouth
road, and at the easy distance of fifty-eight miles from
London.[1] An old mansion, in a state of decay, had
been converted into the fashion and convenience of
a modern house; and if strangers had nothing to see,
the inhabitants had little to desire. The spot was not
happily chosen, at the end of the village and the
bottom of the hill: but the aspect of the adjacent
grounds was various and cheerful; the downs commanded a noble prospect, and the long hanging woods
in sight of the house could not perhaps have been
improved by art or expense. My father kept in his
own hands the whole of the estate, and even rented
some additional land; and whatsoever might be the
balance of profit and loss, the farm supplied him with
amusement and plenty. The produce maintained
a number of men and horses, which were multiplied
by the intermixture of domestic and rural servants;
and in the intervals of labour the favourite team,
a handsome set of bays or greys, was harnessed to the
coach. The economy of the house was regulated by
the taste and prudence of Mrs. Gibbon. She prided
herself in the elegance of her occasional dinners; and
from the uncleanly avarice of Madame Pavilliard,
I was suddenly transported to the daily neatness and
luxury of an English table. Our immediate neighbourhood was rare and rustic; but from the verge of our
hills, as far as Chichester and Goodwood, the western
district of Sussex was interspersed with noble seats
and hospitable families, with whom we cultivated
a friendly, and might have enjoyed a very frequent,
intercourse. As my stay at Buriton was always
voluntary, I was received and dismissed with smiles;
but the comforts of my retirement did not depend on
the ordinary pleasures of the country. My father
could never inspire me with his love and knowledge

---

[1] The estate and manor of Beriton, otherwise Buriton,
were considerable, and were sold a few years ago to Lord
Stawell. S.

of farming. I never handled a gun, I seldom mounted a horse; and my philosophic walks were soon terminated by a shady bench, where I was long detained by the sedentary amusement of reading or meditation. At home I occupied a pleasant and spacious apartment; the library on the same floor was soon considered as my peculiar domain; and I might say with truth, that I was never less alone than when by myself. My sole complaint, which I piously suppressed, arose from the kind restraint imposed on the freedom of my time. By the habit of early rising I always secured a sacred portion of the day, and many scattered moments were stolen and employed by my studious industry. But the family hours of breakfast, of dinner, of tea, and of supper, were regular and long: after breakfast Mrs. Gibbon expected my company in her dressing-room; after tea my father claimed my conversation and the perusal of the newspapers; and in the midst of an interesting work I was often called down to receive the visit of some idle neighbours. Their dinners and visits required, in due season, a similar return; and I dreaded the period of the full moon, which was usually reserved for our more distant excursions. I could not refuse attending my father, in the summer of 1759, to the races at Stockbridge, Reading, and Odiam, where he had entered a horse for the hunters' plate; and I was not displeased with the sight of our Olympic games, the beauty of the spot, the fleetness of the horses, and the gay tumult of the numerous spectators. As soon as the militia business was agitated, many days were tediously consumed in meetings of deputy-lieutenants at Petersfield, Alton, and Winchester. In the close of the same year, 1759, Sir Simeon (then Mr.) Stewart attempted an unsuccessful contest for the county of Southampton, against Mr. Legge, Chancellor of the Exchequer: a well-known contest, in which Lord Bute's influence was first exerted and censured. Our canvass at Portsmouth and Gosport lasted several days; but the interruption of my studies was compensated in some degree by the spectacle of English manners, and the acquisition of some practical knowledge.

If in a more domestic or more dissipated scene my application was somewhat relaxed, the love of knowledge was inflamed and gratified by the command of books ; and I compared the poverty of Lausanne with the plenty of London. My father's study at Buriton was stuffed with much trash of the last age, with much High Church divinity and politics, which have long since gone to their proper place : yet it contained some valuable editions of the classics and the fathers, the choice, as it should seem, of Mr. Law ; and many English publications of the times had been occasionally added. From this slender beginning I have gradually formed a numerous and select library, the foundation of my works, and the best comfort of my life, both at home and abroad. On the receipt of the first quarter, a large share of my allowance was appropriated to my literary wants. I cannot forget the joy with which I exchanged a bank-note of twenty pounds for the twenty volumes of the *Memoirs of the Academy of Inscriptions* ; nor would it have been easy, by any other expenditure of the same sum, to have procured so large and lasting a fund of rational amusement. At a time when I most assiduously frequented this school of ancient literature, I thus expressed my opinion of a learned and various collection, which since the year 1759 has been doubled in magnitude, though not in merit—' Une de ces sociétés, qui ont mieux immortalisé Louis XIV qu'une ambition souvent pernicieuse aux hommes, commençoit déjà ces recherches qui réunissent la justesse de l'esprit, l'aménité et l'érudition : où l'on voit tant de découvertes, et quelquefois, ce qui ne cède qu'à peine aux découvertes, une *ignorance* modeste et *savante* '. The review of my library must be reserved for the period of its maturity ; but in this place I may allow myself to observe, that I am not conscious of having ever bought a book from a motive of ostentation, that every volume, before it

was deposited on the shelf, was either read or sufficiently examined, and that I soon adopted the tolerating
maxim of the elder Pliny, 'nullum esse librum tam
malum ut non ex aliquâ parte prodesset'. I could not
yet find leisure or courage to renew the pursuit of the
Greek language, excepting by reading the lessons of
the Old and New Testament every Sunday, when
I attended the family to church. The series of my
Latin authors was less strenuously completed; but
the acquisition, by inheritance or purchase, of the
best editions of Cicero, Quintilian, Livy, Tacitus, Ovid,
&c., afforded a fair prospect, which I seldom neglected.
I persevered in the useful method of abstracts and
observations; and a single example may suffice, of
a note which had almost swelled into a work. The
solution of a passage of Livy (xxxviii, 38) involved me
in the dry and dark treatises of Greaves, Arbuthnot,
Hooper, Bernard, Eisenschmidt, Gronovius, La Barré,
Freret, &c.; and in my French essay (chapter 20)
I ridiculously send the reader to my own *manuscript*
remarks on the weights, coins, and measures of the
ancients, which were abruptly terminated by the
militia drum.

As I am now entering on a more ample field of
society and study, I can only hope to avoid a vain
and prolix garrulity, by overlooking the vulgar crowd
of my acquaintance, and confining myself to such
intimate friends among books and men, as are best
entitled to my notice by their own merit and reputation, or by the deep impression which they have left
on my mind. Yet I will embrace this occasion of
recommending to the young student a practice which
about this time I myself adopted. After glancing my
eye over the design and order of a new book, I suspended the perusal till I had finished the task of
self-examination, till I had revolved, in a solitary
walk, all that I knew or believed, or had thought on
the subject of the whole work, or of some particular
chapter: I was then qualified to discern how much
the author added to my original stock; and if I was

sometimes satisfied by the agreement, I was sometimes armed by the opposition of our ideas. The favourite companions of my leisure were our English writers since the Revolution : they breathe the spirit of reason and liberty ; and they most seasonably contributed to restore the purity of my own language, which had been corrupted by the long use of a foreign idiom. By the judicious advice of Mr. Mallet, I was directed to the writings of Swift and Addison ; wit and simplicity are their common attributes : but the style of Swift is supported by manly original vigour ; that of Addison is adorned by the female graces of elegance and mildness. The old reproach, that no British altars had been raised to the muse of history, was recently disproved by the first performances of Robertson and Hume, the histories of Scotland and of the Stuarts. I will assume the presumption of saying that I was not unworthy to read them : nor will I disguise my different feelings in the repeated perusals. The perfect composition, the nervous language, the well-turned periods of Dr. Robertson, inflamed me to the ambitious hope that I might one day tread in his footsteps : the calm philosophy, the careless inimitable beauties of his friend and rival, often forced me to close the volume with a mixed sensation of delight and despair.

The design of my first work, the *Essay on the Study of Literature*, was suggested by a refinement of vanity, the desire of justifying and praising the object of a favourite pursuit. In France, to which my ideas were confined, the learning and language of Greece and Rome were neglected by a philosophic age. The guardian of those studies, the Academy of Inscriptions, was degraded to the lowest rank among the three royal societies of Paris : the new appellation of Erudits was contemptuously applied to the successors of Lipsius and Casaubon ; and I was provoked to hear (see M. d'Alembert, *Discours préliminaire à l'Encyclopédie*) that the exercise of the memory, their sole merit, had been superseded by the nobler faculties of the imagination and the judgement. I was ambitious of proving by my own example, as well as by my precepts, that all the faculties of the mind may be exercised and displayed by the study of ancient literature ; I began to select and adorn the various proofs and illustrations which had offered themselves in reading the classics and the first pages or chapters of my essay were composed before my departure from Lausanne. The hurry of the journey, and of the first weeks of my English life, suspended all thoughts of serious application : but my object was ever before my eyes ; and no more than ten days, from the first to the eleventh of July, were suffered to elapse after my summer establishment at Buriton. My essay was finished in about six weeks ; and as soon as a fair copy had been transcribed by one of the French prisoners at Petersfield, I looked round for a critic and judge of my first performance. A writer can seldom be content with the doubtful recompense of solitary approbation ; but a youth ignorant of the world, and of himself, must desire to weigh his talents in some scales less partial than his own : my conduct was natural, my motive laudable, my choice of Dr. Maty judicious and fortunate. By descent and education, Dr. Maty, though born in Holland, might be considered as a Frenchman ; but he was fixed in London by the practice of physic, and an office in the British Museum. His reputation was justly founded on the eighteen volumes of the *Journal Britannique*, which he had supported, almost alone, with perseverance and success. This humble though useful labour, which had once been dignified by the genius of Bayle and the learning of Le Clerc, was not disgraced by the taste, the knowledge, and the judgement of Maty : he exhibits a candid and pleasing view of the state of literature in England during a period of six years (January, 1750—December, 1755) ; and, far different from his angry son, he handles the rod of criticism with the tenderness and reluctance of a parent. The author of the *Journal Britannique* sometimes aspires to the character of a poet and philosopher : his style is pure and elegant; and in his virtues, or even in his defects, he may be ranked as one of the last disciples of the school of Fontenelle. His answer to my first letter was prompt and polite: after a careful examination he returned my manuscript, with some animadversion and much applause; and when I visited London in the ensuing winter, we discussed the design and execution in several free and familiar conversations. In a short excursion to Buriton I reviewed my essay, according to his friendly advice; and after suppressing a third, adding a third, and altering a third, I consummated my first labour by a short preface, which is dated February 3, 1759. Yet I still shrunk from the press with the terrors of virgin modesty: the manuscript was safely deposited in my desk; and as my attention was engaged by new objects, the delay might have been prolonged till I had fulfilled the precept of Horace, 'nonumque prematur in annum'. Father Sirmond, a learned Jesuit, was still more rigid, since he advised a young friend to expect the mature age of fifty before he gave himself or his writings to the public (Olivet, *Histoire de l'Académie Françoise*, tom. ii, p. 143). The counsel was singular; but it is still more singular that it should have been approved by the example of the author. Sirmond was himself fifty-five years of age when he published (in 1614) his first work, an edition of *Sidonius Apollinaris*, with many valuable annotations. (See his life, before the great edition of his works in five volumes folio, Paris, 1696, e Typographia Regia.)

Two years elapsed in silence: but in the spring of 1761 I yielded to the authority of a parent, and complied, like a pious son, with the wish of my own heart.[1]

[1] JOURNAL, March 8, 1758.—I began my *Essai sur l'Étude de la Littérature,* and wrote the 23 first chapters (excepting the following ones, 11, 12, 13, 18, 19, 20, 21, 22) before I left Switzerland.

July 11. I again took in hand my Essay; and in about six weeks finished it, from C. 23–55 (excepting 27, 28, 29, 30, 31, 32, 33, and note to C. 38), besides a number

My private resolves were influenced by the state of
Europe. About this time the belligerent powers had
made and accepted overtures of peace; our English
plenipotentiaries were named to assist at the Congress
of Augsburg, which never met: I wished to attend
them as a gentleman or a secretary; and my father
fondly believed that the proof of some literary talents
might introduce me to public notice, and second the
recommendations of my friends. After a last revisal
I consulted with Mr. Mallet and Dr. Maty, who
approved the design and promoted the execution.
Mr. Mallet, after hearing me read my manuscript,
received it from my hands, and delivered it into those
of Becket, with whom he made an agreement in my
name; an easy agreement: I required only a certain
number of copies; and, without transferring my
property, I devolved on the bookseller the charges and
profits of the edition. Dr. Maty undertook, in my
absence, to correct the sheets: he inserted, without
my knowledge, an elegant and flattering epistle to the

of chapters from C. 55 to the end, which are now struck
out.

Feb. 11, 1759. I wrote the chapters of my Essay,
27, 28, 29, 30, 31, the note to C. 38, and the first part of
the preface.

April 23, 1761. Being at length, by my father's advice,
determined to publish my Essay, I revised it with great
care, made many alterations, struck out a considerable
part, and wrote the chapters from 57–78, which I was
obliged myself to copy out fair.

June 10, 1761. Finding the printing of my book
proceeded but slowly, I went up to town, where I found
the whole was finished. I gave Becket orders for the
presents: twenty for Lausanne; copies for the Duke of
Richmond, Marquis of Carnarvon, Lords Waldegrave,
Litchfield, Bath, Granville, Bute, Shelbourn, Chesterfield,
Hardwicke, Lady Hervey, Sir Joseph Yorke, Sir Matthew
Featherstone, MM. Mallet, Maty, Scott, Wray, Lord
Egremont, M. de Bussy, Mademoiselle la Duchesse
d'Aiguillon, and M. le Comte de Caylus; great part of these
were only my father's or Mallet's acquaintance.

author; which is composed, however, with so much art, that, in case of a defeat, his favourable report might have been ascribed to the indulgence of a friend for the rash attempt of a *young English* gentleman. The work was printed and published, under the title of *Essai sur l'Étude de la Littérature*, à Londres, chez T. Becket et P. A. de Hondt, 1761, in a small volume in duodecimo : my dedication to my father, a proper and pious address, was composed the 28th of May : Dr. Maty's letter is dated the 16th of June ; and I received the first copy (June 23) at Alresford, two days before I marched with the Hampshire militia. Some weeks afterwards, on the same ground, I presented my book to the late Duke of York, who breakfasted in Colonel Pitt's tent. By my father's direction, and Mallet's advice, my literary gifts were distributed to several eminent characters in England and France ; two books were sent to the Count de Caylus, and the Duchesse d'Aiguillon, at Paris : I had reserved twenty copies for my friends at Lausanne, as the first fruits of my education, and a grateful token of my remembrance : and on all these persons I levied an unavoidable tax of civility and compliment. It is not surprising that a work, of which the style and sentiments were so totally foreign, should have been more successful abroad than at home. I was delighted by the copious extracts, the warm commendations, and the flattering predictions of the journals of France and Holland : and the next year (1762) a new edition (I believe at Geneva) extended the fame, or at least the circulation, of the work. In England it was received with cold indifference, little read, and speedily forgotten : a small impression was slowly dispersed ; the bookseller murmured, and the author (had his feelings been more exquisite) might have wept over the blunders and baldness of the English translation. The publication of my History fifteen years afterwards revived the memory of my first performance, and the Essay was eagerly sought in the shops. But I refused the permission which Becket solicited of reprinting it : the public curiosity was imperfectly satisfied by a pirated copy of the booksellers of Dublin ; and when a copy of the original edition has been discovered in a sale, the primitive value of half-a-crown has risen to the fanciful price of a guinea or thirty shillings.

I have expatiated on the petty circumstances and period of my first publication, a memorable era in the life of a student, when he ventures to reveal the measure of his mind : his hopes and fears are multiplied by the idea of self-importance, and he believes for a while that the eyes of mankind are fixed on his person and performance. Whatever may be my present reputation, it no longer rests on the merit of this first essay ; and at the end of twenty-eight years I may appreciate my juvenile work with the impartiality, and almost with the indifference of a stranger. In his answer to Lady Hervey, the Count de Caylus admires, or affects to admire, ' les livres sans nombre que Mr. Gibbon a lus et très bien lus '. But, alas ! my stock of erudition at that time was scanty and superficial ; and if I allow myself the liberty of naming the Greek masters, my genuine and personal acquaintance was confined to the Latin classics. The most serious defect of my Essay is a kind of obscurity and abruptness which always fatigues, and may often elude, the attention of the reader. Instead of a precise and proper definition of the title itself, the sense of the word *Littérature* is loosely and variously applied : a number of remarks and examples, historical, critical, philosophical, are heaped on each other without method or connexion ; and if we except some introductory pages, all the remaining chapters might indifferently be reversed or transposed. The obscurity of many passages is often affected, ' brevis esse laboro, obscurus fio ' ; the desire of expressing perhaps a common idea with sententious and oracular brevity : alas ! how fatal has been the imitation of Montesquieu ! But this obscurity sometimes proceeds from a mixture of light and darkness in the author's mind ; from a partial ray which strikes upon an angle, instead of spreading itself over the surface of an object. After this fair confession I shall presume to say that the Essay does credit to a young writer of two and twenty years of age, who had read with taste, who thinks with freedom, and who writes in a foreign language with spirit and elegance. The defence of the early History of Rome and the new Chronology of Sir Isaac Newton form a specious argument. The patriotic and political design of the Georgics is happily conceived; and any probable conjecture, which tends to raise the dignity of the poet and the poem, deserves to be adopted, without a rigid scrutiny. Some dawnings of a philosophic spirit enlighten the general remarks on the study of history and of man. I am not displeased with the inquiry into the origin and nature of the gods of polytheism, which might deserve the illustration of a riper judgement. Upon the whole, I may apply to the first labour of my pen the speech of a far superior artist, when he surveyed the first productions of his pencil. After viewing some portraits which he had painted in his youth, my friend Sir Joshua Reynolds acknowledged to me that he was rather humbled than flattered by the comparison with his present works; and that after so much time and study, he had conceived his improvement to be much greater than he found it to have been.

At Lausanne I composed the first chapters of my Essay in French, the familiar language of my conversation and studies, in which it was easier for me to write than in my mother tongue. After my return to England I continued the same practice, without any affectation, or design of repudiating (as Dr. Bentley would say) my vernacular idiom. But I should have escaped some anti-Gallican clamour, had I been content with the more natural character of an English author. I should have been more consistent had I rejected Mallet's advice, of prefixing an English dedication to a French book; a confusion of tongues that seemed to accuse the ignorance of my patron. The use of a foreign dialect might be excused by the hope of being

employed as a negotiator, by the desire of being
generally understood on the continent; but my true
motive was doubtless the ambition of new and singular
fame, an Englishman claiming a place among the
writers of France. The Latin tongue had been consecrated by the service of the Church, it was refined by
the imitation of the ancients; and in the fifteenth
and sixteenth centuries the scholars of Europe enjoyed
the advantage, which they have gradually resigned,
of conversing and writing in a common and learned
idiom. As that idiom was no longer in any country
the vulgar speech, they all stood on a level with each
other; yet a citizen of old Rome might have smiled
at the best Latinity of the Germans and Britons;
and we may learn from the *Ciceronianus* of Erasmus,
how difficult it was found to steer a middle course
between pedantry and barbarism. The Romans themselves had sometimes attempted a more perilous task,
of writing in a living language, and appealing to the
taste and judgement of the natives. The vanity of
Tully was doubly interested in the Greek memoirs of
his own consulship; and if he modestly supposes that
some Latinisms might be detected in his style, he is
confident of his own skill in the art of Isocrates and
Aristotle; and he requests his friend Atticus to dis-
perse the copies of his work at Athens, and in the other
cities of Greece (*ad Atticum*, i, 19; ii, 1). But it must
not be forgotten, that from infancy to manhood
Cicero and his contemporaries had read and declaimed,
and composed with equal diligence in both languages;
and that he was not allowed to frequent a Latin school
till he had imbibed the lessons of the Greek gramma-
rians and rhetoricians. In modern times, the language
of France has been diffused by the merit of her writers,
the social manners of the natives, the influence of the
monarchy, and the exile of the Protestants. Several
foreigners have seized the opportunity of speaking to
Europe in this common dialect, and Germany may
plead the authority of Leibnitz and Frederic, of the
first of her philosophers, and the greatest of her kings.

The just pride and laudable prejudice of England has restrained this communication of idioms; and of all the nations on this side of the Alps, my countrymen are the least practised, and least perfect, in the exercise of the French tongue. By Sir William Temple and Lord Chesterfield it was only used on occasions of civility and business, and their printed letters will not be quoted as models of composition. Lord Bolingbroke may have published in French a sketch of his *Reflections on Exile*: but his reputation now reposes on the address of Voltaire, 'Docte sermones utriusque linguae'; and by his English dedication to Queen Caroline, and his *Essay on Epic Poetry*, it should seem that Voltaire himself wished to deserve a return of the same compliment. The exception of Count Hamilton cannot fairly be urged; though an Irishman by birth, he was educated in France from his childhood. Yet I am surprised that a long residence in England, and the habits of domestic conversation, did not affect the ease and purity of his inimitable style; and I regret the omission of his English verses, which might have afforded an amusing object of comparison. I might therefore assume the *primus ego in patriam*, &c., but with what success I have explored this untrodden path must be left to the decision of my French readers. Dr. Maty, who might himself be questioned as a foreigner, has secured his retreat at my expense. ' Je ne crois pas que vous vous piquiez d'être moins facile à reconnoître pour un Anglois que Lucullus pour un Romain.' My friends at Paris have been more indulgent, they received me as a countryman, or at least as a provincial; but they were friends and Parisians.[1] The defects which Maty insinuates, ' Ces traits saillans, ces figures hardies, ce sacrifice de la règle au sentiment,

[1] The copious extracts which were given in the *Journal Étranger* by Mr. Suard, a judicious critic, must satisfy both the author and the public. I may here observe that I have never seen in any literary review a tolerable account of my *History*. The manufacture of journals, at least on the continent, is miserably debased.

et de la cadence à la force ', are the faults of the youth, rather than of the stranger: and after the long and laborious exercise of my own language, I am conscious that my French style has been ripened and improved.

I have already hinted that the publication of my Essay was delayed till I had embraced the military profession. I shall now amuse myself with the recollection of an active scene, which bears no affinity to any other period of my studious and social life.

In the outset of a glorious war, the English people had been defended by the aid of German mercenaries. A national militia has been the cry of every patriot since the Revolution; and this measure, both in parliament and in the field, was supported by the country gentlemen or Tories, who insensibly transferred their loyalty to the house of Hanover: in the language of Mr. Burke, they have changed the idol, but they have preserved the idolatry. In the act of offering our names and receiving our commissions, as major and captain in the Hampshire regiment (June 12, 1759), we had not supposed that we should be dragged away, my father from his farm, myself from my books, and condemned, during two years and a half (May 10, 1760—December 23, 1762), to a wandering life of military servitude. But a weekly or monthly exercise of thirty thousand provincials would have left them useless and ridiculous; and after the pretence of an invasion had vanished, the popularity of Mr. Pitt gave a sanction to the illegal step of keeping them till the end of the war under arms, in constant pay and duty, and at a distance from their respective homes. When the King's order for our embodying came down, it was too late to retreat, and too soon to repent. The south battalion of the Hampshire militia was a small independent corps of four hundred and seventy-six, officers and men, commanded by Lieutenant-Colonel Sir Thomas Worsley, who, after a prolix and passionate contest, delivered us from the tyranny of the Lord Lieutenant, the Duke of Bolton. My proper station, as first captain, was at the head of my own, and afterwards of the grenadier company; but in the absence, or even in the presence, of the two field officers, I was entrusted by my friend and my father with the effective labour of dictating the orders, and exercising the battalion. With the help of an original journal, I could write the history of my bloodless and inglorious campaigns; but as these events have lost much of their importance in my own eyes, they shall be dispatched in a few words. From Winchester, the first place of assembly (June 4, 1760), we were removed, at our own request, for the benefit of a foreign education. By the arbitrary, and often capricious orders of the War Office, the battalion successively marched to the pleasant and hospitable Blandford (June 17); to Hilsea barracks, a seat of disease and discord (September 1); to Cranbrook in the Weald of Kent (December 11); to the seacoast of Dover (December 27); to Winchester camp (June 25, 1761); to the populous and disorderly town of Devizes (October 23); to Salisbury (February 28, 1762); to our beloved Blandford a second time (March 9): and finally, to the fashionable resort of Southampton (June 2); where the colours were fixed till our final dissolution (December 23). On the beach at Dover we had exercised in sight of the Gallic shores. But the most splendid and useful scene of our life was a four months' encampment on Winchester Down, under the command of the Earl of Effingham. Our army consisted of the thirty-fourth regiment of foot and six militia corps. The consciousness of defects was stimulated by friendly emulation. We improved our time and opportunities in morning and evening field-days; and in the general reviews the South Hampshire were rather a credit than a disgrace to the line. In our subsequent quarters of the Devizes and Blandford, we advanced with a quick step in our military studies; the ballot of the ensuing summer renewed our vigour and youth; and had the militia subsisted another year, we might have contested the prize with the most perfect of our brethren.

The loss of so many busy and idle hours was not compensated by any elegant pleasure ; and my temper was insensibly soured by the society of our rustic officers. In every state there exists, however, a balance of good and evil. The habits of a sedentary life were usefully broken by the duties of an active profession : in the healthful exercise of the field I hunted with a battalion, instead of a pack ; and at that time I was ready, at any hour of the day or night, to fly from quarters to London, from London to quarters, on the slightest call of private or regimental business. But my principal obligation to the militia was the making me an Englishman, and a soldier. After my foreign education, with my reserved temper, I should long have continued a stranger to my native country, had I not been shaken in this various scene of new faces and new friends : had not experience forced me to feel the characters of our leading men, the state of parties, the forms of office, and the operation of our civil and military system. In this peaceful service I imbibed the rudiments of the language, and science of tactics, which opened a new field of study and observation. I diligently read, and meditated, the *Mémoires Militaires* of Quintus Icilius (Mr. Guichardt), the only writer who has united the merits of a professor and a veteran. The discipline and evolutions of a modern battalion gave me a clearer notion of the phalanx and the legion ; and the captain of the Hampshire grenadiers (the reader may smile) has not been useless to the historian of the Roman empire.

A youth of any spirit is fired even by the play of arms, and in the first sallies of my enthusiasm I had seriously attempted to embrace the regular profession of a soldier. But this military fever was cooled by the enjoyment of our mimic Bellona, who soon unveiled to my eyes her naked deformity. How often did I sigh for my proper station in society and letters ! How often (a proud comparison) did I repeat the complaint of Cicero in the command of a provincial army ! ' Clitellae bovi sunt impositae. Est incredibile quam me negotii taedeat. Non habet satis magnum campum ille tibi non ignotus cursus animi ; et indus-triae meae praeclara opera cessat. Lucem, *libros,* urbem, domum, vos desidero. Sed feram, ut potero ; sit modo annuum. Si prorogatur, actum est.'[1] From a service without danger I might indeed have retired without disgrace ; but as often as I hinted a wish of resigning, my fetters were riveted by the friendly entreaties of the colonel, the parental authority of the major, and my own regard for the honour and welfare of the battalion. When I felt that my personal escape was impracticable, I bowed my neck to the yoke : my servitude was protracted far beyond the annual patience of Cicero ; and it was not till after the preliminaries of peace that I received my discharge from the act of government which disembodied the militia.[2]

[1] *Epist. ad Atticum,* lib. v, 15.

[2] JOURNAL, January 11, 1761.—In these seven or eight months of a most disagreeably active life, I have had no studies to set down ; indeed, I hardly took a book in my hand the whole time. The first two months at Blandford, I might have done something ; but the novelty of the thing, of which for some time I was so fond as to think of going into the army, our field-days, our dinners abroad, and the drinking and late hours we got into, prevented any serious reflections. From the day we marched from Blandford I had hardly a moment I could call my own, almost continually in motion ; if I was fixed for a day, it was in the guard-room, a barrack, or an inn. Our disputes consumed the little time I had left. Every letter, every memorial relative to them fell to my share ; and our evening conferences were used to hear all the morning hours strike. At last I got to Dover, and Sir Thomas left us for two months. The charm was over ; I was sick of so hateful a service ; I was settled in a com-paratively quiet situation. Once more I began to taste the pleasure of thinking.

Recollecting some thoughts I had formerly had in rela-tion to the System of Paganism, which I intended to make use of in my Essay, I resolved to read Tully *de Natura Deorum,* and finished it in about a month. I lost

When I complain of the loss of time, justice to
myself and to the militia must throw the greatest part

some time before I could recover my habit of application.

Oct. 23.—Our first design was to march through
Marlborough; but finding on inquiry that it was a bad
road, and a great way about, we resolved to push for the
Devizes in one day, though nearly thirty miles. We
accordingly arrived there about three o'clock in the
afternoon.

Nov. 2.—I have very little to say for this and the
following month. Nothing could be more uniform than the
life I led there. The little civility of the neighbouring
gentlemen gave us no opportunity of dining out; the
time of year did not tempt us to any excursions round
the country; and at first my indolence, and afterwards
a violent cold, prevented my going over to Bath. I believe in the two months I never dined or lay from quarters.
I can therefore only set down what I did in the literary
way. Designing to recover my Greek, which I had
somewhat neglected, I set myself to read Homer, and
finished the four first books of the *Iliad*, with Pope's
translation and notes; at the same time, to understand
the geography of the *Iliad*, and particularly the catalogue,
I read the 8th, 9th, 10th, 12th, 13th, and 14th books of
Strabo, in Casaubon's Latin translation: I likewise read
Hume's *History of England to the Reign of Henry the
Seventh*, just published, *ingenious but superficial;* and
the *Journals des Sçavans* for August, September, and
October, 1761, with the *Bibliothèque des Sciences*, &c., from
July to October: both these journals speak very hand-
somely of my book.

December 25, 1761.—When, upon finishing the year,
I take a review of what I have done, I am not dissatisfied
with what I did in it, upon making proper allowances.
On the one hand, I could begin nothing before the middle
of January. The Deal duty lost me part of February;
although I was at home part of March, and all April, yet
electioneering is no friend to the muses. May, indeed,
though dissipated by our sea parties, was pretty quiet;
but June was absolutely lost, upon the march, at Alton,
and settling ourselves in camp. The four succeeding

of that reproach on the first seven or eight months, while I was obliged to learn as well as to teach. The

months in camp allowed me little leisure, and less quiet. November and December were indeed as much my own as any time can be whilst I remain in the militia ; but still it is, at best, not a life for a man of letters. However, in this tumultuous year (besides smaller things which I have set down), I read four books of Homer in Greek, six of Strabo in Latin, Cicero *de Natura Deorum*, and the great philosophical and theological work of M. de Beausobre : I wrote in the same time a long dissertation on the succession of Naples ; reviewed, fitted for the press, and augmented above a fourth, my *Essai sur l'Étude de la Littérature.*

In the six weeks I passed at Beriton, as I never stirred from it, every day was like the former. I had neither visits, hunting, nor walking. My only resources were myself, my books, and family conversations.—But to me these were great resources.

April 24, 1762.—I waited upon Colonel Harvey in the morning, to get him to apply for me to be brigade-major to Lord Effingham, as a post I should be very fond of, and for which I am not unfit. Harvey received me with great good nature and candour, told me he was both willing and able to serve me ; that indeed he had already applied to Lord Effingham for Leake, one of his own officers, and though there would be more than one brigade-major, he did not think he could properly recommend two ; but that if I could get some other person to break the ice, he would second it, and believed he should succeed ; should that fail, as Leake was in bad circumstances, he believed he could make a compromise with him (this was my desire) to let me do the duty without pay. I went from him to the Mallets, who promised to get Sir Charles Howard to speak to Lord Effingham.

August 22.—I went with Ballard to the French church, where I heard a most indifferent sermon preached by M. ******. A very bad style, a worse pronunciation and action, and a very great vacuity of ideas, composed this excellent performance. Upon the whole, which is preferable, the philosophic method of the English, or the rhetoric of the French preachers ? The first (though less

dissipation of Blandford, and the disputes of Portsmouth, consumed the hours which were not employed

glorious) is certainly safer for the preacher. It is difficult for a man to make himself ridiculous, who proposes only to deliver plain sense on a subject he has thoroughly studied. But the instant he discovers the least pretensions towards the sublime or the pathetic, there is no medium; we must either admire or laugh; and there are so many various talents requisite to form the character of an orator, that it is more than probable we shall laugh. As to the advantage of the hearer, which ought to be the great consideration, the dilemma is much greater. Excepting in some particular cases, where we are blinded by popular prejudices, we are in general so well acquainted with our duty, that it is almost superfluous to convince us of it. It is the heart, and not the head, that holds out: and it is certainly possible, by a moving eloquence, to rouse the sleeping sentiments of that heart, and incite it to acts of virtue. Unluckily it is not so much acts, as habits of virtue, we should have in view; and the preacher who is inculcating, with the eloquence of a Bourdaloue, the necessity of a virtuous life, will dismiss his assembly full of emotions, which a variety of other objects, the coldness of our northern constitutions, and no immediate opportunity of exerting their good resolutions, will dissipate in a few moments.

August 24.—The same reason that carried so many people to the assembly to-night, was what kept me away; I mean the dancing.

28.—To-day Sir Thomas came to us to dinner. The Spa has done him a great deal of good, for he looks another man. Pleased to see him, we kept bumperizing till after roll-calling; Sir Thomas assuring us, every fresh bottle, how infinitely soberer he was grown.

29.—I felt the usual consequences of Sir Thomas's company, and lost a morning, because I had lost the day before. However, having finished Voltaire, I returned to Le Clerc (I mean for the amusement of my leisure hours); and laid aside for some time his *Bibliothèque Universelle* to look into the *Bibliothèque Choisie*, which is by far the better work.

September 23.—Colonel Wilkes, of the Buckingham-

in the field ; and amid the perpetual hurry of an inn, a barrack, or a guard-room, all literary ideas were banished from my mind. After this long fast, the longest which I have ever known, I once more tasted at Dover the pleasures of reading and thinking ; and the hungry appetite with which I opened a volume of Tully's philosophical works is still present to my memory. The last review of my Essay before its publication had prompted me to investigate the *nature of the gods* ; my inquiries led me to the *Histoire Critique du Manichéisme* of Beausobre, who discusses many deep questions of Pagan and Christian theology ; and from this rich treasury of facts and opinions I deduced my own consequences, beyond the holy circle of the author. After this recovery I never relapsed into

shire militia, dined with us, and renewed the acquaintance Sir Thomas and myself had begun with him at Reading. I scarcely ever met with a better companion ; he has inexhaustible spirits, infinite wit and humour, and a great deal of knowledge ; but a thorough profligate in principle as in practice, his life stained with every vice, and his conversation full of blasphemy and indecency. These morals he glories in—for shame is a weakness he has long since surmounted. He told us himself, that in this time of public dissension he was resolved to make his fortune. Upon this noble principle he has connected himself closely with Lord Temple and Mr. Pitt, commenced a public adversary to Lord Bute, whom he abuses weekly in the *North Briton* and other political papers in which he is concerned. This proved a very debauched day : we drank a good deal both after dinner and supper ; and when at last Wilkes had retired, Sir Thomas and some others (of whom I was not one) broke into his room, and made him drink a bottle of claret in bed.

October 5.—The review, which lasted about three hours, concluded, as usual, with marching by Lord Effingham, by grand divisions. Upon the whole, considering the camp had done both the Winchester and the Gosport duties all the summer, they behaved very well, and made a fine appearance. As they marched by, I had my usual curiosity to count their files. The following is my field

indolence; and my example might prove that in the life most averse to study, some hours may be stolen,

return : I think it a curiosity ; I am sure it is more exact than is commonly made to a reviewing general.

		No. of Files.	No. of Men.	Establishment.
Berkshire,	Grenadiers, 19 Battalion, 72	91	273	560
W. Essex,	Grenadiers, 15 Battalion, 80	95	285	480
S. Gloster,	Grenadiers, 20 Battalion, 84	104	312	600
N. Gloster,	Grenadiers, 13 Battalion, 52	65	195	360
Lancashire,	Grenadiers, 20 Battalion, 88	108	324	800
Wiltshire,	Grenadiers, 24 Battalion, 120	144	432	800
	Total	607	1821	3600

N.B.—The Gosport detachment from the Lancashire consisted of two hundred and fifty men. The Buckinghamshire took the Winchester duty that day.

So that this camp in England, supposed complete, with only one detachment, had under arms, on the day of the grand review, little more than half their establishment. This amazing deficiency (though exemplified in every regiment I have seen) is an extraordinary military phenomenon : what must it be upon foreign service ? I doubt whether a nominal army of an hundred thousand men often brings fifty into the field.

Upon our return to Southampton in the evening, we found Sir Thomas Worsley.

October 21.—One of those impulses, which it is neither very easy nor very necessary to withstand, drew me from Longinus to a very different subject, the Greek Calendar. Last night, when in bed, I was thinking of a dissertation of M. de la Nauze upon the Roman Calendar, which I read last year. This led me to consider what was the Greek, and finding myself very ignorant of it, I deter-

some minutes may be snatched. Amidst the tumult of Winchester camp I sometimes thought and read

mined to read a short, but very excellent abstract of Mr. Dodwell's book *de Cyclis*, by the famous Dr. Halley. It is only twenty-five pages; but as I meditated it thoroughly, and verified all the calculations, it was a very good morning's work.

October 28.—I looked over a new Greek Lexicon which I had just received from London. It is that of Robert Constantine, Lugdun. 1637. It is a very large volume in folio, in two parts, comprising in the whole 1,785 pages. After the great *Thesaurus*, this is esteemed the best Greek Lexicon. It seems to be so. Of a variety of words for which I looked, I always found an exact definition; the various senses well distinguished, and properly supported, by the best authorities. However, I still prefer the radical method of Scapula to this alphabetical one.

December 11.—I have already given an idea of the Gosport duty; I shall only add a trait which characterizes admirably our unthinking sailors. At a time when they knew that they should infallibly be discharged in a few weeks, numbers, who had considerable wages due to them, were continually jumping over the walls, and risking the losing of it for a few hours' amusement at Portsmouth.

17.—We found old Captain Meard at Alresford, with the second division of the fourteenth. He and all his officers supped with us, and made the evening rather a drunken one.

18.—About the same hour our two corps paraded to march off. They, an old corps of regulars, who had been two years quiet in Dover castle. We, part of a young body of militia, two-thirds of our men recruits, of four months' standing, two of which they had passed upon very disagreeable duty. Every advantage was on their side, and yet our superiority, both as to appearance and discipline, was so striking, that the most prejudiced regular could not have hesitated a moment. At the end of the town our two companies separated: my father's struck off for Petersfield, whilst I continued my route to Alton; into which place I marched my company about noon; two years six months and fifteen days after my first

in my tent; in the more settled quarters of the Devizes,
Blandford, and Southampton, I always secured a

leaving it. I gave the men some beer at roll-calling,
which they received with great cheerfulness and decency.
I dined and lay at Harrison's, where I was received with
that old-fashioned breeding, which is at once so honourable
and so troublesome.

23.—Our two companies were disembodied; mine
at Alton, and my father's at Beriton. Smith marched
them over from Petersfield: they fired three volleys,
lodged the major's colours, delivered up their arms,
received their money, partook of a dinner at the major's
expense, and then separated with great cheerfulness and
regularity. Thus ended the militia; I may say ended,
since our annual assemblies in May are so very precarious,
and can be of so little use. However, our sergeants and
drums are still kept up, and quartered at the rendezvous
of the company, and the adjutant remains at Southampton
in full pay.

As this was an extraordinary scene of life, in which I was
engaged above three years and a half from the date of my
commission, and above two years and a half from the
time of our embodying, I cannot take my leave of it
without some few reflections. When I engaged in it,
I was totally ignorant of its nature and consequences.
I offered, because my father did, without ever imagining
that we should be called out, till it was too late to retreat
with honour. Indeed, I believe it happens throughout,
that our most important actions have been often determined by chance, caprice, or some very inadequate
motive. After our embodying, many things contributed
to make me support it with great impatience:—our con-
tinual disputes with the Duke of Bolton; our unsettled
way of life, which hardly allowed me books or leisure for
study; and, more than all, the disagreeable society in
which I was forced to live.

After mentioning my sufferings, I must say something
of what I found agreeable. Now it is over, I can make
the separation much better than I could at the time.
(1) The unsettled way of life itself had its advantages.
The exercise and change of air and of objects amused me,
at the same time that it fortified my health. (2) A new

separate lodging, and the necessary books; and in the summer of 1762, while the new militia was raising, I enjoyed at Buriton two or three months of literary repose[1]. In forming a new plan of study, I hesitated

field of knowledge and amusement opened itself to me; that of military affairs, which, both in my studies and travels, will give me eyes for a new world of things, which before would have passed unheeded. Indeed, in that respect, I can hardly help wishing our battalion had continued another year. We had got a fine set of new men, all our difficulties were over; we were perfectly well clothed and appointed; and, from the progress our recruits had already made, we could promise ourselves that we should be one of the best militia corps by next summer: a circumstance that would have been the more agreeable to me, as I am now established the real acting major of the battalion. But what I value most is the knowledge it has given me of mankind in general, and of my own country in particular. The general system of our government, the methods of our several offices, the departments and powers of their respective officers, our provincial and municipal administration, the views of our several parties, the characters, connexions, and influence of our principal people, have been impressed on my mind, not by vain theory, but by the indelible lessons of action and experience. I have made a number of valuable acquaintance, and am myself much better known, than (with my reserved character) I should have been in ten years, passing regularly my summers at Beriton, and my winters in London. So that the sum of all is, that I am glad the militia has been, and glad that it is no more.

[1] JOURNAL, May 8, 1762.—This was my birthday, on which I entered into the twenty-sixth year of my age. This gave me occasion to look a little into myself, and consider impartially my good and bad qualities. It appeared to me, upon this inquiry, that my character was virtuous, incapable of a base action, and formed for generous ones; but that it was proud, violent, and disagreeable in society. These qualities I must endeavour to cultivate, extirpate, or restrain, according to their different tendency. Wit I have none. My imagination

between the mathematics and the Greek language; both of which I had neglected since my return from Lausanne. I consulted a learned and friendly mathematician, Mr. George Scott, a pupil of de Moivre; and his map of a country, which I have never explored, may perhaps be more serviceable to others. As soon as I had given the preference to Greek, the example of Scaliger and my own reason determined me on the choice of Homer, the father of poetry, and the Bible of the ancients: but Scaliger ran through the *Iliad* in one and twenty days; and I was not dissatisfied with my own diligence for performing the same labour in an equal number of weeks. After the first difficulties were surmounted, the language of nature and harmony soon became easy and familiar, and each day I sailed upon the ocean with a brisker gale and a more steady course.

> 'Εν δ' ἄνεμος πρῆσεν μέσον ἱστίον, 'ἀμφὶ δὲ κῦμα
> Στείρῃ πορφύρεον μεγάλ' ἴαχε, νηὸς ἰούσης·
> 'Η δ' ἔθεεν κατὰ κῦμα διαπρήσσουσα κέλευθα.[1]
>
> *Iliad,* A. 481.

is rather strong than pleasing. My memory both capacious and retentive. The shining qualities of my understanding are extensiveness and penetration; but I want both quickness and exactness. As to my situation in life, though I may sometimes repine at it, it perhaps is the best adapted to my character. I can command all the conveniencies of life, and I can command too that independence (that first earthly blessing), which is hardly to be met with in a higher or lower fortune. When I talk of my situation, I must exclude that temporary one, of being in the militia. Though I go through it with spirit and application, it is both unfit for, and unworthy of me.

[1] —— Fair wind, and blowing fresh,
Apollo sent them; quick they rear'd the mast,
Then spread th' unsullied canvas to the gale,
And the wind fill'd it. Roar'd the sable flood
Around the bark, that ever as she went
Dash'd wide the brine, and scudded swift away.
                                    Cowper's *Homer.* S.

In the study of a poet who has since become the most intimate of my friends, I successively applied many passages and fragments of Greek writers ; and among these I shall notice a life of Homer, in the *Opuscula Mythologica* of Gale, several books of the geography of Strabo, and the entire treatise of Longinus, which, from the title and the style, is equally worthy of the epithet of *sublime*. My grammatical skill was improved, my vocabulary was enlarged ; and in the militia I acquired a just and indelible knowledge of the first of languages. On every march, in every journey, Horace was always in my pocket, and often in my hand : but I should not mention his two critical epistles, the amusement of a morning, had they not been accompanied by the elaborate commentary of Dr. Hurd, now Bishop of Worcester. On the interesting subjects of composition and imitation of epic and dramatic poetry, I presumed to think for myself ; and thirty close-written pages in folio could scarcely comprise my full and free discussion of the sense of the master and the pedantry of the servant.

After his oracle Dr. Johnson, my friend Sir Joshua Reynolds denies all original genius, any natural propensity of the mind to one art or science rather than another. Without engaging in a metaphysical or rather verbal dispute, I *know*, by experience, that from my early youth I aspired to the character of an historian. While I served in the militia, before and after the publication of my Essay, this idea ripened in my mind ; nor can I paint in more lively colours the feelings of the moment, than by transcribing some passages, under their respective dates, from a journal which I kept at that time.

BURITON, APRIL 14, 1761

(*In a short excursion from Dover*).

' Having thought of several subjects for an historical composition, I chose the expedition of Charles VIII of France into Italy. I read two memoirs of Mr. de

Forcemagne in the *Academy of Inscriptions* (tom. xvii, pp. 539–607), and abstracted them. I likewise finished this day a dissertation, in which I examine the right of Charles VIII to the crown of Naples, and the rival claims of the House of Anjou and Arragon: it consists of ten folio pages, besides large notes.'

BURITON, AUGUST 4, 1761

(In a week's excursion from Winchester camp).

' After having long revolved subjects for my intended historical essay, I renounced my first thought of the expedition of Charles VIII as too remote from us, and rather an introduction to great events, than great and important in itself. I successively chose and rejected the crusade of Richard I, the barons' wars against John and Henry III, the history of Edward the Black Prince, the lives and comparisons of Henry V and the Emperor Titus, the life of Sir Philip Sidney, and that of the Marquis of Montrose. At length I have fixed on Sir Walter Raleigh for my hero. His eventful story is varied by the characters of the soldier and sailor, the courtier and historian; and it may afford such a fund of materials as I desire, which have not yet been properly manufactured. At present I cannot attempt the execution of this work. Free leisure, and the opportunity of consulting many books, both printed and manuscript, are as necessary as they are impossible to be attained in my present way of life. However, to acquire a general insight into my subject and resources, I read the life of Sir Walter Raleigh by Dr. Birch, his copious article in the *General Dictionary* by the same hand, and the reigns of Queen Elizabeth and James I in Hume's *History of England*.'

BURITON, JANUARY, 1762

(In a month's absence from the Devizes).

' During this interval of repose, I again turned my thoughts to Sir Walter Raleigh, and looked more closely into my materials. I read the two volumes in quarto of the *Bacon Papers*, published by Dr. Birch; the *Fragmenta Regalia* of Sir Robert Naunton, Mallet's *Life of Lord Bacon*, and the political treatises of that great man in the first volume of his works, with many of his letters in the second; Sir William Monson's *Naval Tracts*, and the elaborate *Life of Sir Walter Raleigh*, which Mr. Oldys has prefixed to the best edition of his *History of the World*. My subject opens upon me, and in general improves upon a nearer prospect.'

BURITON, JULY 26, 1762

(During my summer residence).

' I am afraid of being reduced to drop my hero; but my time has not, however, been lost in the research of his story, and of a memorable era of our English annals. The *Life of Sir Walter Raleigh*, by Oldys, is a very poor performance; a servile panegyric, or flat apology, tediously minute, and composed in a dull and affected style. Yet the author was a man of diligence and learning, who had read everything relative to his subject, and whose ample collections are arranged with perspicuity and method. Excepting some anecdotes lately revealed in the Sidney and Bacon Papers I know not what I should be able to add. My ambition (exclusive of the uncertain merit of style and sentiment) must be confined to the hope of giving a good abridgement of Oldys. I have even the disappointment of finding some parts of this copious work very dry and barren; and these parts are unluckily some of the most characteristic : Raleigh's colony of Virginia, his quarrels with Essex, the true secret of his conspiracy, and, above all, the detail of his private life, the most essential and important to a biographer. My best resource would be in the circumjacent history of the times, and perhaps in some digressions artfully intro-duced, like the fortunes of the peripatetic philosophy in the portrait of Lord Bacon. But the reigns of Elizabeth and James I are the periods of English history which have been the most variously illus-trated : and what new lights could I reflect on a sub-ject which has exercised the accurate industry of Birch, the lively and curious acuteness of Walpole, the critical spirit of Hurd, the vigorous sense of Mallet and Robertson, and the impartial philosophy of Hume ? Could I even surmount these obstacles, I should shrink with terror from the modern history of England, where every character is a problem, and every reader a friend or an enemy ; where a writer is supposed to hoist a flag of party, and is devoted to damnation by the adverse faction. Such would be *my* reception at home : and abroad, the historian of Raleigh must encounter an indifference far more bitter than censure or reproach. The events of his life are interesting ; but his character is ambiguous, his actions are obscure, his writings are English, and his fame is confined to the narrow limits of our language and our island. I must embrace a safer and more extensive theme.

' There is one which I should prefer to all others, *The History of the Liberty of the Swiss*, of that indepen-dence which a brave people rescued from the House of Austria, defended against a Dauphin of France, and finally sealed with the blood of Charles of Burgundy. From such a theme, so full of public spirit, of military glory, of examples of virtue, of lessons of government, the dullest stranger would catch fire : what might not *I* hope, whose talents, whatsoever they may be, would be inflamed with the zeal of patriotism. But the materials of this history are inaccessible to me, fast locked in the obscurity of an old barbarous German dialect, of which I am totally ignorant, and which I cannot resolve to learn for this sole and peculiar purpose.

'I have another subject in view, which is the contrast of the former history : the one a poor, warlike, virtuous republic, which emerges into glory and freedom ; the other a commonwealth, soft, opulent, and corrupt ; which, by just degrees, is precipitated from the abuse to the loss of her liberty : both lessons are, perhaps, equally instructive. This second subject is, *The History of the Republic of Florence, under the House of Medicis* : a period of one hundred and fifty years, which rises or descends from the dregs of the Florentine democracy, to the title and dominion of Cosmo de Medicis in the Grand Duchy of Tuscany. I might deduce a chain of revolutions not unworthy of the pen of Vertot ; singular men, and singular events ; the Medicis four times expelled, and as often recalled ; and the genius of freedom reluctantly yielding to the arms of Charles V and the policy of Cosmo. The character and fate of Savanarola, and the revival of arts and letters in Italy, will be essentially connected with the elevation of the family and the fall of the republic. The Medicis, 'stirps quasi fataliter nata ad instauranda vel fovenda studia' (*Lipsius ad Germanos et Gallos*, Epist. viii), were illustrated by the patronage of learning ; and enthusiasm was the most formidable weapon of their adversaries. On this splendid subject I shall most probably fix ; but *when*, or *where*, or *how* will it be executed ? I behold in a dark and doubtful perspective ;

Res altâ terrâ, et caligine mersas.'[1]

---

[1] JOURNAL, July 27, 1762.—The reflections which I was making yesterday I continued and digested to-day. I don't absolutely look on that time as lost, but that it might have been better employed than in revolving schemes, the execution of which is so far distant. I must learn to check these wanderings of my imagination.

The youthful habits of the language and manners of France had left in my mind an ardent desire of

Nov. 24.—I dined at the Cocoa Tree with Holt; who, under a great appearance of oddity, conceals more real honour, good sense, and even knowledge than half those who laugh at him. We went thence to the play (*The Spanish Friar*); and when it was over, returned to the Cocoa Tree. That respectable body, of which I have the honour of being a member, affords every evening a sight truly English. Twenty or thirty, perhaps, of the first men in the kingdom, in point of fashion and fortune, supping at little tables covered with a napkin, in the middle of a coffee-room, upon a bit of cold meat, or a sandwich, and drinking a glass of punch. At present, we are full of king's counsellors and lords of the bed-chamber; who, having jumped into the ministry, make a very singular medley of their old principles and language, with their modern ones.

26.—I went with Mallet to breakfast with Garrick; and thence to Drury Lane house, where I assisted at a very private rehearsal, in the Green Room, of a new tragedy of Mallet's, called *Elvira*. As I have since seen it acted, I shall defer my opinion of it till then; but I cannot help mentioning here the surprising versatility of Mrs. Pritchard's talents, who rehearsed, almost at the same time, the part of a furious queen in the Green Room, and that of a coquette on the stage; and passed several times from one to the other with the utmost ease and happiness.

Dec. 30.—Before I close the year I must balance my accounts—not of money, but of time. I may divide my studies into four branches : (1) Books that I have read for themselves, classic writers, or capital treatises upon any science ; such books as ought to be perused with attention, and meditated with care. Of these I read *the twenty last books of the Iliad twice, the three first books of the Odyssey, the Life of Homer, and Longinus περὶ Ὕψους.* (2) Books which I have read, or consulted, to illustrate the former. Such as this year, *Blackwell's Inquiry into the Life and Writings of Homer, Burke's Sublime and Beautiful, Hurd's Horace, Guichardt's Mémoires Militaires,* a great variety of passages of the ancients occasionally useful : large extracts from *Mezeriac, Bayle,* and *Potter;*

revisiting the continent on a larger and more liberal
plan. According to the law of custom, and perhaps
of reason, foreign travel completes the education of
an English gentleman : my father had consented to
my wish, but I was detained above four years by my
rash engagement in the militia. I eagerly grasped the
first moments of freedom : three or four weeks in
Hampshire and London were employed in the preparations of my journey, and the farewell visits of friendship
and civility : my last act in town was to applaud

and many memoirs and abstracts from the *Academy of
Belles Lettres* : among these I shall only mention here
two long and curious suites of dissertations—*the one upon
the Temple of Delphi, the Amphictyonic Council, and the
Holy Wars, by MM. Hardion and de Valois ; the other
upon the Games of the Grecians, by MM. Burette, Gedoyne,
and de la Barre.* (3) Books of amusement and instruction,
perused at my leisure hours, without any reference to a
regular plan of study. Of these, perhaps, I read too
many, since I went through the *Life of Erasmus*, by Le
Clerc and Burigny, many extracts from *Le Clerc's Bib-
liothèques, The Ciceronianus*, and *Colloquies of Erasmus,
Barclay's Argenis, Terasson's Sethos, Voltaire's Siècle de
Louis XIV, Madame de Motteville's Memoirs*, and *Fontenelle's Works.* (4) Compositions of my own. I find hardly
any, except *this Journal*, and the *Extract of Hurd's Horace*,
which (like a chapter of Montaigne) contains many things
very different from its title. To these four heads I must
this year add a fifth. (5) Those treatises of English history
which I read in January, with a view to my now abortive
scheme of the *Life of Sir Walter Raleigh.* I ought indeed
to have known my own mind better before I undertook
them. Upon the whole, after making proper allowances,
I am not dissatisfied with the year.

The three weeks which I passed at Beriton, at the end
of this and the beginning of the ensuing year, are almost
a blank. I seldom went out ; and as the scheme of my
travelling was at last entirely settled, the hurry of impatience, the cares of preparations, and the tenderness
of friends I was going to quit, allowed me hardly any
moments for study.

Mallet's new tragedy of *Elvira* [1]; a post-chaise conveyed me to Dover, the packet to Boulogne, and such

[1] JOURNAL, January 11, 1763.—I called upon Dr. Maty in the morning. He told me that the Duke de Nivernois desired to be acquainted with me. It was indeed with that view that I had written to Maty from Beriton to present, in my name, a copy of my book to him. Thence I went to Becket, paid him his bill (fifty-four pounds), and gave him back his translation. It must be printed, though very indifferent. My comfort is, that my misfortune is not an uncommon one. We dined and supped at the Mallets.

12—I went with Maty to visit the Duke in Albemarle Street. He is a little emaciated figure, but appears to possess a good understanding, taste, and knowledge. He offered me very politely letters for Paris. We dined at our lodgings. I went to Covent Garden to see Woodward in *Bobadil*, and supped with the Mallets at George Scott's.

19.—I waited upon Lady Hervey and the Duke de Nivernois, and received my credentials. Lady Hervey's are for M. le Comte de Caylus, and Madame Geoffrin. The Duke received me civilly, but (perhaps through Maty's fault) treated me more as a man of letters than as a man of fashion. His letters are entirely in that style; for the Count de Caylus and MM. de la Bleterie, de Ste Palaye, Caperonier, du Clos, de Forcemagne, and d'Alembert. I then undressed for the play. My father and I went to the Rose, in the passage of the play-house, where we found Mallet, with about thirty friends. We dined together, and went thence into the pit, where we took our places in a body, ready to silence all opposition. However, we had no occasion to exert ourselves. Notwithstanding the malice of party, Mallet's nation, connexions, and, indeed, imprudence, we heard nothing but applause. I think it was deserved. The plan was borrowed from M. de la Motte, but the details and language have great merit. A fine vein of dramatic poetry runs through the piece. The scenes between the father and son awaken almost every sensation of the human breast; and the counsel would have equally moved, but for the inconvenience unavoidable upon all theatres, that of entrusting fine speeches to indifferent actors. The perplexity

was my diligence, that I reached Paris on the 28th of January, 1763, only thirty-six days after the disbanding of the militia. Two or three years were loosely defined for the term of my absence; and I was left at liberty to spend that time in such places and in such a manner as was most agreeable to my taste and judgement.

In this first visit I passed three months and a half (January 28—May 9), and a much longer space might have been agreeably filled, without any intercourse with the natives. At home we are content to move in the daily round of pleasure and business; and a scene which is always present is supposed to be within our knowledge, or at least within our power. But in a foreign country, curiosity is our business and our pleasure; and the traveller, conscious of his ignorance, and covetous of his time, is diligent in the search and the view of every object that can deserve his attention. I devoted many hours of the morning to the circuit of Paris and the neighbourhood, to the visit of churches and palaces conspicuous by their architecture, to the

of the catastrophe is much, and I believe justly, criticised. But another defect made a stronger impression upon me. When a poet ventures upon the dreadful situation of a father who condemns his son to death, there is no medium, the father must either be a monster or a hero. His obligations of justice, of the public good, must be as binding, as apparent, as perhaps those of the first Brutus. The cruel necessity consecrates his actions, and leaves no room for repentance. The thought is shocking, if not carried into action. In the execution of Brutus's sons I am sensible of that fatal necessity. Without such an example, the unsettled liberty of Rome would have perished the instant after its birth. But Alonzo might have pardoned his son for a rash attempt, the cause of which was a private injury, and whose consequences could never have disturbed an established government. He might have pardoned such a crime in any other subject; and as the laws could exact only an equal rigour for a son, a vain appetite for glory, and a mad affectation of heroism, could alone have influenced him to exert an unequal and superior severity.

royal manufactures, collections of books and pictures, and all the various treasures of art, or learning, and of luxury. An Englishman may hear without reluctance, that in these curious and costly articles Paris is superior to London; since the opulence of the French capital arises from the defects of its government and religion. In the absence of Louis XIV and his successors, the Louvre has been left unfinished: but the millions which have been lavished on the sands of Versailles, and the morass of Marli, could not be supplied by the legal allowance of a British king. The splendour of the French nobles is confined to their town residence; that of the English is more usefully distributed in their country seats; and we should be astonished at our own riches, if the labours of architecture, the spoils of Italy and Greece, which are now scattered from Inverary to Wilton, were accumulated in a few streets between Marylebone and Westminster. All superfluous ornament is rejected by the cold frugality of the Protestants; but the Catholic superstition, which is always the enemy of reason, is often the parents of the arts. The wealthy communities of priests and monks expend their revenues in stately edifices; and the parish church of St. Sulpice, one of the noblest structures in Paris, was built and adorned by the private industry of a late curé. In this outset, and still more in the sequel of my tour, my eye was amused; but the pleasing vision cannot be fixed by the pen; the particular images are darkly seen through the medium of five-and-twenty years, and the narrative of my life must not degenerate into a book of travels [1].

[1] JOURNAL, 21 Février, 1763.—Aujourdhui j'ai commencé ma tournée, pour voir les endroits dignes d'attention dans la ville. D'Augny m'a accompagné. Nous sommes allés d'abord à la bibliothèque de l'Abbaye de St. Germain des Prez, où tout le monde étoit occupé à l'arrangement d'un cabinet de curiosités, et à l'hôpital des invalides, où le dôme étoit fermé à cause des réparations qu'on y faisoit. Il fau donc différer la visite et la description de ces deux endroits. De là nous sommes allés voir

But the principal end of my journey was to enjoy the society of a polished and amiable people, in whose favour I was strongly prejudiced, and to converse with some authors, whose conversation, as I fondly imagined, must be far more pleasing and instructive than their writings. The moment was happily chosen. At the close of a successful war the British name was respected on the continent:

> —— Clarum et venerabile nomen
> Gentibus.

Our opinions, our fashions, even our games, were adopted in France; a ray of national glory illuminated each individual, and every Englishman was supposed to be born a patriot and a philosopher. For myself, I carried a special recommendation; my name and my Essay were already known; the compliment of having written in the French language entitled me to some returns of civility and gratitude. I was considered as a man of letters, who wrote for amusement. Before my departure I had obtained from the Duke de Nivernois, Lady Hervey, the Mallets, Mr. Walpole &c., many letters of recommendation to their private or literary friends. Of these epistles the reception and success were determined by the character and situation

l'école militaire. Comme ce bâtiment s'élève à côté des Invalides, bien des gens y verroient un moyen assez facile d'apprécier les ames différentes de leurs fondateurs. Dans l'un tout est grand et fastueux, dans l'autre tout est petit et mesquin. De petits corps de logis blancs et assez propres, qui, au lieu de 500 gentilshommes, dont on a parlé, en contiennent 258, composent tout l'établissement; car le manège et les écuries ne sont rien. Il est vrai qu'on dit que ces bâtimens ne sont qu'un échaffaudage, qu'on doit ôter, pour élever le véritable ouvrage sur les débris. Il faut bien en effet qu'on n'ait pas bâti pour l'éternité, puisque dans vingt ans la plûpart des poutres se sont pourries. Nous jettâmes ensuite un coup-d'œil sur l'église de St. Sulpice, dont la façade (le prétexte et le fruit de tant de lotteries) n'est point encore achevée.

of the persons by whom and to whom they were
addressed : the seed was sometimes cast on a barren
rock, and it sometimes multiplied an hundred fold in
the production of new shoots, spreading branches,
and exquisite fruit. But upon the whole, I had reason
to praise the national urbanity, which from the court
has diffused its gentle influence to the shop, the cottage,
and the schools. Of the men of genius of the age,
Montesquieu and Fontenelle were no more ; Voltaire
resided on his own estate near Geneva ; Rousseau in
the preceding year had been driven from his hermitage
of Montmorency ; and I blush at my having neglected
to seek, in this journey, the acquaintance of Buffon.
Among the men of letters whom I saw, d'Alembert
and Diderot held the foremost rank in merit, or at least
in fame. I shall content myself with enumerating the
well-known names of the Count de Caylus, of the
Abbé de la Blétérie, Barthélemy, Raynal, Arnaud, of
Messieurs de la Condamine, du Clos, de Ste Palaye,
de Bougainville, Caperonnier, de Guignes, Suard, &c.,
without attempting to discriminate the shades of
their characters, or the degrees of our connexion.
Alone, in a morning visit, I commonly found the
artists and authors of Paris less vain, and more reasonable, than in the circles of their equals, with whom
they mingle in the houses of the rich. Four days in
a week I had a place, without invitation, at the hospitable tables of Mesdames Geoffrin and du Bocage,
of the celebrated Helvetius, and of the Baron d'Olbach.
In these symposia the pleasures of the table were
improved by lively and liberal conversation ; the
company was select, though various and voluntary.[1]

---

[1] JOURNAL, Février 23, 1763.—Je fis une visite à
l'Abbé de la Blétérie, qui veut me mener chez la Duchesse
d'Aiguillon ; je me fis écrire chez M. de Bougainville que
j'ai grande envie de connoître, et me rendis ensuite chez
le Baron d'Olbach, ami de M. Helvétius. C'étoit ma
première visite, et le premier pas dans une fort bonne
maison. Le Baron a de l'esprit et des connoissances, et
surtout il donne souvent et fort bien à dîner.

The society of Madame du Bocage was more soft and moderate than that of her rivals, and the evening conversations of M. de Foncemagne were supported by the good sense and learning of the principal members of the Academy of Inscriptions. The opera and the

Février 24.—L'Abbé Barthélemy est fort aimable et n'a de l'antiquaire qu'une très grande érudition. Je finis la soirée par un souper très agréable chez Madame Bontems avec M. le Marquis de Mirabeau. Cet homme est singulier; il a assez d'imagination pour dix autres, et pas assez de sens rassis pour lui seul. Je lui ai fait beaucoup de questions sur les titres de la noblesse Françoise : mais tout ce que j'en ai pu comprendre, c'est que personne n'a là dessus des idées bien nettes.

Mai, 1763.—Muni d'une double lettre de recommandation pour M. le Comte de Caylus, je m'étois imaginé que je trouverois réunis en lui l'homme de lettres et l'homme de qualité. Je le vis trois ou quatre fois, et je vis un homme simple, uni, bon, et qui me témoignoit une bonté extrême. Si je n'en ai point profité, je l'attribue moins à son caractère qu'à son genre de vie. Il se lève de grand matin, court les atteliers des artistes pendant tout le jour, et rentre chez lui à six heures du soir pour se mettre en robe de chambre, et s'enfermer dans son cabinet. Le moyen de voir ses amis ?

Si ces recommandations étoient stériles, il y en eut d'autres qui devinrent aussi fécondes par leurs suites, qu'elles étoient agréables en elles mêmes. Dans une capitale comme Paris, il est nécessaire, il est juste que des lettres de rècommendation vous ayent distingué de la foule. Mais dès que la glace est rompue, vos connoissances se multiplient, et vos nouveaux amis se font un plaisir de vous en procurer d'autres plus nouveaux encore. Heureux effet de ce caractère léger et aimable du François, qui a établi dans Paris une douceur et une liberté dans la société, inconnues à l'antiquité, et encore ignorées des autres nations. A Londres il faut faire son chemin dans les maisons qui ne s'ouvrent qu'avec peine. Là on croit vous faire plaisir en vous recevant. Ici on croit s'en faire à soi-même. Aussi je connois plus de maisons à Paris qu'à Londres : le fait n'est pas vraisemblable, mais il est vrai.

Italians I occasionally visited; but the French theatre, both in tragedy and comedy, was my daily and favourite amusement. Two famous actresses then divided the public applause. For my own part, I preferred the consummate art of the Clairon, to the intemperate sallies of the Dumesnil, which were extolled by her admirers as the genuine voice of nature and passion. Fourteen weeks insensibly stole away; but had I been rich and independent, I should have prolonged, and perhaps have fixed, my residence at Paris.

Between the expensive style of Paris and of Italy it was prudent to interpose some months of tranquil simplicity; and at the thoughts of Lausanne I again lived in the pleasures and studies of my early youth. Shaping my course through Dijon and Besançon, in the last of which places I was kindly entertained by my cousin Acton, I arrived in the month of May, 1763, on the banks of the Leman Lake. It had been my intention to pass the Alps in the autumn, but such are the simple attractions of the place, that the year had almost expired before my departure from Lausanne in the ensuing spring. An absence of five years had not made much alteration in manners, or even in persons. My old friends, of both sexes, hailed my voluntary return; the most genuine proof of my attachment. They had been flattered by the present of my book, the produce of their soil; and the good Pavilliard shed tears of joy as he embraced a pupil whose literary merit he might fairly impute to his own labours.[1] To my old list I added some new

---

[1] Lausanne, Août 17, 1763.—Après dîner je suis allé en ville. J'ai monté au château, où il y avoit une journée embarrassante. C******** C****** et Mademoiselle de ******* y étoient toutes les deux. Je me suis décidé pour C. Elle a eu toutes les attentions. L'autre en a paru piquée. Avec quel sérieux la vanité des femmes traite ces misères! J'ai soupé chez Pavilliard.

18.—Je suis allé dîner à Mésery. M. le Comte de Golofskin et sa femme. Le Comte est d'une famille très distinguée en Russie. Les dernières révolutions de

acquaintance, and among the strangers I shall distinguish Prince Lewis of Wirtemberg, the brother of the reigning Duke, at whose country-house, near Lausanne, I frequently dined: a wandering meteor, and at length a falling star, his light and ambitious spirit had successively dropped from the firmament of Prussia, of France, and of Austria; and his faults, which he styled his misfortunes, had driven him into philosophic exile in the Pays de Vaud. He could now moralize on the vanity of the world, the equality of mankind, and the happiness of a private station. His address was affable and polite, and as he had shone in courts and armies, his memory could supply, and his eloquence could adorn, a copious fund of interesting anecdotes. His first enthusiasm was that of charity and agriculture; but the sage gradually lapsed in the saint, and Prince Lewis of Wirtemberg is now buried in a hermitage near Mayence, in the last stage of mystic devotion.[1] By some ecclesiastical quarrel,

cet empire leur avoient ôté leurs biens, à l'exception de la terre de Mona, qu'ils avoient achetée au Pays de Vaud. La mort de l'Impératrice Elizabeth les leur rendit; mais le Comte préfère sagement la retraite d'un pays libre aux orages du despotisme. Il est poli, mais froid. On lui donne de l'esprit. Il peut en avoir parmi ses amis. Sa femme, fille du Professeur Mosheim de Göttingen, paroît vive et gaie. Ces deux époux sont un modèle d'affection conjugale.

[1] Août 21.—J'ai dîné à Benans, chez le Prince Louis de Wirtemberg. C'est pour la seconde fois. Il m'avoit prié pour rencontrer le Prince de Ligne, qui nous a fait faux bond. Il paroît que le Prince de Wirtemberg me goute beaucoup. A la politesse aisée et naturelle qu'il a pour tout le monde, il ajoute à mon égard un ton de confiance, d'estime, et presque d'affection. Avec de pareilles manières, il n'est pas possible qu'on Prince vous déplaise. Je trouve à celui-ci de l'esprit, des connoissances, et beaucoup d'usage du monde. Comme il connoit presque toutes les cours de l'Europe, les anecdotes politiques et militaires, dont il assaisonne sa conversation, la rendent très amusante. Je vois qu'il n'a point l'orgueil

Voltaire had been provoked to withdraw himself from
Lausanne, and retire to his castle at Ferney, where
I again visited the poet and the actor, without seeking
his more intimate acquaintance, to which I might now
have pleaded a better title.   But the theatre which
he had founded, the actors whom he had formed,
survived the loss of their master ; and recent from
Paris, I attended with pleasure at the representation
of several tragedies and comedies.   I shall not descend
to specify particular names and characters ; but I
cannot forget a private institution, which will display
the innocent freedom of Swiss manners.   My favourite
society had assumed, from the age of its members,
the proud denomination of the spring (*la société du
printems*).   It consisted of fifteen or twenty young
unmarried ladies, of genteel, though not of the very
first families ; the eldest perhaps about twenty, all

d'un prince Allemand, et l'indignation qu'il faisoit paroître
contre un de ses ancêtres qui avoit voulu vendre un
village pour acheter un cheval, me fait espérer qu'il n'en
a pas la dureté.   Je croirois assez qu'il a toujours un
peu manqué de prudence et de conduite ; des projets
aussi ambitieux que chimériques dont on l'accuse [1], sa vie
ambulante, ses querelles avec son frère, ses dissipations,
sa disgrace à la cour de Vienne ;   tout contribue à m'en
persuader.   Sa situation dans ce pays en est presqu'une
preuve.   Un prince d'une des premières maisons de
l'empire, relégué (dirai-je) ou retiré en Suisse, où il soutient
à peine l'état d'un gentilhomme, doit y être un peu par
sa faute.   Sa femme l'a accompagné dans sa retraite.
C'est une demoiselle Saxonne qu'il a épousé sans biens,
et sans beauté.   Le public ajouteroit, et sans esprit ;
mais je commence à lui en trouver.   Comme le prince
s'est mésallié, les loix orgueilleuses de l'empire excluent
ses enfans de la succession.   Heureusement ils n'ont
encore eu qu'une fille.   A mon retour de Mésery, j'y ai
trouvé deux Anglois qui ont soupé avec nous.

[1] V. le Testament Politique du Maréchal de Belleisle. Ouvrage
digne d'un laquais, mais d'un laquais de ministre, qui a entendu
beaucoup d'anecdotes curieuses.

agreeable, several handsome, and two or three of exquisite beauty. At each other's houses they assembled almost every day, without the control, or even the presence, of a mother or an aunt ; they were trusted to their own prudence, among a crowd of young men of every nation in Europe. They laughed, they sung, they danced, they played at cards, they acted comedies ; but in the midst of this careless gaiety, they respected themselves, and were respected by the men ; the invisible line between liberty and licentiousness was never transgressed by a gesture, a word, or a look, and their virgin chastity was never sullied by the breath of scandal or suspicion : a singular institution, expressive of the innocent simplicity of Swiss manners. After having tasted the luxury of England and Paris, I could not have returned with satisfaction to the coarse and homely table of Madame Pavilliard ; nor was her husband offended that I now entered myself as a *pensionnaire*, or boarder, in the elegant house of Mr. de Mesery, which may be entitled to a short remembrance, as it has stood above twenty years, perhaps, without a parallel in Europe. The house in which we lodged was spacious and convenient, in the best street, and commanding, from behind, a noble prospect over the country and the lake. Our table was served with neatness and plenty ; the boarders were select ; we had the liberty of inviting any guests at a stated price ; and in the summer the scene was occasionally transferred to a pleasant villa, about a league from Lausanne. The characters of master and mistress were happily suited to each other, and to their situation. At the age of seventy-five, Madame de Mesery, who has survived her husband, is still a graceful, I has almost said a handsome woman. She was alike qualified to preside in her kitchen and her drawing-room ; and such was the equal propriety of her conduct, that of two or three hundred foreigners, none ever failed in respect, none could complain of her neglect, and none could ever boast of her favour. Mesery himself, of the noble

family of De Crousaz, was a man of the world, a jovial
companion, whose easy manners and natural sallies
maintained the cheerfulness of his house. His wit
could laugh at his own ignorance : he disguised, by
an air of profusion, a strict attention to his interest ;
and in this situation, he appeared like a nobleman
who spent his fortune and entertained his friends.
In this agreeable society I resided nearly eleven
months (May, 1763—April, 1764) ; and in this second
visit to Lausanne, among a crowd of my English
companions, I knew and esteemed Mr. Holroyd (now
Lord Sheffield) ; and our mutual attachment was
renewed and fortified in the subsequent stages of our
Italian journey. Our lives are in the power of chance,
and a slight variation on either side, in time or place,
might have deprived me of a friend, whose activity
in the ardour of youth was always prompted by
a benevolent heart, and directed by a strong understanding.[1]

[1] JOURNAL, Septembre 16, 1763.—***** et Frey nous
ont quitté. Le premier est une méchante bête, grossier,
ignorant, et sans usage du monde. Sa violence lui a fait
vingt mauvaises affaires ici. On vouloit cependant lui
faire entreprendre le voyage d'Italie, mais Frey refusant
de l'y accompagner, on a pris la partie de le rapeller en
Angleterre en le faisant passer par Paris. Frey est
philosophe, et fort instruit, mais froid et nullement homme
d'esprit. Il est las de courir le monde avec des jeunes
foux. Après avoir rendu celui-ci à sa famille, il compte
venir chercher le repos et la retraite dans ce pays. Qu'il
a raison !

21.—J'ai essuyé une petite mortification au cercle.
Le départ de Frey ayant fait vaquer l'emploi de directeur des étrangers, on m'avoit fait entrevoir qu'on
me le destinoit et ma franchise naturelle ne m'avoit pas
permis de dissimuler que je le recevrois avec plaisir, et
que je m'y attendois. Cependant la pluralité des voix
l'a donné à M. Roel, Hollandois. J'ai vu qu'on a saisi
le premier moment que les loix permettoient de balloter,
et que, si j'avois voulu rassembler mes amis, je l'aurois
emporté ; mais je sais en même tems que je l'aurois eu

If my studies at Paris had been confined to the
study of the world, three or four months would not

il y a trois mois, sans y songer un moment. Ma réputation
baisse ici avec quelque raison, et j'ai des ennemis.

25.—J'ai passé l'après-dîner chez Madame de Bochat.
Je ne l'avois pas vue depuis le 14 de ce mois. Elle
ne m'a point parlé, ni n'a paru s'être apperçue de
mon absence. Ce silence m'a fait de la peine. J'avois
une très belle réputation ici pour les mœurs, mais je vois
qu'on commence à me confondre avec mes compatriotes
et à me regarder comme un homme qui aime le vin et le
désordre.

Octobre 15.—J'ai passé l'après-midi chez Madame
de Mésery. Elle vouloit me faire rencontrer avec une
demoiselle Françoise qu'elle a prié à souper ; cette
demoiselle, qui s'appelle Le Franc, a six pieds de haut.
Sa taille, sa figure, son ton, sa conversation, tout annonce
le grenadier le plus déterminé, mais un grenadier qui
a de l'esprit, des connoissances, et l'usage du monde.
Aussi son sexe, son nom, son état, tout est mystère. Elle
se dit Parisienne, fille de condition, qui s'est retirée dans
ce pays pour cause de religion. Ne seroit-ce pas plûtot
pour une affaire d'honneur ?

Décembre 1.—Nous sommes tous montés à l'église
pour voir la cérémonie du jour. C'étoit la présenta-
tion du Bailif à la grande église, et la prestation du
serment par la ville de Lausanne, les vassaux et tous les
communautés du bailliage. Le grand ministre Polier de
Rollens a prêché à cette occasion. Il nous a étonné ;
au lieu de ces compositions sans chaleur et sans idées qu'il
ne qualifie que trop souvent du nom de sermons, il a fait
paroître aujourdhui les talens d'un orateur et les sentimens
d'un citoyen : il a su parler au souverain de ses devoirs,
et au peuple de ses droits fondés les uns et les autres sur
la volonté des hommes libres qui vouloient se donner un
prince et non pas un tyran. Il a loué peu, avec justesse
et sans fadeur. Son débit et son geste étoient assortis au
ton de son sujet. Ils étoient pleins de dignité, d'onction
et de force. Après le sermon, le Trésorier s'est rendu
au chœur ne l'église suivi du Bailif et de toute l'assemblée.
Là il a présenté au Bailliage leur nouveau gouverneur,
qu'il a annoncé par un discours court, mais qui m'a paru

have been unprofitably spent.   My visits, however
superficial, to the Academy of Medals and the public

rempli de choses.   Le Boursier lui a répondu, mais si
bas, que j'ai perdu tout ce qu'il a dit.   Ce mot de perdu,
est-il à sa place ?   Au reste, jamais cérémonie n'a été
conduite avec moins de décence.   Le désordre étoit
affreux.   Les Grenadiers de George Grand paroissoient
n'y être que pour repousser les honnêtes gens et pour
laisser entrer la canaille.

Je me suis levé tard, et une visite fort amicale de
M. de Chandieu Villars[1], m'a enlevé ce qui me restoit
de la matinée.   M. de Chandieu a servi en France avec
distinction, il s'est retiré avec le grade de maréchal de
camp.   C'est un homme d'une grande politesse, d'un
esprit vif et facile; il seroit aujourdhui, à soixante
ans, l'agrément d'une société de jeunes filles.   C'est
presque le seul étranger qui ait pu acquérir l'aisance
des manières Françoises, sans en prendre en même tems
les airs bruyans et étourdis.

C'étoit un Dimanche de Communion.   Les cérémonies
religieuses sont bien entendues dans ce pays.   Elles
sont rares, et par là même plus respectées; les vieillards
se plaignent à la vérité du refroidissement de la dévo-
tion; cependant un jour, comme celui-ci, offre encore
un spectacle très édifiant.   Point d'affaires, point d'assemblée; on s'interdit jusqu'au *whist*, si nécessaire à
l'existence d'un Lausannois.

Il y a quelques jours que j'ai bien perdu mon temps.
Heureux encore si ce n'étoit que mon temps, que j'eusse
perdu !   J'ai beaucoup joué, ou du moins j'ai beaucoup
parié au cercle ; après quelques commencemens de bonheur
je me suis enfilé au *whist* et au piquet, et j'ai perdu un
quarantaine de Louis.   J'ai eu alors le courage de
m'arrêter tout d'un coup, et sans me laisser éblouir par
de vaines espérances de rattraper ma perte, j'ai renoncé
au gros jeu, du moins pendant quelque temps.   Il voudroit
mieux y renoncer à jamais ; il y a tant d'inconvéniens,
la perte du temps, la mauvaise compagnie ; ces agitations
continuelles de crainte et d'espérance qui aigrissent à la

---

[1] The father of Madame de Severy, whose family were Mr.
Gibbon's most intimate friends, after he had settled at Lausanne
in the year 1783. S.

libraries, opened a new field of inquiry ; and the view
of so many manuscripts of different ages and characters

longue l'humeur et qui dérangent la santé. Le goût
d'étude et la reflexion, peut-il s'associer avec celui du jeu ?
C'est d'ailleurs une remarque que l'expérience m'a souvent
fait faire ; que la partie ne sauroit être égale et qu'une
perte quelconque est sentie bien plus vivement que ne le
seroit un gain pareil. La raison en est claire. On avoit
déjà arrangé sa dépense sur son révenu, et cette perte
inattendue entraine la privation de nécessaire ou du
moins de quelques agrémens sur lesquels on comptoit.
Mais le gain, trop précaire et trop incertain pour devoir
changer les plans d'un homme sensé, ne sert tout au plus
qu'à satisfaire la fantaisie du moment. Voilà de la
sagesse après coup. Si j'avois fait ces reflexions quelques
jours plutôt, je me serois épargné quelques désagrémens
de la part de mon père qui peut ne se point accommoder
de ce surcroit de dépense.

31.—Jettons un coup d'œil sur cette année 1763.
Voyons comment j'ai employé cette portion de mon
existence qui s'est écoulée et qui ne reviendra plus.
Le mois de Janvier s'est passé dans le sein de ma
famille à qui il falloit sacrifier tous mes momens, parcequ'ils étoient les derniers dans les soins d'un départ et
dans l'embarras d'un voyage. Dans ce voyage cependant
je trouvai moyen de lire les lettres de *Busbequius*, Ministre
Impérial à la Porte. Elles sont aussi intéressantes
qu'instructives. Je restai à Paris depuis le 28 Janvier
jusqu'au 9 Mai. Pendant tout ce tems je n'étudiai point.
Les amusemens m'occupoient beaucoup, et l'habitude
de la dissipation, qu'on prend si facilement dans les grandes
villes, ne me permettoient pas de mettre à profit le tems
qui me demeuroit. A la verité, si j'ai peu feuilleté les
livres, l'observation de tous les objets curieux qui se
présentent dans une grande capitale, et la conversation
avec les plus grands hommes du siècle, m'ont instruit de
beaucoup de choses que je n'aurois point trouvé dans les
livres. Les sept ou huit derniers mois de cette année ont
été plus tranquilles. Dès que je me suis vu établi à
Lausanne, j'ai entrepris une étude suivie sur la géographie
ancienne de l'Italie. Mon ardeur s'est très bien soutenue
pendant six semaines jusqu'à la fin du mois de Juin.

induced me to consult the two great Benedictine works, the *Diplomatica* of Mabillon, and the *Palaeo-*

Ce fut alors qu'un voyage de Genève interrompit un peu mon assiduité, que le séjour de Mésery m'offrit mille distractions, et que la société de Saussure acheva de me faire perdre mon tems. Je repris mon travail avec ce Journal au milieu d'*Août*, et depuis ce tems jusqu'au commencement de *Novembre*, j'ai mis à profit tous mes instans; j'avoue que pendant les deux derniers mois mon ardeur s'est un peu ralentie. I^{rement}, Dans cette étude suivie j'ai lu: 1. Près de deux livres de la géographie de *Strabon* sur l'Italie deux fois. 2. Une partie du deuxième livre de l'histoire naturelle de *Pline*. 3. Le quatrième chapitre du deuxième livre de *Pomponius Mela*. 4. Les Itinéraires d'Antonin, et de Jerusalem pour ce qui regarde l'Italie. Je les ai lus avec les Commentaires de Wesseling, &c. J'en ai tiré des tables de toutes les grandes routes de l'Italie, reduisant partout les milles Romains, en milles Anglois, et en lieues de France, selon les calculs de M. d'Anville. 5. L'Histoire des Grands Chemins de l'empire Romain, par M. Bergier, deux volumes in 4°. 6. Quelques Extraits choisis de Cicéron, Tite Live, Velleius Paterculus, Tacite, et les deux Plines. La *Roma Vetus* de Nardini et plusieurs autres opuscules sur le même sujet qui composent presque tout le quatrième tome du Trésor des Antiquités Romaines de Grævius. 7. L'*Italia Antiqua* de Cluvier, en deux volumes in folio. 8. L'*Iter* ou le Voyage de Cl. Rutillius Numatianus dans les Gaules. 9. Les Catalogues de Virgile. 10. Celui de Silius Italicus. 11. Le Voyage d'Horace à Brundusium. N.B. J'ai lu deux fois ces trois derniers morceaux. 12. Le Traité sur les Mesures Itinéraires par M. d'Anville, et quelques Mémoires de l'Académie des Belles Lettres. II^{ment}, On me fit attendre Nardini de la Bibliothèque de Genève. Je voulus remplir ce moment de vuide par la lecture de *Juvenal*, poëte qui je ne connoissois encore que de réputation. Je le lu deux fois avec plaisir et avec soin. III^{ment}, Pendant l'année j'ai lu quelques journaux, entre autres le Journal Etranger depuis son commencement, un tome des Nouvelles de Bayle, et les xxxv premiers volumes de la Bibliothèque raisonnée. IV^{ment}. J'ai beaucoup écrit de mon Recueil Géographique de l'Italie qui est déjà

graphia of Montfaucon. I studied the theory without attaining the practice of the art: nor should I com-

bien ample et assez curieux. V^ment, Je ne dois point oublier ce journal même qui est devenu un ouvrage; 214 pages en quatre mois et demi et des pages des mieux fournies font un objet considérable. Aussi sans compter un grand nombre d'observations détacheés, il s'y trouve des dissertations savantes et raisonnées. Celle du passage d'Annibal contient dix pages, et celle sur la guerre sociale en a douze. Mais ces morceaux sont trop étendus, et le journal même a besoin d'une réforme qui lui retranche quantité de pièces qui sont assez étrangères à son veritable plan. Après avoir un peu réfléchi là dessus, voici quelques règles que je me suis faites sur les objets qui lui conviennent. I^ment, Toute ma vie civile et privée, mes amusemens, mes liaisons, mes écarts même, et toutes mes refléxions qui ne roulent que sur des sujets qui me sont personnels, je conviens que tout cela n'est intéressant que pour moi, mais aussi ce n'est que pour moi que j'écris mon journal. II^ment, Tout ce que j'apprens par l'observation ou la conversation. A l'égard de celle-ci je ne rapporterai que ce que je tiens de personnes tout à la fois instruites et véridiques, lorsqu'il est question de faits, ou du petit nombre de ceux qui méritent le titre de grand homme, s'il s'agit de sentimens et d'opinions. III^ment, J'y mettrai soigneusement tout ce qu'on peut appeller la partie matérielle de mes études; combien d'heures j'ai travaillé, combien de pages j'ai écrit ou lu, avec une courte notice du sujet qu'elles contenoient. IV^ment, Je serois fâché de lire sans refléchir sur mes lectures, sans porter des jugemens raisonnés sur mes auteurs, et sans éplucher avec soin leurs idées et leurs expressions. Mais toute lecture ne fournit pas également. Il y a des livres qu'on parcourt, et il y en a qu'on lit; il y en a enfin qu'on doit étudier. Mes observations sur ceux de la première classe ne peuvent qu'être courtes et détachées. Elles conviennent au journal. Celles qui regardent la seconde classe n'y entreront qu'autant qu'elles auront le même caractère. V^ment, Mes refléxions sur ce petit nombre d'auteurs classiques, qu'on médite avec soin, seront naturellement plus approfondies et plus suivies. C'est pour elles, et pour des pièces plus étendues et plus origi-

plain of the intricacy of Greek abbreviations and Gothic alphabets, since every day, in a familiar

nales, auxquelles la lecture ou la méditation peut donner lieu, que je ferai un recueil séparé. Je conserverai cependant sa liaison avec le journal par des renvois constans qui marqueront le numéro de chaque pièce avec le tems et l'occasion de sa composition. Moyennant ces précautions mon journal ne peut que m'être utile. Ce compte exact de mon tems m'en fera mieux sentir le prix ; il dissipera par son détail, l'illusion qu'on se fait d'envisager seulement les années et les mois et de mépriser les heures et les jours. Je ne dis rien de l'agrément. C'en est un bien grand cependant de pouvoir repasser chaque époque de sa vie, et de se placer, dès qu'on le veut, au milieu de toutes les petites scènes qu'on a joué, ou qu'on a vu jouer.

Avril 6, 1764.—J'ai été éveillé par Pavilliard et Holroyd pour arrêter une fâcheuse affaire qui s'étoit passée au bal après notre départ. Guise, qui faisoit la cour à Mademoiselle d'Illens depuis long tems, voyoit avec peine que Van Berken (un Hollandois) menaçoit de le supplanter. Il ne répondoit jamais aux politesses de son rival, que par des brusqueries ; et à la fin à l'occasion de la main de Mademoiselle d'Illens il s'emporta contre lui le plus mal à propos du monde, et le traita devant tout le monde *d'impertinent*, &c. J'ai appris de Pavilliard que Van Berken lui avoit envoyé un cartel, et que la réponse de Guise ne l'ayant point contenté ils devoient se rencontrer à cinq heures du soir. Au désespoir de voir mon ami engagé dans une affaire qui ne pouvoit que lui faire du tort, j'ai couru chez M. de Crousaz où demeuroit Van Berken. J'ai bientôt vu qu'il ne lui falloit qu'une explication assez légère, jointe à quelque apologie de la part de Guise pour le désarmer, et je suis retourné chez lui avec Holroyd pour l'engager à la donner. Nous lui avons fait comprendre que l'aveu d'un véritable tort ne blessoit jamais l'honneur, et que son insulte envers les dames aussi bien qu'envers Van Berken étoit sans excuse. Je lui ai dicté un billet convenable, mais sans ia moindre bassesse, que j'ai porté au Hollandois. Il a rendu les armes sur le champ, lui a fait la réponse la plus polie, et m'a remercié mille fois du rôle que j'avois fait. En

language, I am at a loss to decipher the hieroglyphics
of a female note. In a tranquil scene, which revived
the memory of my first studies, idleness would have
been less pardonable: the public libraries of Lausanne
and Geneva liberally supplied me with books; and if
many hours were lost in dissipation, many more were
employed in literary labour. In the country, Horace
and Virgil, Juvenal and Ovid, were my assiduous
companions: but in town, I formed and executed
a plan of study for the use of my Transalpine expedition: the topography of old Rome, the ancient
geography of Italy, and the science of medals. (1)
I diligently read, almost always with a pen in my
hand, the elaborate treatises of Nardini, Donatus, &c.,
which fill the fourth volume of the Roman Antiquities
of Graevius. (2) I next undertook and finished the
Italia Antiqua of Cluverius, a learned native of Prussia,
who had measured, on foot, every spot, and has
compiled and digested every passage of the ancient
writers. These passages in Greek or Latin authors
I perused in the text of Cluverius, in two folio volumes:
but I separately read the descriptions of Italy by
Strabo, Pliny, and Pomponius Mela, the Catalogues of
the epic poets, the Itineraries of Wesseling's Antoninus,
and the coasting Voyage of Rutilius Numatianus; and

vérité cet homme n'est pas difficile. Après dîner j'ai vu
nos dames à qui j'ai porté une lettre d'excuses. La
mère n'en veut plus à Guise, mais Mademoiselle d'Illens
est désolée du tort que cette affaire peut lui faire dans
le monde. Cette négociation m'a pris le jour entier;
mais peut on mieux employer un jour qu'à sauver la vie,
peut-être à deux personnes, et à conserver la réputation
d'un ami ? Au reste j'ai vu au fond plus d'un caractère.
Guise est brave, vrai, et sensé, mais d'une impétuosité
qui n'est que plus dangereuse pour être supprimée à
l'ordinaire. C***** est d'une étourderie d'enfant. De
Salis d'une indifférence qui vient plus d'un défaut de
sensibilité, que d'un excès de raison. J'ai conçu une
véritable amitié pour Holroyd. Il a beaucoup de raison
et des sentimens d'honneur avec un cœur des mieux placé.

I studied two kindred subjects in the *Mesures Itiné-raires* of d'Anville, and the copious work of Bergier, *Histoire des grands Chemins de l'Empire Romain.* From these materials I formed a table of roads and distances reduced to our English measure; filled a folio commonplace book with my collections and remarks on the geography of Italy; and inserted in my journal many long and learned notes on the insulae and populousness of Rome, the social war, the passage of the Alps by Hannibal, &c. (3) After glancing my eye over Addison's agreeable dialogues, I more seriously read the great work of Ezechiel Spanheim, *de Praestan-tia et Usu Numismatum,* and applied with him the medals of the kings and emperors, the families and colonies, to the illustration of ancient history. And thus was I armed for my Italian journey.[1]

---

[1] JOURNAL, Lausanne, Avril 17, 1764.—Guise et moi, nous avons donné un dîner excellent et beaucoup de vin à Dupleix, et à beaucoup d'autres. Après dîner nous nous sommes échappés pour faire quelques visites aux Grands, aux Seigneux, et aux d'Illens. Je pars avec quelques regrets : cependant un peu de vin, et une gaieté dont je ne pouvois rendre raison, m'ont rendu d'une étourderie sans pareille, vis-à-vis de ces petites. Je leur ai dit cent folies, et nous nous sommes embrassés en riant. Mésery nous a donné un très beau souper avec une partie de la compagnie du matin, augmentée de Bourgeois et de Pavilliard. Ce souper, les adieux, sur tout à Pavilliard, que j'aime véritablement, et les pré-paratifs du départ, m'ont occupé jusqu'à deux heures du matin.

Je quitte Lausanne avec moins de regret que la pre-mière fois. Je n'y laisse plus que des connoissances. C'étoit la maîtresse et l'ami dont je pleurois la perte. D'ailleurs je voyois Lausanne avec les yeux encore novices d'un jeune homme, qui lui devoit la partie raisonnable de son existence, et qui jugeoit sans objets de comparaison. Aujourdhui j'y vois une ville mal bâtie, au milieu d'un pays délicieux, qui jouit de la paix et du repos, et qui les prend pour la liberté. Un peuple nombreux et bien élevé, qui aime la société, qui y est propre, et qui admet

I shall advance with rapid brevity in the narrative of this tour, in which somewhat more than a year (April, 1764—May, 1765) was agreeably employed. Content with tracing my line of march, and slightly touching on my personal feelings, I shall waive the minute investigation of the scenes which have been viewed by thousands, and described by hundreds of our modern travellers. Rome is the great object of our pilgrimage : and first, the journey ; second, the residence ; and third, the return, will form the most proper and perspicuous division. (1) I climbed Mount Cenis, and descended into the plain of Piedmont, not on the back of an elephant, but on a light osier seat, in the hands of the dexterous and intrepid chairmen of the Alps. The architecture and government of Turin [1] presented the same aspect of tame and tiresome

avec plaisir les étrangers dans ses cotteries, qui seroient bien plus agréables si la conversation n'avoit pas cédé la place au jeu. Les femmes sont jolies, et malgré leur grande liberté, elles sont très sages. Tout au plus peuvent-elles être un peu complaisantes, dans l'idée honnête, mais incertaine, de prendre un étranger dans leurs filets. La maison de M. de Mésery est charmante ; le caractère franc et généreux du mari, les agrémens de la femme, une situation délicieuse, une chère excellente, la compagnie de ses compatriotes, et une liberté parfaite, font aimer ce séjour à tout Anglois. Que je voudrois en trouver un semblable à Londres ! J'y regrette encore Holroyd, mais il nous suit de près.

[1] Turin, Mai 10, 1764.—Nous avons été présentés aux Princesses, et au Duc de Chablais. C'étoit tout ce qui nous restoit de la famille royale que nous avions envie de voir. Il y a trois Princesses qui ont bien l'air de ne jamais changer d'état. L'ainée, la Princesse de Savoye, a un petit visage arrondi qui peut avoir été joli. Louise et Feliceté sont un peu pâles et maigres, mais ce sont bien les meilleures filles du monde. Le Duc de Chablais est grand, bien fait, et un peu noirâtre. Il n'a pas un air aussi prévenant que le Duc de Savoye ; malgré sa grande jeunesse, et la gêne où l'on le tient, il paroît plus libre, et plus formé. C'est le favori du père, qui est aussi

uniformity; but the court was regulated with decent
and splendid economy; and I was introduced to his

prodigue à son égard, qu'il est avare pour le pauvre Duc
de Savoye, qui est obligé de prendre sur son nécessaire, et
sur les revenus de sa femme, les sommes qu'il employe
à des œuvres de charité, et de générosité, surtout à l'égard
des officiers.

11.—Il faut dire deux mots de Turin, et du Souverain qui y règne.   Quand on voit les accroissemens
lents et successifs de la maison de Savoye pendant huit
cens ans, il faut convenir que sa grandeur est plutôt
l'ouvrage de la prudence que de la fortune. Elle se
soutient, comme elle s'est formé, par la sagesse, l'ordre, et
l'économie.   Avec la plus mauvaise partie des Alpes, une
plaine fertile, mais assez resserrée, et une méchante île,
qui lui rapporte, dirai-je, ou qui lui coûte une centaine
de mille livres, le Roi de Sardaigne s'est mis au rang des
puissances.   Il a des places fortes, une armée qu'il a
poussée jusqu'à 50,000 hommes, et une cour nombreuse
et brillante.   On voit dans chaque département un esprit
d'activité, modéré par l'économie qui cherche à tirer
parti de ses avantages, ou à les faire naître.   Sciences,
arts, bâtimens, manufactures, tout s'en ressent.   Il n'y
a pas jusqu'à la navigation qui soit négligée.   Le Roi
pense à faire construire un beau port à Nice, et il a appellé
d'Angleterre notre Capitaine Atkins, pour l'employer dans
sa marine naissante, qui n'est encore composée que d'un
vaisseau de cinquante canons, et une frégate de trente.
Tous les deux sont des prises Espagnoles, achetées des
Anglois.   La frégate est la fameuse *Hermione.*

Gênes, Mai 22.—Nous sommes arrivés à *Gênes* vers
les huit heures et demie du matin.   Notre chemin
n'étoit proprement que le lit d'un grand torrent; mais
les coteaux nous offroient le spectacle très riant d'un
nombre de maisons de campagne très propres, et ornées
d'une belle architecture en peinture.   Le coup d'œil de
Gênes et de son port m'a paru très beau.   Après dîné
nous avons fait une visite à Madame Mac Carthy, qui
voyage avec son fils, et aux Celesia, que j'avois beaucoup
connus en Angleterre.   Je n'ai trouvé que la femme qui
m'a reçu avec beaucoup d'amitié.   Je dois y dîner demain,
et leur présenter Guise.   Madame Celesia est très aimable,

Sardinian majesty, Charles Emanuel, who, after the incomparable Frederic, held the second rank (proximus

son caractère est doux, elle a beaucoup d'esprit, et d'imagination. Il me paroît que l'age et l'usage du monde l'ont guéri d'un tour un peu romanesque qu'elle avoit autrefois. J'ai toujours eu pour elle l'estime et la compassion qu'elle méritoit, et qui font toujours naître une amitié qui tient de la tendresse. Elle est fille du poëte Mallet; la tyrannie de sa belle-mère l'avoit jetté entre les bras de M. Celesia, alors Envoyé de Gênes en Angleterre, qui l'a épousée, et qui la mena bientôt après en sa patrie. Elle se dit fort heureuse; mais elle avoue qu'elle regrette toujours l'Angleterre.

23.—Nous avons dîné chez Celesia. Ils m'ont comblé de politesses, et même d'amitiés; car je dois prendre pour moi tout ce qu'ils ont fait pour Guise. J'ai beaucoup causé avec Celesia sur les affaires du pays, et surtout sur le soulèvement de Gênes en 1746, et sur les révoltes de Corse. Voici quelques circonstances que j'en ai appris. 1^{nt}. Lorsque le peuple a fait cet effort, digne des Romains, il a formé un conseil qu'on appelloit Assemblée du Peuple, qui a continué pendant près d'une année; qu'il y avoit dans l'État deux chefs indépendans. Le Sénat régissoit comme à l'ordinaire toutes les affaires étrangères, et il abandonnoit à cette assemblée tout l'intérieur de la république. Elle demeuroit chargée du soin de la liberté, rendoit ses ordonnances sous peine de la vie, et tenoit son bourreau assis sur les degrés d'une église, et près d'une potence pour les faire exécuter. Ce qu'il y a de plus singulier, c'est que le peuple qui avoit pris ce goût de l'autorité suprême, se dégouta bientôt de ses propres chefs, laissa tomber peu-à-peu son assemblée, et rendit les rênes du gouvernement à la noblesse, sans dispute, et sans conditions. 2^{nt}. Si les Genois ont irrité les Corses, ils ont tâché depuis de les ramener. Il y a quatre ans qu'on fit passer dans l'île une députation illustre, munie de pleins pouvoirs d'accorder aux rébelles tout ce qu'ils demanderoient. Ce fut sans effet. Ces esprits indépendans, nés dans la révolte, et qui se souviennent à peine qu'ils ont été sujets des Genois, n'ont écouté que les conseils violens de Paoli, qui seul sait gouverner ce peuple indocile. Ce chef fameux, dont les mœurs sont

longo tamen intervallo) among the kings of Europe
The size and populousness of Milan could not surprise

encore un peu féroces, égale par ses talens naturels les
grands hommes de l'antiquité. M. Celesia ne pouvoit
le comparer qu'à Cromwell. Comme lui, l'ambition lui
tient lieu des richesses, qu'il méprise, et des plaisirs dont
il ignore l'usage ; comme lui, Dictateur perpétuel d'une
république naissante, il sait la gouverner par un fantôme
de sénat, dont il est le maître ; comme lui, il a su remplir
ses troupes d'un fanatisme religieux qui les rend invincibles.
Les curés de l'île lui sont des instrumens très utiles ; mais
enfin son addresse est d'autant plus singulière, que la
religion n'a été ni le motif, ni le prétexte de la révolte.
La partie la plus saine du Sénat est lasse d'une guerre
qui ne lui a valu que des dépenses immenses, et des dis-
graces. Elle n'y conserve plus que les places maritimes,
dont le territoire est souvent borné par le glacis des fortifications. On abandonneroit avec plaisir les Corses à
eux-mêmes, si on ne craignoit pas le Roi de Sardaigne.
Il est très sur que la Cour de Vienne auroit souhaité
d'acquérir l'île pour le Grand Duc de Toscane, et que
le marché auroit peut-être eu lieu, sans la jalousie de
France.

Juin 3.—J'ai passé la matinée entière à la maison.
Heureux momens de repos, dont on ne sent le prix, que
lorsqu'on a vécu dans le tourbillon. J'ai achevé l'histoire
des Révolutions de Gênes. Le style n'est pas mauvais,
sans être celui de Vertot ; l'ordonnance est claire, sans
être habile. Il est si peu d'abbréviateurs à qui Velleius
Paterculus ait légué son secret, celui de prendre toujours
par grandes masses. Mais dans une histoire politique
j'aurois voulu des idées plus exactes de la constitution
de Gênes, de ses loix, et de ses mœurs.

Nous avons dîné chez Celesia qui est toujours malade.
A huit heures du soir son beau-père nous a présenté au
Doge Brignoletti. C'est un vieillard assez gros, qui a
l'air peu spirituel. Il sait un peu de François, mais il ne
nous a guères parlé qu'Italien. Il nous a poliment reçu,
mais avec un mélange de dignité qui convenoit assez avec
sa sérénité. Cette sérénité reçoit 5,000 livres par an,
et en dépense au moins 25,000 pour avoir le plaisir de
demeurer dans une très vilaine maison, dont il ne peut

an inhabitant of London; but the fancy is amused by a visit to the Boromean Islands, an enchanted

sortir sans une permission du Sénat, d'être vêtu de rouge depuis les pieds jusqu'à la tête, et d'avoir douze pages de 60 ans, habillés à l'Espagnole.

Castel St. Giovanni, Juin 12.—Nous sommes partis de Gênes de très grand matin. Nous espérions de pousser jusqu'à Plaisance, mais les mauvais chemins, et les chicanes qui nous ont arrêtés presqu'à chaque poste, nous ont obligé de nous reposer à neuf heures du soir à Castel St. Giovanni, petit bourg, dans le territoire de Plaisance, à deux postes de la capitale, et à onze et demie de Gênes. Je ne connois rien de plus désagréable, et de plus rude que le passage de la Bouquette, et même que tout le chemin de Gênes à Novi, où commence la plaine de Lombardie. Le Roi de Sardaigne, par une attention sans relâche à profiter des plus petites acquisitions, a réduit enfin les Génois à leurs montagnes nues et stériles, dont ce peuple, tout industrieux qu'il est, peut à peine tirer le moindre avantage. En passant la Bouquette j'ai considéré ce défilé étroit, bordé de précipices, et dominé par des rochers escarpés. J'ai bien compris que sans la politique timide du Sénat, el l'ignorance dans laquelle les paysans étoient encore du soulèvement de Gênes, le Maréchal Botta y auroit laissé ses troupes, et sa liberté, ou sa vie.

Parme, Juin 14.—Vers l'an 1747 des ouvriers qui travailloient à Villora dans les montagnes du Parmesan, déterrèrent une grande table de bronze. On continua à faire des recherches, et peu à peu l'on parvint à découvrir les ruines d'une ville qui ne peut être que l'ancienne Veleia, située dans ces quartiers, et qui doit avoir été écrasée sous la chûte d'une montagne. Ces décombres se trouvoient quelquefois à fleur de terre, et quelquefois à une assez grande profondeur. Je ne pense pas qu'on ait trouvé de maison complette, ni même des vestiges d'aucun édifice public, quoique Veleia ait du en avoir, quand ce ne seroit que des temples. Mais sur la situation des murs, l'on a dressé une espèce de Carte de Veleia, qui paroît avoir été grande. On y a trouvé beaucoup de statues, de lampes, et d'autres antiquités. Le Duc y entretient toujours un Directeur des travaux, avec une

palace, a work of the fairies in the midst of a lake
encompassed with mountains, and far removed from
the haunts of men. I was less amused by the marble
palaces of Genoa, than by the recent memorials of
her deliverance (in December, 1746) from the Austrian
tyranny ; and I took a military survey of every scene
of action within the enclosure of her double walls.
My steps were detained at Parma and Modena, by the
precious relics of the Farnese and Este collections :
but, alas ! the far greater part had been already
transported, by inheritance or purchase, to Naples
and Dresden. By the road of Bologna and the Apennine I at last reached Florence, where I reposed from
June to September, during the heat of the summer
months.[1] In the Gallery, and especially in the Tribune,

quarantaine d'ouvriers, et à mesure qu'on a épuisé un
endroit, on le comble de terre. Voilà tout ce que j'en
ai pu apprendre, graces à un mauvais air de mystère que
la cour affecte d'y mettre. Elle compte un jour, quand
on aura tout trouvé, de rendre compte au public de ses
découvertes, et veut être la première à la rendre. On
vous permet à peine de regarder attentivement, et jamais
de rien copier.

[1] JOURNAL, Florence, Juin 29, 1764.—On a célébré
la fête de St. Jean, protecteur de Florence. A sept heures
du matin nous nous sommes rendus à la place du grand
Duc, pour y voir la cérémonie des présentations, des
hommages, &c., &c. Enfin l'on voyoit avancer la tour
de St. Jean, plus élevée et plus ornée que les aurtes. Le
saint lui-même couronnoit le faîte. Les niches des côtés
étoient remplies de plusieurs autres saints, entre lesquels
on distinguoit St. Sebastien, attaché à un pilier. Tous les
saints étoient des hommes qui jouoient assez bien leurs
rôles. Seulement comme la place de St. Jean paroissoit
un peu dangereuse on avoit substitué une figure de bois au
garçon qui le représentoit auparavant. Cette tour étoit
suivie par ces Chevaux Barbes qui courent l'après-midi,
&c., &c.

L'après-midi nous avons vu la Course des Chevaux
Barbes qui se fait dans le Corso, une grande et belle rue,
mais qui dans bien des endroits n'est point assez large, ni

I first acknowledged, at the feet of the Venus of Medicis, that the chisel may dispute the pre-eminence

assez droite. Nous sommes allés à la suite de M. Mann à six heures du soir. Le Corso étoit déjà rempli de plusieurs centaines de carrosses qui se promenoient pour étaler tout le faste du plus grand gala de Florence. Il faut convenir que les équipages et les habits étoient magnifiques et de goût, et que l'ensemble formoit le plus beau coup-d'œil qu'on puisse s'imaginer. Dans une demie heure les carrosses se sont retirés, et chacun a gagné sa fénêtre, son balcon, ou son échafaud. Nous avons suivi le ministre à la loge de la régence, qui étoit remplie de ce qu'il y avoit de plus distingué dans Florence. On nous y a reçu de la manière la plus polie. Par ce changement de décoration le spectacle devenoit moins brillant, mais plus singulier par la foule innombrable de tous les états qui occupoient les deux côtés d'une grande rue, pendant que la rue même étoit parfaitement libre. Il faut dire que tout se passa sans confusion, et qu'une poignée de grenadiers suffisoit pour retenir dans l'ordre tout ce peuple immense. On fit passer alors les chevaux en procession pour les conduire aux *Carceres*. Ils étoient quinze, parés de rubans de différentes couleurs, et conduits par les palfreniers et la livrée de leurs maîtres. Ils paroissoient en général beaux, mais quoiqu'on les appelle Barbes, ils peuvent être de tous les pays. Il y avoit en particulier un vieux Anglois de l'age de vingt-trois, mais qui remportoit encore à l'ordinaire le prix. On voyoit bien aux acclamations du peuple à quel point il en étoit le favori. Lorsqu'ils étoient arrivés au bout, on les rangea aussi également qu'on le pouvoit ; on lâcha la corde ; ils partirent —je les vis passer avec une vîtesse que l'impétuosité naturelle au cheval, animée encore par l'aiguillon qu'ils portoient m'expliquoit très-bien. Mais j'étois étonné de la constance et de la tranquillité avec laquelle ils poursuivirent leur carrière aussi bien que si les plus habiles cavaliers les eussent montés. Nous les perdîmes bientôt de vue, et toute l'assemblée fixoit les yeux sur le clocher de la cathédrale pour y lire le nom du vainqueur dans les signaux de lumières qui s'y répétoient et qui répondoient au numéro du cheval. Pour suspendre plus long-tems l'impatience publique, il falloit par hasard attendre jusqu'au numéro

with the pencil, a truth in the fine arts which cannot on this side of the Alps be felt or understood.[1] At

treize. Le Prince Neri déclara au peuple (que la curiosité tenoit dans la plus tranquille silence), que le poulain du Chevalier Alessandri avoit remporté la victoire, et ce silence se changea tout-à-coup aux acclamations tumultueuses de trente mille spectateurs. Avant de livrer le prix au vainqueur, on devoit le bénir avec beaucoup de cérémonie à l'église de St. Jean. Autant que j'ai pu juger, les chevaux ont fourni leur carrière de plus de deux milles dans cinq minutes. Le grand diable est arrivé le second, et presqu'au même instant que le premier.

A ne considérer que la vîtesse des chevaux, nos courses l'emportent infiniment sur celle-ci. Cependant l'antiquité de l'institution, l'ardeur d'un peuple entier, qui y assiste, l'intervention du prince, et même de la religion, lui donnent un air bien plus majestueux. On voit que les Florentins chérissent cet usage comme le seul vestige de leur liberté ancienne ; c'est une fureur momentanée qui s'empare de tous les esprits, et depuis les jeux des anciens, c'est peut-être le seul spectacle des plaisirs de tout un état réuni pour s'amuser par les soins, et sous les yeux de ses magistrats.

[1] Juillet 16.—Nous avons fait notre VIIIme *visite à la Galerie*, &c., &c., &c. Je vais parler de ses meubles qui ne consistent qu'en statues, et en bustes antiques, placés alternativement, de manière qu'il se trouve toujours une statue et deux bustes. Ces derniers sont peut-être le trésor le plus précieux de la galerie, puisqu'ils contiennent la suite complette de tous les empereurs, depuis Auguste et Jules César jusqu'à Caracalle, sans compter plusieurs des successeurs de celui-ci ; beaucoup d'impératrices, et des bustes qu'on a assignés à des philosophes, et des poëtes Grecs, sur la foi des descriptions vagues et obscures que les anciens nous ont laissé de leurs personnes. C'est un plaisir bien vif que de suivre les progrès, et la décadence des arts, et de parcourir cette suite des portraits originaux des maîtres du monde. On y voit bien plus distinctement leurs traits que sur leurs médailles, dont le champ est trop petit. Je conviens que ce n'est qu'à l'aide des médailles que nous les reconnoissions ici. C'est pourquoi j'aurois voulu qu'on eût pratiqué dans le piédestal de chaque

home I had taken some lessons of Italian; on the
spot I read, with a learned native, the classics of the

buste, un petit tiroir rempli de ces médailles. Les curieux
auroient trouvé beaucoup d'agrément à les comparer. A
tout ce mérite accessoire il y a beaucoup de ces bustes qui
ajoutent encore celui du travail. Sans vouloir les passer
tous en revue comme l'a fait Cochin, je marquerai ceux
qui m'ont arrêté par quelque endroit. 1. *Jules César*. Il
est singulier. Tous ses traits sont contractés, et l'air du
visage porte les caractères les plus frappans de la vieillesse
et de la caducité. On comprend à peine que ce soit le
buste d'un homme mort à l'âge de cinquante-six ans. Je
n'ai pas pu remarquer sa tête chauve, quoique le front soit
un peu dégarni des cheveux, non plus que la couronne de
laurier, sous laquelle ce héros cachoit un défaut dont il
avoit la foiblesse par quelque endroit. Il est vrai que la plupart des
têtes d'hommes de cette suite, sont sans aucun ornement.
2. *Cicéron*. Un long cou, un visage un peu maigre, beaucoup de rides, un teint un peu jaunâtre, qui vient de la
couleur du marbre, tout annonce ici la force et les travaux
de l'esprit plutôt que du corps. Il est d'une vérité et d'une
finesse extraordinaire. Le sculpteur a marqué un pois
sur la joue gauche ; comme il est joliment fait, il n'est qu'un
agrément qui sert d'ailleurs à le distinguer : mais quoique
le nom fut héréditaire, la marque (Cicer) ne l'étoit pas.
3. *Agrippa*. C'est bien le contraste de Cicéron, quoiqu'il
soit peut-être aussi beau dans son genre. Il est d'une
manière grande et hardie. Un visage large et quarré, des
traits saillans et marqués ; des yeux grands, mais excessivement enfoncés dans la tête ; des cheveux qui couvrent la
moitié du front ; tout y réveille l'idée de la force et de la
vigueur, et présente un ensemble plutôt terrible qu'agréable.
On l'a placé parmi les empereurs que cet homme nouveau
a mis sur le trône du monde. 4. *Sappho*. La sculpture
étoit trop imparfaite au 6ᵐᵉ siècle avant Jesus Christ pour
nous permettre de regarder la tête de cette femme célèbre
comme une originale. Je le croirois encore moins, puisque
Sappho, qui brilloit plutôt par l'esprit que par la beauté,
n'avoit certainement pas ce beau visage ovale, quoiqu'un
peu arrondi par l'embonpoint que le sculpteur lui a donné
ici. Ce morceau est d'une grande beauté. 5. *Caligula*.
Ce buste, qui est d'une exécution libre et hardie, acquiert

Tuscan idiom ; but the shortness of my time, and the
use of the French language, prevented my acquiring

un nouveau prix par la ressemblance parfaite et exacte
qu'il a avec les médailles de ce tyran. Pour un homme
mort dans sa trentième année, ses traits sont extrèmement
formés. 6. *Néron.* Il y a beaucoup d'expression, mais
d'une expression un peu confuse. Dois-je le dire, et le
dire ici ? Néron ne m'a jamais révolté autant que Tibère,
Caligula, ou Domitien. Il avoit beaucoup de vices, mais
il n'étoit pas sans vertus. Je vois dans son histoire peu de
traits d'une méchanceté étudiée. Il étoit cruel, mais il
l'étoit plutôt par crainte que par goût. 7. *Sénèque.* Morceau très estimé et digne de l'être. Sa peau décharnée
paroît ne couvrir que des os et des muscles, qui sont
rendues avec une grande vérité : ses veines sont des tuyaux
qui semblent vuides de sang. Tous les caractères du buste
annoncent un vieillard, et peut-être un vieillard expirant.
8. *Galba.* Buste forte beau. 9. *Otho.* Il n'a d'autre
mérite que celui de sa rareté. Je suis surpris qu'il s'en
trouve. Mille accidens peuvent faire enterrer et conserver
des monnoies ; mais comment s'est-il trouvé quelqu'un
qui ait voulu risquer de garder le buste odieux de ce fantôme
d'empereur ? A la vérité le règne de son ennemi Vitellius
passa presqu'aussi vîte. 10. *Vitellius.* La tête de ce
gourmand et bête stupide est chargée de chair. Il est
singulier que les monumens de cet empereur aussi ne soient
pas plus rares. Je pense que Vespasien le méprisa trop
pour le détruire. 11. *Vespasien.* Si la nature doit être
le modèle des sculpteurs cette tête est d'une beauté merveil-
leuse. Rien n'est plus naturelle que les contours, rien n'est
plus gracieux que l'air, à la fois gai, tranquille et majestueux.
C'est vraiment un visage humain, et quoiqu'il soit plutôt
laid que beau, il est bon et intéressant. Je suis persuadé
que la ressemblance étoit frappante. 12. *Berenice.* La
coeffure de cette reine est en boucles frisées très-artistement,
mais disposées avec une apparence de négligence. Si elle
n'étoit pas plus belle qu'elle n'est représentée ici, on a peine
à comprendre la passion de Titus. 13. *Domitia.* La
manière dont ses cheveux sont ramassés sur le front en
beaucoup de petites boucles détachées, leur donne assez,
selon Cochin, l'air d'une éponge. Nous nous sommes
arrêtés aux Douze Césars, division qui est occasionnée par

any facility of speaking ; and I was a silent spectator in the conversations of our envoy, Sir Horace Mann,

Suétone plutôt que par la raison. Les six Césars auroient été plus naturels.

17.—Nous avons fait notre *IXme visite à la Galerie.* Voici la suite des bustes que nous avons reprise. 14. *Trajan.* Buste facile et naturel. Je vois sur la physionomie un sourire moqueur assez singulier. La tête est extrêmement tournée de côté : mais en général je ne me rappelle pas un seul buste dont la tête soit laissée dans son attitude régulière. Les sculpteurs auront cru avec raison qu'un petit écart de la ligne droite tracée par la nature donnoit plus de grace et d'âme à leurs figures. 15. *Hadrien.* Ce buste est très beau. On voit, selon le témoignage des historiens, que ce prince a commencé le premier à laisser croître sa barbe. Il la coupoit cependant de tems en tems, et ne se piquoit point d'avoir cette longue barbe pendante, et bien nourrie, qui faisoit l'orgueil des philosophes de ce siècle. A l'égard des cheveux, les premiers empereurs les avoient portés courts, frisés avec fort peu de soin, et tombant sur le front. Sur le buste d'Othon on distingue très bien la perruque frisée en grosses boucles par devant dont ce prince fut l'inventeur. Tout ceci ne regarde que les empereurs. Sénèque, qui affichoit la philosophie, a beaucoup de cheveux, et de barbe. 16. *Antinous.* Le buste de ce mignon d'Hadrien est très beau. Le visage est très bien formé, d'un mélange de force et de douceur. Les épaules, la poitrine, et les mammelles, sont traitées avec beaucoup de mollesse. Le plus bel embonpoint ne détruit point ici les graces du contour. Ce buste, plus grand que nature, est entièrement antique, circonstance rare et presqu'unique. Tout au plus a-t-on la tête antique, souvent il en a fallu restaurer une partie, et le nez a presque toujours été cassé. C'est à Antinous seulement que les yeux des bustes commencent à avoir des prunelles ; encore les siens sont-ils à peine perceptibles. On ne sauroit concevoir jusqu'à quel point la prunelle rend la vie et l'expression à tout, et anime tous les traits. Il étoit juste qu'un pareil secours appuyât la sculpture quand elle touchoit au moment de sa décadence. 17. *Antonin le Débonnaire.* Il est plein de verité et d'expression, surtout la partie supérieure du visage, le front, et les yeux. Antonin ajouta

whose most serious business was that of entertaining

à la barbe de petites moustaches frisées. 18. *M. Aurèle.*
Il y en a trois. Celui que le représente jeune, est le meil-
leur. On peut remarquer dans toute cette famille la même
manière de sculpture ; c'est-à-dire plus de beautés de
détail, avec un ensemble moins frappant. 19. *Annius
Verus.* C'est un jeune enfant, qui est vraiment un chef-
d'œuvre. Un petit visage rond, où brillent toutes les
graces de la joie, et de l'innocence. On ne peut se lasser
de le regarder. 20. *Un buste beaucoup plus grand que la
nature.* C'est un visage assez jeune, quoique très formé ;
fort beau, mais qui lève les yeux au ciel avec la plus belle
et la plus forte expression, de la douleur et de l'indignation.
On dit que c'est Alexandre prêt à expirer. Si la conjecture
est un peu avérée on pourroit se flatter de posséder un
morceau unique de la main de Lysippe, le seul sculpteur
à qui Alexandre permettoit de le tailler en marbre. Il
n'y a rien dans ce chef-d'œuvre de noblesse, de simplicité,
et d'expression, qui démente le siècle d'Alexandre, ou l'idée
qu'on peut se former de Lysippe. 21. *Pertinax.* Il me
paroît beau. 22. *Clodius Albinus.* Il est d'albâtre ; à ce
mérite, et celui d'un bon travail, il ajoute celui de la plus
grande rareté. Quand on se rappelle que son ombre de
royauté, à été suivi d'un règne de vingt ans d'un enemi
implacable et cruel, on conçoit bien les raisons de cette
rareté. 23. *Septime Sévère.* Il est bon, mais j'aime mieux
la manière que l'exécution de ce buste. 24. *Geta.* Celui
qui le représente enfant, est fort joli, mais il y paroît plus
formé que l'Annius Verus. 25. *Caracalle.* Bon, mais il
me paroît un peu sec. C'est ici que la sculpture Romaine
est tombée dans le même tems que l'architecture, avec qui
elle a peut-être encore plus de rapports qu'avec la peinture.
Je pense que ces derniers morceaux sont de artistes qui
restoient encore du siècle d'or des Antonins, et qui ne
formèrent point d'élèves dans le siècle de fer des Sévères,
sous qui le gouvernement devint vraiment militaire, et
despotique. Les bustes qui sont les moins mauvais dans
la suite, sont, 26. *Gallien,* et 27. *Eliogabale.* Le total
des bustes des corridors est de quatre vingt douze.

Florence, Juillet 29.—Toute la nation dîna chez M. Mann.
Après dîner nous allâmes voir une course de chevaux. Le
Gran Diavolo a remporté le prix. C'est un vieux Anglois

the English at his hospitable table.[1] After leaving
Florence I compared the solitude of Pisa with the
industry of Lucca and Leghorn, and continued my

qui a vingt deux à vingt trois ans, à qui on n'est point
encore en état de dire *solve senescentem equum*. Ses
victoires, qui sont presqu'aussi fréquentes que ses combats,
ont engagé un prince à offrir dernièrement 1000 sequins
à son maître le Chevalier Alessandri, qui les a refusés.

31.—Lord Palmerston et L. ont dîné avec nous. C'est
un singulier contraste que ces deux jeunes gens. L'un,
posé, tranquille, un peu froid, possède des qualités du cœur,
et de l'esprit, qui le font estimer partout, et l'on voit qu'il
a mis l'attention la plus sérieuse à les cultiver. L. est en
tout d'une impétuosité, qui ne connoit point de bornes ;
d'une vanité qui lui fait rechercher sans l'obtenir l'applau-
dissement de ceux pour qui son orgueil ne lui inspire que
du mépris ; et d'une ambition folle qui ne sert qu'à le
rendre ridicule, sans être accompagnée de cette constance
qui peut seule la faire réussir ; un air de philosophie sans
beaucoup de logique, et une affectation de savoir, soutenue
par une lecture vague et superficielle. Voilà cette homme
extraordinaire qui s'attire partout la haine, ou la pitié. Je
lui trouve cependant un fonds de génie naturel très au-
dessus de son rival Mais ici il sera tout aussi difficile de
retrancher qu'à ajouter. Je vois qu'il me goute beaucoup ;
peu-à-peu sans le savoir nous nous sommes trouvés extrêmement liés. Avec lui il n'y a point de milieu entre une
déclaration de guerre, et l'alliance la plus intime.

[1] Journal, Florence, Août 9, 1764.]—Cocchi à dîné
avec nous. Nous avons beaucoup causé, mais je ne lui
trouve pas le génie qu'on lui attribue, c'est peut-être
parceque les nôtres ne sont pas analogues. J'entrevois de
l'extravagance dans ses idées, de l'affectation dans ses
manières. Il se plaint à tout moment de sa pauvreté. Il
connoit peu la véritable dignité d'un homme de lettres.
S'il a beaucoup de science, elle est bornée à la physique.
Il m'a demandé si Lord Spenser ne pouvoit pas faire des
évêques, et m'a fait un conte de Lord Lyttelton (dont il
ne peut souffrir le fils) où il étoit question des Parlemens
de Campagne. Le soir nous avons suivi le Chevalier Mann
à trois assemblées chez la Comtesse de Gallo, chez la Mar-
quise Gerini, et chez le Duc Strozzi. Cette succession

journey through Sienna to Rome, where I arrived in
the beginning of October. (2) My temper is not very

rapide peut seule m'empêcher de m'ennuyer. Je ne parle
point la langue du pays. J'ignore leurs jeux. Les femmes
sont occupées de leurs Cicisbées, et les hommes paroissent
d'une indifférence extrême.

16.—J'avois oublié de marquer vers le milieu de
Juillet, que le Cardinal Stuart a passé à Florence pour
aller à Pise. C'est dans le Palais Corsini qu'il a logé.
Nous l'avons vu un instant à la Galerie, où il ne s'est
arrêté qu'une demie-heure. C'est un homme d'une petite
mine, et qui a l'air beaucoup plus vieux qu'il ne l'est en
effet. On le dit bon homme, mais excessivement bigot,
et sous le gouvernement des Jésuites. Un certain Abbé
Nicolini, fameux bel esprit, et tyran de la Crusca et bavard
impitoyable, lui a fait son cour, et l'a accompagné partout
avec autant de soin qu'il avoit suivi le Duc de York. Il est
fallu de fort peu que ces deux Sosies ne se soient rencontrés
aux Bains de Pise.

17.—Les deux MM. Damer, fils de Lord Milton, et petits-
fils du Duc de Dorset, sont arrivés. Ils sont tous les deux
fort jeunes, mais sans gouverneur. C'est une mode qui
commence à passer. Le gouverneur est toujours à charge,
et rarement utile ; et quant à la dépense il lui seroit difficile
d'épargner à son élève le quart de ses propres honoraires.

18.—Nous sommes allés avec l'Abbé Pilori pour voir la
Bibliothèque Magliabecchiana, trésor amassé par ce
fameux bibliothécaire des grands Ducs, qu'ils ont depuis
rendu publique. Elle consiste en 40 à 50 mille volumes,
rassemblés dans un assez beau vase. Il est singulier qu'un
particulier d'une fortune des plus médiocres ait pu rassembler un trésor digne des plus grands princes. Mais que
ne pouvoit une vie très longue dont tous les momens
n'avoient qu'un objet unique ? Magliabecchi étoit, pour
parler ainsi, la Mémoire personalisée : un esprit qui ne
pouvoit jamais travailler de lui-même, mais qui auroit été
un Indice parlant des plus utiles à un homme de génie,
occupé de quelque branche de littérature. J'ai vu dans
cette bibliothèque une preuve combien la vie entière de
cet homme étoit consacrée aux sciences. C'est son commerce épistolaire qui remplit centaines de volumes. On
y lit les noms les plus célèbres de l'Europe, et le nombre

susceptible of enthusiasm, and the enthusiasm which I do not feel I have ever scorned to affect. But, at

entier des correspondans monte à plus de trois mille deux cens. Je sens qu'ils n'ont pas été contemporains, mais il y a encore de quoi remplir tous les instans d'une vie ordinaire. Les Réponses de Magliabecchi sont en très petit nombre. On comprend facilement qu'il n'en pouvoit pas conserver beaucoup de copies ; mais on ne soutient point une telle correspondance sans en remplir exactement les devoirs. Peut-être qu'un habile homme pourroit faire dans ce repertoire immense un choix judicieux qui enricheroit l'histoire littéraire du siècle passé. La bibliothèque est plutôt utile que curieuse. Elle se distingue bien plus par les livres imprimés, que par les MSS. qui sont presque tous à St. Laurent. Il y a cependant un beau Recueil des Mathématiciens Grecs, dont il y en a plusieurs qui n'ont jamais été publiés ; une collection nombreuse des premières éditions du quinzième siècle, et un livre imprimé à Venise dans le seizième, qui est très précieux par sa rareté et par son sujet. C'est la Collection des Lois du Royaume de Jérusalem, qui sont passées dans le Royaume de Chypre sous la Maison de Lusignan, et qui paroissent s'y être conservées sous le gouvernement des Vénétiens. Ce livre est en Italien, et ne peut être par conséquent qu'une traduction. J'y ai vu la confirmation d'une circonstance racontée par tous les historiens, que Godefroi de Bouillon n'avoit jamais voulu se faire couronner pour ne pas porter une couronne d'or, dans les lieux même où son Dieu en avoit porté une d'épines. Ce livre a été ignoré de tous les savans. On croit même que Muratori ne le connoissoit pas. Il pourroit servir pour l'histoire des Croisades. De là nous sommes allés à l'église de Santa Croce. L'architecture n'a rien de considérable pour l'architecture : mais ce n'a pas été sans un respect secret que j'ai considéré les tombeaux de Galilée, et de Michel Ange, du restaurateur des arts, et de celui de la philosophie : génies vraiment puissans et originaux. Ils ont illustré leur patrie mieux que les conquérans et les politiques. Les Tartares ont eu un Jenghiz Khan, et les Goths un Alaric, mais nous détournons nos yeux des déserts ensanglantés de la Scythie pour les fixer avec plaisir sur Athènes et sur Florence.

29.—Nous sommes allés en corps avec le Chevalier

the distance of twenty-five years, I can neither forget nor express the strong emotions which agitated my

Mann, pour faire visite au Maréchal Botta, qui est arrivé aujourdhui de Vienne, en dix jours. C'est une course un peu forte pour un vieillard qui a soixante dix-sept ans, mais il paroît encore vert et vigoureux. Il nous a reçu poliment, mais il n'a parlé qu'au chevalier. C'est un homme singulier, qui s'est élevé aux plus grands emplois à force de bévues. Il a eu des ambassades brillantes, et des commandemens d'armées. Aujourdhui il est feld-maréchal, colonel d'un régiment d'infanterie, chef de la régence de Toscane, et vicaire-général de l'empire en Italie. On se plaint beaucoup de sa hauteur et de son avarice. Il se refuse aux dépenses les plus nécessaires pour envoyer beaucoup d'argent à Vienne, et dans sept ou huit ans, qu'il a gouverné la Toscane, il n'a rien fait pour le bien du pays. On compare cette conduite à celle de son prédécesseur le Comte de Richecourt, qui a dignement représenté son prince ; qui a conclu un concordat très-avantageux avec la cour de Rome, supprimé l'inquisition, borné le nombre et la richesse des couvens par une loi de *mortmain*, qui a fait de grand chemin à Bologne, &c., &c.

Septembre 1.—Le Chevalier Mann, comme à l'ordinaire. J'y ai vu un Baron Prussien, dont je ne sais pas le nom. Il y a quatre ou cinq ans qu'il voyage. Il a été en Angleterre, et parle très bon Anglois. Il me paroît joli garçon, et ne manque point de sens. J'ai causé avec lui sur son roi. Il est permis d'être curieux sur le compte d'un pareil homme. Je vois qu'il l'admire plus qu'il ne l'aime. A-t-il tort ? Un de ses oncles s'est fait hacher en pièces pour ne pas essuyer les reproches durs et inévitables de son maître de ce qu'il n'avoit pas fait l'impossible. Le Roi de Prusse se pique de se connoître en physionomie, science qu'il estime, et qui doit plaire aux rois, parcequ'il semble leur donner les connoissances intentives d'un Etre supérieur. Le roi méprise tout homme qui paroît intimidé en sa présence. Mais ne distingueroit-il point entre le courtisan qui tremble devant un roi, et l'homme qui sent la supériorité d'un grand homme ?

Pise, Septembre 24.—J'ai trouvé à Pise mon parent le commandant Acton, avec son neveu, qui nous

mind as I first approached and entered the *eternal city*. After a sleepless night, I trod, with a lofty step, the ruins of the Forum; each memorable spot where Romulus *stood*, or Tully spoke, or Caesar fell, was at once present to my eye; and several days of intoxication were lost or enjoyed before I could descend to a cool and minute investigation. My guide was Mr. Byers, a Scotch antiquary of experience and taste; but, in the daily labour of eighteen weeks, the powers of attention were sometimes fatigued, till I was myself qualified, in a last review, to select and study the capital works of ancient and modern art. Six weeks were borrowed for my tour of Naples, the most populous of cities, relative to its size, whose luxurious inhabitants seem to dwell on the confines of paradise and hell-fire. I was presented to the boy-king by our new envoy, Sir William Hamilton; who, wisely diverting his correspondence from the Secretary of State to the Royal Society and British Museum, has elucidated a country of such inestimable value to the naturalist and antiquarian. On my return, I fondly embraced, for the last time, the miracles of Rome; but I departed without kissing the foot of Rezzonico (Clement XIII), who neither possessed the wit of his predecessor Lambertini, nor the virtues of his successor Ganganelli. (3) In my pilgrimage from Rome to Loretto I again crossed the Apennine; from the coast of the Adriatic I traversed a fruitful and populous country, which could alone disprove the paradox of Montesquieu, that modern Italy is a desert. Without adopting the exclusive prejudice of the natives, I sincerely admire the paint-

ont comblé de politesses. Je plains beaucoup ce pauvre vieillard.' A l'âge de soixante ans il se trouve abandonné de tous les Anglois pour avoir changé de religion; accablé d'infirmité, sans espérance de revoir son pays, il se fixe parmi un peuple dont il n'a jamais pu apprendre la langue. Dans l'univers entier il ne lui reste que son neveu, dont la réputation a beaucoup souffert du changement de son oncle, qu'on attribue à son manège.

ings of the Bologna school. I hastened to escape from
the sad solitude of Ferrara, which in the age of Caesar
was still more desolate. The spectacle of Venice
afforded some hours of astonishment; the University
of Padua is a dying taper; but Verona still boasts
her amphitheatre, and his native Vicenza is adorned
by the classic architecture of Palladio: the road of
Lombardy and Piedmont (did Montesquieu find them
without inhabitants?) led me back to Milan, Turin,
and the passage of Mount Cenis, where I again crossed
the Alps in my way to Lyons.

The use of foreign travel has been often debated as
a general question; but the conclusion must be finally
applied to the character and circumstances of each
individual. With the education of boys, *where* or *how*
they may pass over some juvenile years with the least
mischief to themselves or others, I have no concern.
But after supposing the previous and indispensable
requisites of age, judgement, a competent knowledge
of men and books, and a freedom from domestic
prejudices, I will briefly describe the qualifications
which I deem most essential to a traveller. He should
be endowed with an active, indefatigable vigour of
mind and body, which can seize every mode of conveyance, and support, with a careless smile, every
hardship of the road, the weather, or the inn. The
benefits of foreign travel will correspond with the
degrees of these qualifications; but, in this sketch,
those to whom I am known will not accuse me of
framing my own panegyric. It was at Rome, on the
15th of October, 1764, as I sat musing amidst the
ruins of the Capitol, while the barefooted friars were
singing vespers in the Temple of Jupiter[1], that the
idea of writing the decline and fall of the city first
started to my mind. But my original plan was cir-
cumscribed to the decay of the city rather than of
the empire: and, though my reading and reflections

---

[1] Now the church of the Zocolants, or Franciscan
Friars. S.

began to point towards that object, some years elapsed, and several avocations intervened, before I was seriously engaged in the execution of that laborious work.

I had not totally renounced the southern provinces of France, but the letters which I found at Lyons were expressive of some impatience. Rome and Italy had satiated my curious appetite, and I was now ready to return to the peaceful retreat of my family and books. After a happy fortnight I reluctantly left Paris, embarked at Calais, again landed at Dover, after an interval of two years and five months, and hastily drove through the summer dust and solitude of London. On the 25th of June, 1765, I arrived at my father's house; and the five years and a half between my travels and my father's death (1770) are the portion of my life which I passed with the least enjoyment, and which I remember with the least satisfaction. Every spring I attended the monthly meeting and exercise of the militia at Southampton; and by the resignation of my father, and the death of Sir Thomas Worsley, I was successively promoted to the rank of major and lieutenant-colonel commandant; but I was each year more disgusted with the inn, the wine, the company, and the tiresome repetition of annual attendance and daily exercise. At home, the economy of the family and farm still maintained the same creditable appearance. My connexion with Mrs. Gibbon was mellowed into a warm and solid attachment; my growing years abolished the distance that might yet remain between a parent and a son, and my behaviour satisfied my father, who was proud of the success, however imperfect in his own lifetime, of my literary talents. Our solitude was soon and often enlivened by the visit of the friend of my youth, Mr. Deyverdun, whose absence from Lausanne I had sincerely lamented. About three years after my first departure, he had emigrated from his native lake to the banks of the Oder in Germany. The *res angusta domi*, the waste of a decent patrimony, by an im-

provident father, obliged him, like many of his countrymen, to confide in his own industry; and he was
entrusted with the education of a young prince, the
grandson of the Margrave of Schavedt, of the Royal
Family of Prussia. Our friendship was never cooled,
our correspondence was sometimes interrupted; but
I rather wished than hoped to obtain Mr. Deyverdun
for the companion of my Italian tour. An unhappy,
though honourable passion, drove him from his German
court; and the attractions of hope and curiosity were
fortified by the expectation of my speedy return to
England. During four successive summers he passed
several weeks or months at Buriton, and our free
conversations, on every topic that could interest the
heart or understanding, would have reconciled me to
a desert or a prison. In the winter months of London
my sphere of knowledge and action was somewhat
enlarged, by the many new acquaintance which I had
contracted in the militia and abroad; and I must
regret, as more than an acquaintance, Mr. Godfrey
Clarke of Derbyshire, an amiable and worthy young
man, who was snatched away by an untimely death.
A weekly convivial meeting was established by myself
and other travellers, under the name of the Roman
Club.[1]

The renewal, or perhaps the improvement, of my
English life was embittered by the alteration of my
own feelings. At the age of twenty-one I was, in
my proper station of a youth, delivered from the yoke
of education, and delighted with the comparative
state of liberty and affluence. My filial obedience

---

[1] The members were Lord Mountstuart (now Marquis
of Bute), Colonel Edmonstone, Wm. Weddal, Rev. Mr. Pal-
grave, Earl of Berkley, Godfrey Clarke (Member for Derbyshire), Holroyd (Lord Sheffield), Major Ridley, Thomas
Charles Bigge, Sir William Guize, Sir John Aubrey, the
late Earl of Abingdon, Hon. Peregrine Bertie, Rev. Mr.
Cleaver, Hon. John Damer, Hon. George Damer (late Earl
of Dorchester), Sir Thomas Gascoygne, Sir John Hort,
E. Gibbon. S.

was natural and easy; and in the gay prospect of futurity, my ambition did not extend beyond the enjoyment of my books, my leisure, and my patrimonial estate, undisturbed by the cares of a family and the duties of a profession. But in the militia I was armed with power; in my travels, I was exempt from control; and as I approached, as I gradually passed my thirtieth year, I began to feel the desire of being master in my own house. The most gentle authority will sometimes frown without reason, the most cheerful submission will sometimes murmur without cause; and such is the law of our imperfect nature, that we must either command or obey; that our personal liberty is supported by the obsequiousness of our own dependants. While so many of my acquaintance were married or in parliament, or advancing with a rapid step in the various roads of honour and fortune, I stood alone, immovable and insignificant; for after the monthly meeting of 1770, I had even withdrawn myself from the militia, by the resignation of an empty and barren commission. My temper is not susceptible of envy, and the view of successful merit has always excited my warmest applause. The miseries of a vacant life were never known to a man whose hours were insufficient for the inexhaustible pleasures of study. But I lamented that at the proper age I had not embraced the lucrative pursuits of the law or of trade, the chances of civil office or India adventure, or even the fat slumbers of the church; and my repentance became more lively as the loss of time was more irretrievable. Experience showed me the use of grafting my private consequence on the importance of a great professional body; the benefits of those firm connexions which are cemented by hope and interest, by gratitude and emulation, by the mutual exchange of services and favours. From the emoluments of a profession I might have derived an ample fortune, or a competent income, instead of being stinted to the same narrow allowance, to be increased only by an event which I sincerely deprecated.

The progress and the knowledge of our domestic disorders aggravated my anxiety, and I began to apprehend that I might be left in my old age without the fruits either of industry or inheritance.

In the first summer after my return, whilst I enjoyed at Buriton the society of my friend Deyverdun, our daily conversations expatiated over the field of ancient and modern literature ; and we freely discussed my studies, my first Essay, and my future projects. The *Decline and Fall of Rome* I still contemplated at an awful distance : but the two historical designs which had balanced my choice were submitted to his taste ; and in the parallel between the Revolutions of Florence and Switzerland, our common partiality for a country which was *his* by birth, and *mine* by adoption, inclined the scale in favour of the latter. According to the plan, which was soon conceived and digested, I embraced a period of two hundred years, from the association of the three peasants of the Alps to the plenitude and prosperity of the Helvetic body in the sixteenth century. I should have described the deliverance and victory of the Swiss, who have never shed the blood of their tyrants but in a field of battle ; the laws and manners of the confederate states ; the splendid trophies of the Austrian, Burgundian, and Italian wars ; and the wisdom of a nation, which, after some sallies of martial adventure, has been content to guard the blessings of peace with the sword of freedom.

> ——Manus haec inimica tyrannis
> Ense petit placidam sub libertate quietem.

My judgement, as well as my enthusiasm, was satisfied with the glorious theme ; and the assistance of Deyverdun seemed to remove an insuperable obstacle. The French or Latin memorials, of which I was not ignorant, are inconsiderable in number and weight ; but in the perfect acquaintance of my friend with the German language, I found the key of a more valuable collection. The most necessary books were procured ;

he translated, for my use, the folio volume of Schilling, a copious and contemporary relation of the war of Burgundy; we read and marked the most interesting parts of the great chronicle of Tschudi; and by his labour, or that of an inferior assistant, large extracts were made from the *History* of Lauffer and the *Dictionary* of Lew; yet such was the distance and delay, that two years elapsed in these preparatory steps; and it was late in the third summer (1767) before I entered, with these slender materials, on the more agreeable task of composition. A specimen of my History, the first book, was read the following winter in a literary society of foreigners in London; and as the author was unknown, I listened, without observation, to the free strictures, and unfavourable sentence, of my judges.[1] The momentary sensation was painful; but their condemnation was ratified by my cooler thoughts. I delivered my imperfect sheets

---

[1] Mr. Hume seems to have had a different opinion of this work.

FROM MR. HUME TO MR. GIBBON.

SIR,

It is but a few days ago since M. Deyverdun put your manuscript into my hands, and I have perused it with great pleasure and satisfaction. I have only one objection, derived from the language in which it is written. Why do you compose in French, and carry faggots into the wood, as Horace says with regard to Romans who wrote in Greek? I grant that you have a like motive to those Romans, and adopt a language much more generally diffused than your native tongue: but have you not remarked the fate of those two ancient languages in following ages? The Latin, though then less celebrated, and confined to more narrow limits, has in some measure outlived the Greek, and is now more generally understood by men of letters. Let the French, therefore, triumph in the present diffusion of their tongue. Our solid and increasing establishments in America, where we need less dread the inundation of Barbarians, promise a superior stability and duration to the English language.

Your use of the French tongue has also led you into

to the flames[1], and for ever renounced a design in which some expense, much labour, and more time, had been so vainly consumed. I cannot regret the loss of a slight and superficial essay, for such the work must have been in the hands of a stranger, uninformed by the scholars and statesmen, and remote from the libraries and archives of the Swiss republics. My ancient habits, and the presence of Deyverdun, encouraged me to write in French for the continent of Europe; but I was conscious myself that my style, above prose and below poetry, degenerated into a verbose and turgid declamation. Perhaps I may impute the failure to the injudicious choice of a foreign language. Perhaps I may suspect that the language itself is ill adapted to sustain the vigour and dignity of an important narrative. But if France, so rich in literary merit, had produced a great original historian, his genius would have formed and fixed the idiom to the proper tone, the peculiar mode of historical eloquence.

a style more poetical and figurative, and more highly coloured, than our language seems to admit of in historical productions: for such is the practice of French writers, particularly the more recent ones, who illuminate their pictures more than custom will permit us. On the whole, your History, in my opinion, is written with spirit and judgement; and I exhort you very earnestly to continue it. The objections that occurred to me on reading it were so frivolous, that I shall not trouble you with them, and should, I believe, have a difficulty to recollect them. I am, with great esteem,

Sir,

Your most obedient,

London,   and most humble Servant,
24th of Oct. 1767.   (Signed) DAVID HUME.

[1] He neglected to burn them. He left at Sheffield Place the introduction, or first book, in forty-three pages folio, written in a very small hand, besides a considerable number of notes. Mr. Hume's opinion, expressed in the letter in the last note, perhaps may justify the publication of it. S.

It was in search of some liberal and lucrative employment that my friend Deyverdun had visited England. His remittances from home were scanty and precarious. My purse was always open, but it was often empty; and I bitterly felt the want of riches and power, which might have enabled me to correct the errors of his fortune. His wishes and qualifications solicited the station of the travelling governor of some wealthy pupil; but every vacancy provoked so many eager candidates, that for a long time I struggled without success; nor was it till after much application that I could even place him as a clerk in the office of the Secretary of State. In a residence of several years he never acquired the just pronunciation and familiar use of the English tongue, but he read our most difficult authors with ease and taste: his critical knowledge of our language and poetry was such as few foreigners have possessed; and few of our countrymen could enjoy the theatre of Shakespeare and Garrick with more exquisite feeling and discernment. The consciousness of his own strength, and the assurance of my aid, emboldened him to imitate the example of Dr. Maty, whose *Journal Britannique* was esteemed and regretted; and to improve his model, by uniting with the transactions of literature a philosophic view of the arts and manners of the British nation. Our Journal for the year 1767, under the title of *Mémoires Littéraires de la Grande Bretagne,* was soon finished and sent to the press. For the first article, Lord Lyttelton's *History of Henry II,* I must own myself responsible; but the public has ratified my judgement of that voluminous work, in which sense and learning are not illuminated by a ray of genius. The next specimen was the choice of my friend, *The Bath Guide,* a light and whimsical performance, of local, and even verbal, pleasantry. I started at the attempt: he smiled at my fears: his courage was justified by success; and a master of both languages will applaud the curious felicity with which he has transfused into French prose the spirit, and even the humour, of the English

verse. It is not my wish to deny how deeply I was
interested in these Memoirs, of which I need not surely
be ashamed ; but at the distance of more than twenty
years, it would be impossible for me to ascertain the
respective shares of the two associates. A long and
intimate communication of ideas had cast our sentiments and style in the same mould. In our social
labours we composed and corrected by turns ; and
the praise which I might honestly bestow, would fall
perhaps on some article or passage most properly my
own. A second volume (for the year 1768) was
published of these Memoirs. I will presume to say
that their merit was superior to their reputation ;
but it is not less true that they were productive of
more reputation than emolument. They introduced
my friend to the protection, and myself to the acquaintance, of the Earl of Chesterfield, whose age and infirmities secluded him from the world ; and of Mr. David
Hume, who was under-secretary to the office in which
Deyverdun was more humbly employed. The former
accepted a dedication (April 12, 1769), and reserved
the author for the future education of his successor :
the latter enriched the Journal with a reply to Mr.
Walpole's *Historical Doubts*, which he afterwards
shaped into the form of a note. The materials of the
third volume were almost completed, when I recommended Deyverdun as governor to Sir Richard Worsley,
a youth, the son of my old lieutenant-colonel who was
lately deceased. They set forwards on their travels,
nor did they return to England till some time after
my father's death.

My next publication was an accidental sally of love
and resentment ; of my reverence for modest genius,
and my aversion for insolent pedantry. The sixth
book of the *Aeneid* is the most pleasing and perfect
composition of Latin poetry. The descent of Aeneas
and the Sybil to the infernal regions, to the world of
spirits, expands an awful and boundless prospect,
from the nocturnal gloom of the Cumaean grot,

  Ibant obscuri sola sub nocte per umbram,

to the meridian brightness of the Elysian fields ;

> Largior hic campos aether et lumine vestit
> Purpureo ———

from the dreams of simple nature, to the dreams, alas! of Egyptian theology, and the philosophy of the Greeks. But the final dismission of the hero through the ivory gate, whence

> Falsa ad coelum mittunt insomnia manes,

seems to dissolve the whole enchantment and leaves the reader in a state of cold and anxious scepticism. This most lame and impotent conclusion has been variously imputed to the taste or irreligion of Virgil ; but, according to the more elaborate interpretation of Bishop Warburton, the descent to hell is not a false, but a mimic scene ; which represents the initiation of Aeneas, in the character of a lawgiver, to the Eleusinian mysteries. This hypothesis, a singular chapter in the *Divine Legation of Moses*, had been admitted by many as true ; it was praised by all as ingenious ; nor had it been exposed, in a space of thirty years, to a fair and critical discussion. The learning and the abilities of the author had raised him to a just eminence ; but he reigned the dictator and tyrant of the world of literature. The real merit of Warburton was degraded by the pride and presumption with which he pronounced his infallible decrees ; in his polemic writings he lashed his antagonists without mercy or moderation ; and his servile flatterers (see the base and malignant *Essay on the Delicacy of Friendship* [1]), exalting the master critic far above Aristotle and Longinus, assaulted every modest dissenter who refused to consult the oracle, and to adore the idol. In a land of liberty, such despotism must provoke a general opposition, and the zeal of opposition is seldom candid or impartial. A late professor of Oxford (Dr. Lowth), in a pointed and polished epistle (August 31, 1765), defended himself, and attacked

[1] By Hurd, afterwards Bishop of Worcester.

the Bishop ; and, whatsoever might be the merits of
an insignificant controversy, his victory was clearly
established by the silent confusion of Warburton and
his slaves. *I* too, without any private offence, was
ambitious of breaking a lance against the giant's
shield ; and in the beginning of the year 1770, my
Critical Observations on the Sixth Book of the Aeneid
were sent, without my name, to the press. In this
short essay, my first English publication, I aimed my
strokes against the person and the hypothesis of
Bishop Warburton. I proved, at least to my own
satisfaction, *that* the ancient lawgivers did not invent
the mysteries, and *that* Aeneas was never invested
with the office of lawgiver : *that* there is not any
argument, any circumstance, which can melt a fable
into allegory, or remove the scene from the Lake
Avernus to the Temple of Ceres : *that* such a wild
supposition is equally injurious to the poet and the
man : *that* if Virgil was not initiated he could not, if
he were he would not, reveal the secrets of the initiation : *that* the anathema of Horace (*vetabo qui Cereris
sacrum vulgarit*, &c.) at once attests his own ignorance
and the innocence of his friend. As the Bishop of
Gloucester and his party maintained a discreet silence,
my critical disquisition was soon lost among the
pamphlets of the day ; but the public coldness was
overbalanced to my feelings by the weighty approbation of the last and best editor of Virgil, Professor
Heyne of Gottingen, who acquiesces in my confutation,
and styles the unknown author, *doctus . . . et elegantis-
simus Britannus*. But I cannot resist the temptation
of transcribing the favourable judgement of Mr.
Hayley, himself a poet and a scholar : ' An intricate
hypothesis, twisted into a long and laboured chain of
quotation and argument, the Dissertation on the
Sixth Book of Virgil, remained some time unrefuted.
. . . At length, a superior, but anonymous, critic
arose, who, in one of the most judicious and spirited
essays that our nation has produced, on a point of
classical literature, completely overturned this ill-

founded edifice, and exposed the arrogance and futility of its assuming architect'. He even condescends to justify an acrimony of style, which had been gently blamed by the more unbiassed German; ' *Paullo acrius quam velis . . . perstrinxit* '.[1] But I cannot forgive myself the contemptuous treatment of a man who, with all his faults, was entitled to my esteem [2]; and I can less forgive, in a personal attack, the cowardly concealment of my name and character.

In the fifteen years between my *Essay on the Study of Literature* and the first volume of the *Decline and Fall* (1761–1776), this criticism on Warburton, and some articles in the Journal, were my sole publications. It is more especially incumbent on me to mark the employment, or to confess the waste of time, from my travels to my father's death, an interval in which I was not diverted by any professional duties from the labours and pleasures of a studious life. (1) As soon as I was released from the fruitless task of the Swiss revolutions (1768), I began gradually to advance from the wish to the hope, from the hope to the design, from the design to the execution, of my historical work, of whose limits and extent I had yet a very inadequate notion. The Classics, as low as Tacitus, the younger Pliny, and Juvenal, were my old and familiar companions. I insensibly plunged into the

---

[1] The editor of the *Warburtonian Tracts*, Dr. Parr (p. 192), considers the allegorical interpretation ' as completely refuted in a most clear, elegant, and decisive work of criticism ; which could not, indeed, derive authority from the greatest name : but to which the greatest name might with propriety have been affixed '.

[2] *The Divine Legation of Moses* is a monument, already crumbling in the dust, of the vigour and weakness of the human mind. If Warburton's new argument proved anything, it would be a demonstration against the legislator, who left his people without the knowledge of a future state. But some episodes of the work, on the Greek philosophy, the hieroglyphics of Egypt, &c., are entitled to the praise of learning, imagination, and discernment.

ocean of the Augustan history ; and in the descending
series I investigated, with my pen almost always in
my hand, the original records, both Greek and Latin,
from Dion Cassius to Ammianus Marcellinus, from the
reign of Trajan to the last age of the Western Caesars.
The subsidiary rays of medals, and inscriptions of
geography and chronology, were thrown on their
proper objects ; and I applied the collections of Tille-
mont, whose inimitable accuracy almost assumes the
character of genius, to fix and arrange within my
reach the loose and scattered atoms of historical
information.   Through the darkness of the middle
ages I explored my way in the Annals and Antiquities
of Italy of the learned Muratori ; and diligently
compared them with the parallel or transverse lines
of Sigonius and Maffei, Baronius and Pagi, till I almost
grasped the ruins of Rome in the fourteenth century,
without suspecting that this final chapter must be
attained by the labour of six quartos and twenty
years.   Among the books which I purchased, the
Theodosian Code, with the commentary of James
Godefroy, must be gratefully remembered; I used it
(and much I used it) as a work of history, rather than
of jurisprudence : but in every light it may be considered as a full and capacious repository of the political
state of the empire in the fourth and fifth centuries.
As I believed, and as I still believe, that the propagation
of the Gospel, and the triumph of the Church, are
inseparably connected with the decline of the Roman
monarchy, I weighed the causes and effects of the
revolution, and contrasted the narratives and apologies
of the Christians themselves, with the glances of candour
or enmity which the Pagans have cast on the rising
sects.   The Jewish and heathen testimonies, as they
are collected and illustrated by Dr. Lardner, directed,
without superseding, my search of the originals ; and
in an ample dissertation on the miraculous darkness
of the passion, I privately drew my conclusions from
the silence of an unbelieving age.   I have assembled
the preparatory studies, directly or indirectly relative

to my history; but, in strict equity, they must be spread beyond this period of my life, over the two summers (1771 and 1772) that elapsed between my father's death and my settlement in London. (2) In a free conversation with books and men, it would be endless to enumerate the names and characters of all who are introduced to our acquaintance; but in this general acquaintance we may select the degrees of friendship and esteem. According to the wise maxim, *Multum legere potius quam multa*, I reviewed, again and again, the immortal works of the French and English, the Latin and Italian classics. My Greek studies (though less assiduous than I designed) maintained and extended my knowledge of that incomparable idiom. Homer and Xenophon were still my favourite authors; and I had almost prepared for the press an *Essay on the Cyropaedia*, which, in my own judgement, is not unhappily laboured. After a certain age, the new publications of merit are the sole food of the many; and the most austere student will often be tempted to break the line, for the sake of indulging his own curiosity, and of providing the topics of fashionable currency. A more respectable motive may be assigned for the third perusal of Blackstone's *Commentaries*, and a copious and critical abstract of that English work was my first serious production in my native language. (3) My literary leisure was much less complete and independent than it might appear to the eye of a stranger. In the hurry of London I was destitute of books; in the solitude of Hampshire I was not master of my time. My quiet was gradually disturbed by our domestic anxiety, and I should be ashamed of my unfeeling philosophy had I found much time to waste for study in the last fatal summer (1770) of my father's decay and dissolution.

The disembodying of the militia at the close of the war (1763) had restored the Major (a new Cincinnatus) to a life of agriculture. His labours were useful, his pleasures innocent, his wishes moderate; and my father *seemed* to enjoy the state of happiness which is celebrated by poets and philosophers, as the most agreeable to nature, and the least accessible to fortune.

> Beatus ille, qui procul negotiis
> (Ut prisca gens mortalium)
> Paterna rura bubus exercet suis,
> Solutus omni foenore.[1]   Hor. *Epod.* ii.

But the last indispensable condition, the freedom from debt, was wanting to my father's felicity ; and the vanities of his youth were severely punished by the solicitude and sorrow of his declining age. The first mortgage, on my return from Lausanne (1758), had afforded him a partial and transient relief. The annual demand of interest and allowance was a heavy deduction from his income ; the militia was a source of expense, the farm in his hands was not a profitable adventure, he was loaded with the costs and damages of an obsolete lawsuit ; and each year multiplied the number, and exhausted the patience, of his creditors. Under these painful circumstances I consented to an additional mortgage, to the sale of Putney, and to every sacrifice that could alleviate his distress. But he was no longer capable of a rational effort, and his reluctant delays postponed not the evils themselves, but the remedies of those evils (*remedia malorum potius quam mala differebat*). The pangs of shame, tenderness, and self-reproach, incessantly preyed on his vitals ; his constitution was broken ; he lost his strength and his sight : the rapid progress of a dropsy admonished him of his end, and he sunk into the grave on the 10th of November, 1770, in the sixty-fourth year of his age. A family tradition insinuates that Mr. William Law had drawn his pupil in the light and inconstant character of *Flatus*, who is ever con-

---

[1] Like the first mortals, blest is he,
From debts, and usury, and business free,
With his own team who ploughs the soil,
Which grateful once confess'd his father's toil.

Francis.

fident, and ever disappointed in the chase of happiness. But these constitutional failings were happily compensated by the virtues of the head and heart, by the warmest sentiments of honour and humanity. His graceful person, polite address, gentle manners, and unaffected cheerfulness, recommended him to the favour of every company; and in the change of times and opinions, his liberal spirit had long since delivered him from the zeal and prejudice of a Tory education. I submitted to the order of nature; and my grief was soothed by the conscious satisfaction that I had discharged all the duties of filial piety.

As soon as I had paid the last solemn duties to my father, and obtained, from time and reason, a tolerable composure of mind, I began to form a plan of an independent life, most adapted to my circumstances and inclination. Yet so intricate was the net, my efforts were so awkward and feeble, that nearly two years (November, 1770—October, 1772) were suffered to elapse before I could disentangle myself from the management of the farm, and transfer my residence from Buriton to a house in London. During this interval I continued to divide my year between town and the country; but my new situation was brightened by hope; my stay in London was prolonged into the summer; and the uniformity of the summer was occasionally broken by visits and excursions at a distance from home. The gratification of my desires (they were not immoderate) has been seldom disappointed by the want of money or credit; my pride was never insulted by the visit of an importunate tradesman; and my transient anxiety for the past or future has been dispelled by the studious or social occupation of the present hour. My conscience does not accuse me of any act of extravagance or injustice, and the remnant of my estate affords an ample and honourable provision for my declining age. I shall not expatiate on my economical affairs, which cannot be instructive or amusing to the reader. It is a rule of prudence, as well as of politeness, to reserve such confidence for the ear of a private friend, without exposing our situation to the envy or pity of strangers; for envy is productive of hatred, and pity borders too nearly on contempt. Yet I may believe, and even assert, that in circumstances more indigent or more wealthy, I should never have accomplished the task, or acquired the fame, of an historian; that my spirit would have been broken by poverty and contempt, and that my industry might have been relaxed in the labour and luxury of a superfluous fortune.

I had now attained the first of earthly blessings, independence: I was the absolute master of my hours and actions: nor was I deceived in the hope that the establishment of my library in town would allow me to divide the day between study and society. Each year the circle of my acquaintance, the number of my dead and living companions, was enlarged. To a lover of books, the shops and sales of London present irresistible temptations; and the manufacture of my History required a various and growing stock of materials. The militia, my travels, the House of Commons, the fame of an author contributed to multiply my connexions: I was chosen a member of the fashionable clubs; and, before I left England in 1783, there were few persons of any eminence in the literary or political world to whom I was a stranger.[1] It would most assuredly be in my power to amuse the

---

[1] From the mixed, though polite company of Boodle's, White's and Brooks's, I must honourably distinguish a weekly society, which was instituted in the year 1764, and which still continues to flourish, under the title of the Literary Club. (Hawkins's *Life of Johnson*, p. 415; Boswell's *Tour to the Hebrides*, p. 97.) The names of Dr. Johnson, Mr. Burke, Mr. Topham Beauclerc, Mr. Garrick, Dr. Goldsmith, Sir Joshua Reynolds, Mr. Colman, Sir William Jones, Dr. Percy, Mr. Fox, Mr. Sheridan, Mr. Adam Smith, Mr. Steevens, Mr. Dunning, Sir Joseph Banks, Dr. Warton, and his brother Mr. Thomas Warton, Dr. Burney, &c., form a large and luminous constellation of British stars.

reader with a gallery of portraits and a collection of anecdotes. But I have always condemned the practice of transforming a private memorial into a vehicle of satire or praise. By my own choice I passed in town the greatest part of the year; but whenever I was desirous of breathing the air of the country, I possessed an hospitable retreat at Sheffield Place in Sussex, in the family of my valuable friend Mr. Holroyd, whose character, under the name of Lord Sheffield, has since been more conspicuous to the public.

No sooner was I settled in my house and library, than I undertook the composition of the first volume of my *History*. At the outset all was dark and doubtful; even the title of the work, the true era of the *Decline and Fall of the Empire*, the limits of the introduction, the division of the chapters, and the order of the narrative; and I was often tempted to cast away the labour of seven years. The style of an author should be the image of his mind, but the choice and command of language is the fruit of exercise. Many experiments were made before I could hit the middle tone between a dull chronicle and a rhetorical declamation: three times did I compose the first chapter, and twice the second and third, before I was tolerably satisfied with their effect. In the remainder of the way I advanced with a more equal and easy pace; but the fifteenth and sixteenth chapters have been reduced by three successive revisals from a large volume to their present size; and they might still be compressed, without any loss of facts or sentiments. An opposite fault may be imputed to the concise and superficial narrative of the first reigns from Commodus to Alexander; a fault of which I have never heard, except from Mr. Hume in his last journey to London. Such an oracle might have been consulted and obeyed with rational devotion; but I was soon disgusted with the modest practice of reading the manuscript to my friends. Of such friends some will praise from politeness, and some will criticize from vanity. The author himself is the best judge of his own performance ; no one has so deeply meditated on the subject ; no one is so sincerely interested in the event.

By the friendship of Mr. (now Lord) Eliot, who had married my first cousin, I was returned at the general election for the borough of Leskeard. I took my seat at the beginning of the memorable contest between Great Britain and America, and supported, with many a sincere and silent vote, the rights, though not, perhaps, the interest, of the mother-country. After a fleeting illusive hope, prudence condemned me to acquiesce in the humble station of a mute. I was not armed by nature and education with the intrepid energy of mind and voice,

> Vincentem strepitus, et natum rebus agendis.

Timidity was fortified by pride, and even the success of my pen discouraged the trial of my voice.[1] But I assisted at the debates of a free assembly ; I listened to the attack and defence of eloquence and reason ; I had a near prospect of the characters, views, and passions of the first men of the age. The cause of government was ably vindicated by Lord North, a statesman of spotless integrity, a consummate master of debate, who could wield, with equal dexterity, the arms of reason and of ridicule. He was seated on the Treasury Bench between his Attorney and

[1] A French sketch of Mr. Gibbon's *Life*, written by himself, probably for the use of some foreign journalist or translator, contains no fact not mentioned in his English *Life*. He there describes himself with his usual candour. ‘ Depuis huit ans il a assisté aux délibérations les plus importantes, mais il ne s'est jamais trouvé *le courage*, ni *le talent*, de parler dans une assemblée publique.’ This sketch was written before the publication of his three last volumes, as in closing it he says of his *History* : ‘ Cette entreprise lui demande encore plusieurs années d'une application soutenue ; mais quelqu'en soit le succès, il trouve dans cette application même un plaisir toujours varié et toujours renaissant.’   S.

Solicitor-General, the two pillars of the law and state, *magis pares quam similes ;* and the minister might indulge in a short slumber, whilst he was upholden on either hand by the majestic sense of Thurlow, and the skilful eloquence of Wedderburne. From the adverse side of the house an ardent and powerful opposition was supported by the lively declamation of Barré, the legal acuteness of Dunning, the profuse and philosophic fancy of Burke, and the argumentative vehemence of Fox, who, in the conduct of a party, approved himself equal to the conduct of an empire. By such men every operation of peace and war, every principle of justice or policy, every question of authority and freedom, was attacked and defended ; and the subject of the momentous contest was the union or separation of Great Britain and America. The eight sessions that I sat in parliament were a school of civil prudence, the first and most essential virtue of an historian.

The volume of my *History*, which had been somewhat delayed by the novelty and tumult of a first session, was now ready for the press. After the perilous adventure had been declined by my friend Mr. Elmsly, I agreed, upon easy terms, with Mr. Thomas Cadell, a respectable bookseller, and Mr. William Strahan, an eminent printer ; and they undertook the care and risk of the publication, which derived more credit from the name of the shop than from that of the author. The last revisal of the proofs was submitted to my vigilance ; and many blemishes of style, which had been invisible in the manuscript, were discovered and corrected in the printed sheet. So moderate were our hopes, that the original impression had been stinted to five hundred, till the number was doubled by the prophetic taste of Mr. Strahan. During this awful interval I was neither elated by the ambition of fame, nor depressed by the apprehension of contempt. My diligence and accuracy were attested by my own conscience. History is the most popular species of writing, since it can adapt itself to the highest or the lowest capacity. I had chosen an illustrious subject. Rome is familiar to the schoolboy and the statesman; and my narrative was deduced from the last period of classical reading. I had likewise flattered myself, that an age of light and liberty would receive, without scandal, an inquiry into the human *causes* of the progress and establishment of Christianity.

I am at a loss how to describe the success of the work, without betraying the vanity of the writer. The first impression was exhausted in a few days; a second and third edition were scarcely adequate to the demand; and the bookseller's property was twice invaded by the pirates of Dublin. My book was on every table, and almost on every toilette; the historian was crowned by the taste or fashion of the day; nor was the general voice disturbed by the barking of any *profane* critic. The favour of mankind is most freely bestowed on a new acquaintance of any original merit; and the mutual surprise of the public and their favourite is productive of those warm sensibilities, which at a second meeting can no longer be rekindled. If I listened to the music of praise, I was more seriously satisfied with the approbation of my judges. The candour of Dr. Robertson embraced his disciple. A letter from Mr. Hume overpaid the labour of ten years; but I have never presumed to accept a place in the triumvirate of British historians.

That curious and original letter will amuse the reader, and his gratitude should shield my free communication from the reproach of vanity.

'Edinburgh, March 18, 1776.

' DEAR SIR,

' As I ran through your volume of history with great avidity and impatience, I cannot forbear discovering somewhat of the same impatience in returning you thanks for your agreeable present, and expressing the satisfaction which the performance has given me. Whether I consider the dignity of your style, the depth of your matter, or the extensiveness of your learning, I must regard the work as equally the object of esteem ; and I own that if I had not previously had the happiness of your personal acquaintance, such a performance from an Englishman in our age would have given me some surprise. You may smile at this sentiment, but as it seems to me that your countrymen, for almost a whole generation, have given themselves up to barbarous and absurd faction, and have totally neglected all polite letters, I no longer expected any valuable production ever to come from them. I know it will give you pleasure (as it did me) to find that all the men of letters in this place concur in their admiration of your work, and in their anxious desire of your continuing it.

' When I heard of your undertaking (which was some time ago), I own I was a little curious to see how you would extricate yourself from the subject of your two last chapters. I think you have observed a very prudent temperament ; but it was impossible to treat the subject so as not to give grounds of suspicion against you, and you may expect that a clamour will arise. This, if anything, will retard your success with the public ; for in every other respect your work is calculated to be popular. But among many other marks of decline, the prevalence of superstition in England prognosticates the fall of philosophy and decay of taste ; and though nobody be more capable than you to revive them, you will probably find a struggle in your first advances.

' I see you entertain a great doubt with regard to the authenticity of the poems of Ossian. You are certainly right in so doing. It is indeed strange that any men of sense could have imagined it possible, that above twenty thousand verses, along with numberless historical facts, could have been preserved by oral tradition during fifty generations, by the rudest, perhaps, of all the European nations, the most necessitous, the most turbulent, and the most unsettled. Where a supposition is so contrary to common sense, any positive evidence of it ought never to be regarded. Men run with great avidity to give their evidence in favour of what flatters their passions and their national prejudices.   You are therefore over and above indulgent to us in speaking of the matter with hesitation.

'I must inform you that we are all very anxious to hear that you have fully collected the materials for your second volume, and that you are even considerably advanced in the composition of it.   I speak this more in the name of my friends than in my own, as I cannot expect to live so long as to see the publication of it.   Your ensuing volume will be more delicate than the preceding, but I trust in your prudence for extricating you from the difficulties ; and, in all events, you have courage to despise the clamour of bigots.

I am, with great regard,
Dear Sir,
Your most obedient, and most humble Servant,
DAVID HUME.'

Some weeks afterwards I had the melancholy pleasure of seeing Mr. Hume in his passage through London ; his body feeble, his mind firm.   On the 25th of August of the same year (1776) he died, at Edinburgh, the death of a philosopher.

My second excursion to Paris was determined by the pressing invitation of M. and Madame Necker, who had visited England in the preceding summer. On my arrival I found M. Necker Director-General of the finances, in the first bloom of power and popularity. His private fortune enabled him to support a liberal establishment ; and his wife, whose talents and virtues I had long admired, was admirably qualified to preside in the conversation of her table and drawing-room.   As their friend, I was introduced to the best company of both sexes, to the foreign ministers of all nations, and to the first names and characters of France, who distinguished me by such marks of civility and kindness as gratitude will not suffer me

to forget, and modesty will not allow me to enumerate.
The fashionable suppers often broke into the morning
hours ; yet I occasionally consulted the Royal Library,
and that of the Abbey of St. Germain, and in the
free use of their books at home I had always reason
to praise the liberality of those institutions. The
society of men of letters I neither courted nor declined,
but I was happy in the acquaintance of M. de Buffon,
who united with a sublime genius the most amiable
simplicity of mind and manners. At the table of my
old friend, M. de Forcemagne, I was involved in a
dispute with the Abbé de Mably ; and his jealous
irascible spirit revenged itself on a work which he was
incapable of reading in the original.

As I might be partial in my own cause, I shall
transcribe the words of an unknown critic, observing
only, that this dispute had been preceded by another
on the English constitution, at the house of the Countess
de Froulay, an old Jansenist lady.

'Vous étiez chez M. de Forcemagne, mon cher
Théodon, le jour que M. l'Abbé de Mably et M. Gibbon
y dinèrent en grande compagnie. La conversation
roula presque entièrement sur l'histoire. L'Abbé,
étant un profond politique, la tourna sur l'administration, quand on fut au dessert ; et comme par
caractère, par humeur, par l'habitude d'admirer Tite
Live, il ne prise que le système républicain, il se mit
à vanter l'excellence des républiques ; bien persuadé
que le savant Anglois l'approuveroit en tout, et
admireroit la profondeur de génie qui avoit fait deviner
tous ces avantages à un François. Mais M. Gibbon,
instruit par l'expérience des inconvéniens d'un gouvernement populaire, ne fut point du tout de son
avis, et il prit généreusement la défense du gouvernement monarchique. L'Abbé voulut le convaincre par
Tite Live, et par quelques argumens tirés de Plutarque
en faveur des Spartiates. M. Gibbon, doué de la
mémoire la plus heureuse, et ayant tous les faits présens
à la pensée, domina bientôt la conversation ; l'Abbé
se fâcha, il s'emporta, il dit des choses dures ; l'Anglois,

conservant le phlegme de son pays, prenoit ses avantages, et pressoit l'Abbé avec d'autant plus de succès
que la colère le troubloit de plus en plus. La conversation s'échauffoit, et M. de Forcemagne la rompit
en se levant de table, et en passant dans le salon, où
personne ne fut tenté de la renouer.' *Supplément à
la Manière d'écrire l'Histoire*, p. 125, &c.[1]

Nearly two years had elapsed between the publication of my first and the commencement of my second
volume ; and the causes must be assigned of this long
delay. (1) After a short holiday, I indulged my
curiosity in some studies of a very different nature,
a course of anatomy, which was demonstrated by
Doctor Hunter, and some lessons of chemistry, which
were delivered by Mr. Higgins. The principles of
these sciences, and a taste for books of natural history,
contributed to multiply my ideas and images ; and
the anatomist and chemist may sometimes track me
in their own snow. (2) I dived, perhaps too deeply,
into the mud of the Arian controversy ; and many

[1] Of the voluminous writings of the Abbé de Mably
(see his Eloge by the Abbé Brizard), the *Principes du droit
public de l'Europe*, and the first part of the *Observations
sur l'Histoire de France*, may be deservedly praised ; and
even the *Manière d'écrire l'Histoire* contains several useful
precepts and judicious remarks. Mably was a lover of
virtue and freedom ; but his virtue was austere, and his
freedom was impatient of an equal. Kings, magistrates,
nobles, and successful writers, were the objects of his contempt, or hatred, or envy ; but his illiberal abuse of
Voltaire, Hume, Buffon, the Abbé Reynal, Dr. Robertson,
and *tutti quanti*, can be injurious only to himself.

'Est il rien de plus fastidieux (says the polite Censor)
qu'un M. Gibbon, qui dans son éternelle *Histoire des
Empereurs Romains*, suspend à chaque instant son insipide
et lente narration, pour vous expliquer la cause des faits
que vous allez lire ?' (*Manière d'écrire l'Histoire*, p. 184.
See another passage, p. 280.) Yet I am indebted to the
Abbé de Mably for two such advocates as the anonymous
French Critic and my friend Mr. Hayley. (Hayley's
Works, 8vo. edit., vol. ii, p. 261-3).

days of reading, thinking, and writing were consumed in the pursuit of a phantom. (3) It is difficult to arrange, with order and perspicuity, the various trans- actions of the age of Constantine; and so much was I displeased with the first essay, that I committed to the flames above fifty sheets. (4) The six months of Paris and pleasure must be deducted from the account. But when I resumed my task I felt my improvement; I was now master of my style and subject, and while the measure of my daily performance was enlarged, I discovered less reason to cancel or correct. It has always been my practice to cast a long paragraph in a single mould, to try it by my ear, to deposit it in my memory, but to suspend the action of the pen till I had given the last polish to my work. Shall I add, that I never found my mind more vigorous, nor my composition more happy, than in the winter hurry of society and parliament?

Had I believed that the majority of English readers were so fondly attached even to the name and shadow of Christianity; had I foreseen that the pious, the timid, and the prudent, would feel, or affect to feel, with such exquisite sensibility, I might, perhaps, have softened the two invidious chapters, which would create many enemies, and conciliate few friends. But the shaft was shot, the alarm was sounded, and I could only rejoice, that if the voice of our priests was clamor- ous and bitter, their hands were disarmed from the powers of persecution. I adhered to the wise reso- lution of trusting myself and my writings to the candour of the public, till Mr. Davies of Oxford pre- sumed to attack, not the faith, but the fidelity, of the historian. *My Vindication*, expressive of less anger than contempt, amused for a moment the busy and idle metropolis; and the most rational part of the laity, and even of the clergy, appear to have been satisfied of my innocence and accuracy. I would not print this Vindication in quarto, lest it should be bound and preserved with the history itself. At the distance of twelve years, I calmly affirm my judgement of Davies, Chelsum, &c. A victory over such antagonists was a sufficient humiliation. They, however, were rewarded in this world. Poor Chelsum was indeed neglected; and I dare not boast the making Dr. Watson a bishop; he is a prelate of a large mind and liberal spirit: but I enjoyed the pleasure of giving a royal pension to Mr. Davies, and of collating Dr. Apthorpe to an archiepiscopal living. Their success encouraged the zeal of Taylor the Arian [1], and Milner the Methodist [2], with many others, whom it would be difficult to remember, and tedious to rehearse. The list of my adversaries, however, was graced with the more respectable names of Dr. Priestley, Sir David Dalrymple, and Dr. White; and every polemic, of either University, discharged his sermon or pamphlet against the impenetrable silence of the Roman historian. In his *History of the Corruptions of Christianity*, Dr. Priestley threw down his two gauntlets to Bishop Hurd and Mr. Gibbon. I declined the challenge in a letter, exhorting my opponent to enlighten the world by his philosophical discoveries, and to remember that the merit of his predecessor Servetus is now reduced to a single passage, which indicates the smaller circulation of the blood through the lungs, from and to the heart.[3] Instead of listening to this friendly advice, the dauntless philosopher of Birmingham

[1] The stupendous title, *Thoughts on the Causes of the grand Apostasy*, at first agitated my nerves, till I discovered that it was the apostasy of the whole Church, since the Council of Nice, from Mr. Taylor's private religion. His book is a thorough mixture of *high* enthusiasm and *low* buffoonery, and the Millennium is a fundamental article of his creed.

[2] From his grammar school at Kingston-upon-Hull, Mr. Joseph Milner pronounces an anathema against all rational religion. *His* faith is a divine taste, a spiritual inspiration; *his* church is a mystic and invisible body; the *natural* Christians, such as Mr. Locke, who believe and interpret the Scriptures, are, in his judgement, no better than profane infidels.

[3] *Astrue de la Structure du Cœur*, tom. i, 77, 79.

continued to fire away his double battery against those who believed too little, and those who believed too much. *From my* replies he has nothing to hope or fear: but his Socinian shield has repeatedly been pierced by the mighty spear of Horsley, and his trumpet of sedition may at length awaken the magistrates of a free country.

The profession and rank of Sir David Dalrymple (now a Lord of Session) has given a more decent colour to his style. But he scrutinized each separate passage of the two chapters with the dry minuteness of a special pleader; and as he was always solicitous to make, he may have succeeded sometimes in finding, a flaw. In his *Annals of Scotland*, he has shown himself a diligent collector and an accurate critic.

I have praised, and I still praise, the eloquent sermons which were preached in St. Mary's pulpit at Oxford by Dr. White. If he assaulted me with some degree of illiberal acrimony, in such a place, and before such an audience, he was obliged to speak the language of the country. I smiled at a passage in one of his private letters to Mr. Badcock: 'The part where we encounter Gibbon must be brilliant and striking'.

In a sermon preached before the University of Cambridge, Dr. Edwards complimented a work, 'which can only perish with the language itself'; and esteems the author a formidable enemy. He is, indeed, astonished that more learning and ingenuity has not been shown in the defence of Israel; that the prelates and dignitaries of the Church (alas, good man!) did not vie with each other whose stone should sink the deepest in the forehead of this Goliath.

'But the force of truth will oblige us to confess, that in the attacks which have been levelled against our sceptical historian, we can discover but slender traces of profound and exquisite erudition, of solid criticism and accurate investigation; but we are too frequently disgusted by vague and inconclusive reasoning; by unseasonable banter and senseless witticisms;

by embittered bigotry and enthusiastic jargon; by futile cavils and illiberal invectives. Proud and elated by the weakness of his antagonists, he condescends not to handle the sword of controversy '.[1]

Let me frankly own that I was startled at the first discharge of ecclesiastical ordnance; but as soon as I found that this empty noise was mischievous only in the intention, my fear was converted into indignation; and every feeling of indignation or curiosity has long since subsided in pure and placid indifference.

The prosecution of my history was soon afterwards checked by another controversy of a very different kind. At the request of the Lord Chancellor, and of Lord Weymouth, then Secretary of State, I vindicated, against the French manifesto, the justice of the British arms. The whole correspondence of Lord Stormont, our late ambassador at Paris, was submitted to my inspection, and the *Mémoire Justificatif*, which I composed in French, was first approved by the Cabinet Ministers, and then delivered as a State paper to the courts of Europe. The style and manner are praised by Beaumarchais himself, who, in his private quarrel, attempted a reply; but he flatters me, by ascribing the memoir to Lord Stormont; and the grossness of his invective betrays the loss of temper and of wit; he acknowledged [2] that *le style ne serait pas sans grace, ni la logique sans justesse*, &c., if the facts were true which he undertakes to disprove. For these facts my credit is not pledged; I spoke as a lawyer from my brief, but the veracity of Beaumarchais may be estimated from the assertion that France, by the treaty of Paris (1763), was limited to a certain number of ships of war. On the application of the Duke of Choiseul, he was obliged to retract this daring falsehood.

Among the honourable connexions which I had formed, I may justly be proud of the friendship of

[1] *Monthly Review*, Oct., 1790.
[2] *Oeuvres de Beaumarchais*, tom. iii, pp. 299, 355.

Mr. Wedderburne, at that time Attorney-General, who now illustrates the title of Lord Loughborough, and the office of Chief Justice of the Common Pleas. By his strong recommendation, and the favourable disposition of Lord North, I was appointed one of the Lords Commissioners of Trade and Plantations; and my private income was enlarged by a clear addition of between seven and eight hundred pounds a year. The fancy of an hostile orator may paint, in the strong colours of ridicule, ' the perpetual virtual adjournment, and the unbroken sitting vacation of the Board of Trade '.[1] But it must be allowed that our duty was not intolerably severe, and that I enjoyed many days and weeks of repose, without being called away from my library to the office. My acceptance of a place provoked some of the leaders of the opposition, with whom I had lived in habits of intimacy[2]; and I was

[1] I can never forget the delight with which that diffusive and ingenious orator, Mr. Burke, was heard by all sides of the house, and even by those whose existence he proscribed. (See Mr. Burke's speech on the Bill of Reform, pp. 72-80.) The Lords of Trade blushed at their insignificancy, and Mr. Eden's appeal to the two thousand five hundred volumes of our Reports served only to excite a general laugh. I take this opportunity of certifying the correctness of Mr. Burke's printed speeches, which I have heard and read.

[2] It has always appeared to me, that nothing could be more unjustifiable than the manner in which some persons allowed themselves to speak of Mr. Gibbon's acceptance of an office at the Board of Trade. I can conceive that he may carelessly have used strong expressions in respect to some, or all parties; but he never meant that such expressions should be taken literally; and I know, beyond all possibility of question, that he was so far from being ' in a state of savage hostility towards Lord North ', as it is savagely expressed by Mr. Whitaker, that he always loved and esteemed him. I saw Mr. Gibbon constantly at this time, and was well acquainted with all his political opinions. And although he was not perfectly satisfied with *every* measure, yet he uniformly supported all the *principal ones*

most unjustly accused of deserting a party, in which I had never enlisted.[1]

regarding the American war; and considered himself, and, indeed, was a friend to Administration to the very period of his accepting office. He liked the brilliant society of a club, the most distinguished members of which were notorious for their opposition to Government, and might be led, in some degree, to join in their language; but Mr. Gibbon had little, I had almost said no political acrimony in his character. If the opposition of that or any other time could claim for their own every person who was not perfectly satisfied with all the measures of Government, their party would unquestionably have been more formidable. S.

[1] FROM EDWARD GIBBON, ESQ., TO EDWARD ELLIOT, ESQ., OF PORT ELLIOT (AFTERWARDS LORD ELLIOT).

DEAR SIR, July 2, 1779.

Yesterday I received a very interesting communication from my friend the Attorney-General[a], whose kind and honourable behaviour towards me I must always remember with the highest gratitude. He informed me that, in consequence of an arrangement, a place at the Board of Trade was reserved for me, and that as soon as I signified my acceptance of it, he was satisfied no further difficulties would arise. My answer to him was sincere and explicit. I told him that I was far from approving all the past measures of the administration, even some of those in which I myself had silently concurred; that I saw, with the rest of the world, many capital defects in the characters of some of the present ministers, and was sorry that in so alarming a situation of public affairs, the country had not the assistance of several able and honest men who are now in opposition. But that I had not formed with any of those persons in opposition any engagements or connexions which could in the least restrain or affect my parliamentary conduct; that I could not discover among them such superior advantages, either of measures or of abilities, as could make me consider it as a duty to attach myself to their cause; and that I clearly understood, from the

[a] Alexander Wedderburne, since created Lord Loughborough, Earl of Roslin, and Lord Chancellor.

The aspect of the next session of parliament was stormy and perilous ; county meetings, petitions, and committees of correspondence, announced the public discontent ; and instead of voting with a triumphant majority, the friends of government were often exposed to a struggle, and sometimes to a defeat. The House of Commons adopted Mr. Dunning's motion, 'That the influence of the Crown had increased, was increasing, and ought to be diminished' : and Mr. Burke's bill of reform was framed with skill, introduced with eloquence, and supported by numbers. Our late president, the American Secretary of State, very narrowly escaped the sentence of proscription ; but the unfortunate Board of Trade was abolished in the committee by a small majority (207 to 199) of eight votes. The storm, however, blew over for a time ; a large defection of country gentlemen eluded the sanguine hopes of the patriots : the Lords of Trade were revived ; administration recovered their strength

public and private language of one of their leaders (Charles Fox), that in the actual state of the country, he himself was seriously of opinion that opposition could not tend to any good purpose, and might be productive of much mischief ; that, for those reasons, I saw no objections which could prevent me from accepting an office under the present government, and that I was ready to take a step which I found to be consistent both with my interest and my honour.

It must now be decided whether I may continue to live in England or whether I must soon withdraw myself into a kind of philosophical exile in Switzerland. My father left his affairs in a state of embarrassment, and even of distress. My attempts to dispose of a part of my landed property have hitherto been disappointed, and are not likely at present to be more successful ; and my plan of expense, though moderate in itself, deserves the name of extravagance, since it exceeds my real income. The addition of the salary which is now offered will make my situation perfectly easy ; but I hope you will do me the justice to believe that my mind could not be so, unless I were satisfied of the rectitude of my own conduct. S.

and spirit; and the flames of London, which were
kindled by a mischievous madman, admonished all
thinking men of the danger of an appeal to the people.
In the premature dissolution which followed this
session of parliament I lost my seat. Mr. Elliot was
now deeply engaged in the measures of opposition,
and the electors of Leskeard [1] are commonly of the
same opinion as Mr. Elliot.

In this interval of my senatorial life, I published the
second and third volumes of the *Decline and Fall*.
My ecclesiastical history still breathed the same spirit
of freedom; but Protestant zeal is more indifferent
to the characters and controversies of the fourth and
fifth centuries. My obstinate silence had damped
the ardour of the polemics. Dr. Watson, the most
candid of my adversaries, assured me that he had
no thoughts of renewing the attack, and my impartial
balance of the virtues and vices of Julian was generally
praised. This truce was interrupted only by some
animadversions of the Catholics of Italy, and by some
angry letters from Mr. Travis, who made me personally
responsible for condemning, with the best critics, the
spurious text of the three heavenly witnesses.

The piety or prudence of my Italian translator has
provided an antidote against the poison of his original.
The fifth and seventh volumes are armed with five
letters from an anonymous divine to his friends,
Foothead and Kirk, two English students at Rome;
and this meritorious service is commended by Monsignor Stonor, a prelate of the same nation, who
discovers much venom in the *fluid* and nervous style
of Gibbon. The critical essay at the end of the third
volume was furnished by the Abbate Nicola Spedalieri,
whose zeal has gradually swelled to a more solid
confutation in two quarto volumes.—Shall I be excused
for not having read them?

The brutal insolence of Mr. Travis's challenge can

---

[1] The borough which Mr. Gibbon had represented in
parliament.

only be excused by the absence of learning, judgement, and humanity ; and to that excuse he has the fairest or foulest pretension. Compared with Archdeacon Travis, Chelsum and Davies assume the title of respectable enemies.

The bigoted advocate of popes and monks may be turned over even to the bigots of Oxford ; and the wretched Travis still smarts under the lash of the merciless Porson. I consider Mr. Porson's answer to Archdeacon Travis as the most acute and accurate piece of criticism which has appeared since the days of Bentley. His strictures are founded in argument, enriched with learning, and enlivened with wit ; and his adversary neither deserves nor finds any quarter at his hands. The evidence of the three heavenly witnesses would now be rejected in any court of justice : but prejudice is blind, authority is deaf, and our vulgar bibles will ever be polluted by this spurious text, ' *sedet aeternumque sedebit*.' The more learned ecclesiastics will indeed have the secret satisfaction of reprobating in the closet what they read in the Church.

I perceived, and without surprise, the coldness and even prejudice of the town ; nor could a whisper escape my ear that, in the judgement of many readers, my continuation was much inferior to the original attempts. An author who cannot ascend will always appear to sink : envy was now prepared for my reception, and the zeal of my religious was fortified by the motive of my political enemies. Bishop Newton, in writing his own life, was at full liberty to declare how much he himself and two eminent brethren were disgusted by Mr. Gibbon's prolixity, tediousness, and affectation. But the old man should not have indulged his zeal in a false and feeble charge against the historian [1], who had faithfully and even

---

[1] EXTRACT FROM MR. GIBBON'S COMMONPLACE BOOK.

Thomas Newton, Bishop of Bristol and Dean of St. Paul's, was born at Litchfield on the 21st of December, 1703, O.S. (January 1, 1704, N.S.), and died the 14th of February, 1782,

cautiously rendered Dr. Burnet's meaning by the alternative of 'sleep or repose'. That philosophic

in the seventy-ninth year of his age. A few days before his death he finished the memoirs of his own life, which have been prefixed to an edition of his posthumous works, first published in quarto, and since (1787) re-published in six volumes octavo.

Pp. 173, 174. 'Some books were published in 1781, which employed some of the Bishop's leisure hours, and during his illness. Mr. Gibbon's *History of the Decline and Fall of the Roman Empire* he read throughout, but it by no means answered his expectation; for he found it rather a prolix and tedious performance, his matter uninteresting, and his style affected; his testimonies not to be depended upon, and his frequent scoffs at religion offensive to every sober mind. He had before been convicted of making false quotations, which should have taught him more prudence and caution. But, without examining his authorities, there is one which must necessarily strike every man who has read Dr. Burnet's Treatise *de Statû Mortuorum*. In vol. iii, p. 99, Mr. G. has the following note:—" Burnet (*de S. M.*, pp. 56–84) collects the opinions of the Fathers, as far as they assert the sleep or repose of human souls till the day of judgement. He afterwards exposes (p. 91) the inconveniences which must arise if they possessed a more active and sensible existence. Who would not from hence infer that Dr. B. was an advocate for the sleep or insensible existence of the soul after death ? whereas his doctrine is directly the contrary. He has employed some chapters in treating of the state of human souls in the interval between death and the resurrection; and after various proofs from reason, from scripture, and the Fathers, his conclusions are, that human souls exist after their separation from the body, that they are in a good or evil state according to their good or ill behaviour, but that neither their happiness nor their misery will be complete or perfect before the day of judgement. His argumentation is thus summed up at the end of the fourth chapter—*Ex quibus constat primo, animas superesse extincto corpore; secundo, bonas bene, malas male se habituras; tertio, nec illis summam felicitatem, nec his summam miseriam, accessuram esse ante diem judicii.*" (The Bishop's reading

divine supposes, that, in the period between death and the resurrection, human souls exist without a body,

the whole was a greater compliment to the work than was paid to it by two of the most eminent of his brethren for their learning and station. The one entered upon it, but was soon wearied, and laid it aside in disgust : the other returned it upon the bookseller's hands ; and it is said that Mr. G. himself happened unluckily to be in the shop at the same time.)'

Does the Bishop comply with his own precept in the next page ? (p. 175) ' Old age should lenify, should soften men's manners, and make them more mild and gentle ; but often has the contrary effect, hardens their hearts, and makes them more sour and crabbed.'—He is speaking of Dr. Johnson.

Have I ever insinuated that preferment-hunting is the great occupation of an ecclesiastical life (Memoirs passim) ? that a minister's influence and a bishop's patronage are sometimes pledged eleven deep (p. 151) ? that a prebendary considers the audit week as the better part of the year (p. 127) ? or that the most eminent of priests, the pope himself, would change their religion, if anything better could be offered them (p. 56) ? Such things are more than insinuated in the Bishop's *Life*, which afforded some scandal to the church, and some diversion to the profane laity.

None of the attacks from ecclesiastical antagonists were more malignant and illiberal than some strictures published in the *English Review*, October, 1788, &c., and afterwards reprinted in a separate volume, with the signature of John Whitaker, in 1791. I had mentioned them to Mr. Gibbon, when first published, but so far was he from supposing them worth his notice, that he did not even desire they should be sent to him, and he actually did not see them till his late visit to England a few months before his death. If Mr. Whitaker had only pointed his bitterness against Mr. Gibbon's *opinions*, perhaps no inquiry would have been made into the possible source of his collected virulence and deliberate malignity.

I have in my possession very amicable letters from the Rev. Mr. Whitaker to Mr. Gibbon, written some time after he had read the offensive fifteenth and sixteenth chapters of the *Decline and Fall*. When Mr. Gibbon came to

endowed with internal consciousness, but destitute of all active or passive connexion with the external world. 'Secundum communem dictionem sacrae scripturae, mors dicitur somnus, et morientes dicuntur *obdormire*, quod innuere mihi videtur statum mortis esse statum quietis, silentii, et ἀεργασίας' (*De Statu Mortuorum*, ch. v. p. 98).

I was, however, encouraged by some domestic and foreign testimonies of applause ; and the second and third volumes insensibly rose in sale and reputation to a level with the first. But the public is seldom wrong ; and I am inclined to believe that, especially in the beginning, they are more prolix and less entertaining than the first : my efforts had not been relaxed by success, and I had rather deviated into the opposite fault of minute and superfluous diligence. On the Continent, my name and writings were slowly diffused : a French translation of the first volume had disappointed the booksellers of Paris ; and a passage in the third was construed as a personal reflection on the reigning monarch.[1]

England, in 1787, he read Whitaker's *Mary Queen of Scots,* and I have heard him VERY *incautiously* express his opinion of it. Some *good-natured friend* mentioned it to Mr. Whitaker. It must be an extraordinary degree of resentment that could induce any person, of a liberal mind, to scrape together defamatory stories, true or false, and blend them with the defence of the most benign religion, whose precepts inculcate the very opposite practice. Religion receives her greatest injuries from those champions of the Church who, under the pretence of vindicating the Gospel, outrageously violate both the spirit and the letter of it.

Mr. Whitaker affects principally to review the fourth, fifth, and sixth volumes, but he has allotted the first month's review to an attack on the first three volumes, or rather on the first, which had been published twelve years and a half before it occurred to him that a review of it was necessary. S.

[1] It may not be generally known that Louis the Sixteenth is a great reader, and a reader of English books. On

Before I could apply for a seat at the general election the list was already full; but Lord North's promise was sincere, his recommendation was effectual, and I was soon chosen on a vacancy for the borough of Lymington, in Hampshire. In the first session of the new parliament, administration stood their ground; their final overthrow was reserved for the second. The American war had once been the favourite of the country: the pride of England was irritated by the resistance of her colonies, and the executive power was driven by national clamour into the most vigorous and coercive measures. But the length of a fruitless contest, the loss of armies, the accumulation of debt and taxes, and the hostile confederacy of France, Spain, and Holland, indisposed the public to the American war, and the persons by whom it was conducted; the representatives of the people followed, at a slow distance, the changes of their opinion; and the ministers, who refused to bend, were broken by the tempest. As soon as Lord North had lost, or was about to lose, a majority in the House of Commons, he surrendered his office, and retired to a private station, with the tranquil assurance of a clear conscience and a cheerful temper: the old fabric was dissolved, and the posts of government were occupied by the victorious and veteran troops of opposition. The lords of trade were not immediately dismissed, but the board itself was abolished by Mr. Burke's bill, which decency had compelled the patriots to revive; and I was stripped of a convenient salary, after having enjoyed it about three years.

perusing a passage of my *History* which seems to compare him to Arcadius or Honorius, he expressed his resentment to the Prince of B*****, from whom the intelligence was conveyed to me. I shall neither disclaim the allusion, nor examine the likeness; but the situation of the late King of France excludes all suspicion of flattery; and I am ready to declare that the concluding observations of my third volume were written before his accession to the throne.

So flexible is the title of my *History*, that the final era might be fixed at my own choice; and I long hesitated whether I should be content with the three volumes, the fall of the Western empire, which fulfilled my first engagement with the public. In this interval of suspense, nearly a twelvemonth, I returned by a natural impulse to the Greek authors of antiquity; I read with new pleasure the *Iliad* and the *Odyssey*, the *Histories* of Herodotus, Thucydides, and Xenophon, a large portion of the tragic and comic theatre of Athens, and many interesting dialogues of the Socratic school. Yet in the luxury of freedom I began to wish for the daily task, the active pursuit, which gave a value to every book, and an object to every inquiry: the preface of a new edition announced my design, and I dropped without reluctance from the age of Plato to that of Justinian. The original texts of Procopius and Agathias supplied the events and even the characters of his reign: but a laborious winter was devoted to the Codes, the Pandects, and the modern interpreters, before I presumed to form an abstract of the civil law. My skill was improved by practice, my diligence perhaps was quickened by the loss of office; and, excepting the last chapter, I had finished the fourth volume before I sought a retreat on the banks of the Leman Lake.

It is not the purpose of this narrative to expatiate on the public or secret history of the times: the schism which followed the death of the Marquis of Rockingham, the appointment of the Earl of Shelburne, the resignation of Mr. Fox, and his famous coalition with Lord North. But I may assert, with some degree of assurance, that in their political conflict those great antagonists had never felt any personal animosity to each other, that their reconciliation was easy and sincere, and that their friendship has never been clouded by the shadow of suspicion or jealousy. The most violent or venal of their respective followers embraced this fair occasion of revolt, but their alliance still commanded a majority in the House of Commons;

the peace was censured, Lord Shelburne resigned, and the two friends knelt on the same cushion to take the oath of Secretary of State. From a principle of gratitude I adhered to the coalition: my vote was counted in the day of battle, but I was overlooked in the division of the spoil. There were many claimants more deserving and importunate than myself: the Board of Trade could not be restored; and, while the list of places was curtailed, the number of candidates was doubled. An easy dismission to a secure seat at the Board of Customs or Excise was promised on the first vacancy: but the chance was distant and doubtful; nor could I solicit with much ardour an ignoble servitude, which would have robbed me of the most valuable of my studious hours[1]: at the same time the tumult of London, and the attendance on parliament, were grown more irksome; and, without some additional income, I could not long or prudently maintain the style of expense to which I was accustomed.

From my early acquaintance with Lausanne I had always cherished a secret wish that the school of my youth might become the retreat of my declining age.

---

[1] About the same time, it being in contemplation to send a secretary of embassy to Paris, Mr. Gibbon was a competitor for that office. (See Letter to and from Lord Thurlow.) The credit of being distinguished, and stopped by government when he was leaving England, the salary of £1,200 a year, the society of Paris, and the hope of a future provision for life, disposed him to renounce, though with much reluctance, an agreeable scheme on the point of execution; to engage, without experience, in a scene of business which he never liked; to give himself a master, or at least a principal, of an unknown, perhaps an unamiable character: to which might be added, the danger of the recall of the ambassador, or the change of ministry. Mr. Anthony Storer was preferred. Mr. Gibbon was somewhat indignant at the preference; but he never knew that it was the act of his friend Mr. Fox, contrary to the solicitations of Mr. Craufurd, and other of his friends. S.

A moderate fortune would secure the blessings of ease, leisure, and independence : the country, the people, the manners, the language, were congenial to my taste ; and I might indulge the hope of passing some years in the domestic society of a friend. After travelling with several English [1], Mr. Deyverdun was now settled at home, in a pleasant habitation, the gift of his deceased aunt : we had long been separated, we had long been silent ; yet in my first letter I exposed, with the most perfect confidence, my situation, my sentiments, and my designs. His immediate answer was a warm and joyful acceptance : the picture of our future life provoked my impatience ; and the terms of arrangement were short and simple, as he possessed the property, and I undertook the expense of our common house. Before I could break my English chain, it was incumbent on me to struggle with the feelings of my heart, the indolence of my temper, and the opinion of the world, which unanimously condemned this voluntary banishment. In the disposal of my effects, the library, a sacred deposit, was alone excepted. As my post-chaise moved over Westminster Bridge, I bade a long farewell to the ' fumum et opes strepitumque Romae '. My journey by the direct road through France was not attended with any accident, and I arrived at Lausanne nearly twenty years after my second departure. Within less than three months the coalition struck on some hidden rocks : had I remained on board, I should have perished in the general shipwreck.

Since my establishment at Lausanne, more than seven years have elapsed ; and if every day has not been equally soft and serene, not a day, not a moment, has occurred in which I have repented of my choice. During my absence, a long portion of human life, many changes had happened : my elder acquaintance had left the stage ; virgins were ripened into matrons,

[1] Sir Richard Worsley, Lord Chesterfield, Broderick Lord Midleton, and Mr. Hume, brother to Sir Abraham.

and children were grown to the age of manhood. But the same manners were transmitted from one generation to another : my friend alone was an inestimable treasure ; my name was not totally forgotten, and all were ambitious to welcome the arrival of a stranger and the return of a fellow-citizen. The first winter was given to a general embrace, without any nice discrimination of persons and characters. After a more regular settlement, a more accurate survey, I discovered three solid and permanent benefits of my new situation. (1) My personal freedom had been somewhat impaired by the House of Commons and the Board of Trade ; but I was now delivered from the chain of duty and dependence, from the hopes and fears of political adventure : my sober mind was no longer intoxicated by the fumes of party, and I rejoiced in my escape, as often as I read of the midnight debates which preceded the dissolution of parliament. (2) My English economy had been that of a solitary bachelor, who might afford some occasional dinners. In Switzerland I enjoyed at every meal, at every hour, the free and pleasant conversation of the friend of my youth ; and my daily table was always provided for the reception of one or two extraordinary guests. Our importance in society is less a positive than a relative weight : in London I was lost in the crowd ; I ranked with the first families of Lausanne, and my style of prudent expense enabled me to maintain a fair balance of reciprocal civilities. (3) Instead of a small house between a street and a stable-yard, I began to occupy a spacious and convenient mansion, connected on the north side with the city, and open on the south to a beautiful and boundless horizon. A garden of four acres had been laid out by the taste of Mr. Deyverdun : from the garden a rich scenery of meadows and vineyards descends to the Leman Lake, and the prospect far beyond the Lake is crowned by the stupendous mountains of Savoy. My books and my acquaintance had been first united in London ; but this happy position of my library in town and country was finally reserved for Lausanne. Possessed of every comfort in this triple alliance, I could not be tempted to change my habitation with the changes of the seasons.

My friends had been kindly apprehensive that I should not be able to exist in a Swiss town at the foot of the Alps, after having so long conversed with the first men of the first cities of the world. Such lofty connexions may attract the curious, and gratify the vain ; but I am too modest, or too proud, to rate my own value by that of my associates ; and whatsoever may be the fame of learning or genius, experience has shown me that the cheaper qualifications of politeness and good sense are of more useful currency in the commerce of life. By many, conversation is esteemed as a theatre or a school : but after the morning has been occupied by the labours of the library, I wish to unbend rather than to exercise my mind ; and in the interval between tea and supper I am far from disdaining the innocent amusement of a game at cards. Lausanne is peopled by a numerous gentry, whose companionable idleness is seldom disturbed by the pursuits of avarice or ambition : the women, though confined to a domestic education, are endowed for the most part with more taste and knowledge than their husbands and brothers : but the decent freedom of both sexes is equally remote from the extremes of simplicity and refinement. I shall add as a misfortune rather than a merit, that the situation and beauty of the Pays de Vaud, the long habits of the English, the medical reputation of Dr. Tissot, and the fashion of viewing the mountains and *Glaciers*, have opened us on all sides to the incursions of foreigners. The visits of Mr. and Madame Necker, of Prince Henry of Prussia, and of Mr. Fox, may form some pleasing exceptions ; but, in general, Lausanne has appeared most agreeable in my eyes, when we have been abandoned to our own society. I had frequently seen Mr. Necker, in the summer of 1784, at a country house near Lausanne, where he composed his Treatise on the Administration of the Finances. I have since, in October, 1790, visited him in his present residence, the castle and barony of Copet, near Geneva. Of the merits and measures of that statesman various opinions may be entertained; but all impartial men must agree in their esteem of his integrity and patriotism.

In the month of August, 1784, Prince Henry of Prussia, in his way to Paris, passed three days at Lausanne. His military conduct has been praised by professional men; his character has been vilified by the wit and malice of a demon [1]; but I was flattered by his affability, and entertained by his conversation.

In his tour to Switzerland (September, 1788) Mr. Fox gave me two days of free and private society. He seemed to feel, and even to envy, the happiness of my situation; while I admired the powers of a superior man, as they are blended in his attractive character with the softness and simplicity of a child. Perhaps no human being was ever more perfectly exempt from the taint of malevolence, vanity, or falsehood.

My transmigration from London to Lausanne could not be effected without interrupting the course of my historical labours. The hurry of my departure, the joy of my arrival, the delay of my tools, suspended their progress; and a full twelvemonth was lost before I could resume the thread of regular and daily industry. A number of books most requisite and least common had been previously selected; the academical library of Lausanne, which I could use as my own, contained at least the fathers and councils; and I have derived some occasional succour from the public collections of Berne and Geneva. The fourth volume was soon terminated, by an abstract of the controversies of the Incarnation, which the learned Dr. Prideaux was apprehensive of exposing to profane eyes. It had been the original design of the learned Dean Prideaux to write the history of the ruin of the Eastern Church. In this work it would have been necessary, not only to unravel all those controversies which the Christians made

[1] *Mémoire Secret de la Cour de Berlin,* par Mirabeau.

about the hypostatical union, but also to unfold all the
niceties and subtle notions which each sect entertained
concerning it.　The pious historian was apprehensive
of exposing that incomprehensible mystery to the
cavils and objections of unbelievers ; and he durst not,
' seeing the nature of this book, venture it abroad in so
wanton and lewd an age '.[1]

In the fifth and sixth volumes the revolutions of the
empire and the world are most rapid, various, and
instructive ; and the Greek or Roman historians are
checked by the hostile narratives of the barbarians of
the East and the West.[2]

It was not till after many designs, and many trials,
that I preferred, as I still prefer, the method of grouping
my picture by nations ; and the seeming neglect of
chronological order is surely compensated by the
superior merits of interest and perspicuity.　The style
of the first volume is, in my opinion, somewhat crude
and elaborate ; in the second and third it is ripened
into ease, correctness, and numbers ; but in the three
last I may have been seduced by the facility of my pen,
and the constant habit of speaking one language and
writing another may have infused some mixture of
Gallic idioms.　Happily for my eyes, I have always
closed my studies with the day, and commonly with
the morning ; and a long, but temperate, labour has
been accomplished, without fatiguing either the mind
or body ; but when I computed the remainder of my
time and my task, it was apparent that, according
to the season of publication, the delay of a month
would be productive of that of a year.　I was now
straining for the goal, and in the last winter many
evenings were borrowed from the social pleasures of

[1] See Preface to the *Life of Mahomet*, pp. 10, 11.
[2] I have followed the judicious precept of the Abbé de
Mably (*Manière d'écrire l'Histoire*, p. 110), who advises the
historian not to dwell too minutely on the decay of the
eastern empire ; but to consider the barbarian conquerors
as a more worthy subject of his narrative.　' Fas est et ab
hoste doceri.'

Lausanne. I could now wish that a pause, an interval, had been allowed for a serious revisal.

I have presumed to mark the moment of conception : I shall now commemorate the hour of my final deliverance. It was on the day, or rather night, of the 27th of June, 1787, between the hours of eleven and twelve, that I wrote the last lines of the last page, in a summer-house in my garden. After laying down my pen, I took several turns in a *berceau*, or covered walk of acacias, which commands a prospect of the country, the lake, and the mountains. The air was temperate, the sky was serene, the silver orb of the moon was reflected from the waters, and all nature was silent. I will not dissemble the first emotions of joy on recovery of my freedom, and, perhaps, the establishment of my fame. But my pride was soon humbled, and a sober melancholy was spread over my mind, by the idea that I had taken an everlasting leave of an old and agreeable companion, and that whatsoever might be the future date of my *History*, the life of the historian must be short and precarious. I will add two facts, which have seldom occurred in the composition of six, or at least of five quartos. (1) My first rough manuscript, without any intermediate copy, has been sent to the press. (2) Not a sheet has been seen by any human eyes, excepting those of the author and the printer : the faults and the merits are exclusively my own.[1]

I cannot help recollecting a much more extraordinary fact, which is affirmed of himself by Retif de la Bre-

---

[1] EXTRACT FROM MR. GIBBON'S COMMONPLACE BOOK.

The fourth volume of the *History of the Decline and Fall of the Roman Empire*	begun March 1, 1782—ended June, 1784.
The fifth volume . .	begun July, 1784—ended May 1, 1786.
The sixth volume . .	begun May 18, 1786—ended June 27, 1787.

These three volumes were sent to press August 15, 1787, and the whole impression was concluded April following.

torme, a voluminous and original writer of French
novels. He laboured, and may still labour, in the
humble office of corrector to a printing-house; but
this office enabled him to transport an entire volume
from his mind to the press; and his work was given
to the public without ever having been written by
the pen.

After a quiet residence of four years, during which
I had never moved ten miles from Lausanne, it was
not without some reluctance and terror that I undertook, in a journey of two hundred leagues, to cross
the mountains and the sea. Yet this formidable
adventure was achieved without danger or fatigue;
and at the end of a fortnight I found myself in Lord
Sheffield's house and library, safe, happy, and at
home. The character of my friend (Mr. Holroyd) had
recommended him to a seat in parliament for Coventry,
the command of a regiment of light dragoons, and an
Irish peerage. The sense and spirit of his political
writings have decided the public opinion on the great
questions of our commercial interest with America and
Ireland.[1]

The sale of his *Observations on the American States*
was diffusive, their effect beneficial; the Navigation
Act, the palladium of Britain, was defended, and
perhaps saved, by his pen; and he proves, by the
weight of fact and argument, that the mother-country
may survive and flourish after the loss of America.
My friend has never cultivated the arts of composition;
but his materials are copious and correct, and he
leaves on his paper the clear impression of an active
and vigorous mind. His *Observations on the Trade,
Manufactures, and present State of Ireland,* were
intended to guide the industry, to correct the prejudices, and to assuage the passions of a country which
seemed to forget that she could be free and prosperous
only by a friendly connexion with Great Britain. The
concluding observations are written with so much ease

---

[1] *Observations on the Commerce of the American States,* by
John Lord Sheffield, the 6th edition, London, 1784, in 8vo.

and spirit that they may be read by those who are the least interested in the subject.

He fell [1] (in 1784) with the unpopular coalition; but his merit has been acknowledged at the last general election, 1790, by the honourable invitation and free choice of the city of Bristol.[2] During the whole time of my residence in England, I was entertained at Sheffield Place and in Downing Street, by his hospitable kindness; and the most pleasant period was that which I passed in the domestic society of the family. In the larger circle of the metropolis I observed the country and the inhabitants with the knowledge, and without the prejudices, of an Englishman; but I rejoiced in the apparent increase of wealth and prosperity, which might be fairly divided between the spirit of the nation and the wisdom of the minister. All party-resentment was now lost in oblivion; since I was no man's rival, no man was my enemy. I felt the dignity of independence, and as I asked no more, I was satisfied with the general civilities of the world. The house in London which I frequented with most pleasure and assiduity was that of Lord North. After the loss of power and of sight, he was still happy in himself and his friends, and my public tribute of gratitude and esteem could no longer be suspected of any interested motive. Before my departure from England, I was present at the august spectacle of Mr. Hastings's trial in Westminster Hall. It is not my province to absolve or condemn the Governor of India [3]; but Mr. Sheridan's eloquence commanded my applause; nor could I hear without emotion the

[1] It is not obvious from whence he fell; he never held nor desired any office of emolument whatever, unless his military commissions, and the command of a regiment of light dragoons, which he raised himself, and which was disbanded on the peace in 1783, should be deemed such. S.

[2] See a Letter from Mr. Gibbon to Lord Sheffield, Lausanne, August 7, 1790. S.

[3] He considered the *persecution* of that highly respectable person to have arisen from party views. S.

personal compliment which he paid me in the presence of the British nation.[1]

From this display of genius, which blazed four successive days, I shall stoop to a very mechanical circumstance. As I was waiting in the manager's box, I had the curiosity to inquire of the shorthand writer, how many words a ready and rapid orator might pronounce in an hour ? From 7,000 to 7,500 was his answer. The medium of 7,200 will afford 120 words in a minute, and two words in each second. But this computation will only apply to the English language.

As the publication of my three last volumes was the principal object, so it was the first care of my English journey. The previous arrangements with the bookseller and the printer were settled in my passage through London, and the proofs, which I returned more correct, were transmitted every post from the press to Sheffield Place. The length of the operation, and the leisure of the country, allowed some time to review my manuscript. Several rare and useful books, the *Assises de Jerusalem*, *Ramusius de Bello C. P⁵ʳᵒ*, the *Greek Acts of the Synod of Florence*, the *Statuta Urbis Romae*, &c., were procured, and I introduced in their proper places the supplements which they afforded. The impression of the fourth volume had consumed three months. Our common interest required that we should move with a quicker pace ; and Mr. Strahan fulfilled his engagement, which few printers could sustain, of delivering every week three thousand copies of nine sheets. The day of publication was, however, delayed, that it might coincide with the fifty-first anniversary of my own birthday ; the double festival was celebrated by

---

[1] He said the facts that made up the volume of narrative were unparalleled in atrociousness, and that nothing equal in criminality was to be traced, either in ancient or modern history, in the correct periods of Tacitus or the luminous page of Gibbon. *Morning Chronicle*, June 14, 1788. S.

a cheerful literary dinner at Mr. Cadell's house; and
I seemed to blush while they read an elegant compliment from Mr. Hayley,[1] whose poetical talents had

[1] OCCASIONAL STANZAS, *by* MR. HAYLEY, *read after the
dinner at* MR. CADELL'S, May 8, 1788; *being the day of
the publication of the three last volumes of* MR. GIBBON'S
HISTORY, *and his Birthday.*

> Genii of England, and of Rome!
> In mutual triumph here assume
>   The honours each may claim!
> This social scene with smiles survey!
> And consecrate the festive day
>   To Friendship and to Fame!
>
> Enough, by Desolation's tide,
> With anguish, and indignant pride,
>   Has Rome bewail'd her fate;
> And mourn'd that Time, in Havoc's hour,
> Defaced each monument of power
>   To speak her truly great:
>
> O'er maim'd Polybius, just and sage,
> O'er Livy's mutilated page,
>   How deep was her regret!
> Touched by this Queen, in ruin grand,
> See! Glory, by an English hand,
>   Now pays a mighty debt:
>
> Lo! sacred to the Roman Name,
> And raised, like Rome's immortal Fame,
>   By Genius and by Toil,
> The splendid Work is crown'd to-day,
> On which Oblivion ne'er shall prey,
>   Not Envy make her spoil!
>
> England, exult! and view not now
> With jealous glance each nation's brow,
>   Where History's palm has spread!
> In every path of liberal art,
> Thy Sons to prime distinction start,
>   And no superior dread.
>
> Science for Thee a Newton raised;
> For thy renown a Shakespeare blazed,
>   Lord of the drama's sphere!

more than once been employed in the praise of his friend. Before Mr. Hayley inscribed with my name his epistles on history, I was not acquainted with that amiable man and elegant poet. He afterwards thanked me in verse for my second and third volumes [1]; and in the summer of 1781, the Roman Eagle [2] (a proud

> In different fields to equal praise
>   See History now thy Gibbon raise
>   To shine without a peer !
>
> Eager to honour living worth,
> And bless to-day the double birth,
>   That proudest joy may claim,
> Let artless Truth this homage pay,
> And consecrate the festive day
>   To Friendship and to Fame !

[1] SONNET TO EDWARD GIBBON, ESQ.

On the Publication of his Second and Third Volumes, 1781.

> With proud delight th' imperial founder gazed
>   On the new beauty of his second Rome,
> When on his eager eye rich temples blazed,
>   And his fair city rose in youthful bloom:
> A pride more noble may thy heart assume,
> O Gibbon ! gazing on thy growing work,
> In which, constructed for a happier doom,
> No hasty marks of vain ambition lurk:
> Thou may'st deride both Time's destructive sway,
> And baser Envy's beauty-mangling dirk ;
> Thy gorgeous fabric, planned with wise delay,
>   Shall baffle foes more savage than the Turk ;
> As ages multiply, its fame shall rise,
> And earth must perish ere its splendour dies.

[2] A CARD OF INVITATION TO MR. GIBBON AT BRIGHT-HELMSTONE, 1781.

> An English sparrow, pert and free,
> Who chirps beneath his native tree,
> Hearing the Roman eagle s near,
> And feeling more respect than fear,
> Thus, with united love and awe,
> Invites him to his shed of straw.

title) accepted the invitation of the English Sparrow, who chirped in the groves of Eartham, near Chichester. As most of the former purchasers were naturally desirous of completing their sets, the sale of the quarto edition was quick and easy ; and an octavo size was printed to satisfy at a cheaper rate the public demand. The conclusion of my work was generally read, and variously judged. The style has been exposed to much academical criticism ; a religious clamour was revived, and the reproach of indecency has been loudly echoed by the rigid censors of morals. I never could understand the clamour that has been raised against the indecency of my three last volumes. (1) An

> Tho' he is but a twittering sparrow,
> The field he hops in rather narrow,
> When nobler plumes attract his view
> He ever pays them homage due,
> He looks with reverential wonder,
> On him whose talons bear the thunder ;
> Nor could the Jackdaws e'er inveigle
> His voice to vilify the eagle,
> Tho' issuing from the holy towers,
> In which they build their warmest bowers,
> Their sovereign's haunt they slyly search,
> In hopes to catch him on his perch
> (For Pindar says, beside his God
> The thunder-bearing bird will nod),
> Then, peeping round his still retreat,
> They pick from underneath his feet
> Some molted feather he lets fall,
> And swear he cannot fly at all.——
>   Lord of the sky ! whose pounce can tear
> These croakers, that infest the air,
> Trust him ! the sparrow loves to sing
> The praise of thy imperial wing !
> He thinks thou'lt deem him, on his word,
> An honest, though familiar bird ;
> And hopes thou soon wilt condescend
> To look upon thy little friend ;
> That he may boast around his grove
> A visit from the bird of Jove.

equal degree of freedom in the former part, especially in the first volume, had passed without reproach. (2) I am justified in painting the manners of the times; the vices of Theodora form an essential feature in the reign and character of Justinian; and the most naked tale in my history is told by the Rev. Mr. Joseph Warton, an instructor of youth (*Essay on the Genius and Writings of Pope*, pp. 322–4). (3) My English text is chaste, and all licentious passages are left in the obscurity of a learned language. *Le Latin dans ses mots brave l'honnêteté*, says the correct Boileau, in a country and idiom more scrupulous than our own. Yet, upon the whole, the *History of the Decline and Fall* seems to have struck root, both at home and abroad, and may, perhaps, a hundred years hence still continue to be abused. I am less flattered by Mr. Porson's high encomium on the style and spirit of my history, than I am satisfied with his honourable testimony to my attention, diligence, and accuracy; those humble virtues, which religious zeal had most audaciously denied. The sweetness of his praise is tempered by a reasonable mixture of acid.[1] As the book may not be common in England, I shall transcribe my own character from the *Bibliotheca Historica* of Meuselius [2], a learned and laborious German. 'Summis aevi nostri historicis Gibbonus sine dubio adnumerandus est. Inter Capitolii ruinas stans primum hujus operis scribendi consilium cepit. Florentissimos vitae annos colligendo et laborando eidem impendit. Enatum inde monumentum aere perennius, licet passim appareant sinistrè dicta, minus perfecta, veritati non satis consentanea. Videmus quidem ubique fere studium scrutandi veritatemque scribendi maximum: tamen sine Tillemontio duce ubi scilicet hujus historia finitur saepius noster titubat atque hallucinatur. Quod vel maxime fit, ubi de rebus Ecclesiasticis vel de juris prudentiâ Romanâ (tom. iv) tradit, et in aliis locis.

---

[1] See his preface, pp. 28, 32.

[2] Vol. iv, part 1, pp. 342, 344.

Attamen naevi hujus generis haud impediunt quo minus operis summam et ὀικονομίαν praeclare dispositam, delectum rerum sapientissimum, argutum quoque interdum, dictionemque seu stylum historico aeque ac philosopho dignissimum, et vix à quoque alio Anglo, Humio ac Robertsono haud exceptis (*praereptum ?*), vehementer laudemus, atque saeculo nostro de hujusmodi historiâ gratulemur ... Gibbonus adversarios cum in tum extra patriam nactus est, quia propagationem religionis Christianae, non, ut vulgo fieri solet, aut more Theologorum, sed ut Historicum et Philosophum decet, exposuerat.'

The French, Italian, and German translations have been executed with various success ; but, instead of patronizing, I should willingly suppress such imperfect copies, which injure the character, while they propagate the name of the author. The first volume had been feebly, though faithfully, translated into French by M. Le Clerc de Septchenes, a young gentleman of a studious character and liberal fortune. After his decease the work was continued by two manufacturers of Paris, MM. Desmuniers and Cantwell : but the former is now an active member of the National Assembly, and the undertaking languishes in the hands of his associate. The superior merit of the interpreter, or his language, inclines me to prefer the Italian version : but I wish that it were in my power to read the German, which is praised by the best judges. The Irish pirates are at once my friends and my enemies. But I cannot be displeased with the too numerous and correct impressions which have been published for the use of the Continent at Basil in Switzerland.[1] The conquests of our language and literature are not confined to Europe alone, and a writer who succeeds

---

[1] Of their fourteen octavo volumes, the two last include the whole body of the notes. The public importunity had forced *me* to remove them from the end of the volume to the bottom of the page ; but I have often repented of my compliance.

in London is speedily read on the banks of the Delaware and the Ganges.

In the preface of the fourth volume, while I gloried in the name of an Englishman, I announced my approaching return to the neighbourhood of the Lake of Lausanne. This last trial confirmed my assurance that I had wisely chosen for my own happiness; nor did I once, in a year's visit, entertain a wish of settling in my native country. Britain is the free and fortunate island; but where is the spot in which I could unite the comforts and beauties of my establishment at Lausanne? The tumult of London astonished my eyes and ears; the amusements of public places were no longer adequate to the trouble; the clubs and assemblies were filled with new faces and young men; and our best society, our long and late dinners, would soon have been prejudicial to my health. Without any share in the political wheel, I must be idle and insignificant: yet the most splendid temptations would not have enticed me to engage a second time in the servitude of Parliament or office. At Tunbridge, some weeks after the publication of my *History*, I reluctantly quitted Lord and Lady Sheffield, and, with a young Swiss friend [1], whom I had introduced to the English world, I pursued the road of Dover and Lausanne. My habitation was embellished in my absence, and the last division of books, which followed my steps, increased my chosen library to the number of between six and seven thousand volumes. My seraglio was ample, my choice was free, my appetite was keen. After a full repast on Homer and Aristophanes, I involved myself in the philosophic maze of the writings of Plato, of which the dramatic is, perhaps, more interesting than the argumentative part: but I stepped aside into every path of inquiry which reading or reflection accidentally opened.

Alas! the joy of my return, and my studious ardour, were soon damped by the melancholy state of my friend Mr. Deyverdun. His health and spirits had

[1] M. Wilhelm de Severy.   S.

long suffered a gradual decline, a succession of apoplectic fits announced his dissolution, and before he
expired, those who loved him could not wish for the
continuance of his life. The voice of reason might
congratulate his deliverance, but the feelings of nature
and friendship could be subdued only by time : his
amiable character was still alive in my remembrance ;
each room, each walk, was imprinted with our common
footsteps ; and I should blush at my own philosophy,
if a long interval of study had not preceded and followed
the death of my friend. By his last will he left to me
the option of purchasing his house and garden, or of
possessing them during my life, on the payment either
of a stipulated price, or of an easy retribution to his
kinsman and heir. I should probably have been
tempted by the demon of property, if some legal
difficulties had not been started against my title ;
a contest would have been vexatious, doubtful, and
invidious ; and the heir most gratefully subscribed an
agreement, which rendered my life-possession more
perfect, and his future condition more advantageous.[1]
Yet I had often revolved the judicious lines in which
Pope answers the objections of his long-sighted friend :

> Pity to build without or child or wife ;
> Why, you'll enjoy it only all your life :
> Well, if the use be mine, does it concern one,
> Whether the name belong to Pope or Vernon ?

The certainty of my tenure has allowed me to lay out
a considerable sum in improvements and alterations :
they have been executed with skill and taste ; and
few men of letters, perhaps, in Europe, are so desirably
lodged as myself. But I feel, and with the decline of
years I shall more painfully feel, that I am alone in
paradise. Among the circle of my acquaintance at
Lausanne, I have gradually acquired the solid and
tender friendship of a respectable family [2] ; the four

See Mr. Gibbon's Letters, July 14, August, Sept. 7,
Sept. 9, 1789.

[2] The family of de Severy. S.

persons of whom it is composed are all endowed with
the virtues best adapted to their age and situation;
and I am encouraged to love the parents as a brother,
and the children as a father. Every day we seek
and find the opportunities of meeting: yet even this
valuable connexion cannot supply the loss of domestic
society.

Within the last two or three years our tranquillity
has been clouded by the disorders of France; many
families at Lausanne were alarmed and affected by
the terrors of an impending bankruptcy; but the
revolution, or rather the dissolution of the kingdom,
has been heard and felt in the adjacent lands.

I beg leave to subscribe my assent to Mr. Burke's
creed on the revolution of France. I admire his
eloquence, I approve his politics, I adore his chivalry,
and I can almost excuse his reverence for church
establishments. I have sometimes thought of writing
a dialogue of the dead, in which Lucian, Erasmus, and
Voltaire should mutually acknowledge the danger of
exposing an old superstition to the contempt of the
blind and fanatic multitude.

A swarm of emigrants of both sexes, who escaped
from the public ruin, has been attracted by the vicinity,
the manners, and the language of Lausanne; and our
narrow habitations in town and country are now
occupied by the first names and titles of the departed
monarchy.[1] These noble fugitives are entitled to our
pity; they may claim our esteem, but they cannot,
in their present state of mind and fortune, much
contribute to our amusement. Instead of looking
down as calm and idle spectators on the theatre of
Europe, our domestic harmony is somewhat embittered
by the infusion of party spirit: our ladies and gentlemen assume the character of self-taught politicians;
and the sober dictates of wisdom and experience are
silenced by the clamour of the triumphant *democrates*.

---

[1] See Mr. Gibbon's Letters, Dec. 15, 1789, ditto 1790,
Oct. 5, 13, 20, and Nov. 10, 1792.

The fanatic missionaries of sedition have scattered the seeds of discontent in our cities and villages, which have flourished above two hundred and fifty years without fearing the approach of war or feeling the weight of government. Many individuals, and some communities, appear to be infected with the Gallic frenzy, the wild theories of equal and boundless freedom ; but I trust that the body of the people will be faithful to their sovereign and to themselves ; and I am satisfied that the failure or success of a revolt would equally terminate in the ruin of the country. While the aristocracy of Berne protects the happiness, it is superfluous to inquire whether it be founded in the rights of man : the economy of the State is liberally supplied without the aid of taxes ; and the magistrates *must* reign with prudence and equity, since they are unarmed in the midst of an armed nation.

The revenue of Berne, excepting some small duties, is derived from church lands, tithes, feudal rights, and interest of money. The republic has nearly £500,000 sterling in the English funds, and the amount of their treasure is unknown to the citizens themselves. For myself (may the omen be averted !) I can only declare that the first stroke of a rebel drum would be the signal of my immediate departure.

When I contemplate the common lot of mortality, I must acknowledge that I have drawn a high prize in the lottery of life. The far greater part of the globe is overspread with barbarism or slavery : in the civilized world, the most numerous class is condemned to ignorance and poverty ; and the double fortune of my birth in a free and enlightened country, in an honourable and wealthy family, is the lucky chance of an unit against millions. The general probability is about three to one that a new-born infant will not live to complete his fiftieth year.[1] I have now passed

[1] See Buffon, *Supplément à l'Histoire Naturelle*, tom. vii, pp. 158–64 : Of a given number of new-born infants, one half, by the fault of nature or man, is extinguished before the age of puberty and reason—a melancholy calculation !

that age, and may fairly estimate the present value of my existence in the threefold division of mind, body, and estate.

(1) The first and indispensable requisite of happiness is a clear conscience, unsullied by the reproach or remembrance of an unworthy action.

> ——Hic murus aheneus esto,
> Nil conscire sibi, nulla pallescere culpa.

I am endowed with a cheerful temper, a moderate sensibility, and a natural disposition to repose rather than to activity: some mischievous appetites and habits have perhaps been corrected by philosophy or time. The love of study, a passion which derives fresh vigour from enjoyment, supplies each day, each hour, with a perpetual source of independent and rational pleasure; and I am not sensible of any decay of the mental faculties. The original soil has been highly improved by cultivation; but it may be questioned whether some flowers of fancy, some grateful errors, have not been eradicated with the weeds of prejudice. (2) Since I have escaped from the long perils of my childhood, the serious advice of a physician has seldom been requisite. 'The madness of superfluous health' I have never known, but my tender constitution has been fortified by time, and the inestimable gift of the sound and peaceful slumbers of infancy may be imputed both to the mind and body. (3) I have already described the merits of my society and situation; but these enjoyments would be tasteless or bitter if their possession were not assured by an annual and adequate supply. According to the scale of Switzerland, I am a rich man; and I am indeed rich, since my income is superior to my expense, and my expense is equal to my wishes. My friend Lord Sheffield has kindly relieved me from the cares to which my taste and temper are most adverse: shall I add, that since the failure of my first wishes, I have never entertained any serious thoughts of a matrimonial connexion?

I am disgusted with the affectation of men of letters, who complain that they have renounced a substance for a shadow, and that their fame (which sometimes is no insupportable weight) affords a poor compensation for envy, censure, and persecution.[1] My own experience, at least, has taught me a very different lesson; twenty happy years have been animated by the labour of my *History*, and its success has given me a name, a rank, a character, in the world, to which I should not otherwise have been entitled. The freedom of my writings has indeed provoked an implacable tribe; but, as I was safe from the stings, I was soon accustomed to the buzzing of the hornets: my nerves are not tremblingly alive, and my literary temper is so happily framed, that I am less sensible of pain than of pleasure. The rational pride of an author may be offended, rather than flattered, by vague indiscriminate praise; but he cannot, he should not, be indifferent to the fair testimonies of private and public esteem. Even his moral sympathy may be gratified by the idea, that now, in the present hour, he is imparting some degree of amusement or knowledge to his friends in a distant land; that one day his mind will be familiar to the grandchildren of those who are yet unborn.[2] I cannot boast of the friendship

[1] Mr. d'Alembert relates, that as he was walking in the gardens of Sans Souci with the King of Prussia, Frederic said to him, 'Do you see that old woman, a poor weeder, asleep on that sunny bank? she is probably a more happy being than either of us.' The king and the philosopher may speak for themselves; for my part I do not envy the old woman.

[2] In the first of ancient or modern romances (*Tom Jones*), this proud sentiment, this feast of fancy, is enjoyed by the genius of Fielding.—'Come, bright love of fame, &c., fill my ravished fancy with the hopes of charming ages yet to come. Foretell me that some tender maid, whose grandmother is yet unborn, hereafter, when, under the fictitious name of Sophia, she reads the real worth which once existed in my Charlotte, shall from her sympathetic breast send forth the heaving sigh. Do thou teach me

or favour of princes; the patronage of English literature has long since been devolved on our booksellers,
and the measure of their liberality is the least ambiguous test of our common success. Perhaps the
golden mediocrity of my fortune has contributed to
fortify my application.

The present is a fleeting moment, the past is no
more; and our prospect of futurity is dark and doubtful. This day may *possibly* be my last: but the
laws of probability, so true in general, so fallacious
in particular, still allow about fifteen years.[1] I shall
soon enter into the period which, as the most agreeable
of his long life, was selected by the judgement and
experience of the sage Fontenelle. His choice is
approved by the eloquent historian of nature, who
fixes our moral happiness to the mature season in
which our passions are supposed to be calmed, our
duties fulfilled, our ambition satisfied, our fame and
fortune established on a solid basis.[2] In private conversation, that great and amiable man added the
weight of his own experience; and this autumnal
felicity might be exemplified in the lives of Voltaire,
Hume, and many other men of letters. I am far more
inclined to embrace than to dispute this comfortable
doctrine. I will not suppose any premature decay of

not only to foresee but to enjoy, nay even to feed on
future praise. Comfort me by the solemn assurance that,
when the little parlour in which I sit at this moment
shall be reduced to a worse furnished box, I shall be read
with honour by those who never knew nor saw me, and
whom I shall neither know nor see.' Book xiii, Chap. 1.

[1] Mr. Buffon, from our disregard of the possibility of
death within the four and twenty hours, concludes that
a chance, which falls below or rises above ten thousand to
one, will never affect the hopes or fears of a reasonable
man. The fact is true, but our courage is the effect of
thoughtlessness, rather than of reflection. If a public
lottery were drawn for the choice of an immediate victim,
and if our name were inscribed on one of the ten thousand
tickets, should we be perfectly easy?

[2] See Buffon.

the mind or body; but I must reluctantly observe that two causes, the abbreviation of time, and the failure of hope, will always tinge with a browner shade the evening of life.[1]

[1] The proportion of a part to the whole is the only standard by which we can measure the length of our existence. At the age of twenty, one year is a tenth, perhaps, of the time which has elapsed within our consciousness and memory: at the age of fifty it is no more than the fortieth, and this relative value continues to decrease till the last sands are shaken by the hand of death. This reasoning may seem metaphysical; but on a trial it will be found satisfactory and just. The warm desires, the long expectations of youth, are founded on the ignorance of themselves and of the world: they are gradually damped by time and experience, by disappointment and possession; and after the middle season the crowd must be content to remain at the foot of the mountain; while the few who have climbed the summit aspire to descend or expect to fall. In old age, the consolation of hope is reserved for the tenderness of parents, who commence a new life in their children; the faith of enthusiasts, who sing Hallelujahs above the clouds; and the vanity of authors, who presume the immortality of their name and writings.

LETTERS

IN CONTINUATION OF THE MEMOIR

WHEN I first undertook to prepare Mr. Gibbon's
Memoirs for the press, I supposed that it would be
necessary to introduce some continuation of them,
from the time when they cease, namely, soon after
his return to Switzerland in the year 1788; but the
examination of his correspondence with me suggested
that the best continuation would be the publication
of his letters from that time to his death. I shall
thus give more satisfaction, by employing the language
of Mr. Gibbon, instead of my own; and the public
will see him in a new and admirable light, as a writer
of letters. By the insertion of a few occasional sentences, I shall obviate the disadvantages that are apt
to arise from an interrupted narration. A prejudiced
or a fastidious critic may condemn, perhaps, some
parts of the letters as trivial; but many readers,
I flatter myself, will be gratified by discovering even
in these, my friend's affectionate feelings, and his
character in familiar life. His letters in general bear
a strong resemblance to the style and turn of his
conversation; the characteristics of which were
vivacity, elegance, and precision, with knowledge
astonishingly extensive and correct. He never ceased
to be instructive and entertaining; and in general
there was a vein of pleasantry in his conversation
which prevented its becoming languid, even during
a residence of many months with a family in the
country.

It has been supposed that he always arranged what

he intended· to say before he spoke ; his quickness in conversation contradicts this notion : but it is very true, that before he sat down to write a note or letter, he completely arranged in his mind what he meant to express.   He pursued the same method in respect to other composition ; and he occasionally would walk several times about his apartment before he had rounded a period to his taste. He has pleasantly remarked to me, that it sometimes cost him many a turn before he could throw a sentiment into a form that gratified his own criticism.   His systematic habit of arrangement in point of style, assisted, in his instance, by an excellent memory and correct judgement, is much to be recommended to those who aspire to perfection in writing.

Although the Memoirs extend beyond the time of Mr. Gibbon's return to Lausanne, I shall insert a few Letters, written immediately after his arrival there, and combine them so far as to include even the last note which he wrote a few days previously to his death. Some of them contain few incidents ; but they connect and carry on the account either of his opinions or of his employment. S.

LETTERS

FROM EDWARD GIBBON, ESQ., TO THE RIGHT HON. LORD SHEFFIELD

Lausanne, July 30, 1788.—Wednesday, 3 o'clock.

I HAVE but a moment to say, before the departure of the post, that after a very pleasant journey I arrived here about half an hour ago ; that I am as well arranged as if I had never stirred from this place ; and that dinner on the table is just announced. Severy I dropped at his country-house about two leagues off. I just saluted the family, who dine with me the day after to-morrow, and return to town for some days, I hope weeks, on my account. The son is an amiable and grateful youth ; and even this journey has taught me to know and to love him still better. My satisfaction would be complete, had I not found a sad and serious alteration in poor Deyverdun : but thus our joys are chequered ! I embrace all ; and at this moment feel the last pang of our parting at Tunbridge. Convey this letter or information, without delay, from Sheffield Place to Bath. In a few days I shall write more amply to both places.

October 1, 1788.

After such an act of vigour as my first letter, composed, finished, and dispatched within half an hour after my landing, while the dinner was smoking on the table, your knowledge of the animal must have taught you to expect a proportionable degree of relaxation ; and you will be satisfied to hear, that, for many Wednesdays and Saturdays, I have consumed more time than would have sufficed for the epistle, in devising reasons for procrastinating it to the next post. At this very moment I begin so very late, as I am just going to dress, and dine in the country, that I can take only the benefit of the date, October the first, and must be content to seal and send my letter next Saturday.

October 4.

Saturday is now arrived, and I much doubt whether I shall have time to finish. I rose, as usual, about seven; but as I knew I should have so much time, you know it would have been ridiculous to begin anything before breakfast. When I returned from my breakfast-room to the library, unluckily I found on the table some new and interesting books, which instantly caught my attention; and without injuring my correspondent, I could safely bestow a single hour to gratify my curiosity. Some things which I found in them insensibly led me to other books, and other inquiries; the morning has stolen away, and I shall be soon summoned to dress and dine with the two Severys, father and son, who are returned from the country on a disagreeable errand, an illness of Madame, from which she is however recovering. Such is the faithful picture of my mind and manners, and from a single day *disce omnes*. After having been so long chained to the oar, in a splendid galley indeed, I freely and fairly enjoy my liberty as I promised in my preface; range without control over the wide expanse of my library; converse, as my fancy prompts me, with poets and historians, philosophers and orators, of every age and language; and often indulge my meditations in the invention and arrangement of mighty works, which I shall probably never find time or application to execute. My garden, berceau, and pavilion often varied the scene of my studies; the beautiful weather which we have enjoyed exhilarated my spirits, and I again tasted the wisdom and happiness of my retirement, till that happiness was interrupted by a very serious calamity, which took from me for above a fortnight all thoughts of study, of amusement, and even of correspondence. I mentioned in my first letter the uneasiness I felt at poor Deyverdun's declining health, how much the pleasure of my life was embittered by the sight of a suffering and languid friend. The joy of our meeting appeared at first to revive him; and, though not satisfied, I began to think, at least to hope, that he was every day gaining ground; when, alas! one morning I was suddenly recalled from my berceau to the house, with the dreadful intelligence of an apoplectic stroke; I found him senseless: the best assistance was instantly collected; and he had the aid of the genius and experience of Mr. Tissot, and of the assiduous care of another physician, who for some time scarcely quitted his bedside either night or day. While I was in momentary dread of a relapse, with a confession from his physicians that such a relapse must be fatal, you will feel that I was much more to be pitied than my friend. At length, art or nature triumphed over the enemy of life. I was soon assured that all immediate danger was past; and now for many days I have had the satisfaction of seeing him recover, though by slow degrees, his health and strength, his sleep and appetite. He now walks about the garden, and receives his particular friends, but has not yet gone abroad. His future health will depend very much upon his own prudence: but, at all events, this has been a very serious warning; and the slightest indisposition will hereafter assume a very formidable aspect. But let us turn from this melancholy subject. The Man of the People escaped from the tumult, the bloody tumult of the Westminster election, to the lakes and mountains of Switzerland, and I was informed that he was arrived at the Lyon d'Or. I sent a compliment; he answered it in person, and settled at my house for the remainder of the day. I have eat and drank, and conversed and sat up all night with Fox in England; but it never has happened, perhaps it never can happen again, that I should enjoy him as I did that day, alone, from ten in the morning till ten at night. Poor Deyverdun, before his accident, wanted spirits to appear, and has regretted it since. Our conversation never flagged a moment; and he seemed thoroughly pleased with the place and with his company. We had little politics; though he gave me, in a few words, such a character of Pitt, as one great man should give of another his rival: much of books, from my own, on which he flattered me very pleasantly, to Homer and the *Arabian Nights*: much about the country, my garden (which he understands far better than I do), and, upon the whole, I think he envies me, and would do so were he a minister. The next morning I gave him a guide to walk him about the town and country, and invited some company to meet him at dinner. The following day he continued his journey to Berne and Zurich, and I have heard of him by various means. The people gaze on him as a prodigy, but he shows little inclination to converse with them. . . . Our friend Douglas [1] has been curious, attentive, agreeable; and in every place where he has resided some days, he has left acquaintance who esteem and regret him: I never knew so clear and general an impression.

After this long letter I have yet many things to say, though none of any pressing consequence. I hope you are not idle in the deliverance of Buriton, though the late events and edicts in France begin to reconcile me to the possession of dirty acres. What think you of Necker and the States-General? Are not the public expectations too sanguine? Adieu. I will write soon to my lady separately, though I have not any particular subject for her ear. Ever yours.

Lausanne, Nov. 29, 1788.

As I have no correspondents but yourself, I should have been reduced to the stale and stupid communica-

[1] Lord Glenbervie.

tions of the newspapers, if you had not dispatched me an excellent sketch of the extraordinary state of things. In so new a case the *salus populi* must be the first law; and any extraordinary acts of the two remaining branches of the legislature must be excused by necessity, and ratified by general consent. Till things are settled I expect a regular journal.

From kingdoms I descend to farms. . . . Adieu.

Lausanne, Dec. 13, 1788.

. . . Of public affairs I can only hear with curiosity and wonder; careless as you may think me, I feel myself deeply interested. You must now write often; make Miss Firth copy any curious fragments; and stir up any of my well-informed acquaintance, Batt, Douglas, Adam, perhaps Lord Loughborough, to correspond with me; I *will* answer them.

We are now cold and gay at Lausanne. The Severys came to town yesterday. I saw a good deal of Lords Malmsbury and Beauchamp, and their ladies; Ellis, of the Rolliad, was with them; I like him much: I gave them a dinner.

Adieu for the present. Deyverdun is not worse.

Lausanne, April 25, 1789.

Before your letter, which I received yesterday, I was in the anxious situation of a king, who hourly expects a courier from his general with the news of a decisive engagement. I had abstained from writing, for fear of dropping a word, or betraying a feeling, which might render you too cautious or too bold. On the famous 8th of April, between twelve and two, I reflected that the business was determined; and each succeeding day I computed the speedy approach of your messenger, with favourable or melancholy tidings. When I broke the seal, I expected to read, 'What a damned unlucky fellow you are! Nothing tolerable was offered, and I indignantly withdrew the estate'. I *did* remember the fate of poor Lenborough, and I was afraid of your magnanimity, &c. It is whimsical enough, but it is human nature, that I now begin to think of the deep-rooted foundations of land, and the airy fabric of the funds. I not only consent, but even wish, to have eight or ten thousand pounds on a good mortgage. The pipe of wine you sent to me was seized, and would have been confiscated, if the government of Berne had not treated me with the most flattering and distinguished civility : they not only released the wine, but they paid out of their own pocket the shares to which the bailiff and the informer were entitled by law. I should not forget that the bailiff refused to accept of his part. Poor Deyverdun's constitution is quite broken ; he has had two or three attacks, not so violent as the first : every time the door is hastily opened, I expect to hear of some fatal accident : the best or worst hopes of the physicians are only that he may linger some time longer ; but, if he lives till the summer, they propose sending him to some mineral waters at Aix, in Savoy. You will be glad to hear that I am now assured of possessing, during my life, this delightful house and garden. The act has been lately executed in the best form, and the handsomest manner. I know not what to say of your miracles at home ; we rejoice in the king's recovery, and its ministerial consequences ; and I cannot be insensible to the hope, at least the chance, of seeing in this country a first lord of trade, or secretary at war. In your answer, which I shall impatiently expect, you will give me a full and true account of your designs, which by this time must have dropped, or be determined at least, for the present year. If you come, it is high time that we should look out for a house—a task much less easy than you may possibly imagine. Among new books, I recommend to you the Count de Mira-beau's great work, *Sur la Monarchie Prussienne* ; it is in your own way, and gives a very just and complete idea of that wonderful machine. His *Correspondence Secrète* is diabolically good. Adieu. Ever yours.

Lausanne, June 13, 1789.

You are in truth a wise, active, indefatigable, and inestimable friend; and as our virtues are often connected with our failings, if you were more tame and placid, you would be perhaps of less use and value. A very important and difficult transaction seems to be nearly terminated with success and mutual satisfaction: we seem to run before the wind with a prosperous gale; and, unless we should strike on some secret rocks which I do not foresee, shall, on or before the 31st July, enter the harbour of Content; though I cannot pursue the metaphor by adding we shall *land*, since our operation is of a very opposite tendency. I could not easily forgive myself for shutting you up in a dark room with parchments and attorneys, did I not reflect that this probably is the last material trouble that you will ever have on my account; and that after the labours and delays of twenty years, I shall at last attain what I have always sighed for, a clear and competent income, above my wants, and equal to my wishes. In this contemplation you will be sufficiently rewarded. I hope ***** will be content with our title-deeds, for I cannot furnish another shred of parchment. Mrs. Gibbon's jointure is secured on the Buriton estate, and her legal consent is requisite for the sale. Again and again I must repeat my hope that she is perfectly satisfied, and that the close of her life may not be embittered by suspicion, or fear, or discontent. What new security does she prefer—the funds, the mortgage, or your land? At all events she must be made easy. I wrote to her again some time ago, and begged that if she were too weak to write, she would desire Mrs. Gould or Mrs. Holroyd to give me a line concerning her state of health. To this no answer; I am afraid she is displeased.

Now for the disposal of the money: I approve of the £8,000 mortgage on Buriton; and honour your prudence in not showing, by the comparison of the

rent and interest, how foolish it is to purchase land.
. . . There is a chance of my drawing a considerable
sum into this country, for an arrangement which you
yourself must approve, but which I have not time to
explain at present. For the sake of dispatching, by
this evening's post, an answer to your letter which
arrived this morning, I confine myself to the *needful*,
but in the course of a few days I will send a more
familiar epistle. Adieu. Ever yours.

Lausanne, July 14, 1789.

Poor Deyverdun is no more: he expired Saturday
the 4th instant; and in his unfortunate situation, death
could only be viewed by himself, and by his friends,
in the light of a consummation devoutly to be wished.
Since September he has had a dozen apoplectic strokes,
more or less violent: in the intervals between them
his strength gradually decayed; every principle of
life was exhausted; and had he continued to drag
a miserable existence, he must probably have survived
the loss of his faculties. Of all misfortunes this was
what he himself most apprehended: but his reason
was clear and calm to the last; he beheld his approaching dissolution with the firmness of a philosopher.
I fancied that time and reflection had prepared me
for the event: but the habits of three-and-thirty
years' friendship are not so easily broken. The first
days, and more especially the first nights, were indeed
painful. Last Wednesday and Saturday it would not
have been in my power to write. I must now recollect
myself, since it is necessary for me not only to impart
the news, but to ask your opinion in a very serious
and doubtful question, which must be decided without
loss of time. I shall state the facts, but as I am on
the spot, and as new lights may occur, I do not promise
implicit obedience.

Had my poor friend died without a will, a female
first cousin settled somewhere in the north of Germany,
and whom I believe he had never seen, would have
been his heir-at-law. In the next degree he had

several cousins ; and one of these, an old companion, by name Mr. de Montagny, he has chosen for his heir. As this house and garden was the best and clearest part of poor Deyverdun's fortune ; as there is a heavy duty or fine (what they call *lods*) on every change of property out of the legal descent ; as Montagny has a small estate and a large family, it was necessary to make some provision in his favour. The will therefore leaves me the option of enjoying this place during my life, on paying the sum of £250 (I reckon in English money) at present, and an annual rent of £30 ; or else, of purchasing the house and garden for a sum which, including the duty, will amount to £2,500. If I value the rent of £30 at twelve years' purchase, I may acquire my enjoyment for life at about the rate of £600 ; and the remaining £1,900 will be the difference between that tenure and absolute perpetual property. As you have never accused me of too much zeal for the interest of posterity, you will easily guess which scale at first preponderated. I deeply felt the advantage of acquiring, for the smaller sum, every possible enjoyment, as long as I myself should be capable of enjoying : I rejected, with scorn, the idea of giving £1,900 for ideal posthumous property ; and I deemed it of little moment whose name, after my death, should be inscribed on my house and garden at Lausanne. How often did I repeat to myself the philosophical lines of Pope, which seem to determine the question :

> Pray Heaven, cries Swift, it last as you go on ;
> I wish to God this house had been your own.
> Pity to build without or son or wife :
> Why, you'll enjoy it *only* all your life.
> Well, if the use be mine, does it concern one,
> Whether the name belong to Pope or Vernon ?

In this state of self-satisfaction I was not much disturbed by all my real or nominal friends, who exhort me to prefer the right of purchase : among such friends, some are careless and some are ignorant ;

and the judgement of those who are able and willing to form an opinion, is often biassed by some selfish or social affection, by some visible or invisible interest. But my own reflections have gradually and forcibly driven me from my first propensity; and these reflections I will now proceed to enumerate :

(1) I can make this purchase with ease and prudence. As I have had the pleasure of *not* hearing from you very lately, I flatter myself that you advance on a carpet road, and that almost by the receipt of this letter (July 31) the acres of Buriton will be transmuted into sixteen thousand pounds : if the payment be not absolutely completed by that day, ****** will not scruple, I suppose, depositing the £2,600 at Gosling's, to meet my draught. Should he hesitate, I can desire Darrel to sell *quantum sufficit* of my short annuities. As soon as the new settlement of my affairs is made, I shall be able, after deducting this sum, to square my expense to my income, &c.

(2) On mature consideration, I am perhaps less selfish and less philosophical than I appear at first sight : indeed, were I not so, it would now be in my power to turn my fortune into life-annuities, and let the Devil take the hindmost. I feel (perhaps it is foolish), but I feel that this little paradise will please me still more when it is absolutely my own ; and that I shall be encouraged in every improvement of use or beauty, by the prospect that, after my departure, it will be enjoyed by some person of my own choice. I sometimes reflect with pleasure that my writings will survive me ; and that idea is at least as vain and chimerical.

(3) The heir, Mr. de Montagny, is an old acquaintance. My situation of a life-holder is rather new and singular in this country : the laws have not provided for many nice cases which may arise between the landlord and tenant : some I can foresee, others have been suggested, many more I might feel when it would be too late. His right of property might plague and confine me ; he might forbid my lending to a friend,

inspect my conduct, check my improvements, call for securities, repairs, &c. But if I purchase, I walk on my own terrace fierce and erect, the free master of one of the most delicious spots on the globe.

Should I ever migrate homewards (you stare, but such an event is less improbable than I could have thought it two years ago), this place would be disputed by strangers and natives.

Weigh these reasons, and send me without delay a rational explicit opinion, to which I shall pay such regard as the nature of circumstances will allow. But, alas! when all is determined, I shall possess this house, by whatsoever tenure, without friendship or domestic society. I did not imagine, six years ago, that a plan of life so congenial to my wishes, would so speedily vanish. I cannot write upon any other subject. Adieu. Yours ever.

Lausanne, August, 1789.

After receiving and dispatching the power of attorney, last Wednesday, I opened, with some palpitation, the unexpected missive which arrived this morning. The perusal of the contents spoiled my breakfast. They are disagreeable in themselves, alarming in their consequences, and peculiarly unpleasant at the present moment, when I hoped to have formed and secured the arrangements of my future life. I do not perfectly understand what are these deeds which are so inflexibly required ; the wills and marriage-settlements I have sufficiently answered. But your arguments do not convince ****, and I have very little hope from the Lenborough search. What will be the event ? If his objections are only the result of legal scrupulosity, surely they might be removed, and every chink might be filled, by a general bond of indemnity, in which I boldly ask you to join, as it will be a substantial important act of friendship, without any possible risk to yourself or your successors. Should he still remain obdurate, I must believe, what I already suspect, that **** repents of his purchase, and wishes to elude the conclusion. Our case would be then hopeless, *ibi omnis effusus labor*, and the estate would be returned on our hands with the taint of a bad title. The refusal of mortgage does not please me ; but surely our offer shows some confidence in the goodness of my title. If he will not take eight thousand pounds at *four per cent.* we must look out elsewhere ; new doubts and delays will arise, and I am persuaded that you will not place an implicit confidence in any attorney. I know not as yet your opinion about my Lausanne purchase. If you are against it, the present position of affairs gives you great advantage, &c., &c. The Severys are all well ; an uncommon circumstance for the four persons of the family at once. They are now at Mex, a country-house six miles from hence, which I visit to-morrow for two or three days. They often come to town, and we shall contrive to pass a part of the autumn together at Rolle. I want to change the scene ; and beautiful as the garden and prospect must appear to every eye, I feel that the state of my own mind casts a gloom over them ; every spot, every walk, every bench, recalls the memory of those hours, of those conversations, which will return no more. But I tear myself from the subject. I could not help writing to-day, though I do not find I have said anything very material. As you must be conscious that you have agitated me, you will not postpone any agreeable, or even *decisive* intelligence. I almost hesitate whether I shall run over to England, to consult with you on the spot, and to fly from poor Deyverdun's shade, which meets me at every turn. I did not expect to have felt his loss so sharply. But six hundred miles ! Why are we so far off ?

Once more, what is the difficulty of the title ? Will men of sense, in a sensible country, never get rid of the tyranny of lawyers ? more oppressive and ridiculous than even the old yoke of the clergy. Is not a term of seventy or eighty years, nearly twenty in my own person, sufficient to prove our legal possession ? Will not the records of fines and recoveries attest that

I am free from any bar of entails and settlements ?
Consult some sage of the law, whether their present
demand be necessary and legal. If your ground be
firm, force them to execute the agreement or forfeit
the deposit. But if, as I much fear, they have a right,
and a wish, to elude the consummation, would it not
be better to release them at once, than to be hung
up for five years, as in the case of Lovegrove, which
cost me in the end four or five thousand pounds ?
You are bold, you are wise ; consult, resolve, act.
In my penultimate letter I dropped a strange hint,
that a migration homeward was not impossible. I
know not what to say ; my mind is all afloat ; yet
you will not reproach me with caprice or inconstancy.
How many years did you damn my scheme of retiring
to Lausanne ? I executed that plan ; I found as
much happiness as is compatible with human nature,
and during four years (1783-7) I never breathed
a sigh of repentance. On my return from England
the scene was changed : I found only a faint semblance of Deyverdun, and that semblance each
day fading from my sight. I have passed an anxious
year, but my anxiety is now at an end, and the prospect
before me is a melancholy solitude. I am still deeply
rooted in this country ; the possession of this paradise,
the friendship of the Severys, a mode of society suited
to my taste, and the enormous trouble and *expense*
of a migration. Yet in England (when the present
clouds are dispelled) I could form a very comfortable
establishment in London, or rather at Bath ; and
I have a very noble country-seat at about ten miles
from East Grinstead in Sussex.[1] That spot is dearer
to me than the rest of the three kingdoms ; and I have
sometimes wondered how two men, so opposite in
their tempers and pursuits, should have imbibed so
long and lively a propensity for each other. Sir
Stanier Porten is just dead. He has left his widow
with a moderate pension, and two children, my nearest
relations : the eldest, Charlotte, is about Louisa's age,

[1] Alluding to Sheffield Place.

and also a most amiable sensible young creature. I have
conceived a romantic idea of educating and adopting
her; as we descend into the vale of years our infirmities require some domestic female society: Charlotte
would be the comfort of my age, and I could reward
her care and tenderness with a decent fortune. A
thousand difficulties oppose the execution of the plan,
which I have never opened but to you; yet it would
be less impracticable in England than in Switzerland.
Adieu. I am wounded; pour some oil into my
wounds: yet I am less unhappy since I have thrown
my mind upon paper.

Are you not amazed at the French revolution?
They have the power, will they have the moderation,
to establish a good constitution? Adieu. Ever yours.

Lausanne, Sept. 9, 1789.

Within an hour after the reception of your last,
I drew my pen for the purpose of a reply, and my
exordium ran in the following words: 'I find by
experience, that it is much more rational, as well
as easy, to answer a letter of real business by the
return of the post'. This important truth is again
verified by my own example. After writing three
pages I was called away by a very rational motive,
and the post departed before I could return to the
conclusion. A second delay was coloured by some
decent pretence. Three weeks have slipped away,
and I now force myself on a task which I should have
dispatched without an effort on the first summons.
My only excuse is, that I had little to write about
English business, and that I could write nothing
definitive about my Swiss affairs. And first, as
Aristotle says of the first,

(1) I was indeed in low spirits when I sent what
you so justly style my dismal letter; but I do assure
you that my own feelings contributed much more to
sink me than any events or terrors relative to the
sale of Buriton. But I again hope and trust, from
your consolatory epistle, that, &c., &c.

(2) My Swiss transaction has suffered a great alteration. I shall not become the proprietor of my house and garden at Lausanne, and I relinquish the phantom with more regret than you could easily imagine. But I have been determined by a difficulty, which at first appeared of little moment, but which has gradually swelled to an alarming magnitude. There is a law in this country, as well as in some provinces of France, which is styled *le droit de retrait, le retrait lignagere* (Lord Loughborough must have heard of it), by which the relations of the deceased are entitled to redeem a house or estate at the price for which it has been sold; and as the sum fixed by poor Deyverdun is much below its known value, a crowd of competitors are beginning to start. The best opinions (for they are divided) are in my favour, that I am not subject to *le droit de retrait*, since I take not as a purchaser, but as a legatee. But the words of the will are somewhat ambiguous, the event of law is always uncertain, the administration of justice at Berne (the last appeal) depends too much on favour and intrigue; and it is very doubtful whether I could revert to the life-holding, after having chosen and lost the property. These considerations engaged me to open a negotiation with Mr. de Montagny, through the medium of my friend the judge; and as he most ardently wishes to keep the house, he consented, though with some reluctance, to my proposals. Yesterday he signed a covenant in the most regular and binding form, by which he allows my power of transferring my interest, interprets in the most ample sense my right of making alterations, and expressly renounces all claim, as landlord, of visiting or inspecting the premises. I have promised to lend him twelve thousand livres (between seven and eight hundred pounds), secured on the house and land. The mortgage is four times its value; the interest of four pounds per cent. will be annually discharged by the rent of thirty guineas; so that I am now tranquil on that score for the remainder of my days. I hope that time will gradually reconcile me to

the place which I have inhabited with my poor friend; for in spite of the *cream* of London, I am still persuaded that no other place is so well adapted to my taste and habits of studious and social life.

Far from delighting in the whirl of a metropolis, my only complaint against Lausanne is the great number of strangers, always of English, and now of French, by whom we are infested in summer. Yet we have escaped the superlatively great ones, the Count d'Artois, the Polignacs, &c., who slip by us to Turin. What a scene is France! While the Assembly is voting abstract propositions, Paris is an independent republic; the provinces have neither authority nor freedom, and poor Necker declares that credit is no more, and that the people refuse to pay taxes. Yet I think you must be seduced by the abolition of tithes. If Eden goes to Paris, you may have some curious information. Give me some account of Mr. and Mrs. Douglas. Do they live with Lord North? I hope they do. When will Parliament be dissolved? Are you still Coventry-mad? I embrace my Lady, the sprightly Maria, and the smiling Louisa.[1] Alas! alas! you will never come to Switzerland. Adieu. Ever yours.

Lausanne, Sept. 25, 1789.

Alas! what perils do environ
The man who meddles with cold iron.

Alas! what delays and difficulties do attend the man who meddles with legal and landed business! Yet if it be only to disappoint your expectation, I am not so very nervous at this new provoking obstacle. I had totally forgotten the deed in question, which was contrived in the last year of my father's life, to

---

[1] Maria Josepha Holroyd, eldest daughter of Lord Sheffield, married Sir John Thomas Stanley, of Alderley in Cheshire, Baronet; and Louisa Dorothea Holroyd married Lieutenant-General William Henry Clinton, eldest son of General Sir Henry Clinton, K.B.

tie his hands and regulate the disorder of his affairs ; and which might have been so easily cancelled by Sir Stanier, who had not the smallest interest in it, either for himself or his family. The amicable suit, which is now become necessary, must, I think, be short and unambiguous. Yet I cannot help dreading the crotchets that lurk under the chancellor's great wig ; and at all events, I foresee some additional delay and expense. The golden pill of the two thousand eight hundred pounds has soothed my discontent ; and if it be safely lodged with the Goslings, I agree with you, in considering it as an unequivocal pledge of a fair and willing purchaser. It is indeed chiefly in that light I now rejoice in so large a deposit, which is no longer necessary in its full extent. You are apprised by my last letter that I have reduced myself to the life-enjoyment of the house and garden : and, in spite of my feelings, I am every day more convinced that I have chosen the safer side. I believe my cause to have been good, but it was doubtful. Law in this country is not so expensive as in England, but is more troublesome ; I must have gone to Berne, have solicited my judges in person ; a vile custom ! the event was uncertain ; and during at least two years, I should have been in a state of suspense and anxiety ; till the conclusion of which it would have been madness to have attempted any alteration or improvement. According to my present arrangement I shall want no more than eleven hundred pounds of the two thousand, and I suppose you will direct Gosling to lay out the remainder in India bonds, that it may not lie quite dead, while I am accountable to **** for the interest. The elderly lady in a male habit, who informed me that Yorkshire is a register county, is a certain judge, one Sir William Blackstone, whose name you may possibly have heard. After stating the danger of purchasers and creditors, with regard to the title of estates on which they lay out or lend their money, he thus continues : ' In Scotland every act and event regarding the transmission of property is regularly entered on record; and some of our own provincial divisions, particularly the extended county of York and the populous county of Middlesex, have prevailed with the legislature to erect such registers in their respective districts'. (Blackstone's *Commentaries*, vol. ii, p. 343, edition of 1774, in quarto.) If I am mistaken, it is in pretty good company; but I suspect that we are all right, and that the register is confined to one or two ridings. As we have, alas! two or three months before us, I should hope that your prudent sagacity will discover some sound land, in case you should not have time to arrange another mortgage. I now write in a hurry, as I am just setting out for Rolle, where I shall be settled with cook and servants in a pleasant apartment, till the middle of November. The Severys have a house there, where they pass the autumn. I am not sorry to vary the scene for a few weeks, and I wish to be absent while some alterations are making in my house at Lausanne. I wish the change of air may be of service to Severy the father, but we do not at all like his present state of health. How completely, alas, how completely! could I now lodge you: but your firm resolve of making me a visit seems to have vanished like a dream. Next summer you will not find five hundred pounds for a rational friendly expedition; and should parliament be dissolved, you will perhaps find five thousand for ——. I cannot think of it with patience. Pray take serious strenuous measures for sending me a pipe of excellent Madeira in cask, with some dozens of Malmsey Madeira. It should be consigned to Messrs. Romberg, Voituriers at Ostend, and I must have timely notice of its march. We have so much to say about France, that I suppose we shall never say anything. That country is now in a state of dissolution. Adieu.

Lausanne, December 15, 1789.

You have often reason to accuse my strange silence and neglect in the most important of *my own* affairs;

for I will presume to assert, that in a business of yours of equal consequence, you should not find me cold or careless. But on the present occasion my silence is, perhaps, the highest compliment I ever paid you. You remember the answer of Philip of Macedon: 'Philip may sleep, while he knows that Parmenio is awake'. I expected, and, to say the truth, I wished that my Parmenio would have decided and acted, without expecting my dilatory answer, and in his decision I should have acquiesced with implicit confidence. But since you will have my opinion, let us consider the present state of my affairs. In the course of my life I have often known, and sometimes felt, the difficulty of getting money, but I now find myself involved in a more singular distress, the difficulty of placing it, and if it continues much longer, I shall almost wish for my land again.

I perfectly agree with you, that it is bad management to purchase in the funds when they do not yield four pounds per cent. . . . Some of this money I can place safely, by means of my banker here; and I shall possess, what I have always desired, a command of cash, which I cannot abuse to my prejudice, since I have it in my power to supply with my pen any extraordinary or fanciful indulgence of expense. And so much, indeed, for pecuniary matters. What would you have me say of the affairs of France? We are too near, and too remote, to form an accurate judgement of that wonderful scene. The abuses of the court and government called aloud for reformation; and it has happened, as it will always happen, that an innocent well-disposed Prince has paid the forfeit of the sins of his predecessors; of the ambition of Lewis the Fourteenth, of the profusion of Lewis the Fifteenth. The French nation had a glorious opportunity, but they have abused and may lose their advantages. If they had been content with a liberal translation of our system, if they had respected the prerogatives of the crown, and the privileges of the nobles, they might have raised a solid fabric on the only true foundation, the natural aristocracy of a great country. How different is the prospect! Their king brought a captive to Paris, after his palace had been stained with the blood of his guards; the nobles in exile; the clergy plundered in a way which strikes at the root of all property; the capital an independent republic; the union of the provinces dissolved; the flames of discord kindled by the worst of men (in that light I consider Mirabeau); and the honestest of the Assembly, a set of wild visionaries (like our Dr. Price), who gravely debate, and dream about the establishment of a pure and perfect democracy of five-and-twenty millions, the virtues of the golden age, and the primitive rights and equality of mankind, which would lead, in fair reasoning, to an equal partition of lands and money. How many years must elapse before France can recover any vigour, or resume her station among the Powers of Europe! As yet, there is no symptom of a great man, a Richelieu or a Cromwell, arising, either to restore the monarchy, or to lead the commonwealth. The weight of Paris, more deeply engaged in the funds than *all* the rest of the kingdom, will long delay a bankruptcy; and if it should happen, it will be, both in the cause and the effect, a measure of weakness, rather than of strength. You send me to Chambery, to see a Prince and an Archbishop. Alas! we have exiles enough here, with the Marshal de Castries and the Duke de Guignes at their head; and this inundation of strangers, which used to be confined to the summer, will now stagnate all the winter. The only ones whom I have seen with pleasure are Mr. Mounier, the late President of the National Assembly, and the Count de Lally; they have both dined with me. Mounier, who is a serious dry politician, is returned to Dauphiné. Lally is an amiable man of the world, and a poet: he passes the winter here. You know how much I prefer a quiet select society to a crowd of names and titles, and that I always seek conversation with a view to amusement, rather than information. What happy countries are England and Switzerland, if they know and preserve their happiness!

I have a thousand things to say to my Lady, Maria, and Louisa, but I can add only a short postscript about the Madeira. Good Madeira is now become essential to my health and reputation. May your hogshead prove as good as the last; may it not be intercepted by the rebels or the Austrians. What a scene again in that country! Happy England! Happy Switzerland! I again repeat, adieu.

Lausanne, January 27, 1790.

Your two last epistles, of the 7th and 11th instant, were somewhat delayed on the road; they arrived within two days of each other, the last this morning (the 27th); so that I answer by the first, or at least by the second post. Upon the whole, your French method, though sometimes more rapid, appears to me less sure and steady than the old German highway, &c. . . . But enough of this. A new and brighter prospect seems to be breaking upon us, and few events of *that kind* have ever given me more pleasure than your successful negotiation and ****'s satisfactory answer. The agreement is, indeed, equally convenient for both parties: no time or expense will be wasted in scrutinizing the title of the estate; the interest will be secured by the clause of five per cent., and I lament with you, that no larger sum than eight thousand pounds can be placed on Buriton, without asking (what might be somewhat impudent) a collateral security, &c., &c. . . . But I wish you to choose and execute one or the other of these arrangements with sage discretion and absolute power. I shorten my letter, that I may dispatch it by this post. I see the time, and I shall rejoice to see it at the end of twenty years, when my cares will be at an end, and our friendly pages will be no longer sullied with the repetition of dirty land and vile money; when we may expatiate on the politics of the world and our personal sentiments. Without expecting your answer of business, I mean to write soon in a purer style, and I wish to lay open to my friend the state of my mind, which (exclusive of all worldly concerns) is not perfectly at ease. In the meanwhile, I must add two or three short articles. I am astonished at Elmsley's silence, and the immobility of your picture. Mine should have departed long since, could I have found a sure opportunity, &c., &c. Adieu, yours.

Lausanne, May 15, 1790.

Since the first origin (*ab ovo*) of our connexion and correspondence, so long an interval of silence has not intervened, as far as I remember, between us.

From my silence you conclude that the moral complaint, which I had insinuated in my last, is either insignificant or fanciful. The conclusion is rash. But the complaint in question is of the nature of a slow lingering disease, which is not attended with any immediate danger. As I have not leisure to expatiate, take the idea in three words : ' Since the loss of poor Deyverdun, I am *alone* ; and even in Paradise, solitude is painful to a social mind. When I was a dozen years younger, I *scarcely* felt the weight of a single existence amidst the crowds of London, of parliament, of clubs ; but it will press more heavily upon me in this tranquil land, in the decline of life, and with the increase of infirmities. Some expedient, even the most desperate, must be embraced, to secure the domestic society of a male or female companion. But I am not in a hurry ; there is time for reflection and advice '. During this winter such finer feelings have been suspended by the grosser evil of bodily pain. On the ninth of February I was seized by such a fit of the gout as I had never known, though I must be thankful that its dire effects have been confined to the feet and knees, without ascending to the more noble parts. With some vicissitudes of better and worse, I have groaned between two and three months ; the debility has survived the pain, and though now easy, I am carried about in my chair, without any power, and with a very distant chance of supporting myself, from the extreme weakness and contraction of the joints of my knees. Yet I am happy in a skilful physician, and kind assiduous friends: every evening, during more than three months, has been enlivened (excepting when I have been forced to refuse them) by some cheerful visits, and very often by a chosen party of both sexes. How different is such society from the solitary evenings which I have passed in the tumult of London! It is not worth while fighting about a shadow, but should I ever return to England, Bath, not the metropolis, would be my last retreat.

Your portrait is at last arrived in perfect condition, and now occupies a conspicuous place over the chimney-glass in my library. It is the object of general admiration; good judges (the few) applaud the work; the name of Reynolds opens the eyes and mouths of the many; and were I not afraid of making you vain, I would inform you that the original is not allowed to be more than five-and-thirty. In spite of private reluctance and public discontent, I have honourably dismissed *myself*.[1] I shall arrive at Sir Joshua's before the end of the month; he will give me a look, and perhaps a touch; and you will be indebted to the president one guinea for the carriage. Do not be nervous, I am not rolled up; had I been so, you might have gazed on my charms four months ago. I want some account of yourself, of my Lady (shall we never directly correspond?), of Louisa, and of Maria. How has the latter since her launch supported a quiet winter in Sussex? I so much rejoice in your divorce from that b—— Kitty Coventry, that I care not what marriage you contract. A great city would suit your dignity, and the duties which would kill me in the first session, would supply your activity with a constant fund of amusement. But tread softly and surely; the ice is deceitful, the water is deep, and you may be soused over head and ears before you are aware.

[1] His portrait.

Why did not you or Elmsley send me the African pamphlet [1] by the post ? it would not have cost much. You have such a knack of turning a nation, that I am afraid you will triumph (perhaps by the force of argument) over justice and humanity. But do you not expect to work at Beelzebub's sugar plantations in the infernal regions, under the tender government of a negro-driver ? I should suppose both my Lady and Miss Firth very angry with you.

As to the bill for prints, which has been too long neglected, why will you not exercise the power, which I have never revoked, over all my cash at the Goslings ? The Severy family has passed a very favourable winter ; the young man is impatient to hear from a family which he places above all others : yet he will generously write next week, and send you a drawing of the alterations in the house. Do not raise your ideas ; you know *I* am satisfied with convenience in architecture, and some elegance in furniture. I admire the coolness with which you ask me to epistolize Reynell and Elmsley, as if a letter were so easy and pleasant a task ; it appears less so to me every day.

1790.

Your indignation will melt into pity, when you hear that for several weeks past I have been again confined to my chamber and my chair. Yet I must hasten, generously hasten, to exculpate the gout, my old enemy, from the curses which you already pour on his head. He is not the cause of this disorder, although the consequences have been somewhat similar. I am satisfied that this effort of nature has saved me from a very dangerous, perhaps a fatal, crisis ; and I listen to the flattering hope that it may tend to keep the gout at a more respectful distance, &c., &c., &c.

The whole sheet has been filled with dry selfish business ; but I must and will reserve some lines of

[1] Observations on the Project for abolishing the Slave Trade, by Lord Sheffield.

the cover for a little friendly conversation. I passed four days at the castle of Copet with Necker; and could have wished to have shown him, as a warning to any aspiring youth possessed with the demon of ambition. With all the means of private happiness in his power, he is the most miserable of human beings: the past, the present, and the future, are equally odious to him. When I suggested some domestic amusements of books, building, &c., he answered, with a deep tone of despair, 'Dans l'état où je suis, je ne puis sentir que le coup de vent qui m'a abbattu.' How different from the conscious cheerfulness with which our poor friend Lord North supported his fall! Madame Necker maintains more external composure, *mais le Diable n'y perd rien.* It is true that Necker wished to be carried into the closet, like old Pitt, on the shoulders of the people; and that he has been ruined by the democracy which he had raised. I believe him to be an able financier, and know him to be an honest man; too honest, perhaps, for a minister. His rival Calonne passed through Lausanne, in his way from Turin; and was soon followed by the Prince of Condé, with his son and grandson; but I was too much indisposed to see them. They have, or have had, some wild projects of a counter-revolution: horses have been bought, men levied: and the Canton of Berne has too much countenanced such foolish attempts, which must end in the ruin of the party. Burke's book is a most admirable medicine against the French disease, which has made too much progress even in this happy country. I admire his eloquence, I approve his politics, I adore his chivalry, and I can forgive even his superstition. The primitive church, which I have treated with some freedom, was itself at that time an innovation, and I was attached to the old Pagan establishment. The French spread so many lies about the sentiments of the English nation, that I wish the most considerable men of all parties and descriptions would join in some public act, declaring themselves satisfied with, and resolved to support our present constitution. Such a declaration would have a wonderful effect in Europe ; and, were I thought worthy, I myself would be proud to subscribe it. I have a great mind to send you something of a sketch, such as all thinking men might adopt.

I have intelligence of the approach of my Madeira. I accept with equal pleasure the second pipe, now in the Torrid Zone. Send me some pleasant details of your domestic state, of Maria, &c. If my Lady thinks that my silence is a mark of indifference, my Lady is a goose. I *must* have you all at Lausanne next summer.

Lausanne, August 7, 1790.

I answer at once your two letters ; and I should probably have taken earlier notice of the first, had I not been in daily expectation of the second. I must begin on the subject of what really interests me the most, your glorious election for Bristol. Most sincerely do I congratulate your exchange of a cursed expensive jilt, who deserted you for a rich Jew, for an honourable connexion with a chaste and virtuous matron, who will probably be as constant as she is disinterested.[1] In the whole range of election from Caithness to St. Ives, I much doubt whether there be a single choice so truly honourable to the member and the constituents. The second commercial city invites, from a distant province, an independent gentleman, known only by his active spirit, and his writings on the subject of trade ; and names him, without intrigue or expense, for her representative : even the voice of party is silenced, while factions strive which shall applaud the most.

[1] Lord Sheffield continued to represent the city of Bristol until he was removed to the British House of Peers, in 1802. He can never sufficiently acknowledge the liberality and kindness which he experienced, during the whole period, from the citizens of Bristol. He was not suffered to incur the least expense, not even for the printing of an advertisement. S.

You are now sure, for seven years to come, of never wanting food; I mean business: what a crowd of suitors or complainants will besiege your door! what a load of letters and memorials will be heaped on your table! I much question whether even you will not sometimes exclaim, *Ohe! jam satis est!* but that is your affair. Of the excursion to Coventry I cannot decide, but I hear it is pretty generally blamed: but, however, I love gratitude to an old friend; and shall not be very angry if you damned them with a farewell to all eternity. But I cannot repress my indignation at the use of those foolish, obsolete, odious words, Whig and Tory. In the American war they might have some meaning; and then your Lordship was a Tory, although you supposed yourself a Whig: since the coalition, all general principles have been confounded; and if there ever was an opposition to men, not measures, it is the present. Luckily both the leaders are great men; and, whatever happens, the country must fall upon its legs. What a strange mist of peace and war seems to hang over the ocean! We can perceive nothing but secrecy and vigour; but those are excellent qualities to perceive in a minister. From yourself and politics I now return to my private concerns, which I shall methodically consider under the three great articles of mind, body, and estate.

(1) I am not absolutely displeased at your firing so hastily at the hint, a tremendous hint, in my last letter. But the danger is not so serious or imminent as you seem to suspect; and I give you my word, that, before I take the slightest step which can bind me either in law, conscience, or honour, I will faithfully communicate, and we will freely discuss, the whole state of the business. But at present there is not anything to communicate or discuss; I do assure you that I have not any particular object in view: I am not in love with any of the hyenas of Lausanne, though there are some who keep their claws tolerably well pared. Sometimes, in a solitary mood, I have

fancied myself married to one or another of those whose society and conversation are the most pleasing to me; but when I have painted in my fancy all the probable consequences of such an union, I have started from my dream, rejoiced in my escape, and ejaculated a thanksgiving that I was still in possession of my natural freedom. Yet I feel, and shall continue to feel, that domestic solitude, however it may be alleviated by the world, by study, and even by friendship, is a comfortless state, which will grow more painful as I descend in the vale of years. At present my situation is very tolerable; and if at dinner-time, or at my return home in the evening, I sometimes sigh for a companion, there are many hours, and many occasions, in which I enjoy the superior blessing of being sole master of my own house. But your plan, though less dangerous, is still more absurd than mine: such a couple as you describe could not be found; and, if found, would not answer my purpose; their rank and position would be awkward and ambiguous to myself and my acquaintance; and the agreement of three persons of three characters would be still more impracticable. My plan of Charlotte Porten is undoubtedly the more desirable; and she might either remain a spinster (the case is not without example), or marry some Swiss of my choice, who would increase and enliven our society; and both would have the strongest motives for kind and dutiful behaviour. But the mother has been indirectly sounded, and will not hear of such a proposal for some years. On my side, I would not take her, but as a piece of soft wax which I could model to the language and manners of the country: I must therefore be patient.

Young Severy's letter, which may be now in your hands, and which, for these three or four last posts, has furnished my indolence with a new pretence for delay, has already informed you of the means and circumstances of my resurrection. Tedious indeed was my confinement, since I was not able to move from my house or chair, from the ninth of February to the first of July, very nearly five months. The first weeks were accompanied with more pain than I have ever known in the gout, with anxious days and sleepless nights; and when that pain subsided, it left a weakness in my knees which seemed to have no end. My confinement was however softened by books, by the possession of every comfort and convenience, by a succession each evening of agreeable company, and by a flow of equal spirits and general good health. During the last weeks I descended to the ground floor, poor Deyverdun's apartment, and constructed a chair like Merlin's, in which I could wheel myself in the house and on the terrace. My patience has been universally admired; yet how many thousands have passed those five months less easily than myself. I remember making a remark perfectly simple, and perfectly true: 'At present (I said to Madame de Severy), I am not positively miserable, and I may reasonably hope a daily or weekly improvement, till sooner or later in the summer I shall recover new limbs, and new pleasures, which I do not now possess: have any of you such a prospect?' The prediction has been accomplished, and I have arrived to my present condition of strength, or rather of feebleness: I now can walk with tolerable ease in my garden and smooth places; but on the rough pavement of the town I use, and perhaps shall use, a sedan chair. The Pyrmont waters have performed wonders; and my physician (not Tissot, but a very sensible man) allows me to hope that the term of the interval will be in proportion to that of the fit.

Have you read in the English papers that the government of Berne is overturned, and that we are divided into three democratical *leagues*? true as what I have read in the French papers, that the English have cut off Pitt's head, and abolished the House of Lords. The people of this country are happy; and in spite of some miscreants, and more foreign emissaries, they are sensible of their happiness.

Finally—Inform my Lady, that I am indignant at a false and heretical assertion in her last letter to Severy, ' that friends at a distance cannot love each other, if they do not write '. I love her better than any woman in the world ; indeed I do ; and yet I do not write. And she herself—but I am calm. We have now nearly one hundred French exiles, some of them worth being acquainted with ; particularly a Count de Schomberg, who is become almost my friend ; he is a man of the world, of letters, and of sufficient age, since in 1753, he succeeded to Marshal Saxe's regiment of dragoons. As to the rest, I entertain them, and they flatter me : but I wish we were reduced to our Lausanne society. Poor France ! the state is dissolved, the nation is mad ! Adieu.

Lausanne, April 9, 1791.

First, of my health : it is now tolerably restored, my legs are still weak, but the animal in general is in a sound and lively condition ; and we have great hopes from the fine weather and the Pyrmont waters. I most sincerely wished for the presence of Maria, to embellish a ball which I gave the 29th of last month to all the best company, natives and foreigners, of Lausanne, with the aid of the Severys, especially of the mother and son, who directed the economy, and performed the honours of the *fête*. It opened about seven in the evening ; the assembly of men and women was pleased and pleasing, the music good, the illumination splendid, the refreshments profuse : at twelve, one hundred and thirty persons sat down to a very good supper : at two, I stole away to bed, in a snug corner ; and I was informed at breakfast, that the remains of the veteran and young troops, with Severy and his sister at their head, had concluded the last dance about a quarter before seven. This magnificent entertainment has gained me great credit : and the expense was more reasonable than you can easily imagine. This was an extraordinary event, but I give frequent dinners ; and in the summer I have an assembly every Sunday evening. What a wicked wretch! says my Lady.

I cannot pity you for the accumulation of business, as you ought not to pity *me*, if I complained of the tranquillity of Lausanne; we suffer or enjoy the effects of our own choice. Perhaps you will mutter something, of our not being born for ourselves, of public spirit (I have formerly read of such a thing), of private friendship, for which I give you full and ample credit, &c. But your parliamentary operations, at least, will probably expire in the month of June; and I shall refuse to sign the Newhaven conveyance unless I am satisfied that you will execute the Lausanne visit this summer. On the 15th of June, suppose Lord, Lady, Maria, and maid (poor Louisa!), in a post coach, with Etienne on horseback, set out from Downing Street, or Sheffield Place, cross the channel from Brighton to Dieppe, visit the National Assembly, buy caps at Paris, examine the ruins of Versailles, and arrive at Lausanne, without danger or fatigue, the second week in July; you will be lodged pleasantly and comfortably, and will not perhaps despise my situation. A couple of months will roll, alas! too hastily away: you will all be amused by new scenes, new people; and whenever Maria and you, with Severy, mount on horseback to visit the country, the glaciers, &c., my Lady and myself shall form a very quiet *tête-à-tête* at home. In September, if you are tired, you may return by a direct or indirect way; but I only desire that you will not make the plan impracticable, by grasping at too much. In return, I promise you a visit of three or four months in the autumn of ninety-two: you and my booksellers are now my principal attractions in England. You had some right to growl at hearing of my supplement in the papers: but Cadell's indiscretion was founded on a hint which I had thrown out in a letter, and which in all probability will never be executed. Yet I am not totally idle. Adieu.

Lausanne, May 18, 1791.

I write a short letter, on small paper, to inform you, that the various deeds, which arrived safe and in good condition, have this morning been sealed, signed, and delivered, in the presence of respectable and well-known English witnesses. To have read the aforesaid acts would have been difficult; to have understood them, impracticable. I therefore signed them with my eyes shut, and in that implicit confidence, which we freemen and Britons are humbly content to yield to our lawyers and ministers. I hope, however, most seriously hope, that everything has been carefully examined, and that I am not totally ruined. It is not without much impatience that I expect an account of the payment and investment of the purchase-money. It was my intention to have added a new edition of my will: but I have an unexpected call to go to Geneva to-morrow with the Severys, and must defer that business a few days till after my return. On my return I may possibly find a letter from you, and will write more fully in answer: my posthumous work[1], contained in a single sheet, will not ruin you in postage. In the meanwhile let me desire you either never to talk of Lausanne, or to execute the journey this summer: after the dispatch of public and *private* business, there can be no real obstacle but in yourself. Pray do not go to war with Russia; it is very foolish. I am quite angry with Pitt. Adieu.

Lausanne, May 31, 1791.

At length I see a ray of sunshine breaking from a dark cloud. Your epistle of the 13th arrived this morning, the 25th instant, the day after my return from Geneva; it has been communicated to Severy. We now believe that you intend a visit to Lausanne this summer, and we hope that you will execute that intention. If you are a man of honour, you shall find me one; and, on the day of your arrival at

[1] Mr. Gibbon's will.

Lausanne, I will ratify my engagement of visiting the British Isle before the end of the year 1792, excepting only the fair and foul exception of the gout. You rejoice me, by proposing the addition of dear Louisa; it was not without a bitter pang that I threw her overboard, to lighten the vessel and secure the voyage: I was fearful of the governess, a second carriage, and a long train of difficulty and expense, which might have ended in blowing up the whole scheme. But if you can bodkin the sweet creature into the coach, she will find an easy welcome at Lausanne. The first arrangements which I must make before your arrival, may be altered by your own taste, on a survey of the premises, and you will all be commodiously and pleasantly lodged. You have heard a great deal of the beauty of my house, garden, and situation; but such are their intrinsic value that, unless I am much deceived, they will bear the test even of exaggerated praise. From my knowledge of your lordship, I have always entertained some doubt how you would get through the society of a Lausanne winter; but I am satisfied that, exclusive of friendship, your summer visits to the banks of the Leman Lake will long be remembered as one of the most agreeable periods of your life; and that you will scarcely regret the amuse-ment of a Sussex Committee of Navigation in the dog days. You ask for details: what details? a map of France and a post-book are easy and infallible guides. If the ladies are not afraid of the ocean, you are not ignorant of the passage from Brighton to Dieppe: Paris will then be in your direct road; and even allowing you to look at the Pandemonium, the ruins of Versailles, &c., a fortnight diligently employed will clear you from Sheffield Place to Gibbon Castle. What can I say more?

As little have I to say on the subject of my worldly matters, which seem now, Jupiter be praised, to be drawing towards a final conclusion; since when people part with their money, they are indeed serious. I do not perfectly understand the ratio of the precise sum which you have poured into Gosling's reservoir, but suppose 'it will be explained in a general account.

You have been very dutiful in sending to me, what I have always desired, a cut Woodfall on a remarkable debate; a debate, indeed, most remarkable! Poor Burke is the most eloquent and rational madman that I ever knew. I love Fox's feelings, but I detest the political principles of the man, and of the party. Formerly, you detested them more strongly during the American war than myself. I am half afraid that you are corrupted by your unfortunate connexions. Should you admire the National Assembly, we shall have many an altercation, for I am as high an aristocrat as Burke himself; and he has truly observed, that it is impossible to debate with temper on the subject of that cursed revolution. In my last excursion to Geneva I frequently saw the Neckers, who by this time are returned to their summer residence at Copet. He is much restored in health and spirits, especially since the publication of his last book, which has probably reached England. Both parties, who agree in abusing him, agree likewise that he is a man of virtue and genius; but I much fear that the purest intentions have been productive of the most baneful consequences. Our military men, I mean the French, are leaving us every day for the camp of the Princes at Worms, and support what is called [1]   representation. Their hopes are sanguine; I will not answer for their being well grounded: it is *certain*, however, that the emperor had an interview the 19th instant with the Count of Artois at Mantua; and the aristocrats talk in mysterious language of Spain, Sardinia, the Empire, four or five armies, &c. They will doubtless strike a blow this summer: may it not recoil on their own heads! Adieu. Embrace our female travellers. A short delay!

Lausanne, June 12, 1791.

I now begin to see you all in real motion, swimming from Brighton to Dieppe, according to my scheme, and

[1] The words in the original letter are torn off by the seal.

afterwards treading the direct road, which you cannot well avoid, to the turbulent capital of the late kingdom of France. I know not what more to say, or what further instructions to send ; they would indeed be useless, as you are travelling through a country which has been sometimes visited by Englishmen : only this let me say, that in the midst of anarchy the roads were never more secure than at present. As you will wish to assist at the National Assembly, you will act prudently in obtaining from the French in London a good recommendation to some leading member ; Cazales, for instance, or the Abbé Maury. I soon expect from Elmsley a cargo of books ; but you may bring me any new pamphlet of exquisite flavour, particularly the last works of John Lord Sheffield[1], which the dog has always neglected to send. You will have time to write once more, and you must endeavour, as nearly as possible, to mark the day of your arrival. You may come either by Lyons and Geneva, by Dijon and Les Rousses, or by Dole and Pontarliere. The post will fail you on the edge of Switzerland, and must be supplied by hired horses. I wish you to make your last day's journey easy, so as to dine upon the road, and arrive by tea-time. The pulse of the counter-revolution beats high, but I cannot send you any certain facts. Adieu. I want to *hear* my Lady abusing me for never writing. *All* the Severys are very impatient.

Notwithstanding the high premium, I do not absolutely wish you drowned. Besides all other cares, I must marry and propagate, which would give me a great deal of trouble.

Lausanne, July 1, 1791.

In obedience to your orders I direct a flying shot to Paris, though I have not anything particular to add, excepting that our impatience is increased in the *inverse ratio* of time and space. Yet I almost doubt whether you have passed the sea. The news of the

[1] *Observations on the Corn Laws.*

king of France's escape must have reached you before
the 28th, the day of your departure, and the prospect
of strange unknown disorder may well have suspended
your firmest resolves. The royal animal is again
caught, and all may probably be quiet. I was just
going to exhort you to pass through Brussels and the
confines of Germany; a fair Irishism, since if you
read this, you are already at Paris. The only reasonable advice which now remains, is to obtain, by means
of Lord Gower[1], a sufficiency, or even superfluity, of
forcible passports, such as leave no room for cavil on
a jealous frontier. The frequent intercourse with Paris
has proved that the best and shortest road, instead of
Besançon, is by Dijon, Dole, Les Rousses, and Nyon.
Adieu. I warmly embrace the ladies. It would be
idle now to talk of business.

[1] Then British Ambassador at Paris.

NOTE BY LORD SHEFFIELD

It has appeared from the foregoing Letters, that a visit from myself and my family, to Mr. Gibbon at Lausanne, had been for some time in agitation. This long-promised excursion took place in the month of June, 1791, and occasioned a considerable cessation of our correspondence. I landed at Dieppe immediately after the unfortunate Lewis XVI was brought captive to Paris. During my stay in that capital, I had an opportunity of seeing the extraordinary ferment of men's minds, both in the National Assembly and in private societies, and also in my passage through France to Lausanne, where I recalled to my memory the interesting scenes I had witnessed, by frequent conversations with my deceased friend. I might have wished to record his opinions on the subject of the French Revolution, if he had not expressed them so well in the annexed Letters. He seemed to suppose, as some of his Letters hint, that I had a tendency to the new French opinions. Never was suspicion more unfounded; nor could it have been admitted into Mr. Gibbon's mind, but that his extreme friendship for me, and his utter abhorrence of these notions, made him anxious and jealous, even to an excess, that I should not entertain them. He was, however, soon undeceived; he found that I was fully as averse to them as himself. I had from the first expressed an opinion, that such a change as was aimed at in France, would derange all the regular governments in Europe, hazard the internal quiet and dearest interests of this country, and probably end in bringing on mankind a much greater portion of misery, than the most sanguine reformer had ever promised to himself or others to produce of benefit, by the visionary schemes of liberty and equality, with which the ignorant and vulgar were misled and abused.

Mr. Gibbon at first, like many others, seemed pleased with the prospect of the reform of inveterate abuses; but he very soon discovered the mischief which was intended, the imbecility with which concessions were made, and the ruin which must arise, from the want of resolution or conduct, in the administration of France. He lived to reprobate, in the strongest terms possible, the folly of the first reformers, and the something worse than extravagance and ferocity of their successors. He saw the wild and mischievous tendency of those pretended reformers, which, while they professed nothing but amendment, really meant destruction to all social order; and so strongly was his opinion fixed, as to the danger of hasty innovation, that he became a warm and zealous advocate for every sort of old establishment, which he marked in various ways, sometimes rather ludicrously; and I recollect, in a circle where French affairs were the topic, and some Portuguese present, he, seemingly with seriousness, argued in favour of the Inquisition at Lisbon, and said he would not, at the present moment, give up even that old establishment.

It may, perhaps, not be quite uninteresting to the readers of these Memoirs, to know, that I found Mr. Gibbon at Lausanne in possession of an excellent house; the view from which, and from the terrace, was so uncommonly beautiful, that even his own pen would with difficulty describe the scene which it commanded. This prospect comprehended everything vast and magnificent, which could be furnished by the finest mountains among the Alps, the most extensive view of the Lake of Geneva, with a beautifully varied and cultivated country, adorned by numerous villas, and picturesque buildings, intermixed with beautiful masses of stately trees. Here my friend received us with an hospitality and kindness which I can never forget. The best apartments of the house were appropriated to our use; the choicest society of the place was sought for to enliven our visit, and render every day of it cheerful and agreeable. It was impossible for any man to be more esteemed and admired than Mr. Gibbon was at Lausanne. The preference he had given to that place, in adopting it for a residence, rather than his own country, was felt and acknowledged by all the inhabitants; and he may have been said almost to have given the law to a set of as willing subjects as any man ever presided over. In return for the deference shown to him, he mixed, without affectation, in all the society, I mean all the best society, that Lausanne afforded; he could indeed command it, and was, perhaps, for that reason the more partial to it; for he often declared that he liked society more as a relaxation from study, than as expecting to derive from it amusement or instruction; that to books he looked for improvement, not to living persons. But this I considered partly as an answer to my expressions of wonder, that a man who might choose the most various and most generally improved society in the world, namely, in England, should prefer the very limited circle of Lausanne, which he never deserted but for an occasional visit to M. and Madame Necker. It must not, however, be understood, that in choosing Lausanne for his home, he was insensible to the value of a residence in England: he was not in possession of an income which corresponded with his notions of ease and comfort in his own country. In Switzerland, his fortune was ample. To this consideration of fortune may be added another, which also had its weight; from early youth Mr. Gibbon had contracted a partiality for foreign taste and foreign habits of life, which made him less a stranger abroad than he was, in some respects, in his native country. This arose, perhaps, from having been out of England from his sixteenth to his twenty-first year; yet, when I came to Lausanne, I found him apparently without relish for French society. During the stay I made with him he renewed his intercourse with the principal French who were at Lausanne; of whom there happened to be a considerable number, distinguished for rank or talents ; many indeed respectable for both.[1] I was not absent from my friend's house, except during a short excursion that we made together to M. Necker's at Copet, and a tour to Geneva, Chamouny, over the Col de Balme, to Martigny, St. Maurice, and round the Lake by Vevay to Lausanne. In the social and singularly pleasant months that I passed with Mr. Gibbon, he enjoyed his usual cheerfulness, with good health. After he left England, in 1788, he had had a severe attack, mentioned in one of the foregoing letters, of an erysipelas, which at last settled in one of his legs, and left something of a dropsical tendency ; for at this time I first perceived a considerable degree of swelling about the ankle.

In the beginning of October I quitted this delightful residence ; and some time after my return to England our correspondence recommenced.

[1] Marshal de Castries and several branches of his family, Duc de Guignes and daughters, Duc and Duchesse de Guiche, Madame de Grammont, Princesse d'Henin, Princesse de Bouillon, Duchesse de Biron, Prince de Salm, Comte de Schomberg, Comte de Lally Tolendal, M. Mounier, Madame d'Aguesseau and family, M. de Malsherbes, &c., &c.

LETTERS

FROM EDWARD GIBBON, ESQ.,
TO LORD SHEFFIELD, AND OTHERS

EDWARD GIBBON, ESQ., TO THE HON. MISS HOLROYD

Lausanne, Nov. 9, 1791.

GULLIVER is made to say, in presenting his interpreter, 'My tongue is in the mouth of my friend'. Allow me to say, with proper expressions and excuses, 'My pen is in the hand of my friend'; and the aforesaid friend begs leave thus to continue.[1]

I remember to have read somewhere in Rousseau, of a lover quitting very often his mistress, to have the pleasure of corresponding with her. Though not absolutely your lover, I am very much your admirer, and should be extremely tempted to follow the same example. The spirit and reason which prevail in your conversation, appear to great advantage in your letters. The three which I have received from Berne, Coblentz, and Brussels have given me much real pleasure; first, as a proof that you are often thinking of me; secondly, as an evidence that you are capable of keeping a resolution; and thirdly, from their own intrinsic merit and entertainment. The style, without any allowance for haste or hurry, is perfectly correct; the manner is neither too light, nor too grave; the dimensions neither too long, nor too short: they are such, in

---

[1] The remainder of the letter was dictated by Mr. Gibbon, and written by M. Wilh. de Severy. S.

a word, as I should like to receive from the daughter of my best friend. I attend your lively journal, through bad roads, and worse inns. Your description of men and manners conveys very satisfactory information; and I am particularly delighted with your remark concerning the irregular behaviour of the Rhine. But the Rhine, alas! after some temporary wanderings, will be content to flow in his old channel, while man—man is the greatest fool of the whole creation.

I direct this letter to Sheffield Place, where I suppose you arrived in health and safety. I congratulate my Lady on her quiet establishment by her fireside: and hope you will be able, after all your excursions, to support the climate and manners of Old England. Before this epistle reaches you, I hope to have received the two promised letters from Dover and Sheffield Place. If they should not meet with a proper return, you will pity and forgive me. I have not yet heard from Lord Sheffield, who seems to have devolved on his daughter the task which she has so gloriously executed. I shall probably not write to him, till I have received his first letter of business from England; but with regard to my Lady, I have most excellent intentions.

I never could understand how two persons of such superior merit, as Miss Holroyd and Miss Lausanne, could have so little relish for one another, as they appeared to have in the beginning; and it was with great pleasure that I observed the degrees of their growing intimacy, and the mutual regret of their separation. Whatever you may imagine, your friends at Lausanne have been thinking as frequently of yourself and company, as you could possibly think of them; and you will be very ungrateful, if you do not seriously resolve to make them a second visit, under such name and title as you may judge most agreeable. None of the Severy family, except perhaps my secretary, are inclined to forget you; and I am continually asked for some account of your health, motions, and amusements. Since your departure, no great events have occurred. I have made a short excursion to Geneva and Copet, and found M. Necker in much better spirits than when you saw him. They pressed me to pass some weeks this winter in their house at Geneva; and I may possibly comply, at least in part, with their invitation. The aspect of Lausanne is peaceful and placid; and you have no hopes of a revolution driving me out of this country. We hear nothing of the proceedings of the commission[1], except by playing at cards every evening with Monsieur Fischer, who often speaks of Lord Sheffield with esteem and respect. There is no appearance of Rosset and La Motte being brought to a speedy trial, and they still remain in the castle of Chillon, which (according to the geography of the National Assembly) is washed by the sea. Our winter begins with great severity; and we shall not probably have many balls, which, as you may imagine, I lament much. Angletine does not consider two French words as a letter. Montrond sighs and blushes whenever Louisa's name is mentioned: Philippine wishes to converse with her on men and manners. The French ladies are settled in town for the winter, and they form, with Mrs. Trevor, a very agreeable addition to our society.

---

[1] A commission, at the head of which was Monsieur Fischer, one of the principal members of the government of Berne, a very active and intelligent man, who would have distinguished himself in the administration of any country. This commission, which was accompanied by two or three thousand of the best of the German militia of the Canton of Berne, was sent for the purpose of examining into some attempts to introduce the French revolutionary principles into the Pays de Vaud. Several persons were seized; the greater part were released; the examination was secret, but Rosset and La Motte were confined in the castle of Chillon; and being afterwards condemned, for correspondence with the French, to a long imprisonment, were transferred to the castle of Arbourg, from whence they escaped. S.

It is now enlivened by a visit of the Chevalier de Boufflers, one of the most accomplished men in the *ci-devant* kingdom of France.

As Mrs. Wood[1], who has miscarried, is about to leave us, I must either cure or die; and, upon the whole, I believe the former will be most expedient. You will see her in London, with dear Corea, next winter. My rival magnificently presents me with a hogshead of Madeira; so that in honour I could not supplant him: yet I do assure you, from my heart, that another departure is much more painful to me. The apartment below[2] is shut up, and I know not when I shall again visit it with pleasure. Adieu. Believe me, one and all, most affectionately yours.

EDWARD GIBBON, ESQ., TO THE RIGHT HON. LORD SHEFFIELD

Lausanne, December 28, 1791.

Alas! alas! the demon of procrastination has again possessed me. Three months have nearly rolled away since your departure; and seven letters, five from the most valuable Maria, and two from yourself, have extorted from me only a single epistle, which perhaps would never have been written, had I not used the permission of employing my own tongue and the hand of a secretary. Shall I tell you, that, for these last six weeks, the eve of every day has witnessed a *firm* resolution, and the day itself has furnished some ingenious delay? This morning, for instance, I determined to invade you as soon as the breakfast things should be removed: they were removed; but I had something to read, to write, to meditate, and there was time enough before me. Hour after hour has stolen away, and I finally begin my letter at two o'clock,

---

[1] Madame de Silva.

[2] The apartment principally inhabited during the residence of my family at Lausanne. S.

evidently too late for the post, as I must dress, dine, go abroad, &c. A foundation, however, *shall be* laid, which shall stare me in the face; and next Saturday I shall probably be roused by the awful reflection that it is the last day in the year.

After realizing this summer an event which I had long considered as a dream of fancy, I know not whether I should rejoice or grieve at your visit to Lausanne. While I possessed the family, the sentiment of pleasure highly predominated; when, just as we had subsided in a regular, easy, comfortable plan of life, the last trump sounded, and, without speaking of the pang of separation, you left me to one of the most gloomy, solitary months of October which I have ever passed. For yourself and daughters, however, you have contrived to snatch some of the most interesting scenes of this world. Paris, at such a moment, Switzerland, and the Rhine, Strasburg, Coblentz, have suggested a train of lively images and useful ideas, which will not be speedily erased. The mind of the young damsel, more especially, will be enlarged and enlightened in every sense. In four months she has lived many years; and she will much deceive and displease me, if she does not review and methodize her journal, in such a manner as she is capable of performing, for the amusement of her particular friends. Another benefit which will redound from your recent view is, that every place, person, and object, about Lausanne, are now become familiar and interesting to you. In our future correspondence (do I dare pronounce the word correspondence?) I can talk to you as freely of every circumstance as if it were actually before your eyes. And first, of my own improvements. All those venerable piles of ancient verdure which you *admired* have been eradicated in one fatal day. Your faithful substitutes, William de Severy and Levade, have never ceased to persecute me, till I signed their death-warrant. Their place is now supplied by a number of picturesque naked poles, the foster-fathers of as many twigs of Platanusses, which may afford a grateful but distant shade to the founder, or to his seris Nepotibus. In the meanwhile I must confess that the terrace appears broader, and that I discover a much larger quantity of snow than I should otherwise do. The workmen admire your ingenious plan for cutting out a new bedchamber and book-room; but, on mature consideration, we all unanimously prefer the old scheme of adding a third room on the terrace beyond the library, with two spacious windows, and a fireplace between. It will be larger (28 feet by 21), and pleasanter, and warmer: the difference of expense will be much less considerable than I imagined: the door of communication with the library will be artfully buried in the wainscot; and, unless it be opened by my own choice, may always remain a profound secret. Such is the design; but, as it will not be executed before next summer, you have time and liberty to state your objections. I am much colder about the staircase, but it may be finished, according to your idea, for thirty pounds; and I feel they will persuade me. Am I not a very rich man? When these alterations are completed, few authors of six volumes in quarto will be more agreeably lodged than myself. Lausanne is now full and lively; all our native families are returned from the country; and, praised be the Lord! we are infested with few foreigners, either French or English. Even our democrats are more reasonable or more discreet; it is agreed to waive the subject of politics, and all seem happy and cordial. I have a grand dinner this week, a supper of thirty or forty people on Twelfth Day, &c.; some concerts have taken place, some balls are talked of; and even Maria would allow (yet it is ungenerous to say even Maria) that the winter scene of Lausanne is tolerably gay and active. I say nothing of the Severys, as Angletine has epistolized Maria last post. She has probably hinted that her brother meditates a short excursion to Turin: that worthy fellow Trevor has given him a pressing invitation to his own house. In the beginning of

February I propose going to Geneva for three or four weeks. I shall lodge and eat with the Neckers; my mornings will be my own, and I shall spend my evenings in the society of the place, where I have many acquaintance. This short absence will agitate my stagnant life, and restore me with fresh appetite to my house, my library, and my friends. Before that time (the end of February) what events may happen, or be ready to happen! The National Assembly (compared to which the former was a senate of heroes and demi-gods) seem resolved to attack Germany *avec quatre millions de bayonettes libres;* the army of the princes must soon either fight, or starve, or conquer. Will Sweden draw his sword? will Russia draw her purse? an empty purse! All is darkness and anarchy: neither party is strong enough to oppose a settlement; and I cannot see a possibility of an amicable arrangement, where there are no heads (in any sense of the word) who can answer for the multitude. Send me your ideas, and those of Lord Guildford, Lord Loughborough, Fox, &c.

Before I conclude, a word of my vexatious affairs. Shall I never sail on the smooth stream of good security and half-yearly interest? will everybody refuse my money? I had already written to Darrel and Gosling to obey your commands, and was in hopes that you had already made large and salutary evacuations. During your absence I never expected much effect from the cold indifference of agents; but you are now in England—you will be speedily in London: set all your setting-dogs to beat the field, hunt, inquire, why should you not advertise? Yet I am almost ashamed to complain of some stagnation of interest, when I am witness to the natural and acquired philosophy of so many French, who are reduced from riches, not to indigence, but to absolute want and beggary. A Count Argout has just left us, who possessed ten thousand a year in the island of St. Domingo; he is utterly burnt and ruined; and a brother, whom he tenderly loved, has been murdered by the negroes. These are real misfortunes. I have much revolved the plan of the Memoirs I once mentioned, and, as you do not think it ridiculous, I believe I shall make an attempt: if I can please myself, I am confident of not displeasing; but let this be a profound secret between us: people must not be prepared to laugh, they must be taken by surprise. Have you looked over your, or rather my, letters? Surely, in the course of the year, you may find a safe and cheap occasion of sending me a parcel; they may assist me. Adieu. I embrace my Lady; send me a favourable account of her health. I kiss the Marmaille. By an amazing push of remorse and diligence I have finished my letter (three pages and a half) this same day since dinner; but I have not time to read it. Ever yours.

Half-past six.

To the Same.

Lausanne, December 31, 1791.

To-morrow a New Year, *multos et felices!*

I now most sincerely repent of my late repentance, and do almost swear never to renounce the amiable and useful practice of procrastination. Had I delayed, as I was strongly tempted, another post, your missive of the 13th, which did not reach me till this morning (three mails were due), would have arrived in time, and I might have avoided this second herculean labour. It will be, however, no more than an infant Hercules. The topics of conversation have been fully discussed, and I shall now confine myself to the needful of the new business. *Felix faustumque sit!* may no untoward accident disarrange your Yorkshire mortgage; the conclusion of which will place me in a clear and easy state, such as I have never known since the first hour of property. . . .

The three per cents. are so high, and the country is in such a damned state of prosperity under that fellow Pitt, that it goes against me to purchase at such low interest. In my visit to England next autumn, or in the spring following (alas! you *must* acquiesce in the alternative), I hope to be armed with sufficient materials to draw a sum, which may be employed as taste or fancy shall dictate, in the improvement of my library, a service of plate, &c. I am not very sanguine, but surely this is no uncomfortable prospect. This pecuniary detail, which has not indeed been so unpleasant as it used formerly to be, has carried me further than I expected. I rejoice in Lally's prosperity. Have you reconsidered my proposal of a declaration of constitutional principles from the heads of the party? I think a foolish address from a body of Whigs to the National Assembly renders it still more incumbent on you. Achieve my worldly concerns, *et eris mihi magnus Apollo.* Adieu. Ever yours.

To the Same.

Lausanne, April 4, 1792.

For fear you should abuse me, as usual, I will begin the attack, and scold at you, for not having yet sent me the long-expected intelligence of the completion of my mortgage. *Cospetto di Baccho!* for I must ease myself by swearing a little. What is the cause, the meaning, the pretence of this delay? Are the Yorkshire mortgagers inconstant in their wishes? Are the London lawyers constant in their procrastination? Is a letter on the road, to inform me that all is concluded, or to tell me that all is broken to pieces? Had the money been placed in the three per cents. last May, besides the annual interest, it would have gained by the rise of stock nearly twenty per cent. Your lordship is a wise man, a successful writer, and a useful senator; you understand America and Ireland, corn and slaves; but your prejudice against the funds[1], in which I am often tempted to join, makes

[1] It would be more correct if he had only stated my preference of landed to all other property. S.

you a little blind to their increasing value in the hands of our virtuous and excellent minister. But our regret is vain ; one pull more and we reach the shore ; and our future correspondence will be no longer tainted with business. Shall I then be more diligent and regular ? I hope and believe so ; for now that I have got over this article of worldly interest, my letter seems to be almost finished. A propos of letters, am I not a sad dog to forget my Lady and Maria ? Alas ! the dual number has been prejudicial to both. *How happy could I be with either, were t'other dear charmer away !* I am like the ass of famous memory ; I cannot tell which way to turn first, and there I stand mute and immovable. The baronial and maternal dignity of my Lady, supported by twenty years' friendship, may claim the preference. But the five incomparable letters of Maria !—Next week, however—Am I not ashamed to talk of next week ?

I have most successfully, and most agreeably, executed my plan of spending the month of March at Geneva, in the Necker house, and every circumstance that I had arranged turned out beyond my expectation ; the freedom of the morning, the society of the table and drawing-room, from half an hour past two till six or seven ; an evening assembly and card party, in a round of the best company, and, excepting one day in the week, a private supper of free and friendly conversation. You would like Geneva better than Lausanne ; there is much more information to be got among the men ; but though I found some agreeable women, their manners and style of life are, upon the whole, less easy and pleasant than our own. I was much pleased with Necker's brother, Mr. De Germany, a good-humoured, polite, sensible man, without the genius and fame of the statesman, but much more adapted for private and ordinary happiness. Madame de Staël is expected in a few weeks at Copet, where they receive her, and where, 'to dumb forgetfulness a prey,' she will have leisure to regret 'the pleasing anxious being ', which she enjoyed amidst

the storms of Paris. But what can the poor creature
do ? her husband is in Sweden, her lover is no longer
secretary at war, and her father's house is the only
place where she can reside with the least degree of
prudence and decency. Of that father I have really
a much higher idea than I ever had before; in our
domestic intimacy he cast away his gloom and reserve;
I saw a great deal of his mind, and all that I saw is
fair and worthy. He was overwhelmed by the hurricane, he mistook his way in the fog, but in such a
perilous situation, I much doubt whether any mortal
could have seen or stood. In the meanwhile, he is
abused by all parties, and none of the French in
Geneva will set their foot in his house. He remembers
Lord Sheffield with esteem; his health is good, and
he would be tranquil in his private life, were not his
spirits continually wounded by the arrival of every
letter and every newspaper. His sympathy is deeply
interested by the fatal consequences of a revolution,
in which he had acted so leading a part; and he feels
as a friend for the danger of M. de Lessart, who may
be guilty in the eyes of the Jacobins, or even of his
judges, by those very actions and dispatches which
would be most approved by all the lovers of his country.
What a momentous event is the Emperor's death !
In the forms of a new reign, and of the Imperial
election, the democrats have at least gained time, if
they knew how to use it. But the new monarch,
though of a weak complexion, is of a martial temper;
he loves the soldiers, and is beloved by them; and
the slow fluctuating politics of his uncle may be
succeeded by a direct line of march to the gates of
Strasbourg and Paris. It is the opinion of the master
movers in France (I know it most certainly), that
their troops will not fight, that the people have lost
all sense of patriotism, and that on the first discharge
of an Austrian cannon, the game is up. But what
occasion for Austrians or Spaniards ? the French are
themselves their greatest enemies; four thousand
Marseillois are marched against Arles and Avignon,

the *troupes de ligne* are divided between the two parties, and the flame of civil war will soon extend over the southern provinces. You have heard of the unworthy treatment of the Swiss regiment of Ernest. The canton of Berne has bravely recalled them, with a stout letter to the King of France, which must be inserted in all the papers. I now come to the most unpleasant article, our home politics. Rosset and La Motte are condemned to five and twenty years' imprisonment in the fortress of Arbourg. We have not yet received their official sentence, nor is it believed that the proofs and proceedings against them will be published; an awkward circumstance, which it does not seem easy to justify. Some (though none of note) are taken up, several are fled, many more are suspected and suspicious. All are silent, but it is the silence of fear and discontent; and the secret hatred which rankled against government begins to point against the few who are known to be well-affected. I never knew any place so much changed as Lausanne, even since last year; and though you will not be much obliged to me for the motive, I begin very seriously to think of visiting Sheffield Place by the month of September next. Yet here again I am frightened, by the dangers of a French, and the difficulties of a German, route. You must send me an account of the passage from Dieppe to Brighton, with an itinerary of the Rhine, distances, expenses, &c. As usual, I just save the post, nor have I time to read my letter, which, after wasting the morning in deliberation, has been struck off in a heat since dinner. The views of Sheffield Place are just received; they are admired, and shall be framed. Severy has spent the carnival at Turin. Trevor is only the best man in the world.

To the Same.

Lausanne, May 30, 1792.

After the receipt of your *penultimate*, eight days ago, I expected, with much impatience, the arrival of your next-promised epistle. It arrived this morning, but has not completely answered my expectations. I wanted, and I hoped for a full and fair picture of the present and probable aspect of your political world, with which, at this distance, I seem everyday less satisfied. In the slave question you triumphed last session, in this you have been defeated. What is the cause of this alteration? If it proceeded only from an impulse of humanity, I cannot be displeased, even with an error: since it is very likely that my own vote (had I possessed one) would have been added to the majority. But in this rage against slavery, in the numerous petitions against the slave trade, was there no leaven of new democratical principles? no wild ideas of the rights and natural equality of man? It is these I fear. Some articles in newspapers, some pamphlets of the year, the Jockey Club, have fallen into my hands. I do not infer much from such publications; yet I have never known them of so black and malignant a cast. I shuddered at Grey's motion; disliked the half-support of Fox, admired the firmness of Pitt's declaration, and excused the usual intemperance of Burke. Surely such men as ****, ********, *******, have talents for mischief. I see a club of reform which contains some respectable names. Inform me of the professions, the principles, the plans, the resources, of these reformers. Will they heat the minds of the people? Does the French democracy gain no ground? Will the bulk of your party stand firm to their own interest, and that of their country? Will you not take some active measures to declare your sound opinions, and separate yourselves from your rotten members? If you allow them to perplex government, if you trifle with this

solemn business, if you do not resist the spirit of
innovation in the first attempt, if you admit the smallest
and most specious change in our parliamentary system,
you are lost. You will be driven from one step to
another; from principles just in theory, to consequences most pernicious in practice: and your first
concessions will be productive of every subsequent
mischief, for which you will be answerable to your
country and to posterity. Do not suffer yourselves
to be lulled into a false security; remember the proud
fabric of the French monarchy. Not four years ago
it stood founded, as it might seem, on the rock of
time, force, and opinion, supported by the triple
aristocracy of the church, the nobility, and the parlia-
ments. They are crumbled into dust; they are
vanished from the earth. If this tremendous warning
has no effect on the men of property in England; if
it does not open every eye, and raise every arm, you
will deserve your fate. If I am too precipitate,
enlighten; if I am too desponding, encourage me.

My pen has run into this argument; for, as much
a foreigner as you think me, on this momentous subject
I feel myself an Englishman.

The pleasure of residing at Sheffield Place is, after
all, the first and the ultimate object of my visit to my
native country. But when or how will that visit be
effected? Clouds and whirlwinds, Austrian Croats and
Gallic cannibals, seem on every side to impede my
passage. You appear to apprehend the perils or
difficulties of the German road, and French peace is
more sanguinary than civilized war. I must pass
through, perhaps, a thousand republics or munici-
palities, which neither obey nor are obeyed. The
strictness of passports, and the popular ferment, are
much increased since last summer: *aristocrate* is in
every mouth, lanterns hang in every street, and a
hasty word, or a casual resemblance, may be fatal.
Yet, on the other hand, it is probable that many
English, men, women, and children, will traverse the
country without any accident before next September;

and I am sensible that many things appear more formidable at a distance than on a nearer approach. Without any absolute determination, we must see what the events of the next three or four months will produce. In the meanwhile, I shall expect with impatience your next letter: let it be speedy: my answer shall be prompt.

You will be glad, or sorry, to learn that my gloomy apprehensions are much abated, and that my departure, whenever it takes place, will be an act of choice, rather than of necessity. I do not pretend to affirm that secret discontent, dark suspicion, private animosity, are very materially assuaged; but we have not experienced, nor do we now apprehend, any dangerous acts of violence, which may compel me to seek a refuge among the friendly Bears[1], and to abandon my library to the mercy of the democrats. The firmness and vigour of government have crushed, at least for a time, the spirit of innovation; and I do not believe that the body of the people, especially the peasants, are disposed for a revolution. From France, praised be the demon of anarchy! the insurgents of the Pays de Vaud could not at present have much to hope; and should the *gardes nationales*, of which there is little appearance, attempt an incursion, the country is armed and prepared, and they would be resisted with equal numbers and superior discipline. The Gallic wolves that prowled round Geneva are drawn away, some to the south and some to the north, and the late events in Flanders seem to have diffused a general contempt, as well as abhorrence, for the lawless savages, who fly before the enemy, hang their prisoners, and murder their officers. The brave and patient regiment of Ernest is expected home every day, and as Berne will take them into present pay, that veteran and regular corps will add to the security of our frontier.

I rejoice that we have so little to say on the subject of worldly affairs. This summer we are threatened

[1] Berne.

with an inundation, besides many nameless English
and Irish; but I am anxious for the Duchess of
Devonshire and the Lady Elizabeth Foster, who are
on their march. Lord Malmesbury, the *audacieux*
Harris, will inform you that he has seen me: *him*
I would have consented to keep.

One word more before we part; call upon Mr. John
Nicholls, bookseller and printer, at Cicero's Head,
Red Lion Passage, Fleet Street, and ask him whether
he did not, about the beginning of March, receive a
very polite letter from Mr. Gibbon of Lausanne?
To which, either as a man of business or a civil gentleman, he should have returned an answer. My application related to a domestic article in the *Gentleman's
Magazine* of August, 1788 (p. 698), which had lately
fallen into my hands, and concerning which I requested
some further lights. Mrs. Moss delivered the letters [1]
into my hands, but I doubt whether they will be of
much service to me; the work appears far more
difficult in the execution than in the idea, and as I am
now taking my leave for some time of the library,
I shall not make much progress in the memoirs of
P. P. till I am on English ground. But is it indeed
true, that I shall eat any Sussex pheasants this autumn?
The event is in the book of Fate, and I cannot unroll
the leaves of September and October. Should I reach
Sheffield Place, I hope to find the whole family in
a perfect state of existence, except a certain Maria
Holroyd, my fair and *generous* correspondent, whose
annihilation on proper terms I most fervently desire.
I must receive a copious answer before the end of
next month, June, and again call upon you for a map
of your political world. The chancellor roars; does
he break his chain? *Vale.*

---

[1] His letters to me for a certain period, which he desired
me to send, to assist him in writing his Memoirs. S.

To THE SAME.

Lausanne, August 23, 1792.

When I inform you, that the design of my English expedition is at last postponed till another year, you will not be much surprised. The public obstacles, the danger of one road, and the difficulties of another, would alone be sufficient to arrest so unwieldy and inactive a being; and these obstacles, on the side of France, are growing every day more insuperable. On the other hand, the terrors which might have driven me from hence have, in a great measure, subsided; our State prisoners are forgotten: the country begins to recover its old good humour and unsuspecting confidence, and the last revolution of Paris appears to have convinced almost everybody of the fatal consequences of democratical principles, which lead by a path of flowers into the abyss of hell. I may therefore wait with patience and tranquillity till the Duke of Brunswick shall have opened the French road. But if I am not driven from Lausanne, you will ask, I hope with some indignation, whether I am not drawn to England, and more especially to Sheffield Place? The desire of embracing you and yours is now the strongest, and must gradually become the sole inducement that can force me from my library and garden, over seas and mountains. The English world will forget and be forgotten, and every year will deprive me of some acquaintance, who by courtesy are styled friends: Lord Guilford and Sir Joshua Reynolds! two of the men, and two of the houses in London, on whom I the most relied for the comforts of society.

September 12, 1792.

Thus far had I written in the full confidence of finishing and sending my letter the next post; but six post-days have unaccountably slipped away, and were you not accustomed to my silence, you would almost begin to think me on the road. How dreadfully, since my last date, has the French road been polluted with blood! and what horrid scenes may be acting at this moment, and may still be aggravated, till the Duke of Brunswick is master of Paris! On every rational principle of calculation he must succeed; yet sometimes, when my spirits are low, I dread the blind efforts of mad and desperate multitudes fighting on their own ground. A few days or weeks must decide the military operations of this year, and perhaps for ever; but on the fairest supposition, I cannot look forwards to any firm settlement, either of a legal or an absolute government. I cannot pretend to give you any Paris news. Should I inform you, as we believe, that *Lally is still among the cannibals*, you would possibly answer, that he is now sitting in the library at Sheffield. Madame de Staël, after miraculously escaping through pikes and poignards, has reached the castle of Copet, where I shall see her before the end of the week. If anything can provoke the King of Sardinia and the Swiss, it must be the foul destruction of *his* cousin Madame de Lamballe, and of *their* regiment of guards. An extraordinary council is summoned at Berne, *but resentment may be checked by prudence.* In spite of Maria's laughter, I applaud your moderation, and sigh for a hearty union of all the sense and property of the country. The times require it; but your last political letter was a cordial to my spirits. The Duchess of Devonshire rather dislikes a coalition: amiable creature! The Eliza is furious against you for not writing. We shall lose them in a few days; but the motions of the Eliza and the Duchess for Italy or England are doubtful. Ladies Spencer and Duncannon certainly pass the Alps. I live with them. Adieu. Since I do not appear in person, I feel the absolute propriety of writing to my Lady and Maria; but there is far from the knowledge to the performance of a duty. Ever yours.

To the Same.

Lausanne, October 5, 1792.

As our English newspapers must have informed you of the invasion of Savoy by the French, and as it is possible that you may have some trifling apprehensions of my *being killed and eaten by those cannibals,* it has appeared to me that a short extraordinary dispatch might not be unacceptable on this occasion. It is indeed true, that about ten days ago the French army of the South, under the command of M. de Montesquiou (if any French army can be said to be under any command), entered Savoy, and possessed themselves of Chamberry, Montmelian, and several other places. It has always been the practice of the King of Sardinia to abandon his transalpine dominions; but on this occasion the court of Turin appears to have been surprised by the strange eccentric motions of a democracy, which always acts from the passion of the moment; and their inferior troops have retreated, with some loss and disgrace, into the passes of the Alps. Mount Cenis is now impervious, and our English travellers who are bound for Italy, the Duchess of Devonshire, Ancaster, &c., will be forced to explore a long circuitous road through the Tyrol. But the Chablais is yet intact, nor can our telescopes discover the tricolour banners on the other side of the lake. Our accounts of the French numbers seem to vary from fifteen to thirty thousand men; the regulars are few, but they are followed by a rabble rout, which must soon, however, melt away, as they will find no plunder, and scanty subsistence, in the poverty and barrenness of Savoy. N.B.—I have just seen a letter from Mr. de Montesquiou, who boasts that at his first entrance into Savoy he had only twelve battalions. Our intelligence is far from correct.

The magistrates of Geneva were alarmed by this dangerous neighbourhood, and more especially by the well-known animosity of an exiled citizen, Claviere, who is one of the six ministers of the French Republic. It was carried by a small majority in the General Council, to call in the succour of three thousand Swiss, which is stipulated by ancient treaty. The strongest reason or pretence of the minority was founded on the danger of provoking the French, and they seem to have been justified by the event: since the complaint of the French resident amounts to a declaration of war. The fortifications of Geneva are not contemptible, especially on the side of Savoy; and it is much doubted whether Mr. de Montesquiou is prepared for a regular siege; but the malcontents are numerous within the walls, and I question whether the spirit of the citizens will hold out against a bombardment. In the meanwhile the Diet has declared that the first cannon fired against Geneva will be considered as an act of hostility against the whole Helvetic body. Berne, as the nearest and most powerful canton, has taken the lead with great vigour and vigilance; the road is filled with the perpetual succession of troops and artillery; and, if some disaffection lurks in the towns, the peasants, especially the Germans, are inflamed with a strong desire of encountering the murderers of their countrymen. Mr. de Watteville, with whom you dined at my house last year, refused to accept the command of the Swiss succour of Geneva, till it was made his first instruction that he should never, in any case, surrender himself prisoner of war.

In this situation, you may suppose that we have some fears. I have great dependence, however, on the many chances in our favour, the valour of the Swiss, the return of the Piedmontese with their Austrian allies, eight or ten thousand men from the Milanese, a diversion from Spain, the great events (how slowly they proceed) on the side of Paris, the inconstancy and want of discipline of the French, and the near approach of the winter season. I am not nervous, but I will not be rash. It will be painful to abandon my house and library; but, if the danger should approach, I will retreat before it, first to Berne, and gradually to the North. Should I even be forced to take refuge in England (a violent measure so late in the year), you would perhaps receive me as kindly as you do the French priests—a noble act of hospitality ! Could I have foreseen this storm, I would have been there six weeks ago: but who can foresee the wild measures of the savages of Gaul ? We thought ourselves perfectly out of the hurricane latitudes. Adieu. I am going to bed, and must rise early to visit the Neckers at Rolle, whither they have retired from the frontier situation of Copet. Severy is on horseback, with his dragoons : his poor father is dangerously ill. It will be shocking if it should be found necessary to remove him. While we are in this very awkward crisis, I will write at least every week. Ever yours. Write instantly, and remember all my commissions.

TO THE SAME.

I will keep my promise of sending you a weekly journal of our troubles, that, when the piping times of peace are restored, I may sleep in long and irreproachable silence : but I shall use a smaller paper, as our military exploits will seldom be sufficient to fill the ample size of our English quarto.

October 13, 1792.

Since my last of the 6th, our attack is not more imminent, and our defence is most assuredly stronger, two very important circumstances, at a time when everyday is leading us, though not so fast as our impatience could wish, towards the unwarlike month of November ; and we observe with pleasure that the troops of Mr. de Montesquiou, which are chiefly from the Southern Provinces, will not cheerfully entertain the rigour of an Alpine winter. The 7th instant, Mr. de Chateauneuf, the French resident, took his leave with a haughty mandate, commanding the Genevois, as they valued their safety and the friendship of the Republic, to dismiss their Swiss allies, and to punish the magistrates who had traiterously proposed the calling in these foreign troops. It is precisely the fable of the wolves, who offered to make peace with the sheep, provided they would send away their dogs. You know what became of the sheep. This demand appears to have kindled a just and general indignation, since it announced an edict of proscription; and must lead to a democratical revolution, which would probably renew the horrid scenes of Paris and Avignon. A general assembly of the citizens was convened, the message was read, speeches were made, oaths were taken, and it was resolved (with only three dissentient voices) to live and die in the defence of their country. The Genevois muster above three thousand well-armed citizens; and the Swiss, who may easily be increased (in a few hours) to an equal number, add spirit to the timorous, and confidence to the well-affected: their arsenals are filled with arms, their magazines with ammunition, and their granaries with corn. But their fortifications are extensive and imperfect, they are commanded from two adjacent hills; a French faction lurks in the city, the character of the Genevois is rather commercial than military, and their behaviour, lofty promise, and base surrender, in the year 1782, is fresh in our memories. In the meanwhile, four thousand French at the most are arrived in the neighbouring camp, nor is there yet any appearance of mortars or heavy artillery. Perhaps an haughty menace may be repelled by a firm countenance. If it were worth while talking of justice, what a shameful attack of a feeble, unoffending state! On the news of their danger, all Switzerland, from Schaffhausen to the Pays de Vaud, has risen in arms; and a French resident, who has passed through the country, in his way from Ratisbon, declares his intention of informing and admonishing the National Convention. About eleven thousand Bernois are already posted in the neighbourhood of Copet and Nyon; and new reinforcements of men, artillery, &c., arrive every day. Another army is drawn together to oppose M. de

Ferrieres, on the side of Bienne and the bishopric of
Basle; and the Austrians in Swabia would be easily
persuaded to cross the Rhine in our defence. But we
are yet ignorant whether our sovereigns mean to wage
an offensive or defensive war. If the latter, which is
more likely, will the French begin the attack? Should
Geneva yield to fear or force, this country is open to
an invasion; and though our men are brave, we want
generals; and I despise the French much less than
I did two months ago. It should seem that our hopes
from the King of Sardinia and the Austrians of Milan
are faint and distant; Spain sleeps; and the Duke
of Brunswick (amazement!) seems to have failed in
his great project. For my part, till Geneva falls,
I do not think of a retreat; but, at all events, I am
provided with two strong horses, and an hundred
Louis in gold. Zurich would be probably my winter
quarters, and the society of the Neckers would make
any place agreeable. Their situation is worse than
mine: I have no daughter ready to lie in; nor do
I fear the French aristocrats on the road. Adieu.
Keep my letters; excuse contradictions and repetitions.
The Duchess of Devonshire leaves us next week. Lady
Elizabeth abhors you. Ever yours.

To the Same.

October 20, 1792.

Since my last, our affairs take a more pacific turn;
but I will not venture to affirm that our peace will
be either safe or honourable. Mr. de Montesquiou
and three Commissioners of the Convention, who are
at Carrouge, have had frequent conferences with the
magistrates of Geneva; several expresses have been
dispatched to and from Paris, and every step of the
negotiation is communicated to the deputies of Berne
and Zurich. The French troops observe a very
tolerable degree of order and discipline; and no act
of hostility has yet been committed on the territory
of Geneva.

October 27.

My usual temper very readily admitted the excuse, that it would be better to wait another week, till the final settlement of our affairs. The treaty is signed between France and Geneva ; and the ratification of the Convention is looked upon as assured, if anything can be assured, in that wild democracy. On condition that the Swiss garrison, with the approbation of Berne and Zurich, be recalled before the first of December, it is stipulated that the independence of Geneva shall be preserved inviolate ; that Mr. de Montesquiou shall immediately send away his heavy artillery ; and that no French troops shall approach within ten leagues of the city. As the Swiss have acted only as auxiliaries, they have no occasion for a direct treaty ; but they cannot prudently disarm, till they are satisfied of the pacific intentions of France ; and no such satisfaction can be given till they have acknowledged the new Republic, which they will probably do in a few days, with a deep groan of indignation and sorrow ; it has been cemented with the blood of their countrymen ! But when the Emperor, the King of Prussia, the first general and the first army in Europe have failed, less powerful states may acquiesce, without dishonour, in the determination of fortune. Do you understand this most unexpected failure ? I will allow an ample share to the badness of the roads and the weather, to famine and disease, to the skill of Dumourier, a heaven-born general ! and to the enthusiastic ardour of the new Romans ; but still, still there must be some secret and shameful cause at the bottom of this strange retreat. We are now delivered from the impending terrors of siege and invasion. The Geneva *emigrés*, particularly the Neckers, are hastening to their homes ; and I shall not be reduced to the hard necessity of seeking a winter asylum at Zurich or Constance : but I am not pleased with our future prospects. It is much to be feared that the present government of Geneva will be soon modelled after the

French fashion ; the new republic of Savoy is forming on the opposite bank of the Lake ; the Jacobin missionaries are powerful and zealous ; and the malcontents of this country, who begin again to rear their heads, will be surrounded with temptations, and examples, and allies. I know not whether the Pays de Vaud will long adhere to the dominion of Berne ; or whether I shall be permitted to end my days in this little paradise, which I have so happily suited to my taste and circumstances.

Last Monday only I received your letter, which had strangely loitered on the road since its date of the 29th of September. There must surely be some disorder in the posts, since the Eliza departed indignant at never having heard from you.

I am much indebted to Mr. Nichols for his genealogical communications, which I am impatient to receive ; but I do not understand why so civil a gentleman could not favour me, in six months, with an answer by the post : since he entrusts me with these valuable papers, you have not, I presume, informed him of my negligence and awkwardness in regard to manuscripts. Your reproach rather surprises me, as I suppose I am much the same as I have been for these last twenty years. Should you hold your resolution of writing only such things as may be published at Charing Cross, our future correspondence would not be very interesting. But I expect and require, at this important crisis, a full and confidential account of your views concerning England, Ireland, and France. You have a strong and clear eye ; and your pen is, perhaps, the most useful quill that ever has been plucked from a goose. Your protection of the French refugees is highly applauded. Rosset and La Motte have escaped from Arbourg, perhaps with connivance to avoid disagreeable demands from the republic. Adieu. Ever yours.

To the Same.

November 10, 1792.

Received this day, November 9th, a most amiable dispatch from the too humble secretary[1] of the family of Espee[2], dated October 24th, which I answer the same day. It will be acknowledged that I have fulfilled my engagements with as much accuracy as our uncertain state and the fragility of human nature would allow. I resume my narrative. At the time when we imagined that all was settled, by an equal treaty between two such unequal powers, as the Geneva Flea and the French Leviathan, we were thunderstruck with the intelligence that the ministers of the republic refused to ratify the conditions : and they were indignant, with some colour of reason, at the hard obligation of withdrawing their troops to the distance of ten leagues, and of consequently leaving the Pays de Gez naked, and exposed to the Swiss, who had assembled 15,000 men on the frontier, and with whom they had not made any agreement. The messenger who was sent last Sunday from Geneva is not yet returned; and many persons are afraid of some design and danger in this delay. Montesquiou has acted with politeness, moderation, and apparent sincerity; but he may resign, he may be superseded, his place may be occupied by an *enragé*, by Servan, or Prince Charles of Hesse, who would aspire to imitate the predatory fame of Custine in Germany. In the meanwhile, the General holds a wolf by the ears; an officer who has seen his troops, about 18,000 men (with a tremendous train of artillery), represents them as a black, daring, desperate crew of buccaneers, rather shocking than contemptible ; the officers (scarcely a gentleman among them) without servants, or horses, or baggage, lying *higgledy piggledy* on the ground with the common men, yet maintaining a rough kind of discipline over them. They already begin to accuse and even to suspect their general, and call aloud for blood and

[1] Miss Holroyd.   [2] Meaning Sheffield Place.

plunder : could they have an opportunity of squeezing some of the rich citizens, Geneva would cut up as fat as most towns in Europe. During this suspension of hostilities they are permitted to visit the city without arms, sometimes three or four hundred at a time ; and the magistrates, as well as the Swiss commander, are by no means pleased with this dangerous intercourse, which they dare not prohibit. Such are our fears : yet it should seem, on the other side, that the French affect a kind of magnanimous justice towards their little neighbour, and that they are not ambitious of an unprofitable contest with the poor and hardy Swiss. The Swiss are not equal to a long and expensive war ; and as most of our militia have families and trades, the country already sighs for their return. Whatever can be yielded, without absolute danger or disgrace, will doubtless be granted ; and the business will probably end in our owning the sovereignty, and trusting to the good faith of the republic of France : how that word would have sounded four years ago ! The measure is humiliating ; but after the retreat of the Duke of Brunswick, and the failure of the Austrians, the smaller powers may acquiesce without dishonour. Every dog has his day ; and these Gallic dogs have their day, at least, of most insolent prosperity. After forcing or tempting the Prussians to evacuate their country, they conquer Savoy, pillage Germany, threaten Spain : the Low Countries are ere now invaded ; Rome and Italy tremble ; they scour the Mediterranean, and talk of sending a squadron into the South Sea. The whole horizon is so black, that I begin to feel some anxiety for England, the last refuge of liberty and law ; and the more so, as I perceive from Lord Sheffield's last epistle that his firm nerves are a little shaken : but of this more in my next, for I want to unburden my conscience. If England, with the experience of our happiness and French calamities, should now be seduced to eat the apple of false freedom, we should indeed deserve to be driven from the paradise which we enjoy. I turn aside from the horrid and improbable (yet not impossible) supposition, that, in three or four years' time, myself and my best friends may be reduced to the deplorable state of the French emigrants: they thought it as impossible three or four years ago. Never did a revolution affect, to such a degree, the private existence of such numbers of the first people of a great country: your examples of misery I could easily match with similar examples in this country and the neighbourhood; and our sympathy is the deeper, as we do not possess, like you, the means of alleviating, in some degree, the misfortunes of the fugitives. But I must have, from the very excellent pen of the Maria, the tragedy of the Archbishop of Arles; and the longer the better. Madame de Biron has probably been tempted by some faint and (I fear) fallacious promises of clemency to the women, and which have likewise engaged Madame d'Aguesseau and her two daughters to revisit France. Madame de Bouillon stands her ground, and her situation as a foreign princess is less exposed. As Lord Sheffield has assumed the glorious character of protector of the distressed, his name is pronounced with gratitude and respect. The Duke of Richmond is praised, on Madame de Biron's account. To the Princess d'Henin, and Lally, I wish to be remembered. The Neckers cannot venture into Geneva, and Madame de Staël will probably lie in at Rolle. He is printing a defence of the King, &c., against their republican judges; but the name of Necker is unpopular to all parties, and I much fear that the guillotine will be more speedy than the press. It will, however, be an eloquent performance; and, if I find an opportunity, I am to send you one, to you Lord Sheffield, by his particular desire: he wishes likewise to convey some copies with speed to our principal people, Pitt, Fox, Lord Stormont, &c. But such is the rapid succession of events, that it will appear like the *Pouvoir Executif*, his best work, after the whole scene has been totally changed. Ever yours.

PS.—The revolution of France, and my triple dispatch by the same post to Sheffield Place, are, in my opinion, the two most singular events in the eighteenth century. I found the task so easy and pleasant, that I had some thoughts of adding a letter to the gentle Louisa. I am this moment informed, that our troops on the frontier are beginning to move, on their return home ; yet we hear nothing of the treaty's being concluded.

EDWARD GIBBON, Esq., TO THE HON. MISS HOLROYD.

Lausanne, Nov. 10, 1792.

In dispatching the weekly political journal to Lord Sheffield, my conscience (for I have some remains of conscience) most powerfully urges me to salute, with some lines of friendship and gratitude, the amiable secretary, who might save herself the trouble of a modest apology. I have not yet forgotten our different behaviour after the much-lamented *separation* of October 4, 1791, your meritorious punctuality, and my unworthy silence. I have still before me that entertaining narrative, which would have interested me, not only in the progress of the *carissima famiglia*, but in the motions of a Tartar camp, or the march of a caravan of Arabs ; the mixture of just observation and lively imagery, the strong sense of a man, expressed with the easy elegance of a female. I still recollect with pleasure the happy comparison of the Rhine, who had heard so much of liberty on both his banks, that he wandered with mischievous licentiousness over all the adjacent meadows.[1] The inundation, alas ! has now spread much wider ; and it is sadly to be feared that the Elbe, the Po, and the Danube, may imitate the vile example of the Rhine : I shall be content, how-

---

[1] Mr. Gibbon alludes to letters written to him by Miss Holroyd, when she was returning from Switzerland, along the Rhine, to England. S.

ever, if our own Thames still preserves his fair character of

> Strong without rage, without o'erflowing full.

These agreeable epistles of Maria produced only
some dumb intentions, and some barren remorse;
nor have I deigned, except by a brief missive from
my chancellor, to express how much I loved the author,
and how much I was pleased with the composition.
That amiable author I have known and loved from the
first dawning of her life and *coquetry*, to the present
maturity of her talents; and as long as I remain on
this planet, I shall pursue, with the same tender and
even anxious concern, the future steps of her establishment and life. That establishment must be splendid;
that life must be happy. She is endowed with every
gift of nature and fortune; but the advantage which
she will derive from them depends almost entirely
on herself. You must not, you shall not, think yourself
unworthy to write to any man: there is none whom
your correspondence would not amuse and satisfy.
I will not undertake a task, which my taste would
adopt, and my indolence would too soon relinquish;
but I am really curious, from the best motives, to
have a particular account of your own studies and
daily occupation. What books do you read? and how
do you employ your time and your pen? Except
some professed scholars, I have often observed that
women in general read much more than men; but,
for want of a plan, a method, a fixed object, their
reading is of little benefit to themselves, or others.
If you will inform me of the species of reading to which
you have the most propensity, I shall be happy to
contribute my share of advice or assistance. I lament
that you have not left me some monument of your
pencil. Lady Elizabeth Foster has executed a very
pretty drawing, taken from the door of the green-
house where we dined last summer, and including the
poor acacia (now recovered from the cruel shears of
the gardener), the end of the terrace, the front of the

pavilion, and a distant view of the country, lake, and mountains. I am almost reconciled to d'Apples' house, which is nearly finished. Instead of the monsters which Lord Hercules Sheffield extirpated, the terrace is already shaded with the new acacias and plantains; and although the uncertainty of possession restrains me from building, I myself have planted a bosquet at the bottom of the garden, with such admirable skill that it affords shade without intercepting prospect. The society of the aforesaid Eliza, of the Duchess of Devonshire, &c., has been very interesting; but they are now flown beyond the Alps, and pass the winter at Pisa. The Legards, who have long since left this place, should be at present in Italy; but I believe Mrs. Grimstone and her daughter returned to England. The Levades are highly flattered by your remembrance. Since you still retain some attachment to this delightful country, and it is indeed delightful, why should you despair of seeing it once more? The happy peer or commoner, whose name you may assume, is still concealed in the book of fate; but, whosoever he may be, he will cheerfully obey your commands of leading you from ———— Castle to Lausanne, and from Lausanne to Rome and Naples. Before that event takes place, I may possibly see you in Sussex; and, whether as a visitor or a fugitive, I hope to be welcomed with a friendly embrace. The delay of this year was truly painful, but it was inevitable; and individuals must submit to those storms which have overturned the thrones of the earth. The tragic story of the Archbishop of Arles I have now somewhat a better right to require at your hands. I wish to have it in all its horrid details [1]; and as

---

[1] The answer to Mr. Gibbon's letter is annexed, as giving the best account I have seen of the barbarous transaction alluded to. S.

'Sheffield Place, November, 1792.

' Your three letters received yesterday caused the most sincere pleasure to each individual of this family; to

you are now so much mingled with the French exiles,
I am of opinion, that were you to keep a journal of

none more than myself. Praise (I fear, beyond my deserts),
from one whose opinion I so highly value, and whose
esteem I so much wish to preserve, is more pleasing than
I can describe. I had not neglected to make the collection
of facts which you recommend, and which the great
variety of unfortunate persons whom we see, or with
whom we correspond, enables me to make.

'As to that part of your letter which respects *my studies*,
I can only say, the slightest hint on that subject is always
received with the greatest gratitude, and attended to
with the utmost punctuality; but I must decline that topic
for the present, to obey your commands, which require
from me the horrid account of the *massacre aux Carmes*.—
Eight respectable ecclesiastics landed, about the beginning
of October, from an open boat at Seaford, wet as the
waves. The natives of the coast were endeavouring to
get from them what they had not, viz. money, when
a gentleman of the neighbourhood came to their protection; and, finding they had nothing, showed his good
sense, by dispatching them to Milord Sheffield: they had
been pillaged, and with great difficulty had escaped from
Paris. The reception they met with at this house seemed
to make the greatest impression on them; they were in
ecstasy on finding M. de Lally living: they gradually
became cheerful, and enjoyed their dinner: they were
greatly affected as they recollected themselves, and found
us attending on them. Having dined, and drank a glass of
wine, they began to discover the beauties of the dining-
room, and of the chateau: as they walked about, they
were overheard to express their admiration at the treatment they met, and *from Protestants*. We then assembled
in the library, formed half a circle round the fire, M. de
Lally and Milord occupying the hearth, *à l'Angloise*, and
questioning the priests concerning their escape. Thus
we discovered, that two of these unfortunate men were
in the Carmelite Convent at the time of the massacre of
the one hundred and twenty priests, and had most miraculously escaped, by climbing trees in the garden, and from
thence over the tops of the buildings. One of them,
a man of superior appearance, described, in the most

all the authentic facts which they relate, it would be an agreeable exercise at present, and a future source of entertainment and instruction.

pathetic manner, the death of the Archbishop of Arles, to the following purport, and with such simplicity and feeling, as to leave no doubt of the truth of all that he said. On the second of September, about five o'clock in the evening, at the time they were permitted to walk in the garden, expecting every hour to be released, they expressed their surprise at seeing several large pits, which had been digging for two days past: they said, "The day is almost spent; and yet Manuel told a person who interceded for us last Thursday, that on the Sunday following not one should remain in captivity: we are still prisoners": soon after, they heard shouts, and some musket-shots. An ensign of the national-guard, some commissaries of the sections, and some Marseillois rushed in: the miserable victims, who were dispersed in the garden, assembled under the walls of the church, not daring to go in, lest it should be polluted with blood. One man, who was behind the rest, was shot. "*Point de coup de fusil*," cried one of the chiefs of the assassins, thinking that kind of death too easy. These well-trained fusileers went to the rear; les piques, les haches, les poignards came forward. They demanded the Archbishop of Arles; he was immediately surrounded by all the priests. The worthy prelate said to his friends, "Let me pass; if my blood will appease them, what signifies it, if I die? Is it not my duty to preserve your lives at the expense of my own?" He asked the eldest of the priests to give him absolution: he knelt to receive it; and when he arose, forced himself from them, advanced slowly, and with his arms crossed upon his breast, and his eyes raised to heaven, said to the assassins, "*Je suis celui que vous cherchez.*" His appearance was so dignified and noble, that, during ten minutes, not one of these wretches had courage to lift his hand against him: they upbraided each other with cowardice, and advanced; one look from this venerable man struck them with awe, and they retired. At last, one of the miscreants struck off the cap of the Archbishop with a pike; respect once violated, their fury returned, and another from behind cut him through the

I should be obliged to you, if you would make, or find, sòme excuse for my not answering a letter from your aunt, which was presented to me by Mr. Fowler.

skull with a sabre. He raised his right hand to his eyes; with another stroke they cut off his hand. The Archbishop said, "O! mon Dieu!" and raised the other: a third stroke across the face left him sitting; the fourth extended him lifeless on the ground; and then all pressed forward, and buried their pikes and poignards in the body. The priests all agreed, that he had been one of the most amiable men in France; and that his only *crime* was having, since the revolution, expended his private fortune, to support the necessitous clergy of his diocese. The second victim was the Général des Bénédictines. Then the national guards obliged the priests to go into the church, telling them, they should appear, one after another, before the Commissaires du section. They had hardly entered, before the people impatiently called for them; upon which, all kneeling before the altar, the Bishop of Beauvais gave them absolution: they were then obliged to go out, two by two; they passed before a commissaire, who did not question, but only counted, his victims [1]; they had in their sight the heaps of dead, to which they were going to add. Among the one hundred and twenty priests thus sacrificed were the Bishops of Zaintes and Beauvais (both of the Rochefoucauld family). I should not omit to remark, that one of the priests observed they were assassinated because they would not swear to a constitution which their murderers had destroyed. We had (to comfort us for this melancholy story) the most grateful expressions of gratitude towards the English nation, from whom they did not do us the justice to expect such a reception.

'There can be no doubt that the whole business of the massacres was concerted at a meeting at the Duke of Orleans' house. I shall make you as dismal as myself by this narration. I must change the style. . . . Citoyen Gibbon, je suis ton égal.

'Maria J. Holroyd.'

[1] . . . Visum est lenti quaesisse nocentem
    In numerum pars magna perit;
                              Lucan, lib. ii, vers. 110. S.

I showed him some civilities, but he is now a poor invalid, confined to his room. By her channel and yours I should be glad to have some information of the health, spirits, and situation of Mrs. Gibbon of Bath, whose alarms (if she has any) you may dispel. She is in my debt. Adieu; most truly yours.

EDWARD GIBBON, ESQ., TO THE RIGHT HON. LADY SHEFFIELD.

Lausanne, November 10, 1792.

I could never forgive myself, were I capable of writing, by the same post, a political epistle to the father, and a friendly letter to the daughter, without sending any token of remembrance to the respectable matron, my dearest my Lady, whom I have now loved as a sister for something better or worse than twenty years. No, indeed, the historian may be careless, he may be indolent, he may always intend and most never execute, but he is neither a monster nor a statue; he has a memory, a conscience, a heart, and that heart is sincerely devoted to Lady Sheffield. He must even acknowledge the fallacy of a sophism which he has sometimes used, and she has always and most truly denied; that, where the persons of a family are strictly united, the writing to one is in fact writing to all; and that consequently all his numerous letters to the husband may be considered as equally addressed to his wife. He feels, on the contrary, that separate minds have their distinct ideas and sentiments, and that each character, either in speaking or writing, has its peculiar tone of conversation. He agrees with the maxim of Rousseau, that three friends who wish to disclose a common secret, will impart it only *deux à deux*; and he is satisfied that, on the present memorable occasion, each of the persons of the Sheffield family will claim a peculiar share in this triple missive, which will communicate, however, a triple satisfaction. The experience of what may be effected by vigorous resolution, encourages the historian to hope that he shall cast the skin of the old serpent, and hereafter show himself as a new creature.

I lament, on all our accounts, that the last year's expedition to Lausanne did not take place in a golden period, of health and spirits. But we must reflect, that human felicity is seldom without alloy; and if we cannot indulge the hope of your making a second visit to Lausanne, we must look forwards to my residence next summer at Sheffield Place, where I must find you in the full bloom of health, spirits, and beauty. I can perceive, by all public and private intelligence, that your house has been the open hospitable asylum of French fugitives; and it is a sufficient proof of the firmness of your nerves, that you have not been overwhelmed or agitated by such a concourse of strangers. Curiosity and compassion may, in some degree, have supported you. Everyday has presented to your view some new scene of that strange tragical romance, which occupies all Europe so infinitely beyond any event that has happened in our time, and you have the satisfaction of not being a mere spectator of the distress of so many victims of false liberty. The benevolent fame of Lord S. is widely diffused.

From Angletine's last letter to Maria, you have already some idea of the melancholy state of her poor father. As long as Mr. de Severy allowed our hopes and fears to fluctuate with the changes of his disorder, I was unwilling to say anything on so painful a subject; and it is with the deepest concern that I now confess our absolute despair of his recovery. All his particular complaints are now lost in a general dissolution of the whole frame; every principle of life is exhausted, and as often as I am admitted to his bedside, though he still looks and smiles with the patience of an angel, I have the heartfelt grief of seeing him each day drawing nearer to the term of his existence. A few weeks, possibly a few days, will deprive me of a most excellent friend, and break for ever the most perfect system of domestic happiness, in which I had so large and intimate a share. Wilhelm (who has obtained leave of absence from his military duty) and his sister behave and feel like tender and dutiful children ; but they have a long gay prospect of life, and new connexions, new families, will make them forget, in due time, the common lot of mortality. But it is Madame de Severy whom I truly pity ; I dread the effects of the first shock, and I dread still more the deep perpetual consuming affliction for a loss which can never be retrieved. You will not wonder that such reflections sadden my own mind, nor can I forget how much my situation is altered, since I retired, nine years ago, to the banks of the Leman Lake. The death of poor Deyverdun first deprived me of a domestic companion, who can never be supplied ; and your visit has only served to remind me that man, however amused and occupied in his closet, was not made to live alone. Severy will soon be no more ; his widow for a long time, perhaps for ever, will be lost to herself and her friends, the son will travel, and I shall be left a stranger in the insipid circle of mere common acquaintance. The revolution of France, which first embittered and divided the society of Lausanne, has opposed a barrier to my Sussex visit, and may finally expel me from the paradise which I inhabit. Even that paradise, the expensive and delightful establishment of my house, library, and garden, almost becomes an encumbrance, by rendering it more difficult for me to relinquish my hold, or to form a new system of life in my native country, for which my income, though improved and improving, would be probably insufficient. But every complaint should be silenced by the contemplation of the French ; compared with whose cruel fate, all misery is relative happiness. I perfectly concur in your partiality for Lally ; though nature might forget some meaner ingredients, of prudence, economy, &c., she never formed a purer heart, or a brighter imagination. If he be with you, I beg my kindest salutations to him. I am everyday more closely united with the Neckers. Should France break, and this country be overrun, they would be reduced, in very humble circumstances, to seek a refuge; and where but in England? Adieu, dear Madam, there is, indeed, much pleasure in discharging one's heart to a real friend. Ever yours.

EDWARD GIBBON, ESQ., TO THE RIGHT HON. LORD SHEFFIELD.

Lausanne, November 25, 1792.

After the triple labour of my last dispatch, your experience of the creature might tempt you to suspect that it would again relapse into a long slumber. But, partly from the spirit of contradiction (though I am not a lady), and partly from the ease and pleasure which I now find in the task, you see me again alive, awake, and almost faithful to my hebdomadal promise. The last week has not, however, afforded any events deserving the notice of an historian. Our affairs are still floating on the waves of the Convention, and the ratification of a corrected treaty, which had been fixed for the twentieth, is not yet arrived; but the report of the diplomatic committee has been favourable, and it is generally understood that the leaders of the French republic do not wish to quarrel with the Swiss. We are gradually withdrawing and disbanding our militia. Geneva will be left to sink or swim, according to the humour of the people; and our last hope appears to be, that by submission and good behaviour we shall avert for some time the impending storm. A few days ago, an odd accident happened in the French army; the desertion of the general. As the Neckers were sitting, about eight o'clock in the evening, in their drawing-room at Rolle[1], the door flew open and they were astounded by their servant's announcing *Monsieur le Général de Montesquiou!* On the receipt of some secret intelligence of a *decret d'accusation,* and an order to arrest him, he had only time to get on horseback, to gallop through Geneva, to take boat

---

[1] A considerable town between Lausanne and Geneva.

for Copet, and to escape from his pursuers, who were ordered to seize him alive or dead. He left the Neckers after supper, passed through Lausanne in the night, and proceeded to Berne and Basle, whence he intended to wind his way through Germany, amidst enemies of every description, and to seek a refuge in England, America, or the moon. He told Necker, that the sole remnant of his fortune consisted in a wretched sum of twenty thousand livres; but the public report, or suspicion, bespeaks him in much better circumstances. Besides the reproach of acting with too much tameness and delay, he is accused of making very foul and exorbitant contracts; and it is certain that New Sparta is infected with this vice, beyond the example of the most corrupt monarchy. Kellerman is arrived to take the command; and it is apprehended that on the first of December, after the departure of the Swiss, the French may *request* the permission of using Geneva, a friendly city, for their winter quarters. In that case, the democratical revolution, which we all foresee, will be very speedily effected.

I would ask you, whether you apprehend there was any treason in the Duke of Brunswick's retreat, and whether you have totally withdrawn your confidence and esteem from that once famed general? Will it be possible for England to preserve her neutrality with any honour or safety? We are bound, as I understand, by treaty, to guarantee the dominions of the King of Sardinia and the Austrian provinces of the Netherlands. These countries are now invaded and overrun by the French. Can we refuse to fulfil our engagements, without exposing ourselves to all Europe as a perfidious or pusillanimous nation? Yet, on the other hand, can we assist those allies, without plunging headlong into an abyss, whose bottom no man can discover? But my chief anxiety is for our domestic tranquillity; for I must find a retreat in England, should I be driven from Lausanne. The idea of firm and honourable union of parties pleases me much; but you must frankly unfold what are the great difficulties that may impede so salutary a measure: you write to a man discreet in speech, and now careful of papers. Yet what can such a coalition avail? Where is the champion of the constitution? Alas, Lord Guildford! I am much pleased with the Manchester Ass. The asses or wolves who sacrificed him have cast off the mask too soon; and such a nonsensical act must open the eyes of many simple patriots, who might have been led astray by the specious name of reform. It should be made as notorious as possible. Next winter may be the crisis of our fate, and if you begin to improve the constitution, you may be driven step by step from the disfranchisement of old Sarum to the King in Newgate, the Lords voted useless, the Bishops abolished, and a House of Commons without articles (*sans culottes*). Necker has ordered you a copy of his royal defence, which has met with, and deserved, universal success. The pathetic and argumentative parts are, in my opinion, equally good, and his mild eloquence may persuade without irritating. I have applied to this gentler tone some verses of Ovid (*Metamorph.* l. iii, 302, &c.[1]), which you may read. Madame de Staël has produced a second son. She talks wildly enough of visiting England this winter. She is a pleasant little woman. Poor Severy's condition is hopeless. Should he drag through the winter Madame de Severy would scarcely survive him. She kills herself with grief and fatigue. What a difference in Lausanne! I hope triple answers are on the road. I must write soon; the *times* will not allow me to read or think. Ever yours.

---

[1] Qua tamen usque potest, vires sibi demere tentat.
 Nec, quo centimanum dejecerat igne Typhoea,
 Nunc armatur eo: nimium feritatis in illo.
 Est aliud levius fulmen; cui dextra Cyclopum
 Saevitiae, flammaeque minus, minus addidit irae:
 Tela secunda vocant Superi.

To the Same.

Lausanne, Dec. 14, 1792.

Our little storm has now completely subsided, and we are again spectators, though anxious spectators, of the general tempest that invades or threatens almost every country of Europe. Our troops are everyday disbanding and returning home, and the greatest part of the French have evacuated the neighbourhood of Geneva. Monsieur Barthelemy, whom you have seen secretary in London, is most courteously entertained, as ambassador, by the Helvetic body. He is now at Berne, where a Diet will speedily be convened; the language on both sides is now pacific, and even friendly, and some hopes are given of a provision for the officers of the Swiss guards who have survived the massacres of Paris.

January 1, 1793.

With the return of peace I have relapsed into my former indolence; but now awakening, after a fortnight's slumber, I have little or nothing to add, with regard to the internal state of this country, only the revolution of Geneva has already taken place, as I announced, but sooner than I expected. The Swiss troops had no sooner evacuated the place, than the *Egaliseurs*, as they are called, assembled in arms; and as no resistance was made, no blood was shed on the occasion. They seized the gates, disarmed the garrison, imprisoned the magistrates, imparted the rights of citizens to all the rabble of the town and country, and proclaimed a *National* Convention, which has not yet met. They are all for a pure and absolute democracy; but some wish to remain a small independent state, whilst others aspire to become a part of the republic of France; and as the latter, though less numerous, are more violent and absurd than their adversaries, it is highly probable that they will succeed. The citizens of the best families and fortunes have

retired from Geneva into the Pays de Vaud; but the
French methods of recalling or proscribing emigrants
will soon be adopted. You must have observed that
Savoy is now become *le departement du Mont Blanc.*
I cannot satisfy myself whether the mass of the
people is pleased or displeased with the change; but
my noble scenery is clouded by the democratical
aspect of twelve leagues of the opposite coast, which
every morning obtrude themselves on my view.
I here conclude the first part of the history of our
Alpine troubles, and now consider myself as disengaged
from all promises of periodical writing. Upon the
whole, I kept it beyond our expectation; nor do I
think that you have been sufficiently astonished by
the wonderful effort of the triple dispatch.

You must now succeed to my task, and I shall
expect, during the winter, a regular political journal
of the events of your greater world. You are on the
theatre, and may often be behind the scenes. You
can always see, and may sometimes foresee. My
own choice has indeed transported me into a foreign
land; but I am truly attached, from interest and
inclination, to my native country; and even as a
citizen of the world, I wish the stability of England,
the sole great refuge of mankind, against the opposite
mischiefs of despotism and democracy. I was indeed
alarmed, and the more so, as I saw that you were not
without apprehension; but I now glory in the triumph
of reason and genuine patriotism, which seems to
pervade the country; nor do I dislike some mixture
of popular enthusiasm, which may be requisite to
encounter our mad or wicked enemies with equal arms.
The behaviour of Fox does not surprise me. You
may remember what I told you last year at Lausanne,
when you attempted his defence, that his inmost soul
was deeply tinged with democracy. Such wild opinions
cannot easily be reconciled with his excellent understanding, but *' it is true, 'tis pity, and pity it is 'tis
true.'* He will surely ruin himself in the opinion of
the wise and good men of his own party. You have

crushed the daring subverters of the constitution; but I now fear the moderate well-meaners, reformers. Do not, I beseech you, tamper with parliamentary representation. The present House of Commons forms, in *practice*, a body of gentlemen, who must always sympathize with the interests and opinions of the people; and the slightest innovation launches you, without rudder or compass, on a dark and dangerous ocean of theoretical experiment. On this subject I am indeed serious.

Upon the whole, I like the beginning of ninety-three better than the end of ninety-two. The illusion seems to break away throughout Europe. I think England and Switzerland are safe. Brabant adheres to its old constitution. The Germans are disgusted with the rapine and insolence of their deliverers. The Pope is resolved to head his armies, and the Lazzaroni of Naples have presented St. Januarius with a gold fusee, to fire on the Brigands François. So much for politics, which till now never had such possession of my mind. Next post I will write about myself and my own designs. Alas, your poor eyes! make the Maria write; I will speedily answer her. My Lady is still dumb. The German posts are now slow and irregular. You had better write by the way of France, under cover. Direct to *Le Citoyen Rebours à Pontalier, France*. Adieu; ever yours.

TO THE SAME.

Lausanne, January 6, 1793.

There was formerly a time when our correspondence was a painful discussion of my private affairs; a vexatious repetition of losses, of disappointments, of sales, &c. These affairs are decently arranged: but public cares have now succeeded to private anxiety, and our whole attention is lately turned from Lenborough and Buriton to the political state of France and of Europe. From these politics, however, one letter shall be free, while I talk of myself and of my own plans ; a subject most interesting to a friend, and only to a friend.

I know not whether I am sorry or glad that my expedition has been postponed to the present year. It is true, that I now wish myself in England, and almost repent that I did not grasp the opportunity when the obstacles were comparatively smaller than they are now likely to prove. Yet had I reached you last summer before the month of August, a considerable portion of my time would be now elapsed, and I should already begin to think of my departure. If the gout should spare me this winter (and as yet I have not felt any symptom), and if the spring should make a soft and early appearance, it is my intention to be with you in Downing Street before the end of April, and thus to enjoy six weeks or two months of the most agreeable season of London and the neighbourhood, after the hurry of parliament is subsided, and before the great rural dispersion. As the banks of the Rhine and the Belgic provinces are completely overspread with anarchy and war, I have made up my mind to pass through the territories of the French republic. From the best and most recent information, I am satisfied that there is little or no real danger in the journey ; and I must arm myself with patience to support the vexatious insolence of democratical tyranny. I have even a sort of curiosity to spend some days at Paris, to assist at the debates of the Pandemonium, to seek an introduction to the principal devils, and to contemplate a new form of public and private life, which never existed before, and which I devoutly hope will not long continue to exist. Should the obstacles of health or weather confine me at Lausanne till the month of May, I shall scarcely be able to resist the temptation of passing some part at least of the summer in my own little paradise. But all these schemes must ultimately depend on the great question of peace and war, which will indeed be speedily determined. Should France become impervious to an English traveller, what must I do ? I shall not easily resolve to explore my way through the unknown language and abominable roads of the interior parts of Germany, to embark in Holland, or perhaps at Hamburg, and to be finally intercepted by a French privateer. My stay in England appears not less doubtful than the means of transporting myself. Should I arrive in the spring, it is possible, and barely possible, that I should return here in the autumn: it is much more probable that I shall pass the winter, and there may be even a chance of my giving my own country a longer trial. In my letter to my Lady I fairly exposed the decline of Lausanne; but such an establishment as mine must not be lightly abandoned; nor can I discover what adequate mode of life my private circumstances, easy as they now are, could afford me in England. London and Bath have doubtless their respective merits, and I could wish to reside within a day's journey of Sheffield Place. But a state of perfect happiness is not to be found here below; and in the possession of my library, house, and garden, with the relics of our society, and a frequent intercourse with the Neckers, I may still be tolerably content. Among the disastrous changes of Lausanne, I must principally reckon the approaching dissolution of poor Severy and his family. He is still alive, but in such a hopeless and painful decay, that we no longer conceal our wishes for his speedy release. I never loved nor esteemed him so much as in this last mortal disease, which he supports with a degree of energy, patience, and even cheerfulness, beyond all belief. His wife, whose whole time and soul are devoted to him, is almost sinking under her long anxiety. The children are most amiably assiduous to both their parents, and, at all events, his filial duties and worldly cares must detain the son some time at home.

And now approach, and let me drop into your most private ear a literary secret. Of the Memoirs little has been done, and with that little I am not satisfied. They must be postponed till a mature season: and

I much doubt whether the book and the author can ever see the light at the same time. But I have long revolved in my mind another scheme of biographical writing; the Lives, or rather the Characters, of the most eminent Persons in Arts and Arms, in Church and State, who have flourished in Britain from the reign of Henry the Eighth to the present age. This work, extensive as it may be, would be an amusement, rather than a toil: the materials are accessible in our own language, and, for the most part, ready to my hands: but the subject, which would afford a rich display of human nature and domestic history, would powerfully address itself to the feelings of every Englishman. The taste or fashion of the times seems to delight in picturesque decorations; and this series of British portraits might aptly be accompanied by the respective heads, taken from originals, and engraved by the best masters. Alderman Boydell, and his son-in-law, Mr. George Nicol, bookseller in Pall Mall, are the great undertakers in this line. On my arrival in England I shall be free to consider whether it may suit me to proceed in a mere literary work without any other decorations than those which it may derive from the pen of the author. It is a serious truth, that I am no longer ambitious of fame or money; that my habits of industry are much impaired, and that I have reduced my studies to be the loose amusement of my morning hours, the repetition of which will insensibly lead me to the last term of existence. And for this very reason I shall not be sorry to bind myself by a liberal engagement, from which I may not with honour recede.

Before I conclude, we must say a word or two of parliamentary and pecuniary concerns. (1) We all admire the generous spirit with which you damned the assassins. I hope that your abjuration of all future connexion with Fox was not quite so peremptory as it is stated in the French papers. Let him do what he will, I must love the dog. The opinion of parliament in favour of Louis was declared in a manner worthy of the representatives of a great and a wise nation. It will certainly have a powerful effect; and if the poor king be not already murdered, I am satisfied that his life is in safety: but is such a life worth his care? Our debates will now become everyday more interesting; and as I expect from you only opinions and anecdotes, I most earnestly conjure you to send me *Woodfall's Register* as often (and that must be very often) as the occasion deserves it. I now spare no expense for news.

I want some account of Mrs. G.'s health. Will my Lady never write? How can people be so indolent! I suppose this will find you at Sheffield Place during the recess, and that the heavy baggage will not move till after the birthday. Shall I be with you by the first of May? The gods only know. I almost wish that I had accompanied Madame de Staël. Ever yours.

To the Same.

Begun Feb. 9, ended Feb. 18, 1793.

The struggle is at length over, and poor de Severy is no more. He expired about ten days ago, after every vital principle had been exhausted by a complication of disorders, which had lasted above five months: and a mortification in one of his legs, that gradually rose to the more noble parts, was the immediate cause of his death. His patience and even cheerfulness supported him to the fatal moment; and he enjoyed every comfort that could alleviate his situation, the skill of his physicians, the assiduous tenderness of his family, and the kind sympathy not only of his particular friends, but even of common acquaintance, and generally of the whole town. The stroke has been severely felt: yet I have the satisfaction to perceive that Madame de Severy's health is not affected; and we may hope that in time she will recover a tolerable share of composure and happiness. Her firmness has checked the violent sallies of grief; her gentleness has preserved her from the worst of symptoms, a dry, silent despair. She loves to talk of her irreparable loss, she descants with pleasure on his virtues; her words are interrupted with tears, but those tears are her best relief; and her tender feelings will insensibly subside into an affectionate remembrance. Wilhelm is much more deeply wounded than I could imagine, or than he expected himself: nor have I ever seen the affliction of a son more lively and sincere. Severy was indeed a very valuable man: without any shining qualifications, he was endowed in a high degree with good sense, honour, and benevolence; and few men have filled with more propriety their circle in private life. For myself, I have had the misfortune of knowing him too late, and of losing him too soon. But enough of this melancholy subject.

The affairs of this theatre, which must always be minute, are now grown so tame and tranquil, that they no longer deserve the historian's pen. The new constitution of Geneva is slowly forming, without much noise or any bloodshed; and the patriots, who have stayed in hopes of guiding and restraining the multitude, flatter themselves that they shall be able at least to prevent their mad countrymen from giving themselves to the French, the only mischief that would be absolutely irretrievable. The revolution of Geneva is of less consequence to us, however, than that of Savoy; but our fate will depend on the general event, rather than on these particular causes. In the meanwhile we hope to be quiet spectators of the struggle of this year; and we seem to have assurances that both the Emperor and the French will compound for the neutrality of the Swiss. The Helvetic body does not acknowledge the republic of France; but Barthelemy, their ambassador, resides at Baden, and steals, like Chauvelin, into a kind of extra-official negotiation. All spirit of opposition is quelled in the canton of Berne, and the perpetual banishment of the Van Bercham family has scarcely excited a murmur. It will probably be followed by that of Col. Polier : the crime alleged in their sentence is the having assisted at the federation dinner at Rolle two years ago ; and as they are absent, I could almost wish that they had been summoned to appear, and heard in their own defence.   To the general supineness of the inhabitants of Lausanne I must ascribe that the death of Louis the Sixteenth has been received with less horror and indignation than I could have wished.   I was much tempted to go into mourning, and probably should, had the Duchess been still here ; but, as the only Englishman of any mark, I was afraid of being singular ; more especially as our French emigrants, either from prudence or poverty, do not wear black, nor do even the Neckers.   Have you read his discourse for the king ?   It might indeed supersede the necessity of mourning.   I should judge from your last letter, and from the Diary, that the French declaration of war must have rather surprised you.   I wish, although I know not how it could have been avoided, that we might still have continued to enjoy our safe and prosperous neutrality.   You will not doubt my best wishes for the destruction of the miscreants ; but I love England still more than I hate France.   All reasonable chances are in favour of a confederacy, such as was never opposed to the ambition of Louis the Fourteenth ; but, after the experience of last year, I distrust reason, and confess myself fearful for the event.   The French are strong in numbers, activity, and enthusiasm ; they are rich in rapine ; and, although their strength may be only that of a frenzy fever, they may do infinite mischief to their neighbours before they can be reduced to a strait-waistcoat.   I dread the effects that may be produced on the minds of the people by the increase of debt and taxes, probable losses, and possible mismanagement.   Our trade must suffer ; and though projects of invasion have been always abortive, I cannot forget that the fleets and armies of Europe have failed before the towns in America, which have been taken and plundered by a handful of buccaneers. I know nothing of Pitt as a war minister; but it affords me much satisfaction that the intrepid wisdom of the new Chancellor [1] is introduced into the Cabinet. I wish, not merely on your own account, that you were placed in an active, useful station in government. I should not dislike you Secretary at War.

I have little more to say of myself, or of my journey to England : you know my intentions, and the great events of Europe must determine whether they can be carried into execution this summer. If ***** has warmly adopted *your* idea, I shall speedily hear from him ; but, in truth, I know not what will be my answer : I see difficulties which at first did not occur : I doubt my own perseverance, and my fancy begins to wander into new paths. The amusement of reading and thinking may perhaps satisfy a man who has paid his debt to the public ; and there is more pleasure in building castles in the air than on the ground. I shall contrive some small assistance for your correspondent, though I cannot learn anything that distinguishes him from many of his countrymen ; we have had our full share of poor emigrants : but if you wish that anything extraordinary should be done for this man, you must send me a measure. Adieu. I embrace my Lady and Maria, as also Louisa. Perhaps I may soon write, without expecting an answer. Ever yours.

To the Same.

Lausanne, April 27, 1793.

My dearest Friend, for such you most surely are, nor does there exist a person who obtains, or shall ever obtain, a superior place in my esteem and affection.

After too long a silence I was sitting down to write, when, only yesterday morning (such is now the irregular slowness of the English post), I was suddenly struck, struck indeed to the heart, by the fatal intelli-

[1] Lord Loughborough.

gence [1] from Sir Henry Clinton and Mr. de Lally.
Alas! what is life, and what are our hopes and projects! When I embraced her at your departure from
Lausanne, could I imagine that it was for the last time?
when I postponed to another summer my journey to
England, could I apprehend that I never, never should
see her again? I always hoped that she would spin her
feeble thread to a long duration, and that her delicate
frame would survive (as is often the case) many constitutions of a stouter appearance. In four days! in
your absence, in that of her children! But she is
now at rest; and if there be a future life, her mild
virtues have surely entitled her to the reward of pure
and perfect felicity. It is for you that I feel, and
I can judge of your sentiments by comparing them
with my own. I have lost, it is true, an amiable and
affectionate friend, whom I had known and loved
above three-and-twenty years, and whom I often
styled by the endearing name of sister. But you are
deprived of the companion of your life, the wife of
your choice, and the mother of your children; poor
children! the liveliness of Maria, and the softness of
Louisa, render them almost equally the objects of my
tenderest compassion. I do not wish to aggravate
your grief; but, in the sincerity of friendship, I cannot
hold a different language. I know the impotence of
reason, and I much fear that the strength of your
character will serve to make a sharper and more
lasting impression.

The only consolation in these melancholy trials to
which human life is exposed, the only one at least in
which I have any confidence, is the presence of a real
friend; and of that, as far as it depends on myself,
you shall not be destitute. I regret the few days that
must be lost in some necessary preparations; but
I trust that to-morrow se'nnight (May the fifth) I shall
be able to set forward on my journey to England;
and when this letter reaches you, I shall be considerably advanced on my way. As it is yet prudent to

[1] The death of Lady Sheffield.

keep at a respectful distance from the banks of the French Rhine, I shall incline a little to the right, and proceed by Schaffhausen and Stuttgart to Frankfort and Cologne : the Austrian Netherlands are now open and safe, and I am sure of being able at least to pass from Ostend to Dover; whence, without passing through London, I shall pursue the direct road to Sheffield Place. Unless I should meet with some unforeseen accidents and delays, I hope, before the end of the month, to share your solitude, and sympathize with your grief. All the difficulties of the journey, which my indolence had probably magnified, have now disappeared before a stronger passion ; and you will not be sorry to hear, that, as far as Frankfort or Cologne, I shall enjoy the advantage of the society, the conversation, the German language, and the active assistance of Severy. His attachment to me is the sole motive which prompts him to undertake this troublesome journey ; and as soon as he has seen me over the roughest ground, he will immediately return to Lausanne. The poor young man loved Lady S. as a mother, and the whole family is deeply affected by an event which reminds them too painfully of their own misfortunes. Adieu. I could write volumes, and shall therefore break off abruptly. I shall write on the road, and hope to find a few lines à poste restante at Frankfort and Brussels. Adieu ; ever yours.

TO THE SAME.

Lausanne, May, 1793.

MY DEAR FRIEND,

I must write a few lines before my departure, though indeed I scarcely know what to say. Nearly a fortnight has now elapsed since the first melancholy tidings, without my having received the slightest subsequent accounts of your health and situation. Your own silence announces too forcibly how much you are involved in your feelings ; and I can but too easily conceive that a letter to me would be more painful than to an indifferent person. But that amiable man Count Lally might surely have written a second time; but your sister, who is probably with you; but Maria—alas! poor Maria! I am left in a state of darkness to the workings of my own fancy, which imagines everything that is sad and shocking. What can I think of for your relief and comfort? I will not expatiate on those commonplace topics, which have never dried a single tear; but let me advise, let me urge you to force yourself into business, as I would try to force myself into study. The mind must not be idle; if it be not exercised on external objects, it will prey on its own vitals. A thousand little arrangements, which must precede a long journey, have postponed my departure three or four days beyond the term which I had first appointed; but all is now in order, and I set off to-morrow, the ninth instant, with my *valet de chambre*, a courier on horse-back, and Severy, with his servant, as far as Frankfort. I calculate my arrival at Sheffield Place (how I dread and desire to see that mansion!) for the first week in June, soon after this letter; but I will try to send you some later intelligence. I never found myself stronger, or in better health. The German road is now cleared, both of enemies and allies, and though I must expect fatigue, I have not any apprehensions of danger. It is scarcely possible that you should meet me at Frankfort, but I shall be much disappointed at not finding a line at Brussels or Ostend. Adieu. If there be any invisible guardians, may they watch over you and yours! Adieu.

To the Same.

Frankfort, May 19, 1793.

And here I am, in good health and spirits, after one of the easiest, safest, and pleasantest journeys which I ever performed in my whole life; not the appearance of an enemy, and hardly the appearance of a war. Yet I hear, as I am writing, the cannon of the siege of Mayence, at the distance of twenty miles; and long, very long will it be heard. It is confessed on all sides, that the French fight with a courage worthy of a better cause. The town of Mayence is strong, their artillery admirable; they are already reduced to horse-flesh, but they have still the resource of eating the inhabitants, and at last of eating one another; and, if that repast could be extended to Paris and the whole country, it might essentially contribute to the relief of mankind. Our operations are carried on with more than German slowness, and when the besieged are quiet, the besiegers are perfectly satisfied with their progress. A spirit of division undoubtedly prevails; and the character of the Prussians for courage and discipline is sunk lower than you can possibly imagine. Their glory has expired with Frederick. I am sorry to have missed Lord Elgin, who is beyond the Rhine with the King of Prussia. As I am impatient, I propose setting forwards to-morrow afternoon, and shall reach Ostend in less than eight days. The passage must depend on winds and packets; and I hope to find at Brussels or Dover a letter which will direct me to Sheffield Place or Downing Street. Severy goes back from hence. Adieu. I embrace the dear girls. Ever yours.

To the Same.

Brussels, May 27, 1793.

This day, between two and three o'clock in the afternoon, I arrived at this place in excellent preservation. My expedition, which is now drawing to a close, has been a journey of perseverance rather than speed, of some labour since Frankfort, but without the smallest degree of difficulty or danger. As I have every morning been seated in the chaise soon after sunrise, I propose indulging to-morrow till eleven o'clock, and going that day no farther than Ghent. On Wednesday, the 29th instant, I shall reach Ostend in good time, just eight days, according to my former reckoning, from Frankfort. Beyond that I can say nothing positive ; but should the winds be propitious, it is possible that I may appear next Saturday, June first, in Downing Street. After that earliest date, you will expect me day by day till I arrive. Adieu. I embrace the dear girls, and salute Mrs. Holroyd. I rejoice that you have anticipated my advice by plunging into business ; but I should now be sorry if that business, however important, detained us long in town. I do not wish to make a public exhibition, and only sigh to enjoy you and the precious remnant in the solitude of Sheffield Place. Ever yours.

If I am successful I may outstrip or accompany this letter. Yours and Maria's waited for me here, and overpaid my journey.

NOTE BY LORD SHEFFIELD

THE preceding Letters intimate that, in return for my visit to Lausanne in 1791, Mr. Gibbon engaged to pass a year with me in England; and that the war, which rendered travelling exceedingly inconvenient, especially to a person who, from bodily infirmities, required every accommodation, prevented his undertaking so formidable a journey at the time proposed.

The call of friendship, however, was sufficient to make him overlook every personal consideration, when he thought his presence might prove a consolation. I must ever regard it as the most endearing proof of his sensibility, and of his possessing the true spirit of friendship, that after relinquishing the thought of his intended visit, he hastened to England, in spite of increasing impediments, to soothe me by the most generous sympathy, and to alleviate my domestic affliction : neither his great corpulency, nor his extraordinary bodily infirmities, nor any other consideration, could prevent him a moment from resolving on an undertaking that might have deterred the most active young man. With an alertness by no means natural to him, he, almost immediately, undertook a circuitous journey, along the frontiers of an enemy worse than savage, within the sound of their cannon, within the range of the light troops of the different armies, and through roads ruined by the enormous machinery of war.

The readiness with which he engaged in this kind office, at a time when a selfish spirit might have pleaded a thousand reasons for declining so hazardous a journey, conspired, with the peculiar charms of his society, to render his arrival a cordial to my mind. I had the satisfaction of finding that his own delicate and precarious health had not suffered in the service of his friend. He arrived in the beginning of June at my house in Downing Street, in good health; and after passing about a month with me there, we settled at Sheffield Place for the remainder of the summer; where his wit, learning, and cheerful politeness, delighted a great variety of characters.

Although he was inclined to represent his health as better than it really was, his habitual dislike to motion appeared to increase; his inaptness to exercise confined him to the library and dining-room, and there he joined my friend Mr. Frederick North, in pleasant arguments against exercise in general. He ridiculed the unsettled and restless disposition that summer, the most uncomfortable, as he said, of all seasons, generally gives to those who have the free use of their limbs. Such arguments were little required to keep society, Mr. Jekyll, Mr. Douglas, &c., within doors, when his company was only there to be enjoyed; for neither the fineness of the season, nor the most promising parties of pleasure, could tempt the company of either sex to desert him.

Those who have enjoyed the society of Mr. Gibbon will agree with me that his conversation was still more captivating than his writings. Perhaps no man ever divided time more fairly between literary labour and social enjoyment; and hence, probably, he derived his peculiar excellence of making his very extensive knowledge contribute, in the highest degree, to the use or pleasure of those with whom he conversed. He united, in the happiest manner imaginable, two characters which are not often found in the same person, the profound scholar and the peculiarly agreeable companion.

It would be superfluous to attempt a very minute delineation of a character which is so distinctly marked in the Memoirs and Letters. He has described himself without reserve, and with perfect sincerity. The Letters, and especially the Extracts from the Journal, which could not have been written with any purpose of being seen, will make the reader perfectly acquainted with the man.

Excepting a visit to Lord Egremont and Mr. Hayley, whom he particularly esteemed, Mr. Gibbon was not absent from Sheffield Place till the beginning of October, when we were reluctantly obliged to part with him, that he might perform his engagement to Mrs. Gibbon at Bath, the widow of his father, who had early deserved, and invariably retained his affection. From Bath he proceeded to Lord Spencer's at Althorp, a family which he always met with uncommon satisfaction. He continued in good health during the whole summer, and in excellent spirits (I never knew him enjoy better); and when he went from Sheffield Place, little did I imagine it would be the last time that I should have the inexpressible pleasure of seeing him there in full possession of health.

The few following short letters, though not important in themselves, will fill up this part of the narrative better, and more agreeably, than anything which I can substitute in their place.

EDWARD GIBBON, ESQ., TO THE RIGHT HON. LORD
SHEFFIELD.

October 2, 1793.

THE Cork Street hotel has answered its recommendation; it is clean, convenient, and quiet. My
first evening was passed at home in a very agreeable
tête-à-tête with my friend Elmsley. Yesterday I dined
at Craufurd's with an excellent set, in which were
Pelham and Lord Egremont. I dine to-day with my
Portuguese friend, Madame de Sylva, at Grenier's;
most probably with Lady Webster, whom I met last
night at Devonshire House; a constant, though late,
resort of society. The Duchess is as good, and Lady
Elizabeth as seducing, as ever. No news whatsoever.
You will see in the papers Lord Hervey's memorial.
I love vigour, but it is surely a strong measure to tell
a gentleman you have *resolved* to pass the winter in
his house. London is not disagreeable; yet I shall
probably leave it on Saturday. If anything should
occur, I will write. Adieu; ever yours.

TO THE SAME.

Sunday afternoon I left London and lay at Reading,
and Monday in very good time I reached this place,
after a very pleasant airing; and am always so much
delighted and improved, with this union of ease and
motion, that, were not the expense enormous, I would
travel every year some hundred miles, more especially
in England. I passed the day with Mrs. Gibbon
yesterday. In mind and conversation she is just the
same as she was twenty years ago. She has spirits,
appetite, legs, and eyes, and talks of living till ninety.[1]
I can say from my heart, Amen. We dine at two, and
remain together till nine; but, although we have
much to say, I am not sorry that she talks of intro-
ducing a third or fourth actor. Lord Spencer expects

[1] She was then in her eightieth year. S.

me about the 20th ; but if I can do it without offence, I shall steal away two or three days sooner, and you shall have advice of my motions. The troubles of Bristol have been serious and bloody. I know not who was in fault ; but I do not like appeasing the mob by the extinction of the toll, and the removal of the Hereford militia, who had done their duty. Adieu. The girls must dance at Tunbridge. What would dear little aunt [1] say if I was to answer her letter ? Ever yours, &c.

York House, Bath,
    Oct. 9, 1793.

I still follow the old style, though the Convention has abolished the Christian era, with months, weeks, days, &c.

TO THE SAME.

York House, Bath, October 13, 1793.

I am as ignorant of Bath in general as if I were still at Sheffield. My impatience to get away makes me think it better to devote my whole time to Mrs. Gibbon ; and dear little aunt, whom I tenderly salute, will excuse me to her two friends, Mrs. Hartley and Preston, if I make little or no use of her kind introduction. A *tête-à-tête* of eight or nine hours every day is rather difficult to support ; yet I do assure you that our conversation flows with more ease and spirit when we are alone than when any auxiliaries are summoned to our aid. She is indeed a wonderful woman, and I think all the faculties of her mind stronger, and more active, than I have ever known them. I have settled that ten full days may be sufficient for all the purposes of our interview. I should therefore depart next Friday, the eighteenth instant, and am indeed expected at Althorp on the twentieth ; but I may possibly reckon without my host, as I have not yet apprised Mrs. Gibbon of the term of my visit ;

[1] Mrs. Holroyd.

and will certainly not quarrel with her for a short
delay. Adieu. I must have some political speculations.
The campaign, at least on our side, seems to be at an
end. Ever yours.

To the Same.

Althorp Library, Tuesday, four o'clock.

We have so completely exhausted this morning
among the first editions of Cicero, that I can mention
only my departure hence to-morrow, the sixth instant.
I shall lie quietly at Woburn, and reach London in
good time on Thursday. By the following post I will
write somewhat more largely. My stay in London
will depend partly on my amusement, and your being
fixed at Sheffield Place; unless you think I can be
comfortably arranged for a week or two with you at
Brighton. The military remarks seem good; but now
to what purpose? Adieu. I embrace and much
rejoice in Louisa's improvement. Lord Ossory was
from home at Farning Woods.

To the Same.

London, Friday, November 8, four o'clock.

Walpole has just delivered yours, and I hasten the
direction, that you may not be at a loss. I will write
to-morrow, but I am now fatigued, and rather unwell.
Adieu. I have not seen a soul except Elmsley.

To the Same.

St. James's Street, Nov. 9, 1793.

As I dropped yesterday the word *unwell*, I flatter
myself that the family would have been a little alarmed
by my silence to-day. I am still awkward, though
without any suspicions of gout, and have some idea
of having recourse to medical advice. Yet I creep

out to-day in a chair, to dine with Lord Lucan. But as it will be literally my first going downstairs, and as scarcely anyone is apprised of my arrival, I know nothing, I have heard nothing, I have nothing to say. My present lodging, a house of Elmsley's, is cheerful, convenient, somewhat dear, but not so much as an hotel, a species of habitation for which I have not conceived any great affection. Had you been stationary at Sheffield, you would have seen me before the twentieth; for I am tired of rambling, and pant for my home; that is to say, for your house. But whether I shall have courage to brave ***** and a bleak down, time only can discover. Adieu. I wish you back to Sheffield Place. The health of dear Louisa is doubtless the first object; but I did not expect Brighton after Tunbridge. Whenever dear little aunt is separate from you, I shall certainly write to her; but at present how is it possible? Ever yours.

To the Same, at Brighthelmstone.

St. James's Street, Nov. 11, 1793.

I must at length withdraw the veil before my state of health, though the naked truth may alarm you more than a fit of the gout. Have you never observed, through my *inexpressibles*, a large prominency which, as it was not at all painful, and very little troublesome, I had strangely neglected for many years? But since my departure from Sheffield Place it has increased (most stupendously), is increasing, and ought to be diminished. Yesterday I sent for Farquhar[1], who is allowed to be a very skilful surgeon. After viewing and palping, he very seriously desired to call in assistance, and has examined it again to-day with Mr. Cline, a surgeon, as he says, of the first eminence. They both pronounce it a *hydrocele* (a collection of water), which must be let out by the operation of

[1] Sir Walter Farquhar, Baronet. S.

tapping; but, from its magnitude and long neglect, they think it a most extraordinary case, and wish to have another surgeon, Dr. Baillie, present. If the business should go off smoothly, I shall be delivered from my burden (it is almost as big as a small child), and walk about in four or five days with a truss. But the medical gentlemen, who never speak quite plain, insinuate to me the possibility of an inflammation, of fever, &c. I am not appalled at the thoughts of the operation, which is fixed for Wednesday next, twelve o'clock; but it has occurred to me, that you might wish to be present, before and afterwards, till the crisis was passed; and to give you that opportunity, I shall solicit a delay till Thursday, or even Friday. In the meanwhile, I crawl about with some labour, and much indecency, to Devonshire House (where I left all the fine ladies making flannel waistcoats [1]), Lady Lucan's, &c. Adieu. Varnish the business for the ladies; yet I am afraid it will be public—the advantage of being notorious. Ever yours.

[1] For the soldiers in Flanders. S.

Immediately on receiving the last letter, I went the same day from Brighthelmstone to London, and was agreeably surprised to find that Mr. Gibbon had dined at Lord Lucan's, and did not return to his lodgings, where I waited for him, till eleven o'clock at night. Those who have seen him within the last eight or ten years, must be surprised to hear that he could doubt whether his disorder was apparent. When he returned to England in 1787, I was greatly alarmed by a prodigious increase, which I always conceived to proceed from a rupture. I did not understand why he, who had talked with me on every other subject relative to himself and his affairs without reserve, should never in any shape hint at a malady so troublesome ; but on speaking to his *valet de chambre*, he told me Mr. Gibbon could not bear the least allusion to that subject, and never would suffer him to notice it. I consulted some medical persons, who with me supposing it to be a rupture, were of opinion that nothing could be done, and said that he surely must have had advice, and of course had taken all necessary precautions. He now talked freely with me about his disorder ; which, he said, began in the year 1761 ; that he then consulted Mr. Hawkins, the surgeon, who did not decide whether it was the beginning of a rupture, or a hydrocele ; but he desired to see Mr. Gibbon again when he came to town. Mr. Gibbon not feeling any pain, nor suffering any inconvenience, as he said, never returned to Mr. Hawkins ; and although the disorder continued to increase gradually, and of late years very much indeed, he never mentioned it to any person, however incredible it may appear, from 1761 to November, 1793. I told him that I had always supposed there was no doubt of its being a rupture ; his answer was, that he never thought so, and that he, and the surgeons who attended him, were of opinion that it was a hydrocele. It is now certain that it was originally a rupture, and that a

hydrocele had lately taken place in the same part;
and it is remarkable that his legs, which had been
swelled about the ankle, particularly one of them,
since he had the erysipelas in 1790, recovered their
former shape as soon as the water appeared in another
part, which did not happen till between the time he
left Sheffield Place, in the beginning of October, and
his arrival at Althorp, towards the latter end of that
month. On the Thursday following the date of his
last letter, Mr. Gibbon was tapped for the first time;
four quarts of a transparent watery fluid were discharged by that operation. Neither inflammation nor
fever ensued; the tumour was diminished to nearly
half its size; the remaining part was a soft irregular
mass. I had been with him two days before, and
I continued with him above a week after the first
tapping, during which time he enjoyed his usual
spirits; and the three medical gentlemen who attended
him will recollect his pleasantry, even during the
operation. He was abroad again in a few days, but
the water evidently collecting very fast, it was agreed
that a second puncture should be made a fortnight
after the first. Knowing that I should be wanted at
a meeting in the country, he pressed me to attend it,
and promised that soon after the second operation
was performed he would follow me to Sheffield Place;
but before he arrived I received the two following
letters:

Mr. GIBBON TO LORD SHEFFIELD, AT BRIGHTON.

St. James's Street, Nov. 25, 1793.

Though Farquhar has promised to write a lin
I conceive you may not be sorry to hear directly
from me. The operation of yesterday was much
longer, more searching, and more painful than the
former; but it has eased and lightened me to a much
greater degree.[1] No inflammation, no fever, a delicious

---

[1] Three quarts of the same fluid as before were discharged. S.

night, leave to go abroad to-morrow, and to go out of town when I please, *en attendant* the future measures of a radical cure. If you hold your intention of returning next Saturday to Sheffield Place, I shall probably join you about the Tuesday following, after having passed two nights at Beckenham.[1] The Devons are going to Bath, and the hospitable Craufurd follows them. I passed a delightful day with Burke ; an odd one with Monsignor Erskine, the Pope's Nuncio. Of public news, you and the papers know more than I do, We seem to have strong sea and land hopes ; nor do I dislike the Royalists having beaten the Sans Culottes, and taken Dol. How many minutes will it take to guillotine the seventy-three new members of the Convention, who are now arrested ? Adieu ; ever yours.

St. James's Street, Nov. 30, 1793.

It will not be in my power to reach Sheffield Place quite so soon as I wished and expected. Lord Auckland informs me that he shall be at Lambeth next week, Tuesday, Wednesday, and Thursday. I have therefore agreed to dine at Beckenham on Friday. Saturday will be spent there, and unless some extraordinary temptation should detain me another day, you will see me by four o'clock Sunday, the ninth of December. I dine to-morrow with the Chancellor at Hampstead, and, what I do not like at this time of the year, without a proposal to stay all night. Yet I would not refuse, more especially as I had denied him on a former day. My health is good ; but I shall have a final interview with Farquhar before I leave town. We are still in darkness about Lord Howe and the French ships, but hope seems to preponderate. Adieu. Nothing that relates to Louisa can be forgotten. Ever yours.

[1] Eden Farm. S.

To THE SAME.

St. James's Street, Dec. 6, 1793.
16 du Mois Frimaire.

The man tempted me, and I did eat—and that man
is no less than the Chancellor. I dine to-day, as I
intended, at Beckenham: but he recalls me (the third
time this week) by a dinner to-morrow (Saturday)
with Burke and Windham, which I do not possess
sufficient fortitude to resist. Sunday he dismisses me
again to the aforesaid Beckenham, but insists on finding
me there on Monday, which he will probably do,
supposing there should be room and welcome at the
Ambassador's. I shall not therefore arrive at Sheffield
Place till Tuesday, the 10th instant, and though you may
perceive I do not want society or amusement, I sincerely repine at the delay. You will likewise derive
some comfort from hearing of the spirit and activity
of my motions. Farquhar is satisfied, allows me to go,
and does not think I shall be obliged to precipitate my
return. Shall we never have anything more than
hopes and rumours from Lord Howe? Ever yours.

Mr. Gibbon generally took the opportunity of passing
a night or two with his friend Lord Auckland, at
Eden Farm (ten miles from London), on his passage
to Sheffield Place; and notwithstanding his indisposition, he had lately made an excursion thither from
London; when he was much pleased by meeting the
Archbishop of Canterbury, of whom he expressed an
high opinion. He returned to London, to dine with
Lord Loughborough, to meet Mr. Burke, Mr. Windham, and particularly Mr. Pitt, with whom he was
not acquainted; and in his last journey to Sussex, he
revisited Eden Farm, and was much gratified by the
opportunity of again seeing, during a whole day, Mr.
Pitt, who passed the night there. From Lord Auckland's, Mr. Gibbon proceeded to Sheffield Place; and
his discourse was never more brilliant, nor more enter-

taining, than on his arrival. The parallels which he drew, and the comparisons which he made, between the leading men of this country, were sketched in his best manner, and were infinitely interesting. However, this last visit to Sheffield Place became far different from any he had ever made before. That ready, cheerful, various, and illuminating conversation, which we had before admired in him, was not now always to be found in the library or the dining-room. He moved with difficulty, and retired from company sooner than he had been used to do. On the twenty-third of December, his appetite began to fail him. He observed to me that it was a very bad sign *with him* when he could not eat his breakfast, which he had done at all times very heartily; and this seems to have been the strongest expression of apprehension that he was ever observed to utter. A considerable degree of fever now made its appearance. Inflammation arose, from the weight and the bulk of the tumour. Water again collected very fast, and when the fever went off, he never entirely recovered his appetite even for breakfast. I became very uneasy at his situation towards the end of the month, and thought it necessary to advise him to set out for London. He had before settled his plan to arrive there about the middle of January. I had company in the house, and we expected one of his particular friends; but he was obliged to sacrifice all social pleasure to the immediate attention which his health required. He went to London on the seventh of January, and the next day I received the following billet; the last he ever wrote:

EDWARD GIBBON, ESQ., TO LORD SHEFFIELD.

St. James's Street, four o'clock, Tuesday.

This date says everything. I was almost killed between Sheffield Place and East Grinsted, by hard, frozen, long, and cross ruts, that would disgrace the approach to an Indian wig-wam. The rest was something less painful; and I reached this place half-dead, but not seriously feverish, or ill. I found a dinner invitation from Lord Lucan; but what are dinners to me? I wish they did not know of my departure. I catch the flying-post. What an effort! Adieu, till Thursday or Friday.

By his own desire, I did not follow him till Thursday the ninth. I then found him far from well. The tumour more distended than before, inflamed, and ulcerated in several places. Remedies were applied to abate the inflammation; but it was not thought proper to puncture the tumour for the third time, till Monday, the 13th of January, when no less than six quarts of fluid were discharged. He seemed much relieved by the evacuation. His spirits continued good. He talked, as usual, of passing his time at houses which he had often frequented with great pleasure, the Duke of Devonshire's, Mr. Craufurd's, Lord Spencer's, Lord Lucan's, Sir Ralph Payne's, and Mr. Batt's; and when I told him that I should not return to the country, as I had intended, he pressed me to go; knowing I had an engagement there on public business, he said, ' you may be back on Saturday, and I intend to go on Thursday to Devonshire House'. I had not any apprehension that his life was in danger, although I began to fear that he might not be restored to a comfortable state, and that motion would be very troublesome to him; but he talked of a radical cure. He said that it was fortunate the disorder had shown itself while he was in England, where he might procure the best assistance; and if a radical cure could not be obtained before his return to Lausanne, there was an able surgeon at Geneva, who could come to tap him when it should be necessary. On Tuesday, the fourteenth, when the risk of inflammation and fever from the last operation was supposed to be passed, as the medical gentlemen who attended him expressed no fears for his life, I went that afternoon part of the way to Sussex, and the following day reached Sheffield Place. The next morning, the sixteenth, I received by the post a good account of Mr. Gibbon, which mentioned also that he hourly gained strength. In the evening came a letter by express, dated noon that day, which acquainted me that Mr. Gibbon had had a violent attack the preceding night, and that it was not probable he could live till I came to him. I reached his lodgings in St. James's Street about midnight, and learned that my friend had expired a quarter before one o'clock that day, the sixteenth of January, 1794.

After I left him on Tuesday afternoon, the fourteenth, he saw some company, Lady Lucan and Lady Spencer, and thought himself well enough at night to omit the opium draught, which he had been used to take for some time. He slept very indifferently; before nine the next morning he rose, but could not eat his breakfast. However, he appeared tolerably well, yet complained at times of a pain in his stomach. At one o'clock he received a visit of an hour from Madame de Sylva, and at three, his friend, Mr. Craufurd of Auchinames (for whom he had a particular regard), called, and stayed with him till past five o'clock. They talked, as usual, on various subjects; and twenty hours before his death, Mr. Gibbon happened to fall into a conversation, not uncommon with him, on the probable duration of his life. He said that he thought himself a good life for ten, twelve, or perhaps twenty years. About six, he ate the wing of a chicken, and drank three glasses of Madeira. After dinner he became very uneasy and impatient; complained a good deal, and appeared so weak, that his servant was alarmed. Mr. Gibbon had sent to his friend and relation, Mr. Robert Darell, whose house was not far distant, desiring to see him, and adding, that he had something particular to say. But, unfortunately, this desired interview never took place.

During the evening he complained much of his stomach, and of a disposition to vomit. Soon after nine, he took his opium draught, and went to bed.

About ten, he complained of much pain, and desired that warm napkins might be applied to his stomach. He almost incessantly expressed a sense of pain till about four o'clock in the morning, when he said he found his stomach much easier. About seven, the servant asked whether he should send for Mr. Farquhar ? he answered, no ; that he was as well as he had been the day before. At about half-past eight, he got out of bed, and said he was '*plus adroit*' than he had been for three months past, and got into bed again, without assistance, better than usual. About nine, he said that he would rise. The servant, however, persuaded him to remain in bed till Mr. Farquhar, who was expected at eleven, should come. Till about that hour he spoke with great facility. Mr. Farquhar came at the time appointed, and he was then visibly dying. When the *valet de chambre* returned, after attending Mr. Farquhar out of the room, Mr. Gibbon said, ' *Pourquoi est-ce que vous me quittez ?* ' This was about half-past eleven. At twelve, he drank some brandy and water from a teapot, and desired his favourite servant to stay with him. These were the last words he pronounced articulately. To the last he preserved his senses ; and when he could no longer speak, his servant having asked a question, he made a sign, to show that he understood him. He was quite tranquil, and did not stir ; his eyes half-shut. About a quarter before one, he ceased to breathe.[1]

---

[1] The body was not opened till the fifth day after his death. It was then sound, except that a degree of morti-fication, not very considerable, had taken place on a part of the *colon* ; which, with the whole of the *omentum*, of a very enlarged size, had descended into the *scrotum*, forming a bag that hung down nearly as low as the knee. Since that part had been inflamed and ulcerated, Mr. Gib-bon could not bear a truss ; and when the last six quarts of fluid were discharged, the *colon* and *omentum* descending lower, they, by their weight, drew the lower mouth of the stomach downwards to the *os pubis*, and this probably was the immediate cause of his death.

The *valet de chambre* observed that Mr. Gibbon did not, at any time, show the least sign of alarm or apprehension of death ; and it does not appear that he ever thought himself in danger, unless his desire to speak to Mr. Darell may be considered in that light.

Perhaps I dwell too long on these minute and melancholy circumstances. Yet the close of such a life can hardly fail to interest every reader ; and I know that the public has received a different and erroneous account of my friend's last hours.

I can never cease to feel regret that I was not by his side at this awful period : a regret so strong, that I can express it only by borrowing (as Mason has done on a similar occasion) the forcible language of Tacitus : ' Mihi praeter acerbitatem amici erepti, auget maestitiam quod assidere valetudini, fovere

The following is the account of the appearance of the body, given by an eminent surgeon who opened it :

' Aperto tumore, qui ab inguine usque ad genu se extenderat, observatum est partem eius inferiorem constare ex tunica vaginali testis continenti duas quasi libras liquoris serosi tincti sanguine. Ea autem fuit sacci illius amplitudo ut portioni liquoris longe maiori capiendae sufficeret. In posteriori parte huius sacci testis situs fuit. Hunc omnino sanum invenimus.

' Partem tumoris superiorem occupaverant integrum fere omentum et maior pars intestini coli. Hae partes, sacco sibi proprio inclusae, sibi invicem et sacco suo adeo arcte adhaeserunt ut coivisse viderentur in massam unam solidam et irregularem ; cuius a tergo chorda spermatica sedem suam obtinuerat.

' In omento et in intestino colo haud dubia recentis inflammationis signa vidimus, necnon maculas nonnullas lividi coloris hinc inde sparsas.

' Aperto abdomine, ventriculum invenimus a naturali suo situ detractum usque ad annulum musculi obliqui externi. Pylorum retrorsum et quasi sursum a duodeno retractum. In hepate ingentem numerum parvorum tuberculorum. Vesicam felleam bile admodum distentam. In caeteris visceribus, examini anatomico subjectis, nulla morbi vestigia extiterunt.

deficientem, satiari vultu, complexu non contigit.'
It is some consolation to me that I did not, like
Tacitus, by a long absence, anticipate the loss of my
friend several years before his decease. Although
I had not the mournful gratification of being near him
on the day he expired, yet, during his illness, I had
not failed to attend him with that assiduity which
his genius, his virtues, and, above all, our long, uninterrupted, and happy friendship sanctioned and
demanded.

POSTSCRIPT

Mr. GIBBON's will is dated October 1, 1791, just before I left Lausanne; he distinguishes me, as usual, in the most flattering manner:

'I constitute and appoint the Right Honourable John Lord Sheffield, Edward Darell, Esquire, and John Thomas Batt, Esquire, to be the Executors of this my last Will and Testament; and as the execution of this trust will not be attended with much difficulty or trouble, I shall indulge these gentlemen, in the pleasure of this last disinterested service, without wronging my feelings, or oppressing my heir, by too light or too weighty a testimony of my gratitude. My obligations to the long and active friendship of Lord Sheffield, I could never sufficiently repay.'

He then observes that the Right Hon. Lady Eliot of Port Eliot, is his nearest relation on the father's side; but that her three sons are in such prosperous circumstances, that he may well be excused for making the two children of his late uncle, Sir Stanier Porten, his heirs; they being in a very different situation. He bequeaths annuities to two old servants, three thousand pounds, and his furniture, plate, &c., at Lausanne, to Mr. Wilhelm de Severy; one hundred guineas to the poor of Lausanne, and fifty guineas each to the following persons:—Lady Sheffield and daughters, Maria and Louisa, Madame and Mademoiselle de Severy, the Count de Schomberg, Mademoiselle la Chanoinesse de Polier, and M. le Ministre Le Vade, for the purchase of some token which may remind them of a sincere friend.

The Remains of Mr. Gibbon were deposited in Lord Sheffield's Family Burial-Place, in Fletching, Sussex; whereon is inscribed the following Epitaph, written at my request by a distinguished scholar, the Rev. Dr. Parr :—

EDVARDUS GIBBON

CRITICUS ACRI INGENIO ET MULTIPLICI DOCTRINA

ORNATUS

IDEMQUE HISTORICORUM QUI FORTUNAM

IMPERII ROMANI

VEL LABENTIS ET INCLINATI VEL EVERSI ET FUNDITUS

DELETI

LITTERIS MANDAVERINT

OMNIUM FACILE PRINCEPS

CUIUS IN MORIBUS ERAT MODERATIO ANIMI

CUM LIBERALI QUADAM SPECIE CONIUNCTA

IN SERMONE

MULTA GRAVITATI COMITAS SUAVITER ADSPERSA

IN SCRIPTIS

COPIOSUM SPLENDIDUM

CONCINNUM ORBE VERBORUM

ET SUMMO ARTIFICIO DISTINCTUM

ORATIONIS GENUS

RECONDITAE EXQUISITAEQUE SENTENTIAE

ET IN MONUMENTIS RERUM POLITICARUM OBSERVANDIS

ACUTA ET PERSPICAX PRUDENTIA

VIXIT ANNOS LVI MENS. VII DIES XXVIII

DECESSIT XVII CAL. FEB. ANNO SACRO

MDCCLXXXXIV

ET IN HOC MAUSOLEO SEPULTUS EST

EX VOLUNTATE IOHANNIS DOMINI SHEFFIELD

QUI AMICO BENE MERENTI ET CONVICTORI

HUMANISSIMO

H. TAB. P. C.